September 1993

To Bob Eisner,

    With compliments of the author. Best wishes on the occasion of your retirement. With gratitude for all of your help over the past 20 years.

      Your eternally grateful student,

John Graham

Small Change

Small Change:

The Economics of

Child Support

Andrea H. Beller and John W. Graham

Yale University Press

New Haven and London

Designed by James J. Johnson.
Set in Times Roman type by DEKR Corporation, Woburn, Massachusetts.
Printed in the United States of America by BookCrafters, Inc., Chelsea, Michigan.

A catalogue record for this book is available from the British Library.

The paper in this book meets the guidelines for permanence and durability of the Committee on Production Guidelines for Book Longevity of the Council on Library Resources.

10 9 8 7 6 5 4 3 2 1

Library of Congress Cataloging-in-Publication Data

Beller, Andrea H.
    Small change : the economics of child support / Andrea H. Beller and John W. Graham.
        p.   cm.
    Includes bibliographical references and index.
    ISBN 0-300-05362-2 (alk. paper)
    1. Child support—Economic aspects—United States.   I. Graham, John W.   II. Title.
HV741.B44   1993
338.4'336271—dc20   92–39623

To my parents, Alfred and Helen Gold Beller, who supported me in all my endeavors, and to my children, David and Shira Stolarsky

A.H.B.

To my mother, Ruth Graham Clagett

J.W.G.

Contents

Tables

"In every child who is born," wrote James Agee, "the potentiality of the human race is born again; and in him," as indeed in "each of us, our terrific responsibility towards human life." The abandonment of that responsibility, as represented in a parent's obligation to give his or her child financial support, is what this book is all about. The failure of absent parents, mainly fathers, to pay child support is a national scandal, one that has huge consequences for taxpayers, governments, mothers, and most important, children.

Child support has officially been on the national agenda since 1975 when the "IV-D" program got started and state governments began to work with a new federal office of child support enforcement to establish and collect child support awards in a coordinated manner.

But it was not until the decade of the 1980s that child support truly became a subject of national debate. Census Bureau figures released at the beginning of the decade demonstrated how few children were receiving the support they deserved. Then the neglected children and their hard-pressed mothers put a tragic human face on the cold, hard facts. Grass-roots organizations formed and began to lobby for change, putting pressure on the media to pay attention and on public officials to take action.

That was the genesis of my own involvement in the issue. Despite my exposure to child support problems as an attorney in private practice and as state senate majority leader in Connecticut during the 1970s, it was not until 1981 when I began my campaign for state attorney general that I became aware of just how many mothers and their children were denied their rightful child support payments and how costly it was for the government to support the children of poor families whose fathers had deserted them. I owe my own education to a group of mothers in Connecticut who formed PECOS (Parents for Enforcement of Court Ordered Support) and who helped me work toward the enactment of tougher child support laws in our state during the 1980s.

I have carried that interest to the United States Senate, where I have been pleased to find a growing acceptance of the need for innovative child support collection laws at the federal level and for the stronger enforcement of these laws. The mass media have responded similarly to the pleas of mothers and their children. The result has been a series of hearings and seminars around the country and a wave of stories in popular magazines, newspapers, and television shows about "deadbeat dads" and the kids they've left behind.

A societal consensus has been building for forceful new laws, geared toward improving the identification of absent parents, getting them into court to establish child support obligations, developing effective methods of collection, and punishing those who fail to abide by their child support orders. But what has been the result of the state and federal governments' broader and stronger involvement in child support collection? Are mothers and their children better off because the legal system has begun to care about them? Are taxpayers getting their money's worth from the new investment in child support programs? In short, is the child support system working?

That is the focus of this book. The years of research by Andrea Beller and John Graham into the bottom line of child support—from the establishment of paternity to the awarding of child support to its collection—have yielded a bumper crop of facts that go a long way toward puncturing myths, settling debates, highlighting successes and failures, and furthering our search for better ways to make the system work. I have rarely seen so thorough and so well-documented an analysis of a public-policy problem.

As a result of the authors' thoughtful perspective, this is a book devoid of "conventional wisdom," of politically correct preaching, of pop psychology. It does not stretch or avoid the truth of this terribly complicated social problem. Beller and Graham do not shrink from the difficult task of separating fact from speculation and backing up each fact with a wealth of supporting evidence. Most important—and most refreshing to someone accustomed to political discourse—the authors are not afraid to admit when the answer to certain aspects of the child support problem is not clear. They do not abuse the data to make a point.

That gives added weight to the conclusions reached and recommendations made in *Small Change* and makes the book all the more important for those of us intent on finding ways to make the system work better. For example, the authors show that child support awards, despite more than ten years of legislative and judicial activism, remain low and have actually declined when compared to the father's ability to pay. They also demonstrate that child support awards are generally too low to match the actual costs of raising children in today's world, which means that without changes in the system there is little hope that child support can help families rise out of poverty and off the welfare system.

Such findings are a call to arms for those who want to make government and our laws work better. Lucky for us, Andrea Beller and John Graham supply the arms we will need to do just that. They make a compelling case for the enactment of a national system of guidelines for child support awards, educating judges and lawyers about the need to require awards from *all* fathers, no matter how little money they make, adding criminal penalties for nonsupport to federal child support statutes, and focusing more attention on the special problems of never-married and African-American mothers, many of whom obtain little or no support from the fathers of their children.

Beller and Graham also give evidence of the value of such child support enforcement tools as liens against property, automatic wage withholding, and criminal penalties, suggesting that states and the federal government would do well to ensure their widespread use.

At the heart of *Small Change* is the belief, informed by a thorough analysis of the evidence, that America and America's families function best when children receive love, attention, and support from their mothers *and* their fathers. In an ideal world, all children will have two parents present for their upbringing. But in our imperfect world, we know that this will too often not be the case.

Yet there should never be an excuse for fathers to neglect their obligation to their children. A denial of child support is a denial of love, and that puts tremendous economic and psychological burdens on millions of America's children. To stand up for effective child support awards and collection is to stand up for the family and for the belief that our kids need a mother and a father, even if both cannot be in the same home.

Just as the failure of fathers to pay child support on a massive scale has contributed to a host of social problems in our country today, the more effective collection of child support by government will help us to address the related crises of education, poverty, disease, illiteracy, crime, and other obstacles faced by children as they grow up without adequate support in our troubled world.

The problem of child support crosses all ideological barriers and gives us an important opportunity to unite in a bipartisan manner to enact and promote practical solutions that work. Whatever our personal agendas, I believe we can all agree that it is our "terrific responsibility" as a nation to act when America's children need support.

Small Change establishes that need, proves that it is unmet, and points the way toward big changes in the way we deal with fathers who refuse to pay what their children so genuinely deserve. The potential of the human race, of our nation, is born again in our children, as James Agee said. Meeting the basic economic needs of our children helps us ensure that such tremendous potential is fulfilled.

Sen. Joseph I. Lieberman

This book is about child support payments in the United States during the 1980s, a decade in which changes in the government's child support enforcement system were great and child support emerged on the national agenda for the first time. Nationwide surveys of the child-support-eligible population—first conducted by the Census Bureau in 1979 and repeated at roughly two-year intervals—made possible this detailed analysis of the determinants of, trends in, and consequences of child support payments over this period. Although 1986 was the latest survey we had access to, our detailed analyses and findings have implications for the remainder of the 1980s and into the 1990s. We find that there was at best a small change in child support payments during the 1980s and that for too many mothers and children inadequate child support payments amounted to no more than "small change."

Although this book is the product of scholarly technical research based in the discipline of economics, it is intended for a much wider audience. It is not a comprehensive summary of all that is known to date about child support; rather, it focuses primarily on those questions that can be addressed using census surveys. It is also not a compilation of our previously published work, but it does benefit from the proven methodology established in our earlier papers. Finally, it is neither a how-to book apprising mothers (or fathers) of how to get more child support, nor is it a policy manual advocating any one particular approach to child support reform. Yet it does reach definite conclusions about some of the directions in which we believe public policy ought to be moving. As such, we hope it will prove useful to policymakers.

This book represents the culmination of nearly nine years of collaborative research that began when we were assistant professors at the University of Illinois at Urbana-Champaign. We are grateful to Julian Simon, who first suggested the topic of child support to Beller, who in turn received initial funding under a Hatch grant from the Illinois Agricultural Experiment Station.

In 1983, Andrea Beller approached John Graham with the modest proposal of using newly released census data to analyze the impact of child support payments on the economic well-being of single mothers and their children. That work was presented at a conference of the National Bureau of Economic Research and served as the basis for a research proposal ultimately funded for six years by the Center for Population Research, National Institute for Child Health and Human Development (Grant no. RO1 HD19350). Additional support was provided by the Research Board of the University of Illinois. In 1986, Graham approached Beller with the equally modest proposal of writing a book on child support. Despite numerous obstacles to continued collaboration (Graham moved to Rutgers University and Beller endured a difficult pregnancy), our joint efforts survived thanks to a healthy division of labor, extended telephone conversations, and the good work of Federal Express.

The order of our names on the title page is a simple matter of alphabetical tradition. Although all of the chapters represent a genuine collaboration, Beller could be acknowledged as the custodial parent of chapters 2, 6, and 8, and Graham of chapters 3, 4, 5, and 7. (Chapter 1 truly deserves joint custody.)

Acknowledgments

We gratefully acknowledge the contributions of numerous individuals whose efforts have contributed to this book. First, we thank Ruth A. Sanders, formerly of the Census Bureau, for answering numerous questions about the data, and H. Elizabeth Peters for sharing with us her computer program for extracting the data. Second, we thank the many graduate students at the University of Illinois who helped in our research over the years: Sanghee Sohn Cha, Hyuncha Choe, Seung Sin Chung, Kee-ok Kim Han, Pedro M. Hernandez, Soon-Hee Joung, Yang-Suk Kim, D. Elizabeth Kiss, Lorraine Maddox, John Rearden, Edwin Sexton, and Se-jeong Yang. John Boyd and Jill Hashbarger provided invaluable computer assistance. Betty L. Mathis and Barbara S. Smith did a careful job typing the tables for two chapters.

Several individuals contributed to specific sections of the book. We thank graduate students Karen Fox Folk and Kyung-ja Kim for their assistance with portions of the section "Adequacy of Award

Amounts" in chapter 2. Robert Scott suggested the idea about bar-gaining over award amounts that we use in chapter 4 to explain why new awards rose only half as fast as prices. The section "Issues in Setting State Guidelines" in chapter 6 draws on a report prepared for the state of Illinois (Andrea H. Beller, Barbara J. Phipps, and Sheila Fitzgerald Krein, *An Analysis of Child Support Guidelines Models and Costs of Raising Children,* Illinois Department of Public Aid, 1991.) The discussion in the section "Guideline Models" is taken from part of a report primarily researched and written by Barbara Phipps, and "Measurement of Income," by Phipps and Sheila Krein, who rightfully should be regarded coauthors of these respective sections. The data on actual guidelines in effect in the states were based upon original research by Phipps and data collected by the National Center for the State Courts, 1990. Finally, we found the marvelous Charles Dickens quotation that opens chapter 7 in Arthur A. Adrian, *Dickens and the Parent-Child Relationship* (Athens: Ohio University Press, 1984, 96).

Our colleagues also contributed substantially to our work. We thank Marianne A. Ferber, who carefully read the entire manuscript and offered suggestions on almost every page. Barbara R. Bergmann, Karen Fox Folk, Saul D. Hoffman, Robert Hughes, Jr., Paula Roberts, and Lois B. Shaw offered helpful suggestions on early versions of one or more chapters. In addition, we are indebted to Paula Roberts for offering the point in chapter 8 (under recommendation 5.c. "Further Research") that the Office of Child Support Enforcement made it clear that under mandatory guidelines lowering awards for children born outside marriage violates federal law. We gained useful insights into various aspects of child support from conversations with Barbara R. Bergmann, Irwin Garfinkel, Maurice M. MacDonald, H. Elizabeth Peters, Philip K. Robins, and Robert J. Willis. The book is better for those suggestions we followed and would have been better still had we followed more of them.

We thank our editor at Yale John Covell for his initial interest in our work and his help along the way. Finally, we are especially grateful to our manuscript editor Lorraine Alexson for her very careful editorial work and thoughtful suggestions throughout the manuscript.

John Graham gratefully acknowledges the intellectual support of his former colleagues in the economics department at the University of Illinois, as well as his current colleagues at Rutgers University. Rutgers University provided him an invaluable sabbatical leave during which the book was first outlined. Finally, he is also grateful for the continuing, loving support of Paul Louis Ochman.

Andrea Beller owes an intellectual debt to Gary S. Becker, James J. Heckman, and Irwin Garfinkel, and to all of the other researchers at the Institute for Research on Poverty during 1975–77, whose influence shaped the questions she posed and approaches she took to answering them. She is also grateful to Sharon Y. Nickols for her support over the crucial years of this study. The University of Illinois provided an invaluable sabbatical that was used to launch the book. Finally, Beller owes a great debt to her husband, Kenneth B. Stolarsky, without whose constant support and willingness to undertake extra responsibilities on the home front this book might never have come to fruition.

Small Change

Introduction

The problems women face in collecting child support are not new, but widespread public awareness about them has burgeoned only recently. Between 1960 and 1980 rising rates of divorce and out-of-wedlock births swelled the population of father-absent families and jeopardized the economic well-being of millions of American mothers and their children. The number of single-parent, female-headed families nearly doubled and by 1980 they accounted for roughly half of all poor persons.[1] One factor contributing to the economic plight of many of these families was that too often the fathers of these children—in most cases still alive but living elsewhere—provided little or no financial assistance.[2] As a result, increasingly the public came to view child support—that is, regular, legally mandated payments from a noncustodial parent to a custodial parent—as one of the keys to improving the economic well-being of mothers and their children.

It was not until 1980, however, when the Census Bureau released the preliminary findings of its first national survey of child support and alimony, that the full extent of the problem became widely known.[3] The survey revealed that only 59 percent of an estimated 7.1 million mothers with children under twenty-one whose fathers were living elsewhere as of April 1979 had a child support award. Among the 3.4 million mothers with an award and due payment in 1978, one-quarter received no payment at all, and another quarter received less than the full amount due. Among the 2.5 million women who received some support, the average annual payment was just over $1,800 to help support an average of nearly two children.[4] If the full amount owed had been paid, the average annual child support payment would have been roughly $2,170.[5] The survey also found that on each of the aforementioned child support outcomes, black women and never-married mothers—groups that form a high proportion of both the poor and welfare populations—fared much worse than average.

It had long been recognized that many families without child support suffer personal deprivation, but increasingly nonpayment began to be perceived to have adverse public consequences as well, which society was no longer willing to bear. Most apparent among these was the growing burden of public welfare. Expenditures by the Aid to Families with Dependent Children program (AFDC) ballooned from $1 billion in 1960 to over $12 billion in 1980[6] as the number of families on welfare increased from 800,000 to 3.4 million.[7] Taxpayers who had long accepted the moral obligation of assisting children whose parents are *unable* to provide support, increasingly found themselves called upon to assist children whose fathers were simply *unwilling* to do so.[8] Less immediately apparent but nonetheless important were some of the long-term adverse public consequences. New studies revealed that children living in low-income, single-parent families—whether on welfare or not—are more likely to drop out of school early, become teenage parents, and come to rely upon welfare themselves.[9]

Government efforts to ensure that able-bodied, noncustodial parents fulfilled their financial obligations to their children intensified along with the growth in single-parent, female-headed families and the associated increases in public expenditures on welfare. Federal efforts officially began in 1975 and by the end of the 1980s, child support enforcement had become the first line of defense in the government's long-running war on poverty and welfare dependency. Title I of the Family Support Act of 1988 placed primary responsibility for the support of children squarely on the shoulders of their parents.[10]

Child Support Enforcement as a National Priority

Female-headed, single-parent families had grown in number for more than two decades along with the rapid growth in rates of divorce and out-of-wedlock births. The rate of divorce increased annually from 2.2 per 1,000 total population in 1962 to a peak of 5.3 per 1,000 in 1981.[11] Although thereafter it dropped slightly, the U.S. divorce rate remains the highest in the world.[12] Almost one in four births in 1986 were to unmarried mothers, triple the rate of the mid-1960s.[13] By 1988, female-headed, single-parent families had grown to nearly one-fifth of all families living with their own children under eighteen, almost double their proportion in 1970.[14] By the same year, 21 percent of all children and 51 percent of black children lived with their mother only, roughly double the proportions in 1970.[15] According to recent projections, 6 out of every 10 children born in the mid-1980s, and 9 out of

10 black children, are expected to spend some time in a single-parent family.[16]

Often these women and children fell into poverty and had little choice but to rely on the welfare system.[17] In 1985, 2.8 million of the 8.8 million women with children present whose fathers were absent from the household had incomes below the poverty level, and 2.1 million of them received some form of public assistance income.[18] This increasing "feminization of poverty"[19] and the frequent dependence of these women on welfare raised concerns about the economic situation of women and children following divorce and out-of-wedlock birth. Although some of the economic plight of mother-only families can be traced to larger issues of gender inequality, the nonpayment of child support by noncustodial fathers contributes to it. The census figures released in 1980 revealed not only that many fathers paid little or no child support but also that lack of child support and the poverty rates of women and children were closely linked. In 1978, 42 percent of women without a child support award fell into poverty, but only 18 percent of women with an award and 14 percent of women who received payment were poor.[20]

In retrospect, it is perhaps not surprising that increasing attention was paid to child support reforms in the 1980s. The numbers of women and children on welfare grew rapidly amid large budget deficits, prompting federal policymakers to look elsewhere for sources of support. Moreover, improving child support fitted well with the conservative philosophy of the Reagan administration, which stressed the desirability of private rather than public support whenever possible. In addition, calls to improve the nation's child support system also attracted the support of the increasingly vocal and visible women's movement. Divorce and impoverishment were correctly perceived to be real possibilities for women of all social classes, not just the poor. New statistics showed that the economic status of women and children falls substantially after divorce, while it increases for men.[21] Although they face far less risk of poverty, even remarried women are eligible for child support, but their receipt rates proved to have been particularly low.

A Period of Constancy and Change: 1975–1990

An examination of child support outcomes across the repeated census surveys of the population eligible for child support shows how little things had changed by 1990.[22] As of April 1990, 58 percent of all eligible mothers had a child support award,[23] down from 61 percent in 1986 and 59 percent in 1979. During 1989, 75 percent of all mothers due support actually received some payment, up from less than 72 percent in 1978 but down from the high of 76 percent in 1983 and 1987. Among those receiving support, the average amount of child support received fell 25 percent between 1978 and 1985, adjusted for inflation. After that, receipts rose, but even by 1989 the real value of child support received was 12.5 percent less than in 1978.[24]

In contrast to the apparent lack of progress in child support payments, there have been significant changes in child support laws during the past fifteen years. The federal government's involvement in child support began in 1975 when a part D was added to TITLE IV of the Social Security Act (Public Law 93–647). It created the federal Office of Child Support Enforcement (OCSE) and required that each state establish a separate office to help custodial parents locate absent parents, establish paternity, obtain child support awards, and enforce obligations. Services of these so-called IV-D offices were to be made available to both welfare (AFDC) recipients—who are required to participate—and to nonrecipients upon application. The federal government was to play a major role by providing matching funds to states, by monitoring state programs, and by making public service announcements about the availability of child support enforcement services.[25]

Changes to child support laws continued after 1975. Many states added new enforcement laws and amended existing ones. For example, in 1978 only ten states required employers to initiate mandatory wage withholding if an employee was delinquent in child support obligations; by 1981, twenty-nine states had provisions for mandatory withholding and by 1985, there were forty-one states.[26] The Child Support Enforcement Amendments of 1984 (Public Law 98–378) strengthened the role of OCSE and required all states to use several enforcement tools beginning 1 October 1985, including, among others, the interception of state tax refunds and automatic wage withholding when payments were in arrears by one month. The amendments also required states to develop advisory numeric guidelines by 1 October 1987 that could be used by the courts in setting child support awards.

Since 1985, changes in both state and federal laws have accelerated, culminating in the passage of the Family Support Act of 1988 (Public Law 100–485). This law requires states to make wage withholding immediate in most new or modified orders using the IV-D system beginning 1 October 1990 and in most new orders issued after 1 January 1994. It also requires states to make the guidelines a "rebuttable presumption," meaning that any departure from them must be justified in writing by the court. Further, it provides for the periodic review and updating of the guideline formulas and of individual awards established under the guidelines. Finally, the law requires states to meet certain minimum standards for paternity establishment.

Not only were child support enforcement laws strengthened significantly, but government spending on the child support program increased dramatically over the program's first decade. Total administrative expenditures by the federal government grew from $98 million in fiscal year 1976 to $633 million in 1986 (or to $347 million in constant 1976 dollars).[27] Spending by states rose rapidly, too, so that total government spending on child support programs rose from $139 million in fiscal year 1976 to $941 million in fiscal year 1986 (or to $520 million in 1976 dollars).[28] This 577 percent increase is all the more impressive considering that over the same period total government outlays increased only 152 percent.[29]

As the government increased its activities on behalf of custodial parents and their children, media attention to child support intensified as well. By the late 1970s, newspaper accounts of the failure of non-custodial parents to support their children began to appear with increasing frequency. In 1980, the *New York Times Index* listed "Child Support" as a separate category for the first time, and by 1986, articles under that heading had grown to two full columns. Popular magazines, especially those with a large proportion of black or women readers, carried stories about the recent legal changes in the child support system and offered advice to women on obtaining and enforcing child support awards.[30] Daytime television talk shows[31] and evening news broadcasts documented problems with child support, and even popular entertainment programs focused upon the plight of single mothers and their children.

Looking back over this period of both constancy and change, one obvious question arises. Given the many changes in child support laws, the large increase in government expenditures, and the growth in media attention, why have aggregate child support outcomes changed so little—and in some cases even deteriorated? A major question we address in this book is whether taxpayers have had any return on their investment in new child support enforcement efforts. Have new laws and expenditures since 1975 been ineffective? Does media attention have no impact upon behavior?

Major Themes

In this book we argue that the apparent stability of aggregate child support statistics over the past decade and a half masks some improvements, which we attribute to changes in the legal and social environment surrounding child support. A more detailed analysis of the aggregate statistics than has heretofore been performed reveals that there has been distinct progress for some subgroups of women. Notable gains for both black mothers and never-married mothers are invisible in aggregate statistics because these subgroups form a relatively small proportion of the population eligible for child support. In addition, using statistical analyses, we reveal that opposing forces are responsible for the apparent lack of change in award and receipt rates shown in the aggregate statistics.

Because receipt rates did not fall, and in fact increased for some subgroups of the population, we can infer that changes in public laws and private attitudes have had a positive impact. We also provide evidence that without an improved legal and social environment, the real value of child support awards would have declined even more than they did owing to adverse socioeconomic changes in the composition of the population, to the stagnation of male incomes after 1973, and to the impact of inflation on both existing awards and newly made ones.

Another major theme of this book is that while a more detailed analysis of child support statistics identifies areas of progress, it also reveals persistent problems. Foremost among these is that the real value of child support payments received, already low by almost any standard, fell sharply between 1978 and 1985. As we show, payments declined largely because the real value of awards declined, which can in turn be traced to two principal sources. First, after initial obligations are established, rising prices erode their value because few are adjusted for inflation. When the rate of inflation is high, as it was in the late 1970s, the resulting decline is all the more severe. Second, and even more important, the average dollar value of new awards has been rising more slowly than consumer prices for more than twenty years. Courts appear to have been reticent to adjust the money value of new awards upward by the full amount of price or even income increases, particularly during periods of high inflation. Thus, child support awards have declined as a percentage of male incomes.

Another problem brought out in detailed analyses is that black and never-married mothers fare worse than average at all stages of the child support process. Partly as a result, they are more likely to fall into poverty and to end up on AFDC. Black mothers constitute a disproportionate share not only of the eligible child support population, but also of never-married mothers. Given racial differences in marital status, black fathers are less likely *ever* to have lived in the same household as their children and are more likely to have children in several households, while black mothers are more likely to have children who are supposed to receive financial support from different fathers.[32] Never-married mothers face some important differences in the relevant social, legal, and economic environments from ever-married mothers. The legal environment itself appears to have been better designed for women who become mothers after marriage than for those out of wedlock since the latter must establish paternity as a prerequisite to obtaining a child support award. Furthermore, black fathers tend to have much lower incomes, and hence less ability to pay, than their nonblack counterparts, as do the younger fathers of children born out of wedlock; and black fathers have lower incomes relative to black mothers than do nonblacks. We investigate to what extent racial and marital status differentials in child support might be expected on the basis of differences in the average observable characteristics of custodial mothers and noncustodial fathers grouped by race and marital status and the differential impact of laws on the behavior of these groups.

A related goal of our research was to determine how child support laws have been related to both the progress and the persistent problems we identify. Historically, state laws have varied considerably, but the 1984 Child Support Enforcement Amendments mandated a uniform set of laws for all states, and the 1988 Family Support Act further tightened some of these requirements. We are careful to distinguish changes in laws governing the payment of existing obligations from those governing the establishment of new ones. Until 1988, most new federal and state child support legislation addressed problems of the enforcement of existing awards rather than the creation of new ones. Although we might therefore expect changes in the legal environment between 1975 and 1985 to have caused more progress in receipts than awards, we allow for the intended and unintended feedback effects of enforcement on awards and of the legal environment surrounding awards on receipts. The enforcement techniques mandated by the federal government have generally been believed to be effective without evidence. We study the effects of particular state laws on the progress in child support awards and receipts through 1985 and use the results to draw implications about recent federal legislation. The relative absence of guidelines during this period and the weakness of paternity legislation are probably partly responsible for the problems of the low and declining value of awards and the lack of awards among the never-married. Some provisions of the Family Support Act are scheduled for implementation well into the decade; as more information becomes available, lawmakers will undoubtedly continue to revise and attempt to strengthen these laws.

A final major theme is that the payment (and nonpayment) of child support has consequences, both public and private. One rationale for most child support legislation is that if parents can be made to support their own children, taxpayers will not have to, and dollars invested in child support enforcement can pay dividends in terms of significant savings in welfare payments. We investigate the distribution of benefits between the public and private sectors by comparing the gains in child support for women on AFDC to those for women not on AFDC.[33] Not only may the receipt of child support raise the income of the mother and her children directly, but it may also improve their well-being indirectly. We investigate the consequences of receiving child support income related to choices made by women and children that affect their economic well-being—including AFDC participation, mother's labor supply, mother's remarriage, and children's education.

The Economic Perspective

As our title suggests, we approach the study of child support from an economic perspective and focus primarily on child support as a source of income to families. Alimony is another potentially important source of income, but it does not extend to the same population as child support; it stops with remarriage and does not apply to the never-married. Thus, we do not analyze it, but we do consider it later as an income source to families.[34] We also ignore property settlements, owing to data limitations. An earlier analysis of data from the 1979 survey suggests that child support and property settlements are not substitutes but complements: that is, women who have the largest child support awards also have the largest property settlements.[35] An economic perspective also directs our attention to the costs faced by the mothers and fathers—that is, the incentives for and costs of obtaining child support for mothers and of paying child support for fathers. Some of these costs may be direct, such as lawyer's fees and court costs, but others may be indirect, such as the (psychological) costs of facing an estranged spouse.

Although we rely chiefly on an economic perspective, we recognize the contribution of other concerns beyond the more traditional bounds of economics. In particular, we acknowledge the possible psychological impact of child support, and divorce generally, on children. We also consider the impact of child support on a mother's likelihood of remarriage and on children's educational attainment. In this regard, we rely upon the pioneering work of Gary Becker, who first applied the tools of microeconomic analysis to the study of family behavior.[36]

As perhaps can be deduced from our themes, our approach in the main is one of positive economics, reporting the facts without making value judgments about what *should* be. We recognize that in individual cases there may be legitimate competing claims to limited resources. Since child support involves a redistribution of income, if the father is made to pay more, the mother and her children will be better off, but he (and his second family, if he has one) will be worse off.[37] Nonetheless, in describing changes in child support outcomes, we occasionally use words with normative connotations, such as *good* and *better* or *progress* and *lack of progress*. This reflects our belief that a general public consensus emerged in the 1980s that more child support is preferred to less because too many fathers have paid too little.[38] And to the extent that we compare child support in the United States with other nations, the situation in this country seems even worse.[39] We explicitly depart from the positive approach only in the final chapter, where we point out some of the policy implications of our findings.

Some of the terminology we adopt, widely used in the child support literature, may appear to be potentially misleading. In particular, the term *custodial mother* means the mother has physical custody of the child at the time of the survey but does not necessarily mean she has *sole* legal or even sole physical custody. (In the vast majority of cases, however, the mother does have sole physical custody.) The term *absent father* means the father is absent from the household in which the woman and children reside (consistent with the definition in the census data we are using) but does not necessarily mean he has no contact with his children. As of spring 1990, 62 percent of absent fathers had either visitation privileges or joint custody arrangements.[40]

Data and Methodology

Many of the questions we choose to ask and the approaches we take to answering them are shaped by the availability of data covering the period since 1975. The U.S. Census Bureau surveyed women about their child support experiences for the first time in April 1979. This child support supplement to the Current Population Survey (CPS) covered women ages eighteen and over living with own children under twenty-one years of age whose father was absent from the household.[41] In these surveys, the Census Bureau elicited a brief marital history, information on the number of children, and the award and receipt of child support. These records were then matched with the mother's responses to the March CPS questionnaire, which contained income and demographic data. The April supplement was repeated with some modification in 1982, 1984, and 1986.[42] We used these four surveys in our study. It is important to recognize both the strengths and the limitations of these data for the study of child support.

Foremost among its strengths is that the CPS is one of the few large samples nationally representative of all mothers eligible for child support. Among such data sets, it is the only one that spans nearly the entire period of increasing federal involvement in the child support arena. In addition, when linked sequentially, the four individual CPS surveys can be used to assess changes in child support outcomes arising from government interventions over this period of time. Further, this combined data set is large enough to study separately important subgroups of the population—namely black and never-married mothers. The combined data set contains about 16,000 mothers eligible for child support, including about 4,000 black and 3,000 never-married mothers.[43]

The CPS also has limitations. First, the child support supplement was designed to cover only women with children *currently* eligible for child support, that is, with own children under twenty-one present in the household.[44] Errors in survey design, however, led to the unintentional inclusion of some women (mostly grandmothers) living in a household with their own child aged twenty-one or older and someone else under twenty-one. We adjust the sample to exclude some of these women by placing restrictions (discussed in app. A) on their age and the length of time since the marital disruption.[45] Furthermore, there were three omissions. By intention, the sizable population of teenage mothers (births to teenagers under eighteen years of age constituted 15 percent of all births to unmarried women in 1986)[46] was not surveyed.[47] Inadvertently, women (eighteen or older) who had borne a child out of wedlock before their current marriage, whose child was neither fathered nor adopted by their current husband, were also left out, but we do not know how large this group may be.

Another relatively small group omitted from the survey consists of custodial fathers. According to estimates from the Survey of Income and Program Participation, in 1985 there were 7.1 million children receiving some financial help from an adult provider living elsewhere, with less than 6 percent of these children receiving support from an outside female provider.[48] From a policy perspective, although they are subject to the same laws and guidelines, custodial fathers constitute a less important group, given typical income differences by gender. As for differences in payment behavior, according to data from the National Longitudinal Study of the High School Class of 1972 (NLS72), noncustodial mothers with child support obligations were less likely to pay child support than noncustodial fathers.[49]

A second limitation of the CPS is that it collects data only on *monetary* child support from an absent father to the mother of their children that results from a written agreement between the parents. This is the common notion of child support payments and the one that is legally recognized, but by not including other transfers an absent father could make to his children, it may underestimate the full extent of paternal involvement with children. In-kind payments are possible, such as providing housing space adequate for overnight visits, sending birthday presents, paying for braces or college tuition, or providing health insurance.[50] Recent data from the National Longitudinal Study, however, show that, with the exception of giving presents, a substantial majority of absent fathers never make such *nonmonetary* transfers;[51] and among those who do, these other forms of assistance tend to complement rather than substitute for monetary payments of child support.[52] Nevertheless, these sorts of transfers may be considered in setting guidelines for child support awards.

Finally, perhaps the most important limitations of CPS data derive from their omission of certain relevant information about the father and the history of the child support award. Because it is a household-based survey, CPS collects no information from fathers absent from the household, and after an initial attempt in 1979, mothers were no longer asked to provide any information about them.[53] As a result, we cannot control directly for differences in the incomes of fathers but must rely instead on imperfect proxies, including the relevant socio-economic characteristics of mothers and aggregate data on average male incomes in the year of the marital disruption. We also have to rely solely on the mother's report of how much child support she received, which according to some recent work is often less than the father's reported payments.[54] Finally, we are missing information about several key elements of the child support award: we know how much support was due and received in the year before the survey, but not how much was originally awarded, nor how much was received in other years; we know whether an award was made but not the date of that award,[55] nor how many or which children the award covers. These omissions limit the extent to which we can study, among other things, trends in the value of new child support awards or the effects of past receipts on current payment behavior.[56]

In chapters 2 through 5, we rely almost exclusively upon the four years of CPS data (supplemented, on occasion, by aggregate economic data) to analyze the socioeconomic determinants of, racial and marital status differentials in, and trends over time in child support awards and receipts. In chapter 6, we supplement these national CPS data with some state data to study the effects of changes over time in the legal environment on child support outcomes. We introduce measures of administrative expenditures on child support enforcement obtained from annual reports of OCSE and detailed information about state laws on child support guidelines, paternity determination, and enforcement techniques prepared by the National Conference of State Legislatures. Finally, in chapter 7, we rely again exclusively upon CPS data—and sometimes only a single survey year—to study the impact of child support payments on related economic decisions made by mothers and children.

Although the economic well-being of a custodial mother and her children depends directly upon the amount of child support actually received, not upon the amount awarded, it is often useful to think of child support payments as the end product of four separate outcomes. These include whether or not an award is obtained; if so, how much is awarded (which we approximate by the amount due); whether or not any money is received; and if so, how much is received. We consider each of these four outcomes separately in analyzing causes of trends in child support. The reason for this is that child support payments will change if any one of the outcomes changes; more importantly, payments may fail to change if two or more outcomes move in opposite directions. One example, relevant to the period 1978–85, shows that even when award and receipt rates rise, if award amounts decline sufficiently, the average payments received may also decline. Thus, reversing the decline in child support receipts requires reversing the decline in the value of new award amounts.

Another reason we analyze each of the four child support outcomes separately is that some of the socioeconomic and legal factors that determine awards may be different from the ones that determine receipts. Income at the time of a marital disruption and the formulas of guidelines may influence initial award amounts, while current income and enforcement techniques may affect receipts. Moreover, it is possible that changes in the legal environment governing receipts may improve receipt rates but have an adverse impact on award rates, thereby leaving total receipts unchanged. Finally, we study each outcome separately to understand better the sources of racial and marital status differentials in payments, as well as what might be done to narrow these differentials. For example, we will show that never-married mothers are much less likely than ever-married mothers to have an award, but among those who do, they are just as likely to receive some payment.

Related Studies

Recently, a growing amount of attention has been devoted to child support in the scholarly literature. We do not attempt a comprehensive survey but rather briefly mention here the more significant contributions that directly relate to our present study and cite other pertinent studies in the course of our analyses. Two influential early publications are the books *Child Support and Public Policy* by Judith Cassetty (1978) and *Making Fathers Pay: The Enforcement of Child Support* by David L. Chambers (1979).[57] Since then, the study of child support outcomes has evolved continuously in academic media with progressive improvements in data and methodology.[58]

Beginning in the mid-1980s, theoretical and empirical analyses have extended our understanding of child support issues in many directions.

Yoram Weiss and Robert J. Willis developed and subsequently tested a theoretical model that explains why noncustodial parents prefer to transfer less income to their children than when they live with them.[59] In the empirical literature, using analyses of socioeconomic determinants as a starting point, studies have gone on to analyze differentials in child support outcomes by race and marital status and trends in them over time.[60] A recent innovation has been to combine the legal and socioeconomic determinants of child support receipts in a single unified framework.[61] Finally, studies have only just begun to examine some of the consequences of child support income for welfare, the labor supply, and the educational decisions made by single mothers and their children.[62] Most of these studies have appeared in scholarly journals in the social sciences; as such, this book represents the first attempt to make these analyses available to a wider audience.

All of the analyses of determinants, differentials, and trends presented in this book are new. They provide a comprehensive coverage of child support awards and receipts within a unified framework. Although they build directly on the foundation laid by our earlier studies, they extend the methodology where needed and are based upon a longer time-series of data. The larger number of observations available allows us to examine in more detail various subgroups of the population, such as never-married mothers. For example, we examine for the first time the effects of state paternity legislation and guidelines on the award rates of never-married mothers. The analysis of the legal determinants of support is much more extensive than before, with the first work on the effects of guidelines on awards, the inclusion of state government expenditures, and an analysis of the effects of child support enforcement practices on receipts. We also discuss issues related to the development of guidelines. Finally, we present new results on the consequences of child support for AFDC participation, poverty rates, and the mother's decision about whether and how soon to remarry.[63]

In this book, we confine most theoretical analyses and all technical econometric details to notes and appendixes. A summary of relevant findings is provided at the end of each chapter.

In chapter 2, we present descriptive analyses of the aggregate data that both introduce and summarize many of the main themes of the book; we consider overall trends in child support awards from 1979 to 1986 and receipts from 1978 to 1985, and differentials and trends by race, marital status, and current AFDC status. Chapter 3 serves as a transition between these aggregate analyses and the disaggregate (or individual) analyses found in the next three chapters, developing a theoretical framework and describing the structure of CPS data in detail.

In chapter 4, we make use of more complex statistical analyses to study the socioeconomic determinants of child support awards—in particular the likelihood that a woman will have an award and the value of the award—and in chapter 5, to study child support receipts, including both the likelihood of receiving support and the value of child support received. At the end of chapter 5, we present a summary of the major findings from these two chapters that is designed to stand alone and to inform the reader who prefers to skip details. In chapter 6, we examine the impact of state child support enforcement laws on child support awards and receipts and discuss issues in the formulation of guidelines. These analyses allow us to make predictions about the probable success or failure of the provisions of recent federal child support enforcement legislation.

In chapter 7, we analyze some of the anticipated behavioral consequences of receiving child support payments for mothers and their children. Chapter 8 develops the policy implications of our findings and suggests avenues for future research. We offer seven specific recommendations for the 1990s. How questions about child support are resolved is important: at stake is the economic well-being of millions of American women and children, now and in the future.

Aggregate
Differentials
and Trends in
Child Support
Payments

Child support in the United States has been characterized as a national disgrace.[1] Indeed, many women unexpectedly find themselves to be the sole support of children their husbands or their unmarried lovers presumably wanted as well. According to both law and religious tradition, men and women who have children thereby acquire the moral if not legal responsibility for their support.[2] But as recent statistics make painfully clear, when the parental union breaks up or children are born out of wedlock, fathers too often neglect that responsibility.

Collecting child support has proved difficult for many women as they confront formidable challenges both in obtaining awards and receiving payment. On average, throughout the 1980s only about 60 percent of eligible women had a child support award, and only 50 percent of those due support received full payment. Moreover, judged by almost any standards, payments were low and at least through the mid-1980s declined in real terms. Only black women and never-married mothers made some notable gains during the 1980s.

In this chapter, we analyze in detail aggregate trends and differentials by race and marital status in each child support outcome separately, focusing on the years 1978–86, which was a period during which significant change might have been expected. Child support outcomes encompass both the award and the receipt of child support and cover both rates and amounts. An award may be granted either by voluntary written agreement or court order and specifies an amount of child support to be paid from the noncustodial parent to the custodial parent, also known as the obligation. Among those custodial parents with an award and currently due payment, only some will actually receive any, and the amount they receive may differ from the amount they are due. In particular, we analyze: (1) the percentage of women awarded child support (award rates), (2) the amount of child support currently due, (3) the percentage of women receiving child support (receipt rates), and (4) the amount of child support received, both in dollars and as a proportion of the amount due. We then unite these four outcomes to arrive at the bottom line: the average amount of child support received among the total population eligible for support.

This chapter introduces many of the themes pursued in greater detail later in the book, particularly in chapters 4–6. Our first goal is to identify areas of progress and lack of progress over the period and for awards only, also over an extended period back to 1958. Our second goal is to document differentials by race, which are related to behavioral, cultural, and economic differences, and by marital status, which influences economic decisions and legal obligations. Our final goal is to begin to assess whether the federal child support enforcement program, initiated in 1976, was effective. We conclude that small increases in the award and receipt rates overall combined with larger increases for black mothers and never-married mothers suggest that federal efforts to strengthen child support enforcement may have been at least partially successful. In addition, we find that the real dollar amount of child support payments received has been declining largely because child support awards have not been keeping up with inflation, which largely accounts for the decline in the real value of child support received.

This chapter also considers topics not pursued in greater detail elsewhere—namely, the adequacy of child support awards and differentials in child support outcomes between the AFDC and non-AFDC populations. We show that child support awards are inadequate by almost any reasonable standard. We also find that black mothers not on AFDC have made greater gains in award and receipt rates than those on AFDC, but at the same time many black mothers have escaped from AFDC, suggesting the possible success of the child support enforcement program among AFDC mothers.

The population of women eligible for child support, already large at 7 million in 1979, had grown to 8.6 million by 1986.[3] Our adjusted

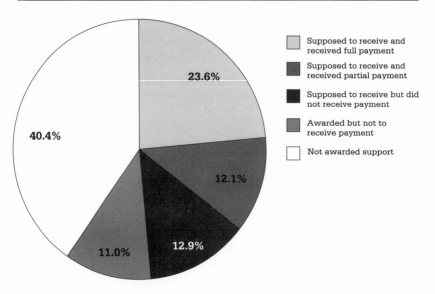

2.1 Child Support Payments to All Mothers with Children from an Absent
Father, 1979–1986

estimates show a slightly smaller population eligible for child support
and a slightly higher award rate than the Census Bureau's published
figures, but a nearly identical receipt rate (see table 2.A1 in app. A).[4]
As shown in figure 2.1, on average, over these years only three in five
eligible mothers had a child support award, only one in three received
some payment from their child's father, and only one in four received
the full amount due.

Roughly one out of four women eligible for child support is black
(one out of ten Hispanic),[5] and one out of five has never been married
(see fig. 2.2). In general, the population of women with children from
an absent father suffers from low economic status, but minority and
never-married mothers tend to be especially poor, with nearly one-
half on welfare (AFDC). The ever-married group of women eligible for
support comprises mothers who are married to but are currently separated from their child's father (17%); who are currently divorced
(one-third); and who are since remarried (one-quarter). Because child
support outcomes have tended to differ among these groups, we analyze each outcome by group and note where its experience diverges
from the average.

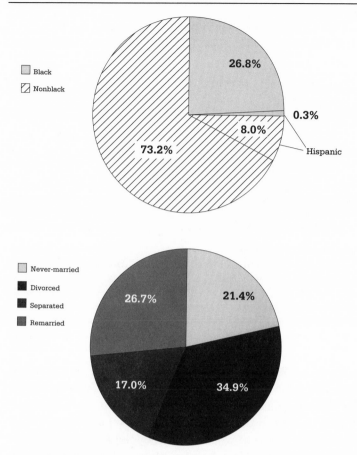

2.2 Race and Current Marital Status of the Female Population Eligible for Child Support, 1979–1986

Award Rates

Obtaining a child support award, the first step in the long process to actual receipt of payments, is perhaps the most difficult one. As previously noted, overall only about 60 percent of eligible mothers secure an award from their children's father. Judged by their low award rates, never-married mothers and minority (black and Hispanic) women have an especially difficult time doing so. Although for most women, the award process seems not to have gotten any easier, more and more black and never-married mothers appear to be succeeding.

Table 2.1   Percentage of Eligible Women with a Child Support
Award as of April 1979, 1982, 1984, and 1986 by Race and Marital
Status[a]

Group (N)[b]	Average	1979	1982	1984	1986
All Women (15,658)	59.6	59.3	59.7	57.8	61.5
Race or National Origin					
Black (3,708)	33.4	28.8	34.0	33.6	36.4
Nonblack (11,950)	69.1	70.4	69.2	66.7	70.4
Hispanic (1,178)	42.8	43.5	44.3	41.2	42.8
Marital Status					
Never-married (3,196)	15.7	10.6	14.3	17.7	18.4
Ever-married (12,462)	71.6	71.3	71.5	68.9	74.5

Source: 1979, 1982, 1984, and 1986 cps March/April Match Files.

[a] Means are weighted averages.

[b] N denotes the total sample size across all four years of data. This sample excludes
65 cases in 1979, 66 in 1982, 74 in 1984, and 77 in 1986 owing to restrictions on the
sample by age and years since divorce or separation of mother (roughly 1.8% of the
sample).

But, as we will see, the most disadvantaged subgroup—black women
on AFDC—have not shared in this progress.

When asked in 1986, a majority of women without an award said
they wanted one.[6] Either their final agreement was still pending (10%),
or they could not obtain an award owing to their inability to locate the
father (30%), to establish paternity (3%), or for other reasons (11%).
But a substantial minority of women said they did not want an award
(38%) or had reached another type of settlement (5%).[7] Women who
do not want an award may fear contact with the absent father for
themselves or their children. Even many of those who say they want
an award may not be willing to incur the costs of getting one, such as
the possible difficulty in locating the father or unwanted contact with
him.

Differentials by Race and Marital Status

Award rates differ most by marital status. Fully 70 percent of the
ever-married, but only 15 percent of the never-married, have awards.
Award rate differentials by race and national origin are only somewhat
less pronounced. Around 70 percent of nonblacks, compared with only
one-third of blacks and 43 percent of Hispanics, have awards (see
table 2.1).

Although race and marital status clearly affect the chances of *not* having an award—as of 1986, almost 82 percent of black, never-married mothers did not compared with just 14 percent of divorced nonblack mothers—they do not dramatically alter the reasons. In 1986, 32 percent of never-married mothers without an award said they were unable to locate the father, while 43 percent said they did not want an award.[8] Among ever-divorced mothers, 24 percent said they were unable to locate the father, while 42 percent said they did not want an award. By race, 40 percent of blacks but only 24 percent of nonblacks were unable to locate the father, while 34 percent of blacks and 40 percent of nonblacks did not want an award.

The Aggregate Award Rate across Survey Years

Over the period since the Census Bureau first began collecting data on child support, award rates have risen little overall; as shown in table 2.1, the overall award rate grew only 2.2 percentage points between 1979 and 1986, from 59.3 to 61.5 percent.[9] The award rate among the ever-married showed a similar trend but rose slightly more, increasing 3.2 percentage points over the period.

The relative constancy of the award rate overall masks a significant improvement in the award for certain subgroups—notably, black and never-married mothers, the groups with the lowest rates. The child support award rate of both groups rose nearly 8 percentage points— among blacks, from 28.8 to 36.4 percent, and among the never-married, from 10.6 to 18.4 percent. In part, these similar trends reflect the groups' overlap: about half of all eligible black women are never married and a majority of never-married mothers are black, albeit declining from 60 percent in 1979 to 53 percent in 1986.

More detailed demographic breakdowns by current marital status and race together reveal further award rate differentials and trends among various subgroups (see table 2.2). Among all ever-married mothers, the divorced and remarried are considerably more likely to have awards than the separated mothers. This is understandable since a separation may be only temporary or a formal child support award may be postponed until the legal hearing, which takes place at divorce.[10] Among black mothers, however, separations often tend to be prolonged and never to be formalized in a written agreement or a divorce.[11] The award rate rose slightly for both divorced and remarried mothers from 1979 to 1986. Although trends are similar for both races,

Table 2.2 Child Support Award Rate by Race and Current Marital Status as of April 1979, 1982, 1984, and 1986[a]

Group (N)[b]	Average	1979	1982	1984	1986	% Change 1979–1986
All Races						
Never-married (799)	15.7	10.6	14.3	17.7	18.4	7.8
Ever-married (3,116)	71.6	71.3	71.5	68.9	74.5	3.2
Separated (633)	43.4	45.7	43.4	41.4	43.4	−2.3
Divorced (1,391)	80.0	79.9	81.3	76.4	82.6	2.7
Remarried (1,092)	78.4	76.8	78.5	76.0	82.0	5.2
Nonblack						
Never-married (344)	16.3	10.6	15.9	17.9	18.5	7.9
Ever-married (2,643)	75.9	77.1	75.1	73.2	78.5	1.4
Separated (421)	48.7	56.2	46.2	47.5	46.6	−9.6
Divorced (1,195)	82.9	83.5	83.1	79.6	85.7	2.2
Remarried (1,028)	79.5	78.6	79.9	76.6	82.7	4.1
Black						
Never-married (455)	15.3	10.6	13.5	17.6	18.4	7.8
Ever-married (472)	50.8	44.5	54.6	48.8	54.8	10.3
Separated (212)	34.0	29.8	37.9	30.5	37.8	8.0
Divorced (196)	64.8	60.6	70.8	61.7	66.3	5.7
Remarried (64)	64.2	53.2	63.8	66.1	72.8	19.6

Source: 1979, 1982, 1984, and 1986 CPS March/April Match Files.

[a] Means are weighted averages.
[b] N denotes the average sample size over the four years of data.

for remarried black mothers the award rate increased an exceptional 20 percentage points.[12] For separated mothers, the award rate fell considerably among nonblacks (10 percentage points) but rose nearly as much among blacks (8 percentage points).

Why did the aggregate award rate rise only 2.2 percentage points over the period 1979–86 although federal and state governments became increasingly involved in the child support system? One reason is the compositional changes in the population of women eligible for support. For instance, the group least likely to have awards, never-married mothers, increased as a proportion of the eligible population. Another reason is that, as we will see later in this chapter, the real incomes of fathers stagnated after 1973 and had not fully recovered by 1984. At lower income levels, judges may simply not issue an award. Finally, perhaps much of the government effort was directed toward the enforcement of existing awards rather than the establishment of new ones. Although it is impossible to tell from our data, an increase in joint custody arrangements may also have exerted a slight downward pressure on the award rate.

Trends in New Award Rates, 1958–1985

The relative constancy of the *aggregate* award rate since 1979 also masks important underlying changes in *new* award rates—the percentage of women newly eligible for child support in a given year who obtain an award. We can study historical trends in new award rates by taking advantage of the fact that each survey consists of a stock of women who entered the child-support-eligible population in various years.[13] Although we do not know the year women first became eligible, among ever-married mothers the divorce or, if not divorced, the separation year is a natural date to choose since most awards are made then, especially if there is a court process. Long-term trends in new award rates can be seen most clearly when we distinguish further between ever-divorced and currently separated mothers and group women from all four surveys according to the year of their marital disruption. This yields a flow of women into the child-support-eligible population over a period of twenty-eight years (1958–85).[14]

By contrast to the aggregate award rate, new award rates among ever-married mothers have risen substantially, although not steadily, over time. Figure 2.3 shows that among newly divorced mothers the award rate exhibits a gradual upward trend from 58 percent in 1963 to 87 percent in 1976, a small decline to 77 percent in 1981, and a slight increase again to 83 percent in 1985. Among newly separated mothers, the rate exhibits an even more pronounced upward trend between 1967 and 1978, from 10 to 53 percent. This is also followed by a slight decline and then rise thereafter, but for this group there is much greater variability around the average than among the divorced. Recalling that the federal government initiated its child support enforcement program in August 1975, an abatement of the long-term upward trend in award rates in its immediate aftermath is somewhat surprising.

When historic trends are displayed by race and marital status, we discover that new award rates appear to have risen more rapidly for blacks than nonblacks and their decline after 1975 to be more pronounced for nonblacks (fig. 2.4). The trend in award rates among divorced nonblacks mirrors the overall trend (see fig. 2.3) at a higher level: the three-year moving average rises from 70 percent in 1964 to a high of 85 percent in 1977, falls to 81 percent in 1981 and rises to 85

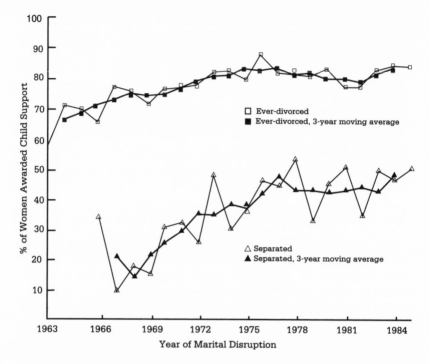

2.3 Rise in Child Support Award Rate among Ever-married Women by Current Marital Status

percent again in 1984. Among divorced blacks, the three-year moving average rises by more and continues to rise longer, from 53 percent in 1966 to 71 percent in 1979; it then declines but shows considerable variability, ending in a high of 68 percent in 1984. Among separated mothers of both races, the three-year moving average award rate rises to a high in 1977 and then fluctuates thereafter, reaching another high in the mid-1980s.

To summarize, among the ever-married, child support award rates have been increasing gradually for at least the past twenty-five years. Yet contrary to expectations, new award rates did not continue to rise after the federal child support enforcement program was initiated in 1975. It might be that stronger child support enforcement legislation actually had the unintended feedback effect of making fathers less likely to agree to and judges less likely to impose an award if the father's ability to pay was in doubt. But around the same time as the federal program commenced, the real income of men began to fall,

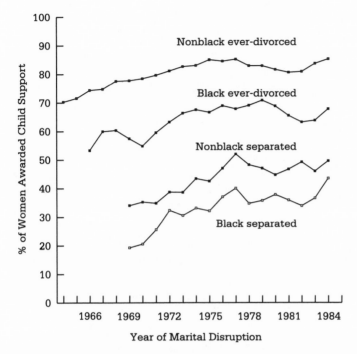

2.4 Rise in Child Support Award Rate among Ever-married Women by Current Marital Status and Race, Three-Year Moving Average

and thus fathers might have become less able to pay child support. In chapter 4 we investigate to what extent the latter factor, and in chapter 6, the former, may have contributed to the recent decline in new award rates.

Award Rates and AFDC Status

We now turn to an examination of trends in aggregate award rates by current AFDC status. This is important for several reasons. First, certain provisions of child support laws, resource efforts of federal and state child support offices, and private incentives to obtain support have all differed historically according to the mother's AFDC status. Second, these differences may shed some light on why trends in new award rates of blacks and nonblacks differed after 1975. Throughout this analysis, it is important to bear in mind that we can only observe *current* AFDC status, not AFDC status at the time of any possible government intervention.

Historically, AFDC mothers have faced a different child support environment from mothers who are not on AFDC. As a condition for receiving AFDC, a woman must assign her child support rights to the state and agree to cooperate in locating the father and establishing an award. Prior to 1984, welfare mothers had little incentive to cooperate since all monies collected on her behalf would go to reimburse the state for the cost of her welfare payments. Her family received only the amount of child support collected in excess of her welfare grant. Since 1 October 1984, the state disregards the first $50 per month per family of any child support collected on her behalf (and passes it through to her) both in determining eligibility and in calculating the amount of benefits.[15] To reduce their welfare costs and take advantage of program cost reimbursement incentives established by the federal government, many states have concentrated their child support efforts on the AFDC caseload. At the close of fiscal year 1979, AFDC recipients represented 85 percent of the child support enforcement (IV-D) caseload, and by fiscal 1985, they still constituted almost 75 percent of all cases.[16]

This concentration of state child support resources on AFDC cases may help to explain why the new award rates of black mothers performed better than those of nonblacks after 1975 and why the aggregate award rate of the never-married rose faster than that of the ever-married between 1979 and 1986.[17] Black and never-married mothers are overrepresented in the AFDC program in proportion to their numbers in the child-support-eligible population: on average between 1979 and 1986, 44 percent of black mothers and 50 percent of never-married mothers were on welfare, compared with only 25 percent of all eligible mothers. Since child support laws and enforcement efforts have largely been directed at the AFDC population, and since blacks and the never-married are disproportionately on AFDC, we might expect their gains to be larger than those of nonblacks and the ever-married.

Evidence about the role of the federal child support enforcement program in generating the stronger award rate gains of never-married and black mothers is found in table 2.3, which breaks down award rates by current AFDC recipient status. For the never-married, the evidence is consistent with the success of the program. Never-married mothers on AFDC improved their award rate 9 percentage points compared with 7 percentage points for those not on AFDC. But, for black

Table 2.3 Percentage of Eligible Women with a Child Support Award as of April 1979, 1982, 1984, and 1986 by Race or Marital Status and Receipt of AFDC[a]

	1979	1982	1984	1986	Change 1979–1986[b]
All Women					
AFDC	41.5	39.0	40.0	36.4	−5.1
Non-AFDC	66.1	66.8	63.4	69.2	3.1
Race					
Black					
AFDC	25.1	26.4	28.3	23.8	−1.3
Non-AFDC	32.0	30.0	37.7	45.6	13.6
Nonblack					
AFDC	55.2	49.9	51.1	47.5	−7.7
Non-AFDC	74.3	73.7	69.9	75.1	0.8
Marital Status					
Never-married					
AFDC	12.5	16.9	18.8	19.2	6.7
Non-AFDC	8.7	11.6	16.7	17.6	8.9
Ever-married					
AFDC	57.2	54.6	55.9	54.2	−3.0
Non-AFDC	75.3	75.5	71.6	78.1	2.8

Source: 1979, 1982, 1984, and 1986 CPS March/April Match files.

[a] Means are weighted averages.

[b] All changes are significant at least at the 5% level except ever-married on AFDC, black on AFDC, and nonblack not on AFDC.

women, a first glance at the evidence in this table only deepens the puzzle. Between 1979 and 1986, the award rate of black women not on AFDC rose nearly 14 percentage points, while for those on AFDC, it declined one percentage point.

How might we explain why award rates of black mothers improved exclusively in the non-AFDC population? One possibility is that state agencies concentrated their resources on collecting existing awards to the neglect of increasing the proportion of eligible women with awards, and black mothers are much more likely than the never-married to have awards. But, the data only weakly support this hypothesis: in fiscal year 1978, obligations were established in roughly two-thirds as many cases as a collection was made.[18] Another possibility is that women who obtained an award were able to escape AFDC or avoid going on it in the first place. Unfortunately, as pointed out above, our data show only current AFDC status and thus do not permit us to evaluate this hypothesis directly.[19] A closer look at the data, however, shows that the proportion (and number) of black women eligible for child support who were on AFDC declined somewhat over this period (as they did for all subgroups except the never-married), from 47 to 42 percent.[20] Furthermore, state IV-D agencies report removing roughly nineteen thousand families from AFDC owing to child support collections during fiscal year 1978.[21] Thus, black women remaining on AFDC may be an adversely selected group in the sense that they are less likely to have awards.

Amount Due

Although award rates tell us about the proportion of eligible women who have a child support agreement, they tell us nothing about the amount agreed upon. If the good news to emerge from census statistics is that award rates have been increasing over time, the bad news is that the value of awards is low and has been declining in real terms. Between 1978 and 1985, inflation seriously eroded the purchasing power of the average child support obligation. For at least twenty years inflation has been eroding the purchasing power of new awards; however, there is some evidence that during the early 1980s, increases in new awards *almost* kept pace with the rate of inflation.

We measure award amounts by the value of child support due in the year prior to the survey among those women due support.[22] This was the only award measure collected in the CPS and may or may not be the same as the amount initially awarded. Amount due and amount awarded will not be the same if the child support award has been renegotiated (formally or informally) or if the contract contains an automatic adjustment clause. Renegotiation may occur if either the father or mother's economic circumstances change. For example, a father might seek a reduction in his support obligation if he becomes involuntarily unemployed or disabled or if there is a change in the living arrangements of his children. A mother might seek an increase in her payments if her expenses rise with changes in her children's needs, increases in the general price level, or unexpectedly large increases in the father's income. Few contracts contain clauses for the automatic adjustment of awards for inflation or increases in the father's income.[23] Moreover, the data we examine in this section (and in greater detail in app. C) support the contention that renegotiations either do not occur or that increases balance decreases in the aggregate. Thus,

Table 2.4   Mean Amount of Child Support Due among All Women Due Support in 1978, 1981, 1983, and 1985 by Race and Marital Status: Total and per Child[a] (in 1985 dollars)

Group (N)[b]	Aver-age	1978	1981	1983	1985	% Change 1978–1985
Total						
All Women (7,706)	2,768	3,279	2,683	2,715	2,494	−23.9
Race or National Origin						
Black (904)	2,238	2,758	2,260	1,906	2,162	−21.6
Nonblack (6,802)	2,850	3,351	2,747	2,840	2,553	−23.8
Hispanic (427)	2,463	2,797	2,566	2,335	2,270	−18.8
Marital Status						
Never-married (359)	1,383	1,550	1,273	1,341	1,419	−8.5
Ever-married (7,347)	2,843	3,335	2,748	2,795	2,575	−22.8
Per Child						
All Women	1,776	2,052	1,701	1,768	1,638	−20.2
Race or National Origin						
Black	1,351	1,733	1,297	1,199	1,278	−26.3
Nonblack	1,843	2,096	1,763	1,856	1,701	−18.8
Hispanic	1,477	1,767	1,495	1,405	1,334	−24.5
Marital Status						
Never-married	1,013	1,300	939	999	964	−25.8
Ever-married	1,818	2,077	1,736	1,813	1,688	−18.7

Source: 1979, 1982, 1984, and 1986 CPS March/April Match Files.

[a] Figures are weighted averages.

[b] Excludes 12 cases in 1978, 12 in 1981, 17 in 1983, and 16 in 1985 owing to restrictions on sample by age and years since divorce or separation of mother (approximately 0.7% of the sample); and 5 in 1981 with negative values on child support due.

we conclude that the measure of child support awards available to us—the amount due—is a good approximation of the amount initially awarded, and we tend to use the words *awarded* and *due* interchangeably.

Differentials by Race and Marital Status

Over the entire period 1978–85, awards averaged $2,768 in 1985 dollars (see table 2.4). As with award rates, award amounts differed most by marital status: on average, award amounts of never-married mothers were roughly one-half those of ever-married mothers. This differential narrowed between 1978 and 1985 as real dollars due declined considerably less among the never-married (9%) than among the ever-married (23%). As a result, at the end of the period, the amount due never-married mothers had reached 55 percent of the amount due ever-married mothers.

Why do award amounts differ by marital status? One reason awards are lower among the never-married may be the differences in the number of children due support. Adjusted for family size, however, awards of the never-married averaged 56 percent of those of the ever-married, suggesting that differences in family size per se account for only a small portion of the overall differential. Another possibility is that even though never-married mothers have almost as many children, their award applies only to one child because their children have different fathers. Unfortunately, the CPS did not ask women how many and which children their award covers. Yet another possible explanation is that on average, never-married mothers tend to be relatively young and disadvantaged (judged, e.g., by education) compared with the ever-married, and this disadvantage is likely to extend to their children's fathers as well.[24]

The differential in amount of child support due by race and ethnic origin is much smaller than by marital status. In three out of the four survey years, black mother's awards averaged between 82 percent and 85 percent of those of nonblack mothers, beginning and ending the period with roughly the same differential. The value of awards among Hispanic mothers averaged roughly 86 percent of those of nonblack mothers.[25]

The most likely reason for the racial difference is the lower ability to pay of black compared with nonblack men. In both 1981 and 1985 median nonwhite male income was only 74 percent of white male income.[26] Given this income difference, black awards are a surprisingly high proportion of nonblack awards (except in 1983). A possible explanation for this may be that because blacks are less likely to have awards than nonblacks, blacks who do have an award may overrepresent the upper end of the income distribution.

Although the overall racial differential in child support due remained relatively constant over the period, 1978–85, trends differed within marital status subgroups (see table 2.5). Among both the never-married and the separated, blacks fared better than nonblacks: their

Table 2.5   Mean Amount of Child Support Due among All Women Due Support in 1978, 1981, 1983, and 1985 by Race and Current Marital Status[a]

(in 1985 dollars)

Group (N)	Average	1978	1981	1983	1985	% Change 1978–1985
All Races						
Never-married (90)	1,383	1,550	1,273	1,341	1,419	−8.5
Ever-married (1,837)	2,843	3,335	2,748	2,795	2,575	−22.8
Separated (213)	3,058	3,338	3,129	3,100	2,655	−20.5
Divorced (974)	2,959	3,427	2,855	2,851	2,797	−18.4
Remarried (650)	2,584	3,202	2,430	2,595	2,216	−30.8
Nonblack						
Never-married (38)	1,506	2,270[b]	1,120	1,353	1,601	−29.5
Ever-married (1,662)	2,884	3,365	2,783	2,876	2,588	−23.1
Separated (161)	3,207	3,490	3,258	3,416	2,617	−25.0
Divorced (876)	3,020	3,452	2,917	2,945	2,848	−17.5
Remarried (625)	2,596	3,206	2,442	2,621	2,215	−30.9
Black						
Never-married (52)	1,230	1,160	1,384	1,333	1,278	10.2
Ever-married (175)	2,512	3,082	2,470	2,106	2,477	−19.6
Separated (52)	2,635	2,855	2,783	2,044	2,743	−3.9
Divorced (98)	2,496	3,216	2,352	2,183	2,421	−24.7
Remarried (25)	2,331	3,095[c]	2,220	1,739[d]	2,232	−27.9

Source: 1979, 1982, 1984, and 1986 CPS March/April Match Files.

[a] Figures are weighted averages.
[b] Cell contains only 17 observations.
[c] This figure includes one edited value changed from $30,000 to $3,000 on the basis of other information in the record.
[d] Cell contains only 12 observations.

award amounts remained roughly constant, while those of nonblacks declined between 25 percent and 30 percent.[27] Among the divorced, blacks fared somewhat worse than nonblacks. Among the remarried, both races experienced the same large decline of around 30 percent. This large decline probably reflects both the fact that the remarried mother tends to have an older award, which has been subject to greater erosion, and that she may be less inclined to seek an increase in her award.[28] Although, on average, racial differentials in the amount due persist, by 1985 the awards of never-married, separated, and remarried black mothers are roughly on a par with those of comparable nonblack mothers.

Trends in Amount Due across Survey Years

The average amount of child support due in current dollars *rose* from $1,988 in 1978 to $2,494 in 1985, up 25 percent; however, after adjusting for inflation, the average real child support award in constant 1985 dollars *declined* from $3,279 in 1978 to $2,494 in 1985, down 24 percent (see table 2.4). Three-quarters of this decline occurred between 1978 and 1981, a period of high inflation when the Consumer Price Index (CPI) increased almost 40 percent.[29] The real value of support due remained constant between 1981 and 1983 while the CPI rose 9.5 percent but then declined 8 percent between 1983 and 1985 while the CPI rose only 8 percent.

Part of the explanation for the decline in real dollars due lies in changes in the composition of the population of women due support. First, the number of children per award fell from 1.8 in 1978 to 1.7 in 1985. Adjusting for this decline in the lower panel of table 2.4, we see that the real value of support due per child declined less than per woman, from $2,052 to $1,638 in 1985, down 20 percent (rather than 24%) from 1978.[30] Second, the composition of the population due support shifted toward women who have traditionally had lower-than-average awards: between 1978 and 1985, never-married mothers increased as a proportion of all mothers due support from 3 to 7 percent, blacks from 12 to 15 percent, and Hispanics from 5 to 6 percent.[31] As we will see in chapter 4, however, these compositional shifts explain only a small portion of the decline in awards. A far greater portion of the decline is attributable to the failure of child support awards, both old and new, to keep up with rising prices and incomes. This is not only because awards are not readjusted to keep up with inflation, as most are not, but also because new awards failed to keep up with prices and incomes. The decline in the value of old and new awards can be seen in the next two tables.

In table 2.6, we display award amounts (in both current and constant dollars) by the year (one prior to the survey) in which they are due and the year of the marital disruption, beginning two years prior to each survey and going back ten or more years.[32] Looking across a given row for a given marital disruption year enables us to see how the value of existing (old) awards changes over time. Looking down a column for a given survey year enables us to see how newly made awards change over time. Finally, examining the first number in each

Table 2.6 Mean Amount of Child Support Due among Ever-married Women Due Support in 1978, 1981, 1983, and 1985 by Year of Marital Disruption[a]
(in current and constant 1985 dollars)

Year of Marital Disruption	Current Dollars				Constant 1985 Dollars[b]			
	1978	1981	1983	1985	1978	1981	1983	1985
1986								
1985								
1984				3,284				3,284
1983				3,260				3,260
1982			2,995	2,998			3,234	2,998
1981			3,283	2,698			3,546	2,698
1980		2,870	3,044	2,312		3,396	3,287	2,312
1979		2,574	2,326	2,481		3,045	2,512	2,481
1978		2,555	2,237	2,462		3,023	2,416	2,462
1977	2,600	2,473	2,966	1,999	4,288	2,925	3,203	1,999
1976	2,369	2,400	2,593	2,101	3,907	2,840	2,800	2,101
1975	2,059	1,962	1,817	2,564	3,395	2,321	1,962	2,564
1974	2,484	1,814	2,233	1,767	4,096	2,146	2,412	1,767
1973	2,105	2,043	2,440		3,472	2,417	2,635	
1972	1,911	1,986	1,832		3,151	2,350	1,979	
1971	1,885	1,970			3,109	2,330		
1970	1,918	1,729			3,162	2,046		
1969	1,609				2,653			
1968	1,423				2,346			
1967	1,611[c]				2,657			

Source: 1979, 1982, 1984, and 1986 cps March/April Match Files.

[a] Figures are weighted averages.

[b] Figures are converted to constant 1985 dollars from the year the support is due (not the marital disruption year).

[c] The last number in each column is computed using data for that year and earlier.

column expressed in constant dollars shows how the real value of the most recent new awards changed across survey years.

Let us first consider how the value of existing awards changes over time. In current dollars, the value of an award would remain roughly constant as we look across a row, if awards are not renegotiated (or if upward and downward renegotiations just balance each other) and contain no cost-of-living adjustment clauses. We see no evidence to the contrary. These data support our earlier contention that the amount of child support due in the year before the survey is a good approximation of the amount awarded at marital disruption, no matter how many years later we observe that amount. In constant dollars, we see the erosion over time in the real value of existing awards caused by inflation. For example, for marital disruptions that took place in 1976, the average award in 1985 dollars declined from $3,900 in 1978 to $2,800 in 1981 and to $2,100 in 1985.[33]

Now let us consider how the value of new awards changes over time. In current dollars, the nominal (current) value of new awards declines as we go back in time to earlier disruption years.[34] For example, among women due support in 1978, if the marital disruption occurred in 1977, awards averaged $2,600, whereas in 1967, they averaged $1,611. In constant dollars, we obtain no further information about new awards as we go back in time because the conversion to 1985 dollars is from the year of the survey, not from the year of the disruption. Looking at the first figure in each column, in 1985 constant dollars, however, we see that across survey years the real value of new awards eroded from $4,288 in 1978 to $3,284 in 1985. Thus, like existing awards, new awards also failed to keep their value at least since the first census survey.

Trends in the Value of New Awards, 1969–1984

Since award amounts do not appear to be renegotiated over time, we can combine ever-married mothers from all survey years together according to their disruption year. In table 2.7, we display the mean child support award and the mean male income by marital disruption year. The decline in the real value of new awards after 1978 in table 2.6 appears to have begun much earlier. In general, at least as far back as 1969, awards remained stagnant while prices rose. The figures in the next to last line of the table show that child support awards rose about half as fast as prices or men's incomes over the entire period, 1969–84. Some of this decline in the real value of awards might have been expected because as seen in column 7, since 1973 male real income generally declined. Yet since the real value of child support declined more than male income, as shown by their ratio in column 8, this cannot be the entire answer.

An examination of year-to-year changes in new child support awards shows that their failure to keep up with inflation was confined to certain limited sets of years. Beginning in 1971, new awards roughly kept pace with inflation and changes in male incomes in all but three periods, 1974–75, 1978–79, and 1982. The first two of these were both intervals of high inflation compared with the years immediately pre-

Table 2.7 Mean Amount of Child Support Awarded among Ever-married Women by Marital Disruption Year and Indicators of Prices and Incomes, 1969–1984

	Current Dollars		Percentage Change from Previous Year			Constant 1985 Dollars[b]			Unemployment Rate of Males Age 20 Years and Over (9)
Year of Marital Disruption	Mean Child Support Award[a] (1)	Mean Male Income (2)	Child Support (3)	CPI (4)	Male Income (5)	Child Support (6)	Male Income (7)	Child Support/ Male Income (8)	
1984	3,284	27,238	0.7	4.3	5.5	3,400	28,197	12.1	6.6
1983	3,260	25,807	8.8	3.2	4.0	3,521	27,869	12.6	8.9
1982	2,996	24,809	-0.6	6.1	6.8	3,340	27,658	12.1	8.8
1981	3,014	23,219	9.4	10.4	8.3	3,567	27,478	13.0	6.3
1980	2,756	21,436	11.8	13.5	7.5	3,598	27,984	12.9	5.9
1979	2,466	19,935	1.8	11.3	8.9	3,653	29,533	12.4	4.2
1978	2,423	18,305	-4.7	7.7	8.1	3,998	30,206	13.2	4.3
1977	2,543	16,929	7.1	6.5	7.8	4,517	30,069	15.0	5.2
1976	2,375	15,701	14.6	5.8	6.7	4,490	29,681	15.1	5.9
1975	2,072	14,714	-4.4	9.1	7.0	4,144	29,428	14.1	6.8
1974	2,167	13,757	5.0	11.0	9.0	4,731	30,037	15.8	3.8
1973	2,064	12,618	6.3	6.2	7.0	4,998	30,552	16.4	3.3
1972	1,942	11,797	5.8	3.3	8.9	4,992	30,326	16.5	4.0
1971	1,836	10,834	9.1	4.3	5.1	4,883	28,814	16.9	4.4
1970	1,683	10,312	-5.2	5.9	5.9	4,662	28,565	16.3	3.5
1969[c]	1,775	9,737	13.2	5.4	10.9	5,205	28,554	18.2	2.1
1969–84	—	—	85.0	183.3	179.7	—	—	—	—
1980–84	—	—	19.2	26.1	27.1	—	—	—	—

Source: 1979, 1982, 1984, and 1986 CPS March/April Match Files (cols. 1 & 6); *Economic Report of the President* (Washington, D.C.: U.S. GPO, 1986), table B-59, 320 (col. 4), table B-35, 293 (col. 9); Census Bureau, CPR, series P-60, no. 159, *Money Income of Households, Families, and Persons in the United States: 1986* (Washington, D.C.: U.S. GPO, 1988), table 29, 103 (col. 2).

[a] The weighted average amount of child support due among ever-married women due support in 1978, 1981, 1983, or 1985, excluding data from the survey year and the previous year owing to part-year awards.

[b] By contrast to table 2.6, the conversion to constant dollars is from the marital disruption year, not the year support was due, so the numbers for new awards differ from those in table 2.6.

[c] Selected to maintain a minimum of 100 observations in a given disruption year

ceding. One can speculate that judges' perceptions simply did not adjust rapidly enough to the price rise. Immediately following each of these periods, in 1976 and 1980, the increase in awards was rather large, indicating that perhaps perceptions had finally caught up with reality. For the most part, during the 1970s, new awards failed to keep up only during periods of unusually high inflation.

The third time new awards did not keep up with price increases was in 1982, the beginning of the deepest recession since the Great Depression. As shown in table 2.7 (col. 9), the unemployment rate of prime age males jumped 2.5 percentage points from 6.3 percent in 1981 to 8.8 percent in 1982. One other time during the previous decade, when the unemployment rate of prime age males jumped 3 percentage points in one year, from 1974 to 1975, new child support awards also experienced a serious setback in the latter year (but this was also a period of high inflation). When fathers are unemployed, awards are likely to be set lower.[35]

The rate at which inflation has been shortchanging women and children may have abated somewhat in the early 1980s. With the exception of 1982, new awards roughly kept pace with inflation (and with changes in male incomes) at least through 1985. As shown in the last line of the table, the value of child support awards increased at nearly three-quarters the rate of prices through the mid-1980s. On the one hand, the finding that new awards kept closer pace with inflation during the 1980s could simply be that inflation remained at modest levels during this period. On the other hand, it could be that new awards benefited from the move by states, as required by the 1984 Child Support Enforcement Amendments, to establish advisory guidelines for awards, which typically tie them to men's incomes. Many states developed guidelines between 1983 and 1985, while a few states had done so even before 1981. We examine the effect of guidelines on awards in chapter 6.

To summarize, we have shown that historically the value of new child support awards has not kept pace with inflation. Small gains in their real value in years of low inflation never compensated for large losses in value in years of high inflation. On average, new awards rose just under half as fast as either male incomes or prices over the period 1969–84. Thus, we conclude that real dollars made available by fathers who do not reside in the same household as their children have deteriorated substantially *at least* since 1969, with negative consequences for the economic well-being of the children.

Adequacy of Award Amounts

Even if new child support awards had kept pace with inflation, would they be adequate? In this chapter, we offer three different vantage points from which to evaluate the adequacy of existing awards. First, we show that child support awards are low and have been declining relative to the father's ability to pay as measured by average male incomes. Second, we show awards are too low to meet children's needs as determined by actual expenditures on children and even by the minimal living standards incorporated into the official poverty line. Finally, we show that at current levels, awards have little potential for reducing poverty and welfare dependency among women and children.

A father's ability to pay and children's needs for support are factors the states consider in setting guidelines for child support award amounts and historically were generally considered by the courts when, prior to guidelines, awards were set on a case-by-case basis. Occasionally, the courts also considered the mother's ability to provide for the children. Unfortunately, the father's ability to pay was often determined by how much income was left over after paying bills, which could include large mortgages and car payments.[36] As a result, awards for parents in similar circumstances varied widely from state to state, county to county, and judge to judge.[37] The recent move to establish uniform guidelines developed in response to growing concern over the disparities and inequities that arose from this system.

Concerning a father's ability to pay, we compare child support award amounts in the year of the award (i.e., the year of the marital disruption) with the incomes of the average male full-time worker in that year.[38] As seen in table 2.7 (col. 8), new awards as a percentage of men's incomes declined from 18 percent in 1969 to 12 percent in 1984. We can also compare the value of the average award due in the year prior to the survey with average male income in that year. This ratio declined from 11 percent in 1978 to 9 percent in 1985 (results not shown).

By almost any standard, these declining percentages would have to be considered alarmingly low for an average of roughly 1.7 children. One standard against which to evaluate these percentages is recent state guidelines for award amounts. Both Massachusetts and Wisconsin base their guideline percentages on the noncustodial parents' gross income, with Massachusetts recommending 25 to 30 percent for one to two children and Wisconsin requiring 17 percent for one child, and 25 percent, 29 percent, 31 percent, and 34 percent, respectively for two, three, four, and five or more children.[39] Thus, it would appear that, since at least 1970, new awards as a proportion of male incomes have fallen well below these mandated guidelines.

As for adequacy, we compare average awards to children's needs for support. The average amount due per child in 1985 among all women due support was $1,638 and the average new award per child (in 1984) among ever-married women due support was $2,044. What portion of the annual needs of a child in 1985 does $1,638 ($2,044) meet? Assessing children's needs is not a simple task because their "needs" tend to vary with the level of living of the family they reside with. We take two approaches. The first, based on studies of the costs of raising children, is designed to capture what parents at particular socioeconomic levels spend on their children. The second, based on the official poverty line, is designed to capture what society deems the minimum acceptable level of living for children to be.

The most widely known study of the costs of raising children is that by Thomas J. Espenshade. Another study of parental expenditures on children is that by Edward P. Lazear and Robert T. Michael.[40] While the former arrives at estimates for three socioeconomic status levels, the latter estimates how much the average family spends on a child. Both studies are based on data from the 1972–73 Consumer Expenditure Survey (CEX), a national survey of household expenditure patterns conducted by the Bureau of Labor Statistics,[41] but they use different methodologies with the result that the Espenshade estimates turn out to be higher than the Lazear and Michael estimates. Some have argued that the approach used by Espenshade tends to overestimate costs, whereas that used by Lazear and Michael tends to underestimate them.[42] We return to discuss these and other studies on the costs of raising children in detail in chapter 6, when we address the development of guidelines for child support awards.

For each study, we convert the estimates of child costs into 1985 dollars using the CPI.[43] According to Lazear and Michael, the average annual parental expenditure on a child is $3,245, roughly twice the average amount of child support due per child and 1.6 times the average new award among the ever-married. According to Espenshade, however, even at his lowest socioeconomic status level (husband with a blue-collar job, less than high school education, and the wife working part-time), the average annual cost of raising a child from birth to age eighteen is $4,925, roughly 3 times the average amount of child support due and 2.4 times the average new award.

Can the mother provide the difference between the average child support award and the average expenditures on children, and should she be expected to? Since few married women earn as much as their husbands, it is unrealistic to assume that they can provide an amount equal to that of the man. It may also be unreasonable to expect them to do so since they provide valuable services as custodial parents, which are not incorporated in these estimates. On average, women who worked year-round, full-time in 1985 actually contributed 38.5 percent of total family earnings.[44] Assuming that the mother works year-round, full-time, the amount of money available for meeting the children's needs would still be inadequate based upon all of the comparisons of awards to needs above, except for new awards to ever-married mothers relative to Lazear and Michael's estimates of parental expenditures on children.

Of course, even by this latter comparison, awards are adequate only under the best of circumstances. A mother must have been married to the child's father, she must work year-round, full-time, and she must spend all of the earnings on the child. Moreover, the average single mother must earn as much as the average married woman who works year-round, full-time, which is unlikely because married women who are drawn into the labor force tend to be the ones with relatively high wages.[45] Finally, the single mother's expenses must be no higher, which is also unlikely because she is more likely to have to pay for full-time child care.[46] Furthermore, even if new awards are adequate by this comparison, they are just barely so, and unless awards are renegotiated, they will quickly cease to be adequate as inflation erodes their real purchasing power.

Our second approach, designed to capture minimal needs, is to compare child support awards to poverty-level income, a minimum living standard developed by the Social Security Administration.[47] In 1985 it took $5,593 to maintain one adult at the poverty line, an additional $1,817 if she had one child living with her, and an additional $3,069 if she had two children. Since women due support in 1985 had an average of 1.68 children, we estimate by interpolation that they needed $2,668 to maintain them at the poverty level, more than the $2,494 average amount of child support due in 1985. Referring back to table 2.4, the only demographic subgroups for whom awards even approach the poverty level of living are ever-married mothers ($2,575) and nonblack mothers ($2,553). Looking at table 2.7, among the ever-married, only those divorced or separated during the 1980s are due adequate support to maintain their children at or above the poverty line in 1985. Stated another way, the average poverty line for a single parent in 1985 would be $8,261 ($5,593 + $2,668). Even if the woman receives $2,494 in child support, this leaves her $5,767 below the poverty line; she would thus need to provide 70 percent of her family's income just in order to maintain them at the poverty level of living.

From the third vantage point, we show that given the low award amounts, particularly among AFDC recipients, the potential of the present child support system for reducing the poverty rate and welfare dependency (the AFDC participation rate) is likely to be minimal. Even if all existing awards were paid, declines in poverty and welfare dependency would be minimal according to the results presented in chapter 7. Under the same scenario, Philip K. Robins provides evidence of possible savings in welfare benefits of up to 15 percent, but limited possibilities of removing women and children from welfare.[48] Both studies conclude that to achieve substantial reductions in poverty and welfare dependency requires addressing the inadequacy of award amounts.

The Family Support Act of 1988 has several provisions designed to attack two sources of the problem of the inadequacy of awards—that is, that new awards are a low percentage of men's incomes and that old awards are neither renegotiated nor indexed, so their real value declines over time with increases in prices. First, it makes the use of guidelines by the states mandatory, that is, they must be used as a rebuttable presumption, such that a departure from them must be justified in writing; and second, it provides, beginning in 1990, for the periodic review of awards established under the state IV-D program by request, for adjustment of the awards to the guidelines if necessary, and beginning in 1993, for the periodic review and adjustment of such awards every three years. Although the guidelines vary widely, awards are specified as a percentage of the noncustodial parent's income, and these percentages are at least loosely based upon estimates of the costs of raising children, a topic we return to in chapter 6.[49]

Receipt Rates

Obtaining an award or negotiating an adequate one does not guarantee payment. As seen in figure 2.1 overall roughly three-quarters of

Table 2.8 Percentage of Women Receiving Child Support among All Women Due Support in 1978, 1981, 1983, and 1985 by Race and Marital Status[a]

Group (*N*)	Average	1978	1981	1983	1985
All Women (7,711)	73.5	71.7	71.8	76.2	74.0
Race or National Origin					
Black (908)	68.3	62.7	67.1	69.1	72.2
Nonblack (6,803)	74.3	72.9	72.5	77.3	74.3
Hispanic (427)	65.3	64.5	65.6	62.7	67.8
Marital Status					
Never-married (359)	73.9	81.5	63.1	75.9	76.2
Ever-married (7,352)	73.5	71.3	72.2	76.2	73.8

Source: 1979, 1982, 1984, and 1986 CPS March/April Match Files.

[a] Means are weighted averages.

women due support receive some payment. Among those who receive some, only around two-thirds receive full payment. Another way to say this is that one-quarter of women due child support receive none, another quarter receive partial payment, and only one-half receive full payment.

By contrast to award rates, child support receipt rates, defined as the proportion of women who receive child support among those due support in the year prior to the survey, vary relatively little according to demographic subgroup (see table 2.8). On average, three out of four mothers—both ever-married and never-married—receive support. It is not surprising that receipt rates differ little by marital status because those few never-married mothers who obtain an award are likely to be a relatively select group.[50] By race and ethnicity, some differentials emerge, and as with award rates, minority groups do worse. Around two-thirds of black and Hispanic mothers receive payment compared with three-fourths of nonblack mothers.

The story about trends in receipt rates across survey years is a familiar one—minimal overall gains masking significant gains for the most disadvantaged groups. Although initially lower than average, the receipt rate of black mothers rose continuously: by 1985 it exceeded its 1978 level by 10 percentage points and approached parity with the stable rate of nonblack mothers. Among the never-married, the receipt rate increased 13 percentage points between 1981 and 1985 after an initial large drop of 18 percentage points. By contrast, the receipt rate of the ever-married increased only 2.5 percentage points.

Table 2.9   Child Support Receipt Rate among All Women Due
Support in 1978, 1981, 1983, and 1985 by Race and Current Marital
Status[a]

Group (N)	Average	1978	1981	1983	1985	Change 1978–1985
All Races						
Never-married (90)	73.9	81.5	63.1	75.9	76.2	−5.3
Ever-married (1,838)	73.5	71.3	72.2	76.2	73.8	2.5
Separated (213)	80.9	72.4	79.8	87.3	84.6	12.2
Divorced (974)	74.7	73.0	73.9	76.5	75.1	2.1
Remarried (651)	68.8	68.4	66.6	71.7	68.5	0.1
Nonblack						
Never-married (38)	74.7	93.2	49.6	78.9	81.1	−12.1
Ever-married (1,663)	74.3	72.6	73.0	77.2	74.1	1.5
Separated (161)	83.0	75.8	83.6	87.5	85.6	9.8
Divorced (876)	76.4	74.3	75.0	79.2	76.5	2.2
Remarried (626)	68.8	69.3	67.0	71.3	68.0	−1.3
Black						
Never-married (52)	73.4	75.2	72.8	74.1	72.4	−2.8
Ever-married (176)	66.8	60.2	65.8	67.4	72.1	11.9
Separated (52)	75.0	61.6	70.1	86.4	82.4	20.8
Divorced (98)	62.4	62.4	65.0	57.2	65.2	2.8
Remarried (25)	67.5	48.7	59.5	86.5	76.6	27.9

Source: 1979, 1982, 1984, and 1986 CPS March/April Match Files.

[a] Means are weighted averages.

Further analysis by race and current marital status together (table
2.9) reveals large increases in child support receipt rates among separated mothers of both races and among remarried black mothers.
Between 1978 and 1985, the receipt rate of separated blacks increased
20 points, while that of separated nonblacks increased 10 points. By
1985, the receipt rate of separated women of both races had climbed
above 80 percent, higher than for any other marital status subgroup.
To some extent, we anticipate a higher receipt rate among the separated because the average separation occurred more recently than the
average divorce and more recent disruptions tend to have higher payment rates. But, in addition, with a considerably lower award rate
than other marital statuses, separated mothers due support are likely
to be a select group in the sense that their children's fathers are more
willing to pay. Furthermore, during the transition of a separation, a
father may see his children more often, leading to a higher payment
rate.[51] Although remarried black mothers also experienced a large

increase in their receipt rate (28 points), they form only a small minority of the population receiving support.[52]

The failure of child support receipt rates, overall, to increase more rapidly may be a result of compositional changes in the population due support, particularly the increase noted earlier in the proportion blacks, and to falling real income, reducing the ability of the average father to pay support. (See chap. 5.)

To summarize, receipt rates increased slightly for ever-married mothers over the entire period and for never-married mothers beginning in 1981. As with award rates, black mothers made the most progress starting from the lowest base, with most of their progress concentrated among the separated and remarried. Since the separation of a black mother lasts about two years longer on average than that of a nonblack mother,[53] the rising receipt rate of black separated mothers bodes well for the maintenance of gains among blacks. Nonblack separated mothers also experienced a greater than average increase in receipt rates. The increase in receipt rates, especially among blacks, again suggests some modest success of the child support enforcement program.

Receipt Rates and AFDC Status

Why did receipt rates increase among blacks, the never-married, and separated mothers due support, while remaining relatively steady overall? One thing these subgroups have in common is their disproportionate representation on AFDC: 34 percent of the blacks, 54 percent of the never-married, and 30 percent of the separated are on AFDC compared with only 16 percent overall. Since AFDC recipients are required to cooperate with the IV-D agency in obtaining child support on their behalf and since the resources of the child support enforcement program have been disproportionately directed at the AFDC and other low-income clientele,[54] we can surmise that a considerable amount of effort has gone into increasing the receipt rates of these groups. In part, to determine whether these efforts have in some sense paid off, we examine receipt rates by AFDC recipient status.[55]

In table 2.10, we display receipt rates by AFDC and non-AFDC recipient status. First, let us consider the general question of whether the child support enforcement efforts of the federal government beginning in 1975 and heavily concentrated in the AFDC population were

Table 2.10   Percentage of Women Receiving Child Support among All Women Due Support in 1978, 1981, 1983, and 1985 by Race or Marital Status and Receipt of AFDC[a]

	1978	1981	1983	1985	Change 1978–1985[b]	Change 1981–1985[c]
All Women						
AFDC	60.3	53.8	58.7	63.7	3.4	9.9
Non-AFDC	74.5	75.3	79.4	75.7	1.2	0.4
Race						
Black						
AFDC	61.4	59.5	64.1	64.1	2.7	4.6
Non-AFDC	63.7	70.7	71.9	75.1	11.4	4.4
Nonblack						
AFDC	59.9	51.7	56.4	63.6	3.7	11.9
Non-AFDC	75.4	75.8	80.2	75.8	0.4	0.0
Marital Status						
Never-married						
AFDC	76.9	60.7	64.7	71.2	−5.7	10.5
Non-AFDC	88.5	66.2	89.1	81.3	−7.2	15.1
Ever-married						
AFDC	58.5	52.5	57.3	61.3	2.8	8.8
Non-AFDC	74.2	75.5	79.1	75.5	1.3	0.0
Separated						
AFDC	64.7	58.3	78.9	66.5	1.8	8.2
Non-AFDC	77.5	90.4	90.2	89.0	11.5	−1.4

Source: 1979, 1982, 1984, and 1986 CPS March/April Match Files.

[a] Means are weighted averages.

[b] The only significant changes are for separated mothers not on AFDC and black mothers not on AFDC.

[c] Changes are significant at least at the 5% level for all women on AFDC, never-married women not on AFDC, and nonblack women on AFDC.

successful. Did the receipt rates of women on AFDC show significant improvement over the period 1978–85? Over the entire period, the answer is no: the increase in the receipt rate for all women on AFDC is statistically indistinguishable from zero. But, between 1981 and 1985, the receipt rate of women on AFDC increased 10 percentage points after an initial large decline between 1978 and 1981, mirroring the pattern we observed earlier for all never-married mothers. This pattern also holds for all subgroups of AFDC mothers and is most pronounced for nonblacks, with their 1981–85 increase approaching 12 percentage points.

We noted when considering award rates by AFDC recipient status that the success of the federal program in obtaining awards might have helped women escape from AFDC. As with women eligible for child support, both the number and proportion of women due support on AFDC declined between 1978 and 1985 for all subgroups except the never-married (for whom the proportion declined but the number increased). The majority of the decline in the proportion of women on AFDC (60%), which created substantial adverse selection of those remaining on, coincided with the decline in receipt rates of women on AFDC between 1978 and 1981. Despite the continued decline in the proportion on AFDC subsequently, receipt rates recovered fully. Gains in the receipt rate of women on AFDC despite their increasingly adverse selection may be taken as evidence of success of the child support enforcement program. Further evidence of such success are the gains in receipt rates among black women due support not on AFDC combined with a dramatic downturn in their proportion on AFDC to which we now turn.[56]

As with award rates, receipt rates rose only among those black mothers not on AFDC—by 11 percentage points to 75 percent in 1985. By contrast, the receipt rate of black mothers on AFDC increased only 3 percentage points to 64 percent.[57] At the same time, the proportion (and number) of black women due support on AFDC declined dramatically, from 45 percent in 1978 to 27 percent in 1985. This suggests that many women receiving child support escaped AFDC, leaving those who remained on a highly adversely selected group with respect to prospects for receiving child support. They may have escaped AFDC because they received child support and because of an increase in the stringency in the rules for welfare eligibility. The pattern of gains for separated women due support is quite similar except that the entire gain among those not on AFDC came by 1981. Further evidence that black women exiting from AFDC were relatively advantaged is that between 1978 and 1985 receipt amounts of black women on AFDC declined more than twice as much as those of black women not on AFDC (results not shown).

Amount Received

As indicated earlier, only around two-thirds of women receiving support get the full amount they are due. We next examine trends and differentials in the total amount of child support received; then we examine trends in receipts per child (that is, receipts divided by the number of children covered by the award) to provide a clearer picture

Table 2.11   Mean Amount of Child Support Received among Women Receiving Support in 1978, 1981, 1983, and 1985 by Race and Marital Status: Total and per Child[a] (in 1985 dollars)

Group (*N*)	Average	1978	1981	1983	1985	% Change 1978–1985
Total						
All Women (5,629)	2,520	2,960	2,490	2,523	2,212	−25.3
Race or National Origin						
Black (619)	1,824	2,127	1,951	1,575	1,754	−17.5
Nonblack (5,010)	2,621	3,059	2,567	2,654	2,291	−25.1
Hispanic (274)	2,165	2,240	2,442	2,004	2,030	− 9.4
Marital Status						
Never-married (265)	1,246	1,609	1,201	1,223	1,147	−28.7
Ever-married (5,364)	2,590	3,011	2,542	2,598	2,295	−23.8
Per Child						
All Women	1,588	1,785	1,551	1,633	1,429	−19.9
Race or National Origin						
Black	1,089	1,314	1,047	999	1,068	−18.7
Nonblack	1,660	1,841	1,623	1,721	1,491	−19.0
Hispanic	1,233	1,344	1,372	1,102	1,162	−13.5
Marital status						
Never-married	925	1,452	798	925	788	−45.7
Ever-married	1,624	1,798	1,581	1,674	1,479	−17.7

Source: 1979, 1982, 1984, and 1986 cps March/April Match Files.

[a] Means are weighted averages.

of what is actually available to each child. Total receipts and receipts per child exhibit somewhat different trends by race and marital status because the number of children receiving support changed differentially among demographic subgroups: it increased among the never-married, remained constant among blacks and Hispanics, and decreased among the ever-married and among nonblacks.

The amount of child support received in current dollars rose from $1,795 in 1978 to $2,212 in 1985, an *increase* of 23 percent; by contrast, in constant 1985 dollars the amount *declined* 25 percent from $2,960 to $2,212 (see table 2.11). As with award amounts, differentials in receipt amounts tend to favor the majority—nonblack mothers previously married to their children's father. Never-married mothers receive roughly half as much child support as the ever-married, about $1,250 compared with $2,590 on average, and experienced roughly the same decline in real dollars between 1978 and 1985 as the ever-married. Black mothers' receipts relative to those of nonblack mothers varied between 59 and 77 percent. These black-nonblack ratios fall below those in amount due, indicating that blacks face a further disadvantage when it comes to collecting the child support allotment. For Hispanics, however, these ratios relative to all nonblacks are nearly the same as in amount due. But both blacks and Hispanics experienced smaller percentage declines in total real dollars received than nonblacks.

The amount of support received per child, like the amount due, declined less (20%) than the total amount because the number of children per woman receiving support declined (from 1.8 to 1.7) (table 2.11). Most striking is that this is far less true among the never-married, reflecting the big increase in the number of children per never-married mother. On a per child basis, real dollars of child support received by the never-married declined an astonishing 46 percent to $788 in 1985. As pointed out in chapter 1, however, we cannot determine whether the award of the never-married mother covers only one or all of her children.[58] On a per child basis, the apparent gains in the amount received by blacks and Hispanics relative to nonblacks all but disappear, reflecting the fact that the decrease in number of children per woman took place largely among nonblacks.

Examining the amount of child support received by current marital status and race together, we find that among nonblacks receipts deteriorated more than average for separated and never-married mothers,[59] whereas among blacks they deteriorated about the same amount for all marital status categories except remarried, for whom they did not change[60] (see table 2.12).

Amount of Child Support Received Relative to Amount Due

Because the amount of child support received is largely determined by the amount due, much of the variation over time in the former comes from variation in the latter. Thus, in our discussion of receipts we naturally compare amounts received with amounts due. In these comparisons, the figures on the amount due pertain to women who actually receive support rather than to women merely due it. In fact, the three out of four women due support who receive it are a relatively

Table 2.12 Mean Amount of Child Support Received among Women Receiving Support in 1978, 1981, 1983, and 1985 by Race and Current Marital Status[a] (in 1985 dollars)

Group (N)	Average	1978	1981	1983	1985	% Change 1978–1985
All Races						
Never-married (66)	1,246	1,609	1,201	1,223	1,147	−28.7
Ever-married (1,341)	2,590	3,011	2,542	2,598	2,295	−23.8
Separated (171)	2,708	3,074	2,820	2,896	2,082	−32.3
Divorced (730)	2,747	3,231	2,627	2,698	2,541	−21.4
Remarried (441)	2,274	2,643	2,263	2,294	1,970	−25.5
Nonblack						
Never-married (28)	1,353	2,204	812	1,278	1,306	−40.7
Ever-married (1,225)	2,652	3,073	2,593	2,688	2,331	−24.1
Separated (132)	2,941	3,349	2,967	3,223[b]	2,207	−34.1
Divorced (668)	2,811	3,284	2,680	2,793	2,588	−21.2
Remarried (424)	2,302	2,673	2,309	2,329	1,958	−26.7
Black						
Never-married (38)	1,172	1,209	1,392	1,188	1,009	−16.5
Ever-married (117)	2,033	2,360	2,097	1,724	2,020	−14.4
Separated (39)	1,983	2,002	2,365	1,792	1,776	−11.3
Divorced (61)	2,155	2,715	2,127	1,765	2,139	−21.2
Remarried (17)	1,718	1,683	1,362	1,352	2,125	26.3

Source: 1979, 1982, 1984, and 1986 CPS March/April Match Files.

[a] Means are weighted averages.
[b] Includes one outlier value with around $52,000 child support received.

advantaged group—their awards average roughly $900, or 42 percent, more in 1985 dollars than those of women due support who do *not* receive it ($600, or 20%, more if they are black, and $300, or 26%, more if never-married).

Among all women who received support, the decline in the amount received was roughly the same as the decline in the amount due over the entire period. But this close relation did not hold for all subgroups. Among the never-married and among blacks, real dollars received declined more than real dollars due, while among Hispanics, they declined less.

A more direct way to compare the amount received with the amount due is to examine their ratio.[61] Over the period under study, the average woman receiving support received 83 percent of what she was owed[62] (see table 2.13). Once again blacks face an apparent dis-

Table 2.13   Ratio of Amount of Child Support Received to Amount Due among Women Receiving Support in 1978, 1981, 1983, and 1985 by Race and Marital Status[a]

	Average	1978	1981	1983	1985
All Women[b]	0.831	0.835	0.855	0.824	0.811
Race or National Origin					
Black	0.785	0.810	0.803	0.798	0.747
Nonblack	0.837	0.838	0.862	0.828	0.823
Hispanic	0.827	0.780	0.907	0.828	0.793
Marital Status					
Never-Married	0.837	0.925	0.932	0.855	0.745
Ever-Married	0.830	0.832	0.852	0.823	0.817

Source: 1979, 1982, 1984, and 1986 CPS March/April Match Files.

[a] Means are weighted averages.

[b] Sample size same as table 2.12, except that here and in table 2.14, 13 observations were excluded for which the ratio of child support received to child support due exceeded 4; includes one edited observation changed from $18,000 to $1,800 due for a black mother in 1978 on the basis of other information in the record.

advantage: they received around 78 percent of the amount due on average compared with 84 percent for nonblacks. Although never-married mothers collected the same proportion of child support as ever-married mothers on average over this period, at the end of the period they joined black mothers in collecting a smaller proportion. Recently, blacks and the never-married have faced greater difficulty collecting child support than nonblack, ever-married mothers. We will see how this came about as we examine trends in the ratio of child support received to child support due.

For women overall, the ratio of child support received to due declined 2 percentage points between 1978 and 1985.[63] This decline was confined to certain demographic subgroups. Among blacks, the ratio declined from 81 to 75 percent, with most of the decline confined to the 1983–85 period. Among the never-married, it declined from 93 to 75 percent, from well above average to well below average, with the entire decline coming after 1981. For both groups, these declines surfaced in the face of progress in other child support outcomes examined earlier. Both groups had experienced significant increases in their award rates over the entire period and significant increases in their receipt rates over the entire period for blacks and after 1981 for the never-married. Furthermore, among both groups, the real value of their awards had held up somewhat better than average.

Table 2.14   Ratio of Amount of Child Support Received to Amount Due among Women Receiving Support in 1978, 1981, 1983, and 1985 by Race and Current Marital Status[a]

	Average	1978	1981	1983	1985	Change 1978–1985
All Races[b]						
Never-married	0.837	0.925	0.932	0.855	0.745	−0.180
Ever-married	0.830	0.832	0.852	0.823	0.817	−0.015
Separated	0.834	0.848	0.873	0.830	0.783	−0.065
Divorced	0.841	0.842	0.851	0.840	0.833	−0.009
Remarried	0.810	0.808	0.842	0.789	0.803	−0.005
Nonblack						
Never-married	0.837	0.928	0.926	0.903	0.738	−0.190
Ever-married	0.837	0.837	0.861	0.826	0.826	−0.011
Separated	0.851	0.852	0.902	0.823	0.823	−0.029
Divorced	0.848	0.850	0.857	0.846	0.839	−0.011
Remarried	0.815	0.811	0.852	0.793	0.807	−0.004
Black						
Never-married	0.837	0.923	0.935	0.824	0.751	−0.172
Ever-married	0.768	0.781	0.769	0.788	0.746	−0.035
Separated	0.779	0.831	0.784	0.854	0.685	−0.146
Divorced	0.779	0.765	0.792	0.772	0.782	0.017
Remarried	0.709	0.716	0.653	0.682	0.753	0.037

Source: 1979, 1982, 1984, and 1986 cps March/April Match Files.

[a] Means are weighted averages.
[b] Sample size reported in table 2.12, except see note b, table 2.13

A more detailed examination of these trends by current marital status and race together reveals that the decline in the ratio of amount received to amount due was also confined to the nondivorced population. Among blacks, the decline occurred for separated and never-married mothers (although the latter decline is not statistically significant), and among nonblacks, for never-married mothers (see table 2.14). What do these three demographic subgroups have in common? All experienced unusual progress in some of the other child support outcomes considered earlier. For all three groups, the award rate increased, child support due maintained its value better than average, and the receipt rate increased over the entire period for black separated mothers and after 1981 for never-married mothers. The juxtaposition of declining collections with improvements in these other outcomes suggests that fathers who are somewhat less willing or less able to pay have been brought reluctantly into the system by reforms in the child support enforcement program. A lesson to be learned is that such efforts at child support reform may result in a decline in the proportion of awards collected.

Trends in child support payments in the United States between 1978 and 1986 show a mixed picture. Small increases in the award and receipt rates were accompanied by large declines in the real value of awards and receipts. Overall, both award and receipt rates rose around 2 percentage points, while the real value of support due and received declined around 25 percent.

What do these gains and losses imply about changes in child support received overall? Is the average woman who finds herself eligible for child support in 1986 better off or worse off than she was in 1979? To answer this question, we need to look across all the different stages of the child support process to arrive at a final outcome, the expected child support payment received by the average woman. In 1985, the 8.6 million women eligible for child support received an average of $822. The majority of them (63%) received nothing, while 37 percent received $2,212 on average. In 1978, the 7 million women eligible for support received an average of $1,036 (in 1985 dollars). Sixty-five percent received nothing, while 35 percent received $2,960 on average. Thus, considering changes in all child support outcomes, expected payments on average dropped around 20 percent between 1978 and 1985. (See fig. 2.5.)

Minority groups, especially black mothers, experienced greater improvements than the majority, but their position was considerably worse to begin with. The award rate of black women increased 8 percentage points, while their receipt rate rose 10 percentage points. Despite these gains, the real value of their child support payments per child declined no less than among nonblacks, and their ratio of child support received to child support due fell more. Despite this latter decline, the expected child support payment of the average black woman increased between 1978 and 1985. In 1978, the average black woman eligible for support could expect payment of only $297 (in 1985 dollars), whereas by 1985 she could expect payment of $364, an improvement of about 23 percent (see fig. 2.5). The expected payment rate alone rose from 14 to 21 percent, or by about 50 percent. We should note, however, that compared with all women, a black woman could expect child support payments only 29 percent as large in 1978

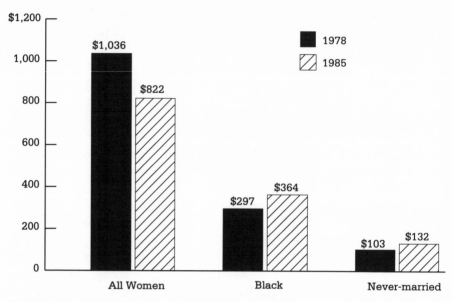

2.5 Average Child Support Payments Received among Women Eligible for Support

and 44 percent in 1985. Thus, despite their considerable progress relative to all women, black women still have some distance to go.

The progress of never-married mothers was also noteworthy. Between 1979 and 1986 their award rate rose almost 8 percentage points, and between 1981 and 1985 their receipt rate rose 13 points. Furthermore, the real value of their awards declined less than of most other subgroups. Like blacks, however, never-married mothers also received an increasingly smaller proportion of their awards. In 1978, the average never-married mother could expect payment of only $103 (in 1985 dollars); by 1985, her expected payments had grown to $132, an improvement of 28 percent (see fig. 2.5). Her expected payment rate alone rose from 6 to 11 percent. If, instead, we take 1981 as the benchmark, when her expected payments averaged only $79, then the improvement to 1985 grows to 67 percent. Some of the big increase in expected payments among the never-married is attributable to the increase in their proportion due support from 74 to 82 percent, whereas the proportion of the ever-married due support remained roughly constant at 82 percent over the period. This suggests that new awards, which are generally still due, became an increasing proportion of all awards among the never-married. But these gains should not be construed to mean that there is no longer a problem for this group. The expected payments of a never-married mother, which averaged 10 percent of those of all women in 1978, had grown to only 16 percent by 1985. Given how extremely low these expected payments are, it is clear why a never-married mother would have little incentive to seek actively a child support award.

Despite the fact that black and never-married mothers showed some gains, the glaring fact is that overall expected child support payments declined 20 percent between 1978 and 1985, and almost two-thirds of women eligible for child support continued to receive nothing. The major cause of this is the decline in the amount of child support due over this period. And, as we have been able to show, the general deterioration in award amounts extends back at least to the beginning of the 1970s. New award amounts rose only about half as fast as prices or incomes, and over time existing awards decline in value because few are renegotiated. Although both of these problems pose challenges for public policy, there are some grounds for optimism. First, we have shown that between 1980 and 1984, new awards kept closer pace with rising prices. This may have occurred because inflation was lower or because some states initiated guidelines that set awards as a proportion of the absent father's income. According to recently released census statistics, the upward trend in new awards appears to have continued, if not accelerated.[64] Second, the Family Support Act of 1988 mandated the periodic review of child support awards being enforced under the IV-D program.

There is some evidence that child support reform and increased government spending had a positive impact on child support outcomes. First, the overall 20 percent decline in expected payments would almost certainly have been larger owing to some adverse compositional shifts in the population without government efforts that helped raise award and receipt rates. Second, the increase in expected payments experienced by black and never-married mothers may be attributed in part to government efforts that were concentrated on the AFDC population, to which blacks and the never-married belong disproportionately. Furthermore, the growth in receipt rates during the 1980s among nonblack mothers on AFDC and in award and receipt rates of black mothers not on AFDC at the same time as the proportion of mothers on AFDC declined suggests both that child support enforcement efforts reached an increasingly disadvantaged population and that their efforts helped some women escape from AFDC. Moreover, evidence of declines in the relative amount of child support paid in the face of rising award and payment rates suggests that increasingly reticent fathers have been brought into the system, in all likelihood by child support enforcement efforts. (See chap. 6.)

The detailed analyses of aggregate data in this chapter raise various questions, which we will explore in more detail in the disaggregated analyses to follow. A first set of questions concerns demographic *differentials* among women at a point in time. Why do some women have more favorable child support outcomes than other women, that is, have an award, have a higher award, receive support, or receive more of the support they are due? Why do black and never-married mothers fare so much worse than nonblack and ever-married mothers on most of these outcomes?

A second set of questions concerns trends across survey years in child support outcomes. What accounts for the small overall increases in award and receipt rates and the large declines in the real value of child support due and received between 1979(78) and 1986(85)? Why did award rates rise more for never-married and black women, award amounts decline less for never-married women, and receipt rates rise more for black women, separated women, and after 1981, for never-married women than for other women? Why did the ratio of amount received to amount due fall, especially for blacks and the never-married?

A final set of questions concerns historical long-term trends in *new* child support awards among ever-married mothers. What accounts for the secular trend in new award rates over the past twenty-five years—the strong upward trend to 1976 (or 1980 for blacks) and the downward trend thereafter? Why was the decline greater for nonblack and ever-divorced women than for black and separated women? Why did the value of new awards rise less than half as much as consumer prices or male incomes and decline from 18 to 12 percent of male incomes over a decade and a half?

Before considering these questions and examining the impact of government child support enforcement efforts, we develop in chapter 3 the theoretical and empirical framework that forms the basis for the disaggregated analyses to follow.

An Economic Model of
Child Support

Happy families are all alike;
every unhappy family is
unhappy in its own way.
—LEO TOLSTOY

Like Tolstoy's unhappy family, parents who live apart from each other confront some challenges in providing for their children's well-being that most two-parent families never do. For example, couples who divorce or have a child out of wedlock need to decide who will retain primary physical custody of the child(ren) and how often the other parent will be permitted to visit. Perhaps most important, they must decide to what extent the noncustodial parent will be required to share in the children's ongoing financial support. Increasingly, many single parents in the United States have opted for child support, which may be defined as the legally obligated financial exchanges between parents who do not live with each other to support the children who live with one of them. Even today, however, a substantial minority make no such provisions, leaving the entire burden of support to be borne by only one of them.

The decisions single parents make concerning child support (and to a lesser degree, child custody and visitation) are fundamentally economic choices because they are about the allocation of scarce resources, especially time and money. But these decisions are also shaped by psychological factors and by the prevailing social and legal environments. In this chapter we construct an economic model of child support awards and receipts, but we also pay attention to the impact of relevant noneconomic influences, whenever possible.

This chapter, in two parts, provides a theoretical and empirical foundation for the chapters that follow. The first part is a theoretical analysis of marital dissolution and the child support process. In this discussion we translate recent technical work by ourselves and other economists into lay terms and summarize recent findings on the inter-action of economic, social, and psychological forces that shape child support outcomes. The second part of the chapter shows how this theoretical model of child support can be implemented given the limited socioeconomic data available in the four supplements to the Current Population Survey. We compare the average characteristics of women who have a child support award with those who do not, and of women receiving support with those who do not. We also examine racial and marital status differences in these characteristics and show how the demographic composition of the child support population has shifted over time. Finally, we identify some determinants of child support that we are unable to control for with CPS data. We offer evidence from other studies how these factors may be expected to influence child support outcomes and discuss how their omission is likely to affect our results. In an appendix to this chapter (see app. B), we offer a short introduction to regression and decomposition analyses to enable readers without a background in statistics to understand the basic methodology behind the results in the chapters that follow.

A Theoretical Model of Child Support

The goal of this section is to develop a theoretical model of child support payments. As a prelude, we review the costs and benefits of marriage and divorce from an economic perspective. We also look at typical custody and child support arrangements when couples with children divorce or a child is born out of wedlock. Using some basic tools of microeconomics, we model the behavior of a noncustodial father and custodial mother and use the model to ask what factors are likely to make fathers offer to pay more child support and mothers to request more. Finally, we look at some differences between the determinants of child support awards and receipts.

A Brief Introduction to the Economics of the Family

Between 1960 and 1985 the proportion of all families with own children under age eighteen headed solely by a woman increased from 7.4 to 19.3 percent.[1] This dramatic growth has been attributed to increased divorce rates and decreased remarriage rates and after 1970, to an increase in the number of out-of-wedlock births, especially among blacks.[2] To understand the financial hardships faced by these mother-only families, it is useful to contrast their disadvantages with the economic advantages of two-parent families. There are substantial economic gains to be derived when a mother and father agree to share resources and expenses. Many, if not all, of these same gains are lost when they separate.

Two-parent families enjoy higher total incomes and lower per capita expenditures than single-parent families.[3] According to recent statistics, the median income of married-couple families in 1986 was $32,805, compared with $24,962 for families headed by a male only and $13,647 for families headed by a female only.[4] Household budget studies find that when family size increases, expenditures increase less than proportionately to the increase in family size. This occurs, in part, because many household goods are public or shared goods that can be consumed by more than one person at the same time, and in part, because larger consumer units benefit from economies of scale or lower per unit costs in bulk purchases.

Two-parent families not only have twice as much time to earn income compared with a single parent, but they also have twice as much time to devote to productive activities within the home. Since many types of so-called home production (such as cooking, cleaning, or gardening) can be accomplished by one person, coordination and cooperation allows each parent to specialize in those activities in which he or she has a "comparative advantage," thereby increasing the family's total output of home produced-goods. Other activities (especially child rearing) may benefit from shared participation, either through time saved or better quality of work generated, or owing to the pure enjoyment of sharing time together. Economists identify the latter as the *positive externalities* associated with cohabitation. In other words, if his well-being is increased by her consumption, and vice versa, then the couple is better off living together so that each can enjoy the other's consumption directly.

If marriage—or at least cohabitation—offers so many economic benefits, why do so many couples break up, and why do an increasing number of parents choose not to marry at all? Simply put, the economic argument for marital dissolution is that, given voluntary associations, one or both parties believe they will be better off alone (or with a different partner, since new partners are sometimes selected before a divorce occurs).[5] Marriages begin with incomplete information about the potential contributions of each party: over time, one partner may be disappointed with the other's willingness or capacity to earn income or to cooperate in home production. In addition, the formerly positive externalities of cohabitation may turn negative: one or both parties now feel their well-being is diminished by observing the other's consumption.

If marital dissolution occurs, one important issue is how any capital accumulated during the marriage will be distributed. There are financial assets, household durables, and perhaps a house that have to be allocated. Most often this division is resolved with a one-time property settlement. One party, with the help of the other, may have accumulated substantial amounts of human capital: if, for example, the wife sacrificed her career to advance the husband's, she may be entitled to some portion of his lifetime income as a return on her investment in him. This could take the form of either a one-time payment, payments for a fixed time period while she invests or reinvests in her own human capital, or payments known as alimony or maintenance income that continue as long as she does not remarry.

The most difficult problems of equitable distribution generally involve another type of capital accumulated during the marriage—the children. First, who shall have legal and physical custody of the children and to what extent is the other party entitled to visitation? Second, since children's maintenance requires continued expenditures of time and money, who shall bear the costs of child rearing? The noncustodial parent may be required to pay child support to help meet some of these costs. In general, state laws and family courts are expected to resolve each of these issues of custody, visitation, and child support "in the best interests of the child," but in many cases problems persist long after the marriage has been dissolved or the out-of-wedlock birth occurred.

In theory, either parent may retain custody of the children, and either may be ordered to pay child support; in practice, it is almost always the mother who retains physical custody (although joint legal custody has become increasingly popular),[6] and it is the father who is likely to be ordered to pay child support. In a national survey conducted during 1984–85, of nearly 4 million persons providing financial support to children living elsewhere, 93 percent were men.[7] Thus, let us suppose that children live with their mother and fathers are ordered to pay child support. We examine the economic position of each new household following the marital disruption. It is likely that both parties find their household income reduced, their per capita expenditures increased, and their home production time greatly diminished.

Following divorce, a father's well-being is likely to decline in several ways. If his former wife had worked outside the home, his total family income will fall. If he increases his home production time at the expense of his market work, his personal earnings will also fall. Although his total expenditures may fall, his per capita spending is likely to rise, particularly if he has to maintain a house large enough to accommodate his children when they visit. Moreover, any reduction in spending may be only temporary: if he remarries or has a child out of wedlock, his new children will compete with his old ones for his limited resources. Finally, his well-being is most certainly diminished in one important way: although he may still care about his children, he has fewer opportunities to observe or monitor their consumption directly. He sees them less often the farther away they live and the greater his dislike for his former wife is.

The new mother-only family also experiences a reduction in its living standard and generally by substantially more than the father.[8] In 1986, the income of single female-headed families was 58 percent lower than that of all married couples and 64 percent lower than families in which both husband and wife work.[9] The mother finds that her per capita expenditures have increased as she loses some of the benefits of shared goods and economies of scale in large purchases. In addition, she loses not only her former husband's income but also his potential home production time. The demands on her time increase: with the loss of his income and home production time, she is more likely to work outside of the home, and she will probably need to purchase child care services to supplement her own home time. Finally, to the extent that she expects to receive alimony or child support, a large portion of her income may be subject to considerable risk or variability. If the children's father fails to pay or pays less than he owes, her income can fall dramatically. The uncertainty associated with its receipt makes long-term planning difficult and reduces her family's well-being.

Child support presents problems for both the mother and the father. She worries that he may not pay what he owes, and that if he does pay, he may try to exert too much control over her and the children. He worries that she will spend the money on herself rather than the children or that she will spend it on the children in a different way than he prefers. In the next section we develop a theoretical model to explain why some couples agree to child support and why some do not. We look at what factors affect the amount of child support awarded, and given that child support is due, what factors affect whether or not it is actually paid.

An Economic Model of Child Support

We begin with the assumption that, even after divorce, most parents still care about their children's well-being (although the degree of caring may vary among individuals). If fathers care about their children, why do so many fail to support them? As we saw in chapter 2, only about 60 percent of all absent fathers in the 1980s have an obligation to pay anything, and only half of those owing support in any year actually pay the full amount owed. If mothers care about their children, why do so many not insist that the father help support his children? As we also saw, 38 percent of mothers without a child support award as of April 1986 said they did not even want one.

HOW MUCH SUPPORT DOES THE FATHER OFFER TO PAY? We begin by examining the behavior of the noncustodial father.[10] Suppose his well-being (or *utility,* as economists term it) increases with his own consumption and that of his children. He must decide how to allocate his income between satisfying his own wants and those of his children who live with their mother. He knows that each dollar he spends on himself increases his own consumption by $1, but each dollar he transfers in the form of child support payments to his children's mother increases their consumption by less than $1. The reason for this is that, from the perspective of the children's mother, child support is fungible (i.e., interchangeable) with income from other sources, and it is she who decides how her family's total income—including child support—will be allocated between satisfying her own needs and those of the children. For simplicity, suppose she always spends *1-a* percent of total income on herself and *a* percent on his children.[11] (It is important to note that *a* represents the fraction spent on *his* not on *her* children, since she may also have other children who have a different father. The presence of other children is likely to reduce the value of *a*.) Thus, the father knows that when he allocates X of his income to child support, his own children's consumption increases by only a fraction of that amount, aX. As a rational planner, he will divide his income between child support and his own needs so that the last dollar

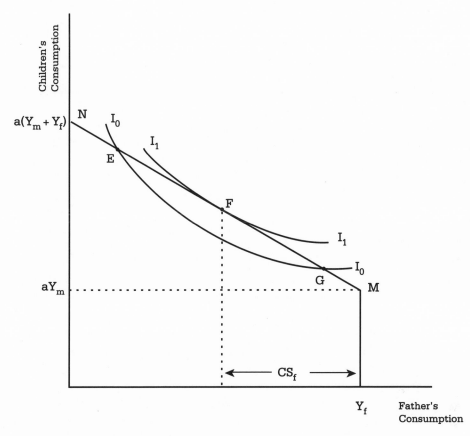

3.1 A Father's Offer to Pay Child Support

increases his well-being equally whether it is distributed to his children or to himself.

Let us call CS the level of child support the father would elect to pay in the absence of outside constraints (such as state guidelines, which we introduce below). The determination of CS_f is shown diagrammatically in figure 3.1, where the horizontal axis measures his own consumption and the vertical axis measures his children's. The curves I_0 and I_1 (called his indifference curves) represent combinations of his own and his children's consumption that leave him equally well off. Their negative slopes reflect the implicit trade-off that a decrease in his own consumption must be offset by an increase in his children's consumption to keep his well-being constant. The flatter are his indifference curves, the more he "cares" about his children in the sense that he is willing to decrease his own consumption by more to obtain a given increase in their consumption. All of the combinations shown by I_1 represent a higher level of well-being than any of those shown by I_0.

Suppose the father's income is Y_f. The straight line MN in figure 3.1 (called the budget line) equals potential allocations of his income between himself and his children. At end point M he spends all of his income on himself and pays no child support, leaving his children's consumption to be financed completely by their mother. (If her income is denoted Y_m, and she spends a percent of it on his children, their consumption is aY_m.) At end point N he pays all of his income as child support, raising his children's consumption to $a(Y_m + Y_f)$. The slope of MN is $(-a)$, which says that reducing his own consumption by \$1 raises his children's consumption by \$$a$ (because their mother uses $1-a$ for her own consumption).

In short, we might say that the budget line MN represents the father's ability to support himself and pay child support (or, more precisely, his ability to increase his children's consumption), while indifference curves such as I_0 and I_1 summarize his desire to pay. He selects the best (or most desired) payment level from among all those he is able to afford (i.e., that lie on his budget line). In figure 3.1, points E, F, and G are all affordable, but F is preferred to either E or G. At point F, he offers to pay CS_f in child support and retains $Y_f - CS_f$ for his own needs. No other income allocation that is affordable to him is preferred to point F (since all other affordable points are on lower indifference curves).

What affects the level of support offered by the father, CS_f? We can show that CS_f depends, in part, upon the father's ability to increase his children's consumption (i.e., his budget line), which in turn, depends upon his income (Y_f), the mother's income (Y_m), and the fraction of income she spends on his children (a). If his income increases from Y_f to Y_f', as in figure 3.2, the budget line shifts rightward to $M'N'$, parallel to MN. He is likely to spend some of this additional income on himself and some of it on his children, thus raising the amount of child support he offers to pay to CS_f'. If the mother's income increases from Y_m to Y_m', as in figure 3.3, the budget line shifts upward to $M''N''$. This raises his children's consumption and allows him to increase his own consumption as well, by reducing the amount of child support he offers to pay to CS_f''. Finally, if the mother

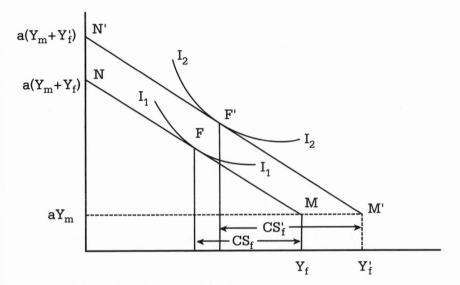

3.2 Increase in Father's Income Raises Offer to Pay

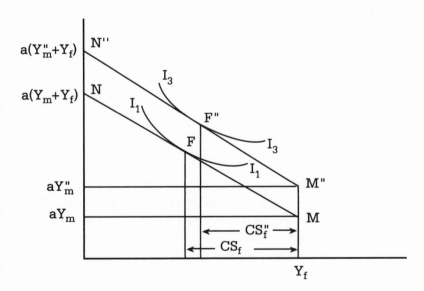

3.3 Increase in Mother's Income Reduces Father's Offer to Pay

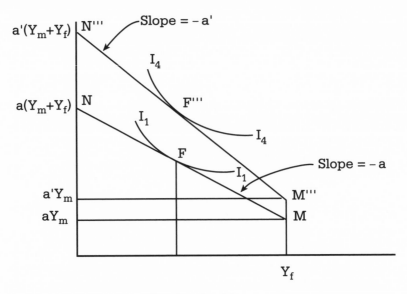

3.4   Increase in Share of Income Mother Allocates to Children May Raise or
Lower Father's Offer to Pay

increases the fraction of income she spends on his children's consumption from a to a', as in figure 3.4, the budget line both steepens
and shifts upward to $M'''N'''$. In response to this, he may either raise
or lower the amount of child support he offers to pay: the steeper
slope induces him to pay more since his ability to "transfer" resources
to his children has increased, but the upward shift also induces him
to raise his own consumption by paying less child support.[12] To summarize, the father will offer to pay more child support when his income
increases or when the mother's income decreases, but he may raise
or lower his offer when she increases the fraction of income she
transfers to the children.

CS_f also depends, in part, on the slope of his indifference curves,
or in other words, on his desire to pay. As can be seen in figure 3.5,
the flatter are his indifference curves (I_1 compared with I'_1), the more
child support he offers to pay. As argued above, his indifference curves
will be flatter the more he cares about his children. In turn, his degree
of caring might be expected to increase with the number and ages of
his children because a man who cares more about children may have
fathered more of them, and a man with older children is likely to have
spent more time with them before his marital disruption. (In this sense,

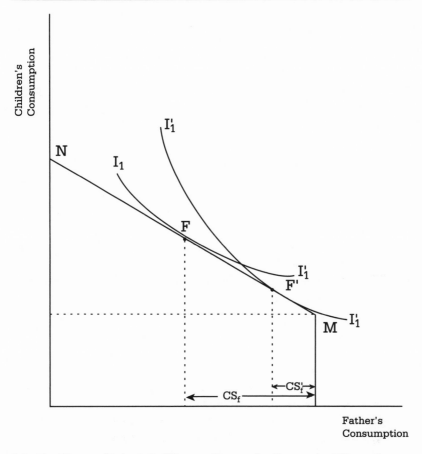

3.5 The Flatter a Father's Indifference Curves, the Greater the Offer to Pay

a father who was never married may care less about children than one who was.) The steeper are his indifference curves, the less support he offers to pay from any given income. They will be steeper the greater are his needs, which in turn will be greater if he has remarried or has fathered other children.

HOW MUCH SUPPORT DOES THE MOTHER REQUEST? Now we turn to the behavior of the custodial mother, whose well-being (or utility) is assumed to depend on her own consumption and that of her children. Her family's income consists of her own labor market earnings and her nonwage income (such as interest, dividends, public assistance, and the earnings of other family members), plus any alimony and child support she receives. She spends this income on her own consumption and that of her children, allocating it among them so that the last dollar increases her well-being equally whether she spends it on herself or on her children. (For simplicity, it is assumed that all goods are private goods, so that income she spends on herself does not also benefit her children and vice versa.) Following our earlier notation, we can call a the fraction of income she spends on her children and $1-a$ the fraction she spends on herself.

How much child support will the mother request? Since child support adds to her family's income and thus increases both her own potential consumption and that of her children, it might appear the answer is simply that "the more the better." Assuring the receipt of child support, however, has both pecuniary and nonpecuniary costs. She may have to incur out-of-pocket legal expenses and may have to take time off from work to take the father to court to ensure that he pays the support he owes. In addition, she may expect to experience considerable emotional distress negotiating with an estranged husband over initial custody and visitation and support arrangements and may expect this distress to be exacerbated by continuing disagreements over visitation rights and the way she is spending the money he provides. Given these costs, she will want to weigh the expected costs of receiving child support against the expected benefits of its receipt.

These costs and benefits are shown in figure 3.6, where the horizontal axis measures dollars of child support requested, and the vertical axis measures either the marginal (i.e., additional) cost or benefit derived from the last dollar of child support received. We draw the marginal benefit curve to slope downward, assuming each additional dollar of child support income received raises her well-being by less than the previous dollar. We draw the marginal cost curve to slope upward, assuming she faces increasing pecuniary and nonpecuniary costs of obtaining ever-larger amounts of child support.[13] The mother may be expected to increase her demand for child support as long as the additional benefit derived from its receipt exceeds the additional cost of obtaining it. In figure 3.6, her request is represented by CS_m, where the marginal cost and benefit curves intersect. Beyond this point, the extra costs do not cover the extra benefits of receiving it.

What factors affect the level of support she requests, CS_m? The higher the marginal benefit curve, the greater is CS_m. The marginal benefit of a dollar of child support is higher the smaller are a mother's combined other sources of income (owing to the assumption of dimin-

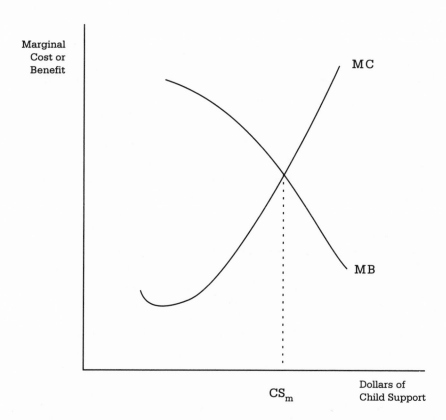

3.6 A Mother's Request for Support

ishing marginal utility of income). Mothers with fewer years of education and previous work experience can expect to earn less; mothers who live in states with smaller AFDC benefits can expect to receive less public assistance; and mothers without an extensive family support network can expect to receive less help from other relatives. The marginal benefit of child support is also greater the higher are her family needs. Total expenditures are higher the more children she has to support and the higher the standard of living to which she and the children had become accustomed prior to her marital disruption.

CS_m will also increase if the marginal cost curve shifts downward. Costs will be lower the less bitter the marital disruption, since this may increase the mother's expectation that the father will pay voluntarily. Mothers with more education may be more efficient at seeking legal assistance in case he fails to pay. Costs may also vary with the mother's state of residence. Some states offer more help than others in securing an award and collecting payments. If the father lives in a different state, it may be especially difficult to collect payments. Finally, costs vary with marital status: if a mother was never married to her children's father, she may have to locate him and establish paternity as a prelude to obtaining an award.

THE ACTUAL CHILD SUPPORT AWARD. How much child support, if any, will be awarded? Ignoring for the moment the role of the state in setting levels of support, we can say that the actual amount of support voluntarily agreed to, CS, will equal: $CS = $ minimum (CS_f, CS_m). In other words, the actual award will be the minimum of the amount offered by the father or requested by the mother. It is possible that CS will equal zero—that is, no child support will be agreed to. This will occur if either CS_f or CS_m is zero. Fathers with sufficiently low abilities or desires to pay may offer nothing, or mothers with sufficiently low expected benefits or high expected costs may prefer to receive nothing.

Since 1975, some states have introduced advisory or mandatory child support guidelines. Let CS_s represent the state's minimum standard of support, which will vary with the number of children due support, with the income of the father, and in some states, also with the income of the mother. In this case, the actual child support obligation will be the larger of CS from the equation or CS_s. That is, some couples will voluntarily agree to a level of support in excess of the state minimum, while others will be constrained by that minimum standard. In practice, there may be an important difference between mandatory and advisory guidelines. By law, mandatory guidelines are meant to represent a *minimum* suggested payment level; in practice, in some states, advisory guidelines have been interpreted as providing an upper bound or *maximum* payment level.

THE AMOUNT OF CHILD SUPPORT RECEIVED. The above model describes the process of establishing a child support award. But not all awards are paid in full every year; indeed, some fathers fail to pay any of what they owe. In this section we argue that the specific factors that govern the receipt of child support may differ somewhat from those that govern its award. And, although receipts, like awards, will be affected by the actions of both the father and the mother, ultimately, it is the father who decides whether or not he will pay and how much he will pay. Of course, the mother may influence his decision by initiating (or threatening to initiate) enforcement proceedings against him if he fails to pay. New state laws that require automatic wage withholding lessen his discretion in this matter.

Just as with awards, a father's ability and desire to pay are likely to be the principal determinants of whether or not he pays. The difference is that awards are more likely to depend upon his expected or *long-run* ability and desire to pay, while receipts will depend upon his *current* circumstances.[14] If his current income is less than expected, perhaps because of illness or unemployment, he may pay less than the full amount he owes. Based upon a sample of California divorces, H. Elizabeth Peters and Laura M. Argys report that the single most important predictor of child support receipts is the father's unemployment experience.[15] If he sees that the income of his children's mother (excluding child support) is higher than he had anticipated, he may attempt to reduce his support payments. His desire to pay may diminish over time, particularly if there have been conflicts over visitation or how the mother is spending the support he provides, or if he develops a stronger allegiance to a new family. For example, Frank F. Furstenberg, Jr., argues that many men tend to exhibit a pattern of "child swapping"—that is, they relinquish responsibilities for biological children in favor of children in their current household.[16]

Whether or not he continues to fulfill his support obligation when his ability or desire to pay changes will depend in part upon the expected consequences of nonpayment (or underpayment). These, in turn, depend upon the likelihood of his apprehension and conviction and the severity of the penalties imposed if he is caught. These probabilities vary by state of residence because, at least traditionally, states have differed in their child support enforcement laws and the extent to which they have actually used these laws to apprehend and convict nonpaying fathers. The consequences will also depend upon particular actions taken by the children's mother, since it is she who usually will initiate collection proceedings against him. In cases where the mother receives AFDC benefits, however, the state itself can initiate legal action against nonpaying fathers.

The likelihood that a custodial mother will initiate enforcement proceedings against her children's nonpaying father depends upon the expected benefits and costs of doing so.[17] The benefits are likely to be positively related to the value of her award and the amount of the accumulated arrearage in these payments and inversely related to her own income. Mothers receiving AFDC may perceive few benefits from initiating collection proceedings since under current law, after a $50 "disregard" per month, child support collections reduce AFDC benefits dollar for dollar. The costs will depend upon a mother's ability to obtain legal assistance from her state's child support (IV-D) office or from a private attorney and upon her confidence in the legal system.[18] More educated women are likely to be better informed about their options and more efficient at using the legal system. Never-married mothers and racial minorities may have a greater distrust of government and the courts.

Implementing the Child Support Model

In subsequent chapters we employ multivariate statistical techniques to estimate the importance of socioeconomic and legal determinants of child support award and receipt outcomes among mothers in four April supplements to the CPS conducted between 1979 and 1986. As a prelude to these analyses, we show how information contained in the CPS data can be used to approximate some of the determinants of child support from our theoretical model. We also point out some determinants of child support that we cannot observe directly and may not be able to capture indirectly. We review relevant findings from other studies that have been able to control for at least some of these missing determinants and assess the implications of their omission for our empirical work.

Determinants We Can Observe Directly or Capture Indirectly

The theoretical model of child support developed here suggests that awards and receipts depend primarily upon the father's ability and desire to pay support and upon the mother's expected benefits from and costs of obtaining support. To implement this model, we need to find appropriate empirical counterparts to these theoretical constructs. This task is made more difficult because although the Census Bureau collected detailed demographic and income information on custodial mothers, they collected none on absent fathers. We may, however, be able to control indirectly for his ability and desire to pay on the basis of certain characteristics of mothers and, for our study of awards, aggregate data on male income in the year of the marital disruption.

CAPTURING THE FATHER'S ABILITY AND DESIRE TO PAY. Ideally, we might capture the father's ability to pay child support (i.e., his budget constraint) by his current income, his expected future income, and his income at the time of the award. Because none of these income measures is available to us, we will attempt to approximate his ability to pay on the basis of certain socioeconomic characteristics of his children's mother that are known. In his classic study of the marriage market, Gary Becker uses the term *positive assortative mating* to describe the notion that, unlike magnets, opposites do not usually attract: spouses are likely to exhibit similar socioeconomic characteristics, including intelligence, education, age, race, wealth, religion, and ethnic origin.[19] We have information on the custodial mother's education, age, race, Spanish ethnicity, and residential location. It is well known that earnings are positively correlated with age and education and negatively correlated with nonwhite race and Spanish ethnicity; it is likely that earnings also correlate negatively with central city residence given the large underclass in many inner cities.[20] These variables are good proxies for a mother's own earnings potential and should be suitable ones for his income as well.[21]

To improve our measure of the father's ability to pay, especially as it relates to award determination, we introduce some aggregate time-series data from outside CPS. Whether or not a woman obtains an award and how much support she is due may depend largely upon the father's income at the time of the award. It is unlikely that the mother's current age and education fully control for differences in income of fathers at the time of the original award determination. Thus, in our analysis of awards we also approximate the father's income by the mean income of all year-round, full-time male workers, by race, in the year of the mother's marital disruption. This approximation assumes that the distribution of income around the mean did not change over our period of analysis and that the income of all year-round, full-time male workers represents the average income of newly divorced or separated fathers who are likely to be somewhat younger than average.[22]

A priori, it is not obvious how best to capture the father's desire to support his children (i.e., his indifference curves). In most empirical work, tastes and preferences are approximated by an individual's socioeconomic characteristics. Following this practice, we employ certain information about the mother to represent his desire to pay—including her current marital status, the number and ages of her children, whether her award was court-ordered or agreed to voluntarily, and (for ever-married mothers) the number of years since the marital disruption. We would hypothesize that a father is less willing to support his children if their mother has remarried or if the child support award was court-ordered rather than voluntarily agreed to. He may be more willing to support older children or more children to whom his emotional attachment is potentially greater. But his willingness to pay support is likely to diminish over time, as his contact with his children attenuates. In their analysis of father-child contacts based upon data from the National Survey of Children, Furstenberg and Kathleen Mullan Harris report that the percentage of fathers who maintain regular contact with their children following divorce declines rapidly, falling from about 50 percent within the first three years to less than 30 percent four to nine years after divorce.[23] Interestingly, however, they find that father-child contacts decline less for older children than for younger ones.

CAPTURING THE MOTHER'S EXPECTED BENEFITS AND COSTS. Awards and receipts also depend, in part, upon the mother's expected benefits and costs of support. In our empirical analysis we capture expected benefits by the mother's current marital status and the number and ages of her children to reflect current expenditures, and by education, age, race, and national origin to reflect her own potential income. Although we know a mother's current income, it would not be correct to use this as a proxy for her expected benefits, because, rather than being a determinant of child support outcomes, current income (even when it excludes child support) itself depends in part upon these outcomes. That is, whether or not a mother has a child support award and how much support she receives is likely to affect whether or not she works, how much she works, and whether or not she seeks alternative sources of support such as public assistance or the help of extended family members.

We use some of the same socioeconomic characteristics to proxy a mother's expected costs of obtaining support, including her current marital status and education. As noted earlier, the costs may be greater for never-married mothers who may need to locate their child's father and establish paternity before obtaining an award, and costs may also be greater for separated than for divorced mothers since the latter will already have had more contact with the legal system. Mothers with more education may be more aware of their legal options and better able to seek enforcement assistance. Costs of collecting support also depend upon the effectiveness of the enforcement program in her state of residence.

SOCIOECONOMIC CHARACTERISTICS AND CHILD SUPPORT OUT-COMES. Many socioeconomic characteristics of mothers can be used to represent more than one theoretical component of the child support model. For example, we have seen that her education is related to *his* ability to pay, *her* expected benefits from support, and *her* costs of obtaining it. One implication of this is that we cannot always separate the effect on child support outcomes of his ability and desire to pay from her benefits and costs of support, and in some cases even the direction of the effect may be ambiguous. For example, the higher the mother's educational attainment, the greater the father's ability to pay and the lower her expected costs of collection—which should raise child support receipts—but the smaller are her expected benefits—which should lower them.

Table 3.1 lists the socioeconomic characteristics of mothers used in the empirical analyses of the next three chapters. It identifies which of the four underlying theoretical determinants each characteristic is likely to represent, using the abbreviations *FA* for father's ability to pay, *FD* for father's desire to pay, *MB* for mother's expected benefits and *MC* for mother's expected costs. The last two columns of the table summarize the overall expected effect of each characteristic on both awards and receipts. For example, as discussed above, the effect of mother's education is likely to be ambiguous because although more education raises *FA* and lowers *MC* (which in turn increases awards and receipts), it also lowers *MB* (which in turn decreases them). In most cases the mother's characteristics are likely to affect awards and receipts in the same direction, but in a few cases, they may have different effects.

Table 3.2 shows the average values of each of these characteristics in the CPS data. On average, mothers with an award are older, have more education, and are less likely to be black, Hispanic, or to live in a central city—characteristics that indicate, in part, a father with a greater ability to pay. Women with an award are also somewhat more likely to have at least one child aged six to seventeen and are much

Table 3.1 Type of Determinant and Expected Effect of Selected Socioeconomic Characteristics of Mothers in Child Support Models

Socioeconomic Characteristics	Type of Determinant	Expected Effect on	
		Awards	Receipts
Education and age			
Years of education	FA, MB, MC	?	?
Current age	FA, MB	?	?
Race and ethnicity			
Black[a]	FA	—	—
Hispanic[a]	FA	—	—
Current marital status			
Separated[b]	FD, MC	—	?
Remarried[b]	FD, MB	NA	—
Never-married[b]	FD, MC	—	?
Number and ages of children			
Number	FD, MB	+	+
Age 6–17[a]	FD, MB	+	+
Region and location			
Northeast[c]	MC	?	?
North central[c]	MC	?	?
South[c]	MC	?	?
SMSA[a]	MB, MC	+	+
Central city[a]	FA, MB	—	—
Years since marital disruption	FD, MC	—	—
Voluntary award agreement[a]	FD, MC	NA	+
Amount of support due	FA, FD, MB, MC	NA	+

Note: FA = father's ability to pay; FD = father's desire to pay; MB = mother's expected benefits from support; MC = mother's expected costs of obtaining support; NA = not applicable

[a] Relative to not having this characteristic
[b] Relative to being currently divorced
[c] Relative to living in the West

more likely to have been married to their children's father—characteristics that are positively related to the father's desire to pay. Mothers with and without an award have the same number of children, indicating that their needs for support may be similar. The expected costs of obtaining support, however, may be lower for women with an award: they have more education, are more likely to have been married, and more likely to have gone through a formal divorce settlement. The costs of obtaining an award may also vary by region: women with an award are more likely to live in metropolitan areas and in western or north central states.

In table 3.2, we also compare mothers who receive support with

Table 3.2 Average Socioeconomic Characteristics of Mothers by Whether or not Awarded and Receiving Child Support[a]

Socioeconomic Characteristics	Total Eligible Population		Population Due Support	
	Awarded	Not awarded	Receiving	Not receiving
Years of education	12.2	11.3	12.5	11.9
Current age	35.0	31.7	34.8	34.0
Number of children	1.7	1.7	1.7	1.7
Years since divorce[b]	6.1	6.1	5.2	6.7
Percentage				
College graduates	9.8	5.0	11.7	6.2
Black	15.0	44.1	12.6	16.2
Hispanic	6.0	11.7	5.3	7.9
Never-married	5.6	44.7	5.2	5.1
Separated	12.4	23.8	13.0	8.5
Remarried	35.1	14.3	30.5	38.4
Divorced	46.9	17.3	51.3	48.1
Child, age 6–17	76.9	54.5	79.5	77.5
Northeast	16.7	22.7	18.3	13.3
North central	27.7	20.7	26.2	29.8
South	34.3	38.8	35.1	32.6
West	21.3	17.8	20.4	24.4
SMSA	63.1	69.6	63.2	62.5
Central city	27.4	44.6	25.6	29.4
Voluntary award	—	—	39.0	14.5
Weighted percentage of total sample	59.6	40.4	73.5	26.5

Source: 1979, 1982, 1984, and 1986 cps March/April Match files.

[a] Figures are weighted averages.

[b] Among ever-married mothers only

those who do not (among those due support). Many socioeconomic characteristics appear to vary with receipts the same way they do with awards. For example, mothers who receive child support tend to be older, have more education, and are less likely to be black or Hispanic than women who do not receive any of the support they are due—again, factors that may reflect differences in the father's ability to pay. Similarly, mothers receiving support are more likely to live in a metropolitan area, live outside of the inner city, have children aged six to seventeen, and have more children—factors that may reflect differences in both the mother's expected benefits and the father's desire to pay.

Some socioeconomic characteristics exhibit a different pattern for receipts than awards. For example, never-married mothers make up an equal proportion of recipients and nonrecipients; separated women are more likely to receive child support due them than not; remarried women are much less likely to be among those receiving child support. Regional patterns are also different between awards and receipts: mothers who receive child support are more likely to live in the Northeast and less likely to live in the West than mothers who do not receive any of the support they are due. Finally, there are two characteristics that, although not relevant to award determination, are related to the receipt process: women receiving support are more likely than those not receiving any to have a voluntary (rather than court-ordered) child support award and among the ever-married, to have experienced a more recent marital disruption.

As we saw in chapter 2, blacks and never-married mothers are less likely to have a child support award and are due and receive less support than other mothers. Part of the reason for these differential outcomes is that mothers who are black or never married are more likely to exhibit some characteristics that are associated with lower-than-average awards and receipts. These demographic differences can be seen clearly in table 3.3, which displays the average characteristics of mothers eligible for child support by race and marital status. These data show that compared with nonblacks, black mothers have less education, are more likely to be separated or never-married than divorced or remarried, and are more likely to live in the South or an inner city. They also show that compared with the ever-married, never-married mothers are younger, have less education, have younger children, and are more likely to be black or Hispanic, and to live in an inner city. As we will see, these differences in average characteristics may account for some of the differences in child support outcomes by race and marital status (chaps. 4 and 5).

As we have seen, child support award and receipt rates rose while the value of support due and received declined between 1978(79) and 1985(86). Some part of these changes might have been expected if the composition of the child support population had shifted over time toward mothers with characteristics associated with lower-than-average awards and receipts. These compositional shifts can be seen in table 3.4, which shows the average characteristics of all mothers eligible for child support in 1979 and 1986 and ever-married mothers due support in 1978 and 1985. Among all mothers eligible for child support,

Table 3.3 Average Socioeconomic Characteristics of All Mothers
Eligible for Child Support by Race and Marital Status[a]

Socioeconomic Characteristics	Race		Marital Status	
	Nonblack	Black	Ever-married	Never-married
Years of education	12.0	11.6	12.0	11.3
Current age	34.3	31.9	35.6	26.5
Number of children	1.7	1.9	1.7	1.7
Years since divorce[b]	6.0	6.4	6.1	—
Percentage				
College graduates	9.0	4.7	9.2	3.0
Black	0.0	100.0	17.4	61.2
Hispanic	10.9	1.3	7.8	10.3
Never-married	11.4	49.0	0.0	100.0
Separated	14.8	23.0	21.6	0.0
Remarried	33.9	7.1	34.0	0.0
Divorced	40.0	21.0	44.4	0.0
Child, age 6–17	70.3	61.5	75.6	38.8
Northeast	19.2	18.9	18.3	22.2
North central	25.5	23.1	25.1	23.9
South	31.3	49.4	35.3	39.2
West	24.0	8.6	21.3	14.7
SMSA	61.5	77.4	64.1	71.7
Central city	24.3	61.8	29.4	52.7
Weighted percentage of total sample	73.2	26.8	78.6	21.4

Source: 1979, 1982, 1984, and 1986 CPS March/April Match files.

[a] Figures are weighted averages.
[b] Among ever-married mothers only

the percentage who were never married increased between 1979 and
1986, while the percentage separated or remarried declined. Among
ever-married mothers due child support, the percentage who were
black or had a voluntary award increased between 1978 and 1985,
while the average number of children declined.

Determinants We Cannot Observe Directly or Capture Indirectly

Child support outcomes are also affected by a variety of economic
and noneconomic factors that we are unable to observe directly and
may not be able to control for indirectly. Some of these, such as the
absent father's income, are missing from our data but in principle can

Table 3.4   Average Socioeconomic Characteristics of All Mothers Eligible for Child Support in 1979 and 1986 and of Ever-married Mothers Due Support in 1978 and 1985[a]

Socioeconomic Characteristics	All Mothers Eligible for Support		Ever-married Mothers Due Support	
	1979	1986	1978	1985
Years of education	11.6	12.0	12.0	12.5
Current age	33.4	34.0	34.7	35.6
Number of children	1.7	1.8	1.8	1.7
Years since divorce[b]	6.0	6.4	5.3	6.0
Percentage				
College graduates	6.4	8.5	8.2	11.3
Black	26.6	26.3	10.4	11.9
Hispanic	7.3	9.2	5.7	6.2
Never-married	19.7	23.2	0.0	0.0
Separated	17.6	15.5	13.9	11.2
Remarried	28.9	26.8	35.1	35.5
Divorced	33.8	34.5	51.0	53.4
Child, age 6–17	66.0	69.4	79.1	81.3
Northeast	19.0	18.8	17.2	15.4
North central	25.2	25.7	28.3	26.0
South	35.8	36.5	30.9	36.1
West	20.1	19.0	23.6	22.5
SMSA	66.2	64.3	63.5	61.2
Central city	35.4	33.7	25.7	24.4
Voluntary award	—	—	30.3	33.0

Source: 1979, 1982, 1984, and 1986 CPS March/April Match files.

[a] Figures are weighted averages.
[b] Among ever-married mothers only

be measured. Others, such as the quality of the parents' ongoing relationship, may be more difficult to measure. Next we discuss some of those determinants of child support we are unable to control for and offer evidence from recent studies as to how these factors might be expected to affect child support outcomes.

MISSING INFORMATION ABOUT THE FATHER. Many of the limitations of our empirical analysis stem from the absence of data obtained directly from the absent father.[24] Perhaps most important, there is no information about the father's income, employment status, or wealth either at the time of the survey or the award. Previous studies, where the absent father could be interviewed, consistently show that his "current" income (at the time of the survey) is strongly and positively related to his payment behavior.[25] No study has been able to match award amounts to the father's income at the time of the award. Ron Haskins, in a small study of absent fathers in rural North Carolina, provides some information on employment status and wealth.[26] He reports that more than half of the fathers in his study whose children received AFDC had been unemployed at least once during the previous two years. He also found that the level of average wealth was low: only 10 percent of fathers in his study owned a home, only 25 percent had any financial assets, and only 50 percent owned a car.

We do not know the father's current living arrangements, including where he lived, whether or not he had remarried, or if he had other children to support. Martha Hill, using data from the Panel Study of Income Dynamics, found evidence that child support collections are lower when a father and mother live in different states.[27] Evidence is mixed on the impact of the father's remarriage on his payment behavior: Hill reports that his remarriage has no impact on payments, while Freya L. Sonenstein and Charles A. Calhoun found that fathers who remarry are actually more likely to meet their child support obligations. Hill also reports that the more other children there are who live with the father, the less child support he pays. No studies have looked at payment rates among fathers who owe child support to more than one mother.

MISSING INFORMATION ABOUT THE MOTHER. Even though we have extensive data on the socioeconomic characteristics of mothers eligible for child support, they are not likely to capture fully all the differences among mothers in their expected benefits and costs of child support. In terms of benefits, we cannot observe a mother's willingness to seek financial support other than from her children's father. She may, on the one hand, seek more child support if she has no extensive family network to turn to or if she feels a strong stigma from accepting public assistance. On the other hand, she may seek less child support if she intends to remarry soon after her divorce (although remarriage per se does not preclude her from receiving child support). In terms of costs, we cannot observe a mother's willingness to use the legal system to obtain and enforce a support order. She may seek more support the more willing or able she is to obtain legal assistance from a private attorney or to make use of the services provided by her state's child support enforcement office.

OTHER MISSING INFORMATION. We also have no data on custody
and visitation, two important legal arrangements that may be closely
linked to child support obligations. In their study of absent fathers,
Sonenstein and Calhoun find that a father is most likely to pay the
support he owes when parents have joint legal custody of the children
who reside with the mother. In a study of recent California divorce
cases, however, joint legal custody (relative to mother-only custody)
seems to be associated neither with higher award amounts nor with
higher payment rates.[28] A number of studies have found a strong link
between visitation and child support payments: not surprisingly, visitation and payments appear to be positively related and may be simultaneously determined by a common set of predictors.[29] In all of
these studies, however, the frequency of visitation appears to be low
and declines over time.[30]

Another determinant of child support that is difficult to quantify is
the quality of the ongoing relationship between the mother and the
father. For mothers with a child support award, we know only whether
the award was court ordered or voluntarily agreed to. Court-ordered
awards may indicate a greater degree of discord between parents than
if the award was agreed to voluntarily, or they may suggest there was
more to bargain over. We have no comparable information for mothers
without an award, and we know nothing about the parents' ongoing
relationship since the time of the award. Although it may be hard to
distinguish cause from effect, Sonenstein and Calhoun report that
mothers who characterize their current relationship with their children's father as "very friendly," are more likely to receive support
and receive higher payments on average.[31]

EMPIRICAL IMPLICATIONS. The omission of certain relevant information about the absent father, the custodial mother and their
ongoing interpersonal relationship has important implications for our
empirical analyses of determinants, differentials, and trends. Because
we are unable to observe at least some dimensions of the father's
ability and desire to pay support and the mother's expected benefits
and costs of support, we are not able to explain all of the individual
variation in child support outcomes. This means that a substantial
portion of the observed cross-sectional variation in both award and
receipt outcomes remains unexplained. But since our main objective
is to try to account for racial and marital status differentials and trends
over time in these outcomes, the omission of these determinants may

not be critical as long as they are not correlated with race or current marital status per se and did not change appreciably over time.

In this chapter we developed a simple economic model of child support payments to mothers with children from an absent father. We have argued that both award and receipt outcomes are likely to depend upon the ability and desire of the father to pay support and upon the expected costs and benefits of support to mothers. Each of these four determinants has important socioeconomic dimensions, although each may also be influenced by certain relevant social and psychological factors. In addition, awards may be affected by state-mandated child support guidelines and paternity laws, and receipts may be influenced by federal and state child support enforcement laws and practices.

We have also shown how this theoretical model of child support can be estimated empirically, given the information available to us in the child support supplements to the 1979, 1982, 1984, and 1986 CPS. Both the father's ability and desire to pay and the mother's expected benefits and costs of support will be approximated by several socioeconomic characteristics of the children's mother and by some aggregate economic data from the year of the mother's marital disruption. But because none of these four determinants of child support can be measured perfectly, all the observed variation in child support outcomes cannot be explained on the basis of socioeconomic indicators alone, nor can we expect to separate the effects of the various components. Fortunately, as we have argued, this limitation is not particularly constraining given the goals of our empirical analysis to account for racial and marital status differentials and trends over time in child support outcomes. It is to these analyses that we now turn.

Child Support
Awards:
Determinants,
Differentials,
and Trends

The first steps toward receiving child support payments from an absent parent are to obtain an award and negotiate an adequate amount of support. As we have seen, as of April 1986, only about 60 percent of mothers with children from an absent father had taken the first step successfully, and among mothers due payments in 1985, the average amount due was only $2,500. In this chapter we shift our focus from aggregate to individual analyses of these outcomes to provide answers to some of the questions posed at the end of chapter 2.

As in chapter 2, we study each award outcome separately. First, we examine award rates—that is, the percentage of the eligible population with a child support award—and second, the dollar value of awards among women due support. We begin both sections with an analysis of determinants—that is, the statistical association between the observable socioeconomic characteristics of mothers eligible for child support (as specified in table 3.1) and their award outcomes. This provides the framework to account first for racial and marital status differentials and second trends over time to 1986 in aggregate award rates and amounts. To the extent that the differentials and trends are unexpected on this basis, we speculate on their causes, including especially changes over time in the legal environment. In our analysis of trends, we are careful to distinguish between changes over time in existing awards and in new ones. We end both sections by making inferences about the probable causes of some recent changes in aggregate award outcomes (from 1986 to 1990) in light of our disaggregated findings to 1986.

Award Rates

We begin by attempting to answer the question: why do some mothers have an award while others do not? We find that award rates differ significantly[1] by the mother's race, current marital status, educational attainment, age, residential location, and by the number and ages of her children. Using these results, we next examine the racial and marital status differentials averaged over the period 1979–86 in more detail. We show that somewhat more than half of the differential in award rates between black and nonblack women—but less than one-third of that between ever-married and never-married women—can be accounted for by racial or marital status differences in average socioeconomic characteristics. We then assess the impact of various changes over time in the population eligible for child support on the aggregate award rate, which rose 2.2 percentage points between 1979 and 1986. Among other things, we show that its rise would have been nearly twice as large had the proportion of the eligible population never married not increased.

Finally, by restricting our attention to ever-married mothers, for whom we know the year of marital disruption, we study historical trends in the likelihood that a mother who becomes newly eligible for child support will obtain an award. Extending our analysis in chapter 2, we show that new award rates have been rising at least since 1958 and have risen more quickly for blacks than nonblacks. We also show that the secular increase in new award rates, especially among nonblacks, slowed considerably after 1975, coincident with the introduction of federal child support enforcement legislation. We speculate on the causes of this apparent slowdown in the growth of new awards and offer evidence that much of it can be attributed to the stagnation in the growth of real incomes of men after 1973.

Demographic Determinants of Award Rates

In this section we examine the statistical association between certain socioeconomic characteristics of a mother and her children and the likelihood that she has a child support award. As we argued in chapter 3, whether or not a mother obtains a child support award depends in part upon her own behavior and in part upon that of the children's father. Her decision to seek an award depends upon her expected needs for support and her perceived costs of obtaining it, whereas his decision to offer one depends upon his financial ability to pay and his desire to support his children. Although we cannot observe these factors directly (in part, because the absent father could not be interviewed), the behavior of both the mother and father is likely to vary systematically with some characteristics of the mother that can be observed (see table 3.1). The results discussed here, which are derived from multivariate probit analyses, show the effect of a one unit change in a given characteristic on the likelihood of having a child support award, all else being equal.[2]

We present these estimates in table 4.1, for all women eligible for child support, and for ever-married and never-married mothers separately.[3] Rather than discussing the effect of all characteristics in detail, we highlight only the most significant ones, relating them back to the underlying concepts of mother's needs for and costs of support and the father's ability and desire to pay. Our discussion focuses on all women, but we note significant differences by marital status where they occur.[4]

Ex ante, a mother's education has an indeterminate effect on award rates since it serves as a proxy (substitute) for both her expected needs and his ability to pay. All else being equal, the greater her education the less likely she is to require financial assistance from the father, but given positive assortative mating, the more able he is to provide it. Ex post, we find a positive relation: among all mothers, each additional year of education is on average associated with a 2.8 percentage point increase in the likelihood of having a child support award. The effect of education, however, is nonlinear at the upper end: college graduates are only 4.3 percentage points (rather than 11.2 points) more likely to have an award than high school graduates.[5] Among the never married, the only significant (and positive) association between award rates and education is whether or not the mother has graduated from high school.

Like education, the mother's age may reflect the earnings potential of both parents. Age, however, may also be a proxy for the date of the marital disruption. Older women whose disruptions occurred longer ago may be less likely to have an award if the likelihood of obtaining support has risen over time (as evidence presented in chap. 2 suggested). When we do not control for the date of the marital

Table 4.1   Effect of Selected Socioeconomic Characteristics of Mothers on Likelihood of Having a Child Support Award as of April 1979, 1982, 1984, or 1986 by Marital Status

	All Mothers	Ever-married	Never-married
Education and age			
Years of education	2.8**	2.5**	−0.04
College graduate[a]	−6.9*	−6.3*	—
High school graduate[a]	—	—	4.9*
Current age	−0.2**	—	−0.3*
Age at divorce	—	−0.05	—
Race and ethnicity			
Black[a]	−15.4**	−16.1**	−3.7*
Hispanic[a]	−11.5**	−9.0**	−8.5*
Current marital status			
Never-married[b]	−62.7**	—	—
Separated[b]	−33.2**	−28.5*	—
Remarried[b]	−4.3*	−2.8*	—
Number and ages of children			
Number	2.2**	1.6*	1.5
Age 6–17[a]	11.2**	11.3**	3.4*
Region or location			
Northeast[c]	−2.4**	−2.6*	0.8
North central[c]	5.3**	5.2**	2.3
South[c]	−0.6	−1.8	3.5
SMSA[a]	1.8	1.4	1.6
Central city[a]	−3.0*	−3.0*	0.5
Indicator of year of marital disruption	—	0.6**	—
Mean award rate	61.0%	72.6%	15.2%
Sample size	15,099	12,043	3,056

Note: Figures represent the percentage point change in the probability of having an award for a one-unit change in a given variable, holding all others constant. Estimates are derived from probit regressions, which also control for year of survey. The indicator of year of marital disruption is coded as the last two digits of the divorce or separation year minus 57.

*(**) Indicates statistical significance at a 5% (1%) level.
[a] Relative to not having this characteristic
[b] Relative to being currently divorced
[c] Relative to living in the West

disruption, the mother's current age has a small but significantly negative effect. All else equal, women who are ten years older than average are 2 percentage points less likely to have an award or 3 points less likely if they have never been married. But when we control for the date of marital disruption directly, age is no longer significantly related to award status, suggesting that, among ever-married mothers, age primarily captures differences in dates of disruption.[6]

As we saw in chapter 2, the likelihood of obtaining an award differs sharply by race and ethnicity, which reflect a variety of cultural and economic factors. Holding differences other than race (or ethnicity) constant, we find that the award rate of black (Hispanic) women is 15.4 (11.5) percentage points lower than that of nonblacks (non-Hispanics). These ceteris paribus differentials are less than half the size of the aggregate differentials observed in chapter 2. This suggests, as we show in detail in the next section, that more than half of the aggregate racial differential in award rates can be explained by differences in characteristics of the mother.

Like race, current marital status reflects a variety of factors, including differences in mother's needs, father's ability to pay, and the legal environment. We find that a mother who has never married is 62.7 percentage points less likely to have an award compared with a mother with the same socioeconomic characteristics who is currently divorced. A separated (remarried) woman is 33.2 (4.3) percentage points less likely to have an award than an otherwise identical divorced women. These ceteris paribus differentials by marital status are almost as large as the aggregate differentials we reported in chapter 2. This suggests that unlike racial differentials, marital status differentials in award rates are largely unexplained by differences in the mother's socioeconomic characteristics.

The number and ages of the children affect both the mother's needs and the father's desire to pay (see chap. 3). All else equal, we find that each additional child raises the probability of having an award by 2.2 percentage points. If one or more of the children is aged six to seventeen, the likelihood of an award is 11.2 percentage points higher than if all the children are younger or older.

Award rates also differ by geographic location. We find that women living within the boundaries of a central city of a metropolitan area (SMSA) are 3 percentage points less likely to have an award than those who live in the suburbs. Like central city residence, region may reflect cultural and cost-of-living differences, but it is also likely to capture legal differences pertaining to marital dissolution and child support. Although laws concerning divorce, paternity establishment, child custody, and child support awards differ from state to state, states that share a common boundary often have a history or tradition of similar legislation.[7] We find that women in north central states are 5.3 percentage points more likely to have an award, while women in the Northeast are 2.4 points less likely to have an award than otherwise identical women living in the West.

Accounting for Racial and Marital Status Differentials

Some of the most striking findings to emerge from our aggregate analyses in chapter 2 were the large differentials in award rates by race and marital status. Of course, we might expect some differential by race (or marital status) because, on average, black (never-married) women differ from nonblack (ever-married) women in some important respects. For example, as we have just seen (table 4.1), women with more education and those living outside of the central city are more likely to have a child support award. We have also seen (table 3.3) that on average black women have less education and are less likely to live outside of the central city than nonblacks. Thus, we might expect that, on average, blacks will have a lower award rate than nonblack women. In what follows, we attempt to divide racial and marital differentials in award rates into the portions that can be explained by observable demographic differences and the portions that remain unexplained. We identify particular factors that contribute the most to explaining the differential in award rates and speculate on why some of the differential remains unexplained.[8]

RACIAL DIFFERENTIALS. Averaged over the period 1979–86, the aggregate award rate of black women was about half that of nonblacks. Among all women eligible for child support, 33.4 percent of blacks had an award, compared with 69.1 percent of nonblacks, for a racial differential of 35.7 percentage points (see table 2.1). Although there are no discernible racial differentials in award rates among the never-married, among the ever-married, blacks were 25.1 percentage points less likely to have an award (see table 2.2). In table 4.2 we decompose these racial differentials in award rates for all eligible women and for ever-married mothers into the portions that can and cannot be explained by racial differences in demographic characteristics.

Among all women eligible for child support, we find that racial differences in socioeconomic characteristics can account for around 73 percent of the 35.7 percentage point racial differential in award rates (table 4.2).[9] The racial difference in the percentage of mothers who have never been married accounts for much of this: blacks are

Table 4.2   Accounting for Racial and Marital Status Differentials in Award Rates on the Basis of Mother's Characteristics and Male Real Incomes

	Total Percentage Differential	Differential Explained by		Unexplained differential
		Mother's character-istics	Male real incomes	
By race				
All nonblack vs. black[a]	35.7 (100%)	26.1 (73%)	—	9.6 (27%)
Ever-married Nonblack vs. black[a]	25.1 (100%)	9.2 (37%)	8.0 (32%)	7.9 (31%)
By marital status				
Ever-married vs. never-married[b]	55.9 (100%)	18.5 (33%)	—	37.4 (67%)
Ever-divorced vs. separated[c]	35.6 (100%)	6.4 (18%)	—	29.2 (88%)

Note: Mother's socioeconomic characteristics are listed in table 4.1, and male real income is the mean income of year-round, full-time male workers, by race, in year of mother's marital disruption (measured in 1985 constant dollars).

[a] Uses nonblack probit coefficients to evaluate differences in the means of explanatory variables
[b] Uses ever-married probit coefficients to evaluate differences in the means of explanatory variables
[c] Uses ever-divorced probit coefficients to evaluate differences in the means of explanatory variables

over four times as likely as nonblacks never to have been married, and the incidence of child support awards is much lower among the never married. Simply on the basis of this, we could expect black mothers to be 24 percentage points less likely than nonblacks to have an award. Blacks are also more likely than nonblacks to exhibit certain other characteristics associated with lower award rates (according to table 4.1). They are nearly twice as likely to be separated, almost three times as likely to live within the central city of an SMSA, more likely not to have children between the ages of six and seventeen, and have fewer years of education (see table 3.3). On the other hand, black women are younger and have more children to support than nonblacks, two characteristics associated with higher award rates. These factors, however, are not enough to offset the ones associated with lower award rates; thus, on balance, we expect black mothers to be 26.1 percentage points less likely than nonblack mothers to have an award, leaving an unexplained differential of only 9.6 percentage points.

Looking only at mothers who have been married to their children's father, we can explain more than two-thirds of the overall 25.1 percentage point racial differential in award rates. As shown in table 4.2, we conclude that about one-third of the differential is a result of differences in the mother's characteristics and one-third a result of differences in the absent father's ability to pay.[10] Large income differences by race are an obvious source of racial differentials in award rates. But since the actual income of fathers is unknown, we approximated it by the mean income of year-round, full-time, male workers by race in the mother's marital disruption year.[11] (In our sample, black income was 71% of nonblack income, or approximately $8,000 less in 1985 dollars.) We then estimated the statistical association between our approximation of father's income and award rates, holding constant the mother's socioeconomic characteristics. We found each additional $1,000 in income associated with about a 1 percent increase in the likelihood of having an award. Given this association, we calculate that the gap in income can account for about 8 percentage points of the racial differential in award rates, or in other words, for 32 percent of the actual 25.1 percentage point differential.[12]

To summarize, once we control for differences in marital status, age, education, family size, geographic location, and (for ever-married women) an estimate of the absent father's income, we can explain around 70 percent of the racial gap in award rates. Among all women, the difference in marital status is the single most important explanatory factor; among the ever-married, differences in the mother's characteristics and father's income are about equally important. Thus, we conclude that around 30 percent of the differential in award rates between black and nonblack women cannot be attributed to differences in observable socioeconomic factors other than race itself. As argued earlier, race per se represents a complex set of cultural, behavioral, and economic factors that are difficult to disentangle; however, we will try to consider some of the more important components.

In part, race may reflect economic and behavioral differences between black and nonblack absent fathers. When we do not control for male incomes directly, race certainly reflects the lower ability to pay of black fathers relative to their nonblack counterparts. When we approximate father's income by the income of full-time black and white male workers, we still may fail to control fully for racial differences in the ability to pay to the extent that black men are less likely to be full-time employees. In addition to ability, race may also represent differences in the father's desire to pay. Yoram Weiss and Robert Willis report that by 1985, 50 percent of black mothers who had graduated high school in 1972, compared with only 5 percent of similar white mothers, had borne one or more children before their first marriage.[13] For one thing, a father is less likely to agree to a child support award if the mother has other children to support since he cannot be certain that all of his payment will go to his children. For another, if a father has children by several different women, his allegiance may be spread rather thin.

Among mothers, race may reflect differences in needs, especially if there are racial differences in access to alternative sources of support. For example, the social stigma attached to receiving public assistance may be less in predominantly black communities where large segments of the population already receive it. In addition, black women have been more likely to be in the labor force, at least historically, and more willing to turn to their own extended families (especially, the mother's own mother) for help in the support of their children.[14] Finally, the black mother may be reluctant to try to formalize a child support agreement if her child's father is already providing support on an informal basis. This informality is consistent with patterns of marital disruptions among black women, for whom separations often do not end with a formal divorce.

Racial differences in access to the legal system may also contribute to the unexplained differential in award rates. Black women may be less knowledgeable about the types of legal assistance available or how to obtain help when fathers fail to offer support. Blacks may be less able to afford private attorneys and less willing to seek public legal assistance, owing perhaps to a historical distrust of government and the courts. The lower incidence of both marriage and divorce among blacks relative to nonblacks is consistent with the notion that black women are less likely to use the legal system to formalize family arrangements.[15]

MARITAL STATUS DIFFERENTIALS. Averaged over the 1979–86 period, 15.7 percent of never-married mothers had an award, compared with 71.6 percent of ever-married mothers, for an overall differential of 55.9 percentage points (see table 2.1). Among the ever-married, award rates of currently separated women were 35.6 percentage points lower than those of the ever-divorced (i.e., currently divorced or remarried). In table 4.2 we decompose each of these differentials into the portions explained and unexplained; we identify important explanatory factors and speculate on why large residuals remain unexplained.

Never-married mothers have many characteristics that tend to lower award rates. Compared with the ever-married, they have almost one year less education; are only half as likely to have a child between the ages of six and seventeen; are nearly twice as likely to live within a central city; are more likely to live in the Northeast; are slightly more likely to be Hispanic; and are more than three times as likely to be black (see table 3.3). Taken together, these differences explain one-third, or 18.5 percentage points, of the overall differential (table 4.2).[16] The most important explanatory factor is the higher proportion of never-married mothers who are black, followed by their lower incidence of children aged six to seventeen, fewer years of education, a higher incidence of central city residence, and higher proportion Hispanic.

Within the ever-married group, differences in the mother's characteristics explain less of the award rate differential. Taken together, all observable differences in characteristics account for less than 20 percent, or 6.4 percentage points, of the differential between ever-divorced and separated women.[17] Compared with ever-divorced women, currently separated women are three times as likely to be black, have fewer years of education, and are less likely to have a child aged six to seventeen. As above, race is the single most important explanatory factor, but 88 percent of the differential remains unexplained.

Some of the unexplained marital status differentials in award rates may be owing to differences in the father's ability and desire to pay. Income differences are likely to be large between the ever-married and the never-married. According to recent aggregate data, the average income of never-married males (age eighteen years and over who work year-round, full-time) was $19,959 in 1985, compared with $27,781 for those men currently divorced.[18] Given even this admittedly crude approximation of income differences, we can account for an 8.1 percentage point differential in award rates between ever-married and never-married mothers, thereby reducing the unexplained residual from 37.4 percentage points to 27.3 points.[19] In addition, fathers who have been married to their children's mother are likely to have a greater emotional attachment to their children (and to be more certain of paternity) than single fathers who may never even have shared the same household with their children. Since some never-married women have children with different men, the father of one child may be reluctant to provide support if he believes some of it will benefit children who are not his. Finally, fathers who are only separated from their children's mother may abstain from offering child support as a bargaining tactic to either speed a divorce settlement or a reconciliation.

Some of the unexplained marital status differentials may also be from differences in the mother's costs and benefits of obtaining a child support award. Unlike the ever-married, never-married mothers may have to locate their child's father and establish paternity before even attempting to secure an award. Thus, they incur not only higher legal expenses but also the social stigma of being labeled an unwed mother. In addition, even if an award is obtained, its expected value is likely to be very low, as we saw in chapter 2. Thus, given the high costs and meager benefits, many never-married mothers never attempt to obtain an award from their child's father, preferring instead to make other arrangements for the child's support, such as living with their own parents. Even among the ever-married, mothers may behave differently. Unlike the ever-divorced, separated women may believe their current living arrangements to be only temporary. They may not want to insist on a formal child support order if the absent father is already providing support informally, particularly if that may further destabilize already tenuous marital relations.

Accounting for Trends in Award Rates across Survey Years

As we saw in tables 2.1 and 2.2, between April 1979 and April 1986 the proportion of women with a child support award rose from 59.3 to 61.5 percent of the eligible population. While the aggregate award rate rose 2.2 percentage points overall, it increased 3.2 points among ever-married and 7.8 points among never-married mothers. The award rate remained unchanged among nonblacks but rose 7.6 percentage points among blacks. Here we will try to account for these trends in award rates by race and marital status.

Why would aggregate award rates be expected to change over time? We have seen that not all groups of women are equally likely to obtain a child support award. Never-married and currently separated mothers are less likely than ever-divorced mothers (with otherwise similar characteristics) to have an award (see table 4.1). We have also seen that the proportion of all mothers eligible for child support who were never married increased substantially between 1979 and 1986, while the proportion separated decreased (see table 3.4). Given the increase in the former, we might expect the aggregate award rate to fall, while given the decrease in the latter, we might expect it to rise. We seek to determine what change in award rates could have been expected on the basis of all observable changes in the composition of the population eligible for child support between 1979 and 1986. Our results are summarized in table 4.3 for women overall, by marital status, and among the ever-married by race.[20]

What accounts for the 2.2 percentage point rise in the award rate of all women? As shown in table 4.3, given all observable changes in the socioeconomic characteristics of mothers except for the increase in the percent never married (which we analyze separately), the award rate could have been expected to rise 1.2 percentage points.[21] Although some changes could actually have been expected to lower the award rate (including an increase in the Hispanic percentage and a decrease in the average number of children), they were more than offset by changes that could have been expected to raise it (including a decrease in the percentage separated and an increase in educational attainment). The increase in the proportion of the population never married is shown separately in table 4.3 because of its large impact on the award rate. As we have seen, on average, never-married mothers are 62.7 percentage points less likely than otherwise similar divorced women to have an award (see table 4.1), and between 1979 and 1986 they increased from 19.7 to 23.2 percent of the eligible child support population (see table 3.4). Had this been the only change over the period, the aggregate award rate would have declined 1.5 percentage points.[22] Combining this decline with the increase owing to other demographic changes discussed above, the aggregate award rate should have fallen 0.3 percentage points between 1979 and 1986 (i.e., $-1.5 + 1.2$). Because it actually rose 2.2 percentage points, we conclude that the aggregate award rate is 2.5 percentage points higher in 1986 than would

Table 4.3 Accounting for Changes in Aggregate Award Rates from 1979 to 1986 by Marital Status and Race

Marital Status and Race	Actual Change in Award Rates 1979–1986[a]	Explained by Demographic Changes in			Change unexplained by these factors[d]
		Mother's characteristics[b]	% Never-married	Male real incomes[c]	
All women	2.2 (100%)	1.2 (54%)	-1.5 (-68%)	—	2.5 (114%)
Never-married	7.8 (100%)	0.3 (4%)	—	—	7.5 (96%)
Ever-married	3.2 (100%)	1.4 (44%)	—	0.3 (9%)	1.5 (47%)
Black	10.3 (100%)	3.5 (34%)	—	2.4 (23%)	4.4 (43%)
Nonblack	1.4 (100%)	0.7 (50%)	—	-0.4 (-29%)	1.1 (79%)

Note: Results are based upon separate probit regressions by marital status, and for the ever-married, by race, using all four years of data. Figures are adjusted to reflect weighted averages in chap. 2.

[a] From tables 2.1 and 2.2
[b] Mother's characteristics are those listed in table 4.1, other than never-married, which is analyzed separately.
[c] Male real income is the mean income of year-round, full-time male workers, by race, in the year of the mother's marital disruption (measured in 1985 constant dollars).
[d] Actual minus explained change

have been expected solely on the basis of shifts in the composition of the eligible population.

Next, we turn our attention to never-married mothers who experienced the greatest increase in award rates of all marital status groups, up 7.8 percentage points between 1979 and 1986. We could have expected their award rate to have risen only 0.3 percentage points owing to slight increases in the average ages of mothers and their children, an increase in the percentage of mothers who were high school graduates, and a decrease in the percentage who were black.[23] Thus, as shown in the second row of table 4.3, the award rate of never-married mothers increased 7.5 percentage points more than would have been predicted on the basis of observable demographic changes.

Shifting our focus to ever-married mothers, for whom the award rate rose 3.2 percentage points between 1979 and 1986, we can trace the impact not only of changes over time in the observable socioeconomic characteristics of mothers, but also of changes in the ability to pay of fathers. As shown in table 4.3, changes in the characteristics of ever-married mothers (including decreases in the proportion black, currently separated, or residing in central cities and an increase in average years of education) could have been expected to raise their award rate 1.4 percentage points. A father's ability to pay appears to have increased only slightly between the 1979 and 1986 surveys (rising from $28,230 to $28,420) when we approximate it by the mean real income in 1985 dollars of year-round, full-time male workers during the year of the mother's marital disruption.[24] Given the statistical association between male income and award rates, we can predict that this $190 increase in income could have been expected to raise the aggregate award rate by 0.3 percentage points between 1979 and 1986.[25] Thus, taken together, changes in the characteristics of ever-married mothers eligible for child support along with the modest increase in their former husbands' ability to pay support could have been expected to raise their award rate by 1.7 percentage points between 1979 and 1986, leaving an unexpected increase of 1.5 percentage points.

In table 4.3, we divide the increases in the award rates of ever-married black and nonblack mothers separately into expected and unexpected parts. (We restrict our attention to the ever-married so that we can control for changes over time in the father's income, an important source of racial differences.) Among black mothers, the award rate rose 10.3 percentage points; among nonblacks, it rose 1.4 percentage points. Changes over time in the average socioeconomic characteristics of mothers explain some of the increase for both racial groups. They predict a 3.5 percentage point rise for blacks and a 0.7 point rise for nonblacks. Changes across survey years in average male incomes (in the year of the marital disruption), however, have very different effects by race. Among blacks, male incomes rose $1,324, leading us to expect a 2.4 percentage point increase in award rate. Among nonblacks, it fell $302, leading us to expect a 0.4 percentage point decline in award rate. Overall, we conclude that nearly 43 percent of the 10.4 percentage point increase in the black award rate and 71 percent of the 1.4 percentage point increase in the nonblack award rate would not have been expected.

To summarize, for all marital and racial subgroups, we find that between 1979 and 1986 award rates rose by more than would have been expected on the basis of observable shifts in the composition of the population eligible for child support. What might account for these unexpected increases? In what follows we show that they can be attributed to higher award rates among those women who became *newly* eligible for child support between 1979 and 1986. Higher new award rates, in turn, may be associated with improvements in the social and legal environment surrounding the child support award process per se, a topic we investigate in greater detail in chapter 6.

It may be observed that the aggregate award rate in a given survey year represents the percentage of all women currently eligible for child support (the eligible pool) who have an award. Each year this pool changes as some mothers who are no longer eligible for support exit and other mothers who are newly eligible enter.[26] Over time, the aggregate award rate is subject to change as women who newly enter the pool find themselves more (or less) likely than those already in it to obtain an award at the time of their marital disruption.[27] In other words, unexpected changes in the aggregate award rate allow us to make inferences about changes in the new award rates of women who have only recently become eligible for support. If we find that the aggregate rate has risen across survey years even after adjusting for demographic changes in the eligible population, we can deduce that new award rates have been rising.

It turns out that it is possible to look behind these aggregate statistics to investigate historical trends in new award rates directly from 1958 to 1985. We then use our findings from this analysis to account for the unexpected portion of the increase in the aggregate award rate between 1979 and 1986 and to predict future trends in the award rate.

Trends in New Award Rates, 1958–1985

As in chapter 2, we define the *new* award rate as the likelihood that a mother who becomes newly eligible for child support obtains an award in a given year. Since mothers were not asked to provide the date they obtained (or attempted to obtain) an award, we restrict our attention to the ever-married and use the date of the marital disruption as a proxy for the date of the award (which allows us to trace new award rates back to 1958).[28] As we saw in figures 2.3 and 2.4, new award rates of ever-married mothers have generally risen over time.[29] They rose more for blacks than nonblacks and more for separated than divorced women. As we also noted, the upward trend in new award rates, particularly among nonblacks, appears to have slowed in the mid-1970s, coincident with the introduction of federal child support legislation in August 1975.

Why might we expect new award rates to have risen over time? As we argued in chapter 3, award outcomes depend upon the prevailing economic, social, and legal environments at the time of the marital disruption. The period since 1958 has seen rapid economic, social and legal changes—especially ones favorable to increasing award rates. On the economic front, real incomes of men (working full-time) rose 44 percent between 1958 and 1986,[30] although most of the increase occurred before 1974. On the social front, divorce rates more than doubled between 1965 and 1980 (from 10.6 to 22.6 per 1,000 women fifteen years or older), and the number of families headed by women alone rose sharply (from 5 to 8.7 million).[31] As a result, the stigma of divorce and single parenthood diminished, family courts dealt increasingly with the problems of marital dissolution, and social scientists, the press, and government bodies paid increasing attention to the economic impoverishment of mothers and their children. On the legal front, one result of this increased attention was the introduction of many new child support enforcement laws, particularly after 1975.[32]

WHAT WE FOUND. The generally upward trends in new award rates shown in figures 2.3 and 2.4 are supported by more detailed statistical analyses summarized in table 4.4 that also control for changes over time in the demographic composition of the newly eligible child support population.[33] For this work, it is particularly important to control for the ages of the children, which we do. As noted in chapter 2, because the Census Bureau surveyed mothers *currently*

Table 4.4   Annual Percentage Point Increase in New Award Rates of Ever-married Mothers, by Race, for Marital Disruptions Occurring 1958–1985, not Controlling and Controlling for Male Real Incomes in Year of Disruption

	Annual Percentage Point Increase in New Award Rates		
Race	1958–1985	1958–1975	1976–1985
Controlling for mother's socioeconomic characteristics only			
All ever-married	0.47	0.88	0.06[a]
Black (1,743)[b]	0.73	0.88	0.56
Nonblack (9,753)	0.42	0.84	0.002[a]
Controlling for mother's characteristics and male real incomes			
All ever-married	0.36	0.32	0.39
Black	0.58	0.34	0.65
Nonblack	0.36	0.39	0.36

Note: Estimates are derived from separate probit equations by race, which control for mother's socioeconomic characteristics listed in table 4.1. Male real income equals the mean income of year-round, full-time male workers, by race, in year of mother's marital disruption (measured in 1985 constant dollars).

[a] Significantly different from 1958–75 rate
[b] Sample size

eligible rather than *ever* eligible for child support, mothers with older marital disruptions will be in the sample only if their children were very young at the time of the disruption. Thus, unless we control for the ages of the children, we are likely to confound the effect of the children's ages with the effect of the year of the disruption on award rates.[34] In the top half of table 4.4, we report the average annual percentage point increase in new award rates for all ever-married women, as well as for black and nonblack ever-married women separately, holding constant the mother's socioeconomic characteristics.[35] We estimate an average annual trend rate for the entire period 1958 to 1986 and for the two subperiods 1958–75 and 1976–86.

As shown in table 4.4, we find that among all ever-married women the likelihood of obtaining a child support award rose 0.47 percentage points per year between 1958 and 1985 or, in other words, by almost 1 percentage point every two years. Overall, the upward trend in new award rates was significantly greater for black women (0.73 points per year) than for nonblack women (0.42 points per year). In results not shown, we found the upward trend somewhat greater for separated than for divorced women, but the difference was not statistically significant. Black women constitute a disproportionate share of all separated women,[36] which may account for the apparent differential trend by marital status in figures 2.3 and 2.4.

We also estimated the statistical analyses underlying table 4.4 in such a way as to permit the possibility of a differential trend before and after the introduction of federal child support legislation in August 1975 (which, allowing for a short time lag, we take to be 1976).[37] Table 4.4 gives the average annual percentage point change in new award rates for 1958–75 and 1976–85 separately and indicates (see note) when the two rates are significantly different.[38] As shown there, the likelihood of obtaining a new award rose at about the same rate for both black and nonblack women between 1958 and 1975 (at 0.88 and 0.84 percentage points per year, respectively). After 1975, black award rates continued to rise (albeit at a somewhat slower 0.56 points per year), while nonblack award rates virtually stopped rising.

ACCOUNTING FOR WHAT WE FOUND. The estimates in table 4.4 raise several important questions. First, what factors account for the overall increase between 1958 and 1986 in the likelihood of obtaining a child support award? Second, why was the increase in new award rates greater for blacks than for nonblacks? And third, why did the upward trend appear to stop for nonblacks but not for blacks after 1975, coincident with the introduction of federal child support legislation? As we have argued, we might expect changes over time in the likelihood of obtaining an award to be related to changes in the economic, social, and legal environments. Because these factors are so closely intertwined, it is not always possible to isolate the influence of a single factor. In what follows, however, we show that controlling for changes over time in at least one measure of aggregate economic conditions—real incomes of men—allows us to account for at least some of the observed changes in award rates.

We might expect some of the rise in new award rates since 1958 to be a result of improvements in the economic well-being of absent fathers. As we argued in chapter 3, the greater is the absent father's ability to pay, the more likely he will be to agree to an award voluntarily or the more likely is the court to order one. After some experimentation with various alternative indices of change, we found that we could best capture the father's ability to pay by the average real incomes of men in the year of the award (approximated, as in our analysis of racial differentials, by the mean income in 1985 constant dollars of year-round, full-time male workers, by race, in the year of the mother's marital disruption).[39] We then reestimated the award relation underlying the estimates (see table 4.4), adding this time series on male incomes.[40]

We find that the upward trend in real incomes of men is significantly related to the increase in new award rates over time, accounts for about one-fourth of the overall trend in new award rates, and evens out the trends before and after 1975. For all ever-married women, each $1,000 increase in male real income between 1958 and 1986 is associated with a 1.1 percentage point increase in new award rates, and this effect is somewhat stronger for nonblacks than for blacks.[41] Yet even though male real incomes and new award rates are positively and significantly related to each other, changes over time in the former cannot account for more than 25 percent of the increase in the latter. As we can see in the bottom half of table 4.4, after controlling for income, we still find new award rates rose 0.36 percentage points per year for all women, 0.58 points for black women, and 0.36 points for nonblack women. In other words, overall, about 75 percent (i.e., 0.36/0.47) of the upward trend in new award rates from 1958 to 1986 remains unexplained by the secular rise in the real income of men.

Although they leave most of the increase in new award rates over the entire period unexplained, trends in male real incomes can account for the differential trend in award rates before and after 1975. It might be recalled from table 2.7 that average male real incomes grew steadily through 1973 but then stagnated and declined sharply from 1978 to 1981. This means that many mothers who sought an award after 1973 found their children's fathers increasingly less able to provide support. Controlling for the effect of this real-income stagnation, we find that for all ever-married mothers the rate of increase in new awards that remains unaccounted for by changes in male real incomes was approximately the same before and after 1975 (0.32 percentage points per year from 1958 to 1975, and 0.39 percentage points per year after 1975).[42]

Changes over time in male real incomes also explain the racial differential in trends in new award rates after 1975. Between 1958 and 1986, average real incomes of nonblack men increased only 44 percent, while those of black men increased 90 percent. As a consequence, the ratio of black to nonblack income rose from .686 in 1973 to .754 in 1986.[43] Controlling for male real incomes by race, we find that black and nonblack women experienced essentially similar increases in new award rates since 1975: black rates grew 0.65 percentage points per year while nonblack rates grew 0.35 percentage points per year, but this difference (unlike those in the top half of the table) is not statistically significant. In other words, we can no longer reject the hypothesis that black and nonblack mothers experienced identical rates of increase in new awards after 1975.

To summarize, among all ever-married mothers eligible for child support, the likelihood of obtaining a child support award upon marital disruption increased at an average annual rate of 0.47 percentage points or at a rate of 0.88 points per year from 1958 to 1975 and 0.06 points per year from 1976 to 1986. We find that we are able to account for about one-fourth of the upward trend in new award rates over the entire period and all of the apparent slowdown in the trend after 1975 on the basis of changes over time in the real income of year-round, full-time male workers in the year of the award. Controlling for these changes, we conclude that new award rates grew at an average annual rate of 0.36 percentage points over the entire period 1958 to 1986 or, in other words, rose about 1 percentage point every three years. We might attribute this remaining upward trend to changes over time in the social and legal environments surrounding the award of child support. As we will see in chapter 6, however, the first state laws about awards were established only in 1975, and even after 1975 we find no significant effect of laws on award rates.

IMPLICATIONS AND PROJECTIONS FOR THE AGGREGATE AWARD RATE. In this final section on award rates, we look at the relation between changes over time in new award rates and changes across survey years in the aggregate award rate. First, we show that the increase in the aggregate award rate from 1979 to 1986 that we would not have expected on the basis of changes in demographic factors (i.e., the "unexpected change" in table 4.3) is consistent with our finding of the secular upward trend in new award rates between 1958 and 1985 (in the bottom half of table 4.4). Second, looking at recent census data that postdate our analyses, we show that changes in the aggregate award rate between 1986 and 1990 might have been predicted on the basis of trends in new award rates prior to 1986 and of changes in the marital composition of the population since 1986.

We have argued that the unexpected increase of 1.5 percentage points in the aggregate award rate of ever-married mothers between 1979 and 1986 (or 4.4 points for blacks and 1.1 points for nonblacks) might be a result of the more favorable award experiences of women who entered the child support pool after 1979. These unexpected increases are roughly consistent with the annual rate of increase in new award rates displayed in table 4.4. When new award rates rise, the aggregate award rate will also rise, and it can be shown that the two will change over time at approximately the same rate (when the relative size of each new marital disruption cohort remains constant over time).[44] Thus, with new award rates rising 0.36 percentage points per year, we might expect the aggregate award rate to rise 0.36 points per year also, or by 2.5 percentage points over the seven years between 1979 and 1986. By race, the cumulative rise in the aggregate award rate predicted on the basis of the upward trend in new award rates would be 4.1 percentage points for blacks and 2.5 points for nonblacks. For blacks, this predicted rise is almost the same as the unexpected change in the aggregate award rate (4.1 vs. 4.4); for both all ever-married mothers and nonblacks, the predicted rise is slightly greater than the unexpected increase in the aggregate award rate (2.5 vs. 1.5 and 2.5 vs. 1.1). For these two groups, it is not entirely clear why aggregate award rates failed to rise quite as much as would have been anticipated on the basis of the upward trend in new award rates. One explanation may be that in contrast to our assumption of constant size cohorts over time, new disruptions (and thus new awards) represented a progressively smaller fraction of the total eligible child support population after 1981 as divorce rates began to decline.[45] As a result, rising new award rates after 1981 had a smaller impact on changes over time in the aggregate award rate.

In September 1991, the Census Bureau released findings from a more recent child support survey conducted in April 1990. According to this report, the aggregate award rate of all mothers eligible for support was 57.7 percent. It was 23.9 percent for never-married mothers and 71.9 percent for ever-married mothers. Thus, compared with 1986, the aggregate award rate in 1990 was 3.8 percentage points lower overall, 5.5 points higher for never-married mothers, and 2.6 points lower for ever-married mothers. We might ask whether or not these changes could have been expected on the basis of our knowledge about trends in new award rates prior to 1986 as well as information about changes in the composition of the child support pool since 1986.

The decline in the aggregate award rate of all women after 1986 can be attributed almost entirely to a single factor—the disproportionate increase in the never-married population, which rose from 23.2 to 29.6 percent of the total population eligible for child support between 1986 and 1990. How might this shift in marital composition be expected to affect the aggregate award rate? If award rates for both ever-married and never-married mothers had remained constant at their 1986 levels (i.e., 74.5% and 18.4 %, respectively), then given the disproportionate increase in the never-married population, we could have expected the aggregate award rate to fall from 61.5 to 57.9 percent, a decline of 3.6 percentage points, which is very close to the actual decline of 3.8 points.

Evidence from the 1990 survey on award rates by marital status presents a mixed picture about recent progress in awards. On the one hand, the decline in the award rate of ever-married mothers is disturbing but perhaps not entirely unexpected given the stagnation in new award rates after 1975, which we recorded in table 4.4. On the other hand, the increase in the aggregate award rate of never-married mothers is reassuring, suggesting that the upward trend in the award rate among never-married mothers that we observed between 1979 and 1986 has continued unabated.

Award Amounts

Securing a child support award is only part of the first step toward ultimately receiving payment; negotiating an adequate award amount is the other part. As we saw in chapter 2, the amount of child support due varies considerably by race and marital status and in real terms declined sharply between 1978 and 1985.

We begin our analysis of award amounts by estimating how the real value of support currently due (measured in 1985 dollars) varies with the socioeconomic characteristics of the mother, the year in which the award was made, and the sample year in which it is due. Then, we use these results to try to account for racial and marital status differentials in the value of child support due and to identify reasons why the real value of support due declined during the 1980s. We conclude that about two-thirds of the differential in the value of support due between ever-married black and nonblack mothers can be explained on the basis of racial differences in mother's characteristics and in male incomes. About half of the differential in awards between ever-married and never-married mothers can be explained on the basis of differences in socioeconomic characteristics alone.

We show that demographic changes over time in the population due support and the erosion from inflation in the real value of old (i.e., existing) awards account for only a small portion of the decline in the real value of child support due between 1978 and 1985. Rather, we argue that the decline stems from the failure of new awards made after 1978 to keep up with increases in consumer prices or male incomes. Looking at historical trends in new awards directly, we show that, at least since 1958, the value of new awards obtained by ever-married mothers (measured in current dollars) has been rising only half as fast as either consumer prices or average male incomes. As a result, the real value of awards has been declining at an average annual rate of about 3.5 percent. We offer several hypotheses to explain the persistence of this decline.

A brief reminder about our terminology may be in order. Given the construction of the CPS questionnaire, we know how much child support a mother is due in the year prior to the survey but not how much she was originally awarded. In an appendix to this chapter (app. C), we offer indirect evidence that the two amounts are almost always the same. Thus, throughout our discussion of determinants, differentials, and trends, we often use the phrase *award amount* rather than the more cumbersome *value of child support due*.

Demographic Determinants of the Value of Awards

The average value of child support due among all mothers due support in 1978, 1981, 1983, or 1985 was $2,768, measured in constant 1985 dollars (see table 2.4).[46] In this section we make use of multivariate statistical analysis (as reviewed in app. B) to examine how award amounts differ by race, marital status, and a variety of other observable socioeconomic characteristics. Table 4.5 reports the effect of these characteristics on the value of child support due for all women due support and for ever-married mothers separately, ceteris paribus.[47] (Too few never-married mothers are due support to warrant a separate analysis.) The figures in the table can be interpreted as the dollar increase in child support due associated with a one unit increase in a given characteristic, holding all other characteristics constant. We discuss each of these estimates in turn, relating them back to the underlying child support model developed in chapter 3.

Table 4.5 Effect of Selected Socioeconomic Characteristics of Mothers Due Child Support in 1978, 1981, 1983, or 1985 on Amount of Support Due by Marital Status (in 1985 dollars)

	All Women	Ever-married
Education and age		
Years of education	145**	145**
College graduate[a]	419*	389*
Current age	9*	—
Age at divorce	—	29*
Race and ethnicity		
Black[a]	−653**	−655**
Hispanic[a]	−270	−210
Current marital status		
Never-married[b]	−797**	—
Separated[b]	201	160
Remarried[b]	−269**	−58
Number and ages of children		
Second child[a]	948**	895**
Third child[a]	632**	635**
Fourth child (or more)[a]	500**	556**
Age 6–17[a]	281**	359**
Region or location		
Northeast[c]	219*	228*
North central[c]	229**	228*
South[c]	217*	205*
SMSA[a]	373**	375**
Central city[a]	−189*	−138
Voluntary agreement[a]	413**	315**
Indicator of year of marital disruption	—	94**
Mean amount due	$2,785	$2,854
Sample size	7,497	7,146

Note: Figures represent the dollar change in child support due for a unit change in a given variable, holding all else constant. OLS estimates also control for year of survey and for the ever-married, whether payments are due only part of the year. The indicator of year of marital disruption is coded as last two digits of marital disruption year minus 57.

*(**) Indicates statistical significance at a 5% (1%) level.
[a] Relative to not having this characteristic
[b] Relative to being currently divorced
[c] Relative to living in the West

As we argued in chapter 3, the value of a child support award is likely to vary directly with the income of the absent father. Although his income is not observed, several socioeconomic characteristics of the mother are likely to be correlated with it, including her age, education, and ethnicity.[48] We find that years of education, college graduation, and current age (or age at divorce or separation for ever-married women) have positive and significant effects on the amount of support due. Black women are due about 23 percent less support than nonblack women with comparable socioeconomic characteristics.[49] Hispanic women are due almost 10 percent less support than other women, but the ceteris paribus difference is not significant.

Support also varies with the ages and number of children. Women with at least one child between the ages of six and seventeen are due between $281 and $359 more child support than similar women with only younger or older children. On average, between 1978 and 1985, mothers with one child were due $2,162. Holding all else constant, the presence of a second child raises support due by an average of $948; a third child raises support by another $632; each additional child beyond that adds $500 more.

It is interesting to compare the magnitude of these increments in award amounts with increments in actual expenditures on children as reported by Edward Lazear and Robert Michael in their analysis of the 1972–73 Consumer Expenditure Survey. Although most of their work is for two-parent families, at one point Lazear and Michael show how total expenditures on children in households with one adult rise with the number of children present, by race and income level.[50] Among both white and black families, they report increments to expenditures on children that are consistently greater (even in their smaller 1972–73 dollars) than our increments to actual awards for all incomes above $5,000 and $10,000, respectively. Thus, extending our earlier analysis of the adequacy of awards, we conclude that not only does the average level of child support awards seem to be too low, but increments to awards with increases in the number of children due support are also too low to meet the needs of most families.

The amount of support due varies by marital status, reflecting a variety of factors, including differences in the amount of time elapsed since the award was established, economic conditions at the time of the award, the absent father's ability and desire to pay, and the mother's expected needs for and costs of obtaining support. Compared with currently divorced women (who are due, on average, $2,974), otherwise identical never-married mothers are due 27 percent (or $797) less support. Fathers obligated to pay child support who were never married to their child's mother are likely to offer less support than other fathers because their emotional bond with their child is presumably weaker. Never-married mothers may settle for less because they believe the cost of obtaining more support is too high given the meager benefits they expect.

Among ever-married mothers, award amounts differ by current marital status, but these differences largely reflect differences in the year of the award (the marital disruption). When we do not control directly for the disruption year (col. 1), remarried women are due significantly less support ($269) than comparable divorced women. But once we control for the disruption year, the differential shrinks to $58 and is no longer significant. In other words, remarried women appear in the first column to be due less support than divorced women largely because their awards were established longer ago when price levels were lower. (According to the results in col. 2, the value of support currently due is $94 less for each additional year since the marital disruption occurred.) In addition, a remarried woman may permit her child support award to be renegotiated downward (or cease to request upward adjustments), if her new husband helps to support her children.[51]

Support amounts also differ by geographic location. Women in western states are due significantly less child support than otherwise similar women living elsewhere.[52] Regional differences may be due in part to state variations in the presence of child support guidelines governing award amounts. The lower value of awards in western states may also be related to the impact of no-fault divorce laws that began there. For example, Elizabeth Peters offers evidence that alimony, child support, and property settlements received by women were lower in 1979 in states with no-fault divorce laws.[53] Women living within an SMSA are due about $375 more child support than women not in an SMSA. Among SMSA residents, those living within the central city are due about $189 less, although this effect is not significant among ever-married mothers.[54] In large part, these ceteris paribus locational differences may be related to variations in housing expenditures and other costs of living.

Finally, women who report that their child support award was agreed to voluntarily are due between $315 and $413 more support than women with court-ordered settlements. This may reflect differ-

Table 4.6   Accounting for Racial and Marital Status Differentials in Amount of Child Support Due in 1978, 1981, 1983, or 1985 (in 1985 dollars)

| Total Differential[a] | Explained by Differences in | | Unexplained differential[d] |
	Mother's characteristics[b]	Male real incomes[c]	
Nonblack ever-married vs. black ever-married			
$372 (100%)	$−163 (−44%)	$408 (110%)	$127 (34%)
All ever-married vs. all never-married			
$1,460 (100%)	$674 (46%)	—	$786 (54%)

ᵃ Differentials obtained from table 2.5

ᵇ Mother's characteristics are those listed in table 4.5.

ᶜ Mean male incomes of year-round, full-time workers, by race, in year of mother's marital disruption (in 1985 constant dollars)

ᵈ For race, the unexplained differential equals the total minus explained differential, where the explained differential evaluates racial differences in characteristics and income using black regression coefficients. For marital status, the unexplained differential equals the coefficient on the variable *never-married* from the regression for all women reported in table 4.5.

ences in the father's desire to pay support and differences in the mother's expected costs of obtaining support or the impact of the courts per se on award amounts.

Accounting for Racial and Marital Status Differentials

On average, black mothers are due considerably less child support than nonblacks, and never-married mothers are due much less than the ever-married. We examine to what extent we can account for these differentials on the basis of differences in average demographic characteristics by race or marital status, and we also speculate on why a part of the differentials remains unexplained. Our results are summarized in table 4.6.

RACIAL DIFFERENTIALS. On average, between 1978 and 1985, black women were due $2,238 in 1985 constant dollars, or $612 (21%) less than the $2,850 due nonblack women (see table 2.4). In statistical analyses, the details of which are not reported here, we find that we can attribute as much as one-third of this overall racial differential in dollars due to the much lower percentage of black mothers who have ever married their children's father.[55] But even among ever-married mothers, the racial differential remains large: blacks are due $2,512, or $372 (13%) less than the $2,884 due nonblacks (see table 2.5). Unlike racial differences in marital status, however, most other differences in the mother's characteristics by race actually tend to raise the expected awards of blacks relative to nonblacks. For example, black women tend to have more children to support, to have somewhat older children, and are considerably less likely to be living in the West (see table 3.4). Taken together, as shown in table 4.6, these racial differences in mother's characteristics lead us to expect ever-married blacks to be due, on average, $146 more child support than ever-married nonblacks.[56]

In contrast to racial differences in the mother's characteristics, which only deepen the puzzle of why ever-married black mothers are due less support, racial differences in the absent father's income can account for more than 100 percent of the racial gap in awards. If we proxy the father's income by the mean income of year-round, full-time male workers by race, in the year of the mother's marital disruption, we find that black income averages only 73 percent of nonblack income or, expressed in 1985 dollars, $16,205 for blacks compared with $22,108 for nonblacks.[57] Holding the mother's socioeconomic characteristics constant, we estimated the association between the father's income and the value of child support due, allowing that association to differ by race. We found that among black women, each $1,000 increase in the absent father's income is associated with a $62 increase in the value of child support due, while among nonblack women, the same increase raises dollars due by $79. Given even the lower estimate of $62, we calculate that the racial difference in the father's income can account for a $408 racial differential in average dollars due, which exceeds the actual differential of $372.[58]

To summarize, while among ever-married women, we expect blacks to be due less child support than nonblacks on the basis of racial differences in the father's income, we expect blacks to be due more support on the basis of their socioeconomic characteristics. Combining these two effects, we expect ever-married black women to be due, on average, $245 less child support than nonblack women. In other words, as shown in table 4.6, only about one-third of the total racial differential ($127/$372) cannot be accounted for by racial differences in either the mother's characteristics or the father's income.

What accounts for the lower award amounts of blacks that cannot be explained by either demographic or income differences? As we have already suggested in our discussion of racial differences in award rates, one possibility is that our income proxy based upon the earnings of full-time workers may underestimate actual racial differences in income. In addition, even when correctly measured, income may not fully capture the full racial difference in the father's ability to pay. Recent research on racial differences in wealth show that among young families in the 1970s, the assets of blacks were about one-sixth the value of those of whites and that this wealth difference is far greater than could be expected on the basis of income differences alone.[59] Given their lower wealth, higher unemployment rates, and lower labor force participation rates, black men may offer to pay less support than nonblacks, and many court judges may expect them to be less able to pay.

The racial differences in mother's socioeconomic characteristics that we can observe may not fully control for all differences between black and nonblack mothers. Given the lower ability to pay of black fathers, many black mothers may not believe it is worth their while to press for higher awards, particularly if that means going to court. Black women may be more willing to seek alternative sources of support for their children, including their own extended families, and public assistance. Some recent work finds that race is an important factor in explaining welfare participation: black women are significantly more likely to be on AFDC than are similar nonblacks.[60] But another study by Robert Moffitt found no racial difference in a variable measuring "welfare stigma," that is, the mother's distaste for going on AFDC.[61]

MARITAL STATUS DIFFERENTIALS. Even larger than the racial differential in award amounts is that between never-married and ever-married mothers. As we saw in table 2.4, on average between 1978 and 1985, never-married mothers were due $1,383, or $1,460 less than the $2,843 due ever-married mothers (measured in constant 1985 dollars). Our statistical analysis (summarized in table 4.6) suggests that somewhat less than half (46%) of this differential can be accounted for by socioeconomic factors. None of the differential can be explained by differences in family size per se, since both ever-married and never-married mothers have an average of 1.7 children.[62] Compared to the ever-married, however, never-married mothers are younger, have less education, and are more likely to be black—all characteristics associated with lower-than-average child support awards. On the basis of differences in all observable socioeconomic characteristics (listed in table 4.5), we can expect never-married mothers to be due $674 less support on average than the ever-married.[63] The $786 residual unexplained by these factors may reflect unobservable differences among mothers in their cost of obtaining support (due, in part, to additional legal hurdles for the never-married) and differences between fathers in their ability and desire to support their children.[64]

It is likely that we could account for a substantial portion of this $786 unexplained differential in award amounts if we were able to control for differences in the father's income. On average, we would expect fathers of children of never-married mothers to have much lower incomes than those of ever-married mothers. We might approximate their income by average incomes in 1985 of men by current marital status. According to these data, the income of never-married men averaged $19,959, or 72 percent of that of divorced men of $27,781. Among ever-married mothers only, we find that each $1,000 increment to the father's income raises the value of child support due by $73. Using this relation to evaluate the $7,822 income difference by marital status, we would expect a never-married mother to be due $571 less support than an otherwise identical ever-married mother. In other words, it appears that marital status differences in father's incomes alone would be able to account for about 73 percent of the $786 unexplained differential in award amounts.

Accounting for Trends in the Amount Due across Survey Years

We now return to a question raised in chapter 2 that has both puzzled and frustrated child support advocates and public policymakers: Why did the real value of child support due decline so sharply between 1978 and 1985? Adjusted for the increase in the cost of living, we know the average value of child support due to have been 24 percent lower in the 1985 survey than in the 1978 survey. If this downward trend in expected real payments is to be arrested—much less reversed—we need to know why it occurred. A variety of possible explanations have been advanced. Our goal is to assess the relative importance of each, since each explanation calls for a different remedy.

Throughout most of the analysis that follows we focus our attention on ever-married mothers because we need to approximate the year of the award by the year of the marital disruption, but where possible, we draw some conclusions for the never-married as well.

The pool of ever-married mothers due child support in a given survey year consists of all women who obtained an award at the time of their marital disruption (or perhaps, subsequently) and who still expect to receive payment.[65] Over time, as some women with old awards exit and others with new awards enter, three principal factors will cause the average real value of child support due to change. These are changes in the demographic composition of the population, changes in the inflation rate, which affect the extent to which old awards not indexed to the price level decline in value, and changes in the real value of new awards. We evaluate the relative contribution of each of these factors to the decline in support due between 1978 and 1985.

One factor that affects the average value of child support due is the demographic composition of the pool of women due support. The average socioeconomic characteristics of women in the pool may change over time, and these characteristics are important determinants of the real value of support due (table 4.5). If, for example, the composition of the pool due support shifts across survey years towards a greater proportion of mothers with characteristics that are associated with lower than average awards, we would expect the real value of child support due to decline.

A second factor that affects the real value of child support due is the extent to which prices have risen since obligations were originally established. Few child support awards are written as *indexed* contracts—that is, automatically adjusted over time as consumer prices rise—and, as we show in appendix C, few awards are ever renegotiated. As a result, when prices rise, the average real value of old (i.e., existing) awards declines, and the faster prices rise, the greater is the rate of decay. Thus, when we compare the real value of child support due in two different survey years, we expect its real value to be lower in the survey whose average participant has experienced more inflation between the date of the award and the date of the survey.

The third factor that affects the real value of support due is the change over time in the real value of awards of new entrants into the pool (i.e., new awards). At least since 1970, the nominal value of new awards has been rising only about half as fast as either consumer

Table 4.7   Accounting for Changes in Real Value of Child Support Due Ever-married Mothers between 1978 and 1985 (in 1985 constant dollars)

Time Period	Overall Change in the Real Value of Child Support Due[a] (1)	Change in Support Due Explained by		Change unex-plained by these factors[d] (4)
		Demographic shifts in population due support[b] (2)	Cumulative inflation on old awards[c] (3)	
1978–85	$−760	$66	$−131	$−695
	(100%)	(−8.6%)	(17.2%)	(91.4%)
1978–81	$−587	$59	$−270	$−376
	(100%)	(−10.1%)	(46.0%)	(64.1%)
1981–85	$−173	$−22	$77	$−228
	(100%)	(12.8%)	(−44.3%)	(131.5%)

Note: Since explained changes relative to 1978 (1981) are based upon a child support due regression using 1978 (1981) data only, changes for each subperiod will not equal the change for the full time period.

[a] Average amount of child support due in the later minus earlier sample year, expressed in 1985 constant dollars

[b] Change across sample years in average socioeconomic characteristics (from table 4.5) multiplied by corresponding coefficients from 1978 or 1981 regression

[c] Change across sample years in the cumulative increase in CPI (between year of award and sample year) multiplied by its coefficient from 1978 or 1981 regression

[d] Col. 1 minus cols. 2 and 3

prices or male incomes (see table 2.7). As a result, the real value of new awards has been declining. (In the next section we investigate several hypotheses why this has occurred.) As a consequence, when the real value of new awards declines over time, the average real value of child support due across survey years declines as well.[66]

How important was each of these factors in contributing to the sharp decline in the real value of child support due between 1978 and 1985? Among ever-married mothers, the average real value of child support due (measured in 1985 dollars) fell from $3,335 in 1978 to $2,575 in 1985—a decline of $760, or 22.8 percent (see table 2.4). Over three-quarters of this decline, or $587, occurred between 1978 and 1981, while the remaining $173 decline occurred between 1981 and 1985. In table 4.7 we identify what portion of each of these declines could have been expected on the basis of either demographic changes in the population due support or changes in the *cumulative* rate of inflation between the average year of the award and the year the support was due.[67] Changes that could not have been expected on either of these grounds we label as "unexpected." We argue that this unexpected decline is largely associated with the declining real value of new awards.[68]

Between 1978 and 1985 the average number of children (per ever-married mother) due support fell and the proportion of mothers who were black or Hispanic increased (see table 3.4). These changes could have been expected to reduce the real value of support due because women with fewer children and minority women are due less child support (see table 4.5). At the same time, average years of education rose and the proportion of women with older children or voluntary child support settlements increased—changes that could have been expected to raise the real value of support due. In table 4.7, we show what changes in child support due could have been expected between one survey and another when we evaluate all the changes in characteristics together given the award environment that prevailed at the time of the earlier survey.[69]

We find that the changes in the composition of the pool fail to account for any of the decline in real support due up to 1981 but do account for some of the decline thereafter. Between 1978 and 1981, when the largest average decline occurred, demographic changes worked to raise support due by $59, given the award environment prevailing up to 1978. Between 1981 and 1985, when the average real value of support due declined less, demographic changes worked to lower it by $22, given the award environment prevailing up to 1981. Yet over the entire period 1978 to 1985, we could have expected the average real value of support due to rise $66.

In results not shown in the table, changes in demographic composition become a slightly more important part of the explanation for the decline if we include never-married mothers in the analysis. Among all marital status groups taken together, the average real value of support due declined from $3,279 in 1978 to $2,494 in 1985—a decline of $785 or 23.9 percent (see table 2.4). Taken together, all socioeconomic changes other than in the percentage never married appear to be nearly offsetting, leading to the prediction that real support due should have remained roughly constant between 1978 and 1985. But by itself, the increase in never-married mothers from 2.9 percent of all women due support in 1978 to 6.3 percent in 1985 can account for a $33 decline in real support due between 1978 and 1985.[70] Thus, we conclude that about 4 percent of the overall decline in expected child support payments between 1978 and 1985 (i.e., $33/$775) might be attributable to the recent disproportionate increase of the never-married among those due support.

We also show in table 4.7 the change in child support due that can be attributed to the decline in the real value of old awards. Inflation reduces the real value of child support currently due if awards made in years prior to the survey year (i.e., old awards) are not indexed to the price level. We can measure the magnitude of this effect by estimating the statistical association between the real value of support due in a given survey year and the *cumulative* amount of inflation that occurred from the date of each award to the date of the survey.[71] For short, we refer to this estimate as the *cumulative inflation effect*. Then, if the average cumulative rate of inflation increases from one survey (say 1978) to another (say 1985), we can expect the real value of support due to decline (between 1978 and 1985) by an amount equal to the change in the cumulative inflation rate times the size of the cumulative inflation effect.

Because the inflation rate accelerated in the late 1970s and early 1980s, among mothers due support in 1978, prices had risen an average of 36 percent since their award, while among mothers due support in 1981(85), the cumulative inflation rate since their award was 53 percent (44%). As shown in table 4.7, we estimate that women due support in 1981(85) were due $270 ($131) less than women due support in 1978.[72] After 1981, because the inflation rate declined, the average cumulative inflation rate experienced by women due support in 1985 was actually 9 percentage points less than for women due support in 1981. This leads us to expect the real value of support due to have risen $77 between 1981 and 1985.[73]

To summarize our findings to this point, changes in the socioeconomic characteristics of ever-married mothers due support and the erosion of old awards resulting from inflation account for little of the $760 decline in the average real value of child support due between 1978 and 1985. During a period of very high inflation, 1978 to 1981, they do account for more than one-third of the decline, but during the period of relatively little inflation, 1981 to 1985, they account for none of the decline, and in fact make the unexplained decline appear even larger.

Intuitively, when we hold the observable determinants of child support due constant, the unexplained decline in the real value of support due represents changes in the underlying award process or experience itself.[74] Hence, we can attribute unexplained changes across survey years in child support due to the entry of mothers with new awards. As we now show, the real value of *new* awards declined at an average annual rate of 3.5 percent between 1958 and 1985, causing the real value of both new awards and support due to decline almost 22 percent between 1978 and 1985.

Trends in the Value of New Awards, 1958–1985

Consistent with evidence presented in chapter 2, new awards rose about half as quickly as consumer prices or male incomes between 1958 and 1985. We offer several hypotheses why this occurred. Throughout this analysis we restrict our attention to ever-married mothers and approximate the value of child support originally awarded (which we do not know) by the value of support currently due (which we do). While these two amounts will differ if awards are renegotiated (either formally or informally) when the economic circumstances of the mother or father change, we provide indirect statistical evidence in appendix C that they are almost always the same.

DO NEW AWARDS RISE AS QUICKLY AS PRICES AND INCOMES? Although, as might well be expected, the value of new awards measured in current dollars has risen over time, we have already seen some evidence (in table 2.7) that, at least since 1969, new award amounts have tended to rise more slowly than consumer prices or average male incomes. In table 4.8 we report the average value of new awards obtained between 1958 and 1985, for all mothers together and for mothers in each survey separately, expressed in current dollars and in 1985 constant dollars.[75] We also report the annual percentage point change in new awards in both current and constant dollars, and we compare changes over time in the value of new awards to changes in the Consumer Price Index and average male incomes in the year of the award.

On average between 1958 and 1985, controlling for changes in the demographic composition of the population, the nominal value of new child support awards rose 3.4 percent per year (row 2).[76] The real value of new awards, however, declined at an annual rate of 3.5 percent (row 6).[77] On average, each 10 percent increase in consumer prices was associated with a 4.8 percent increase in the nominal value

Table 4.8 Relation between Changes in Value of New Awards to Ever-married Mothers, 1958–1985, and Male Incomes or Consumer Prices, for All Mothers and by Year Support is Due (in current and constant 1985 dollars)

	All Mothers	Mothers Due Support in			
		1978	1981	1983	1985
Current dollars[a]					
Average new award value	$2,388	2,038	2,329	2,547	2,606
Annual percentage change in new awards	3.4%	3.7	3.6	2.6	3.9
Percentage change in new awards given a 10% increase in:					
Consumer prices[b]	4.8%	6.6	5.1	3.4	5.0
Nominal male incomes[c]	4.7%	5.3	4.8	3.4	5.4
Constant 1985 dollars[d]					
Average new award value	$3,995	4,445	4,044	3,991	3,545
Annual percentage change in new awards	−3.5%	−1.6	−3.3	−5.2	−3.7
Percentage change in new awards given a 10% increase in:					
Consumer prices	−5.2%	−3.4	−4.9	−6.6	−4.9
Nominal male incomes	−5.0%	−2.6	−4.6	−7.0	−5.3

[a] Current value of child support due in year prior to survey

[b] Coefficient on natural log of CPI (1967 = 100) in year of marital disruption, from an OLS regression on natural log of award value, controlling for socioeconomic characteristics in table 4.5.

[c] Coefficient on natural log of male income from an OLS regression on natural log of award value, controlling for socioeconomic characteristics in table 4.5

[d] Value of child support due in year prior to survey times CPI in 1985 and divided by CPI in year of marital disruption

of new awards, or equivalently, with a 5.2 percent decrease in their real value.[78] The situation did not appear to improve during the 1980s, contrary to some evidence in table 2.7. We allowed the historical relation between the value of new awards and the CPI to differ before and after 1980,[79] and we experimented by splitting the time period at dates other than 1980, but we found no statistical evidence that new awards did better at keeping up with inflation in more recent than in earlier years.[80]

Over time, we might expect the current value of child support awards to rise not only with consumer prices, but also male incomes. Indeed, the model of child support formulated in chapter 3 suggests that award amounts should vary directly with the father's ability to pay. Sen. Joseph Lieberman has argued that, following English common law, court-ordered child support awards in the United States have almost always been based upon the father's income.[81] Since their introduction in 1975, child support guidelines have formally linked award amounts to the noncustodial parent's income. In some states (see chap. 6), such as Wisconsin, awards are established as a fixed percentage of the noncustodial parent's income; in others, such as Delaware, the precise association between awards and income may vary somewhat with the custodial parent's own ability to support the children.[82]

Thus, in table 4.8 we also show the historical association between changes in new award amounts and changes in the mean income of year-round full-time male workers in current dollars. We find that, on average between 1958 and 1985, each 10 percent increase in the current value of male income was associated with a 4.7 percent increase in the nominal value of new awards and with a 5.0 percent decrease in their real value.[83] Furthermore, grouping mothers by survey year, we see no evidence of a change in the relation between awards and income over time.[84] Thus, we can conclude that, at least since 1958, new award amounts have increased only about half as fast as male incomes.

WHY HAS THE REAL VALUE OF NEW AWARDS BEEN FALLING? As we have confirmed, the real value of new awards fell steadily between 1958 and 1986. We offer several noncompeting hypotheses why this decline occurred. By noncompeting, we mean that each hypothesis is consistent with the observed decline, and none precludes any of the others from also accounting for part of the decline.

One hypothesis is that the decline in the real value of newly made awards is simply an unintended consequence of high rates of unanticipated inflation. Just as in wage and salary negotiations, individuals and institutions tend to negotiate child support contracts in nominal rather than real terms (i.e., they exhibit "money illusion"). Thus, during periods of high inflation, perceptions often lag behind increases in consumer prices. We have already seen evidence of this in table 2.7: the real value of new awards tended to decline the most during years of the highest rates of inflation. There is, however, one important difference between the consequences of money illusion in wage and salary negotiations and in child support negotiations. Real wages may fall during years of unusually high inflation, but they tend to recover completely in subsequent years of lower inflation. Real child support awards, however, never completely recover their lost value. The reason for this is that in wage negotiations the very same workers who have experienced a decline in their real wages often return to the bargaining table the following year, but in child support negotiations, a different group of mothers participate each year. Because of this lack of continuity, adverse outcomes in one year are not likely to affect the bargaining process the next year.

There may also be a built-in mechanism in the bargaining process at divorce that causes awards to lag behind price increases. Typically, the mother's lawyer requests an increase in award amounts over those given the previous year equal to the most recent twelve-month increase in the CPI, while the father's lawyer suggests the same amount as was given last year to individuals in comparable circumstances. The judge effects a compromise by splitting the difference between the two, and as a result, new award amounts rise about half as fast as prices over time.

Alternatively, the decline in the real value of new awards may be a direct consequence of the stagnation in real incomes of men that occurred during the 1970s. As previously noted, the mean real income of year-round full-time male workers declined about 10 percent from a peak of $30,552 in 1973 to a low of $27,478 in 1981, measured in 1985 constant dollars. We found some support for the hypothesis that real incomes and awards move in the same direction by relating the real value of new awards to both a linear time trend (to control for the downward trend in real awards) and male real incomes simultaneously. We estimated that while real awards declined at an average annual rate of 3.65 percentage points overall, they rose a statistically significant 0.6 percentage points for each 1 percentage point increase in male real income.[85] In other words, given the 10 percent decline in male real income that occurred between 1973 and 1981, we could have expected the real value of new awards to decline about 6 percent. Of course, there is reason to suspect that this cannot be the only reason why the real value of new awards declined because, as we have seen, the ratio of new awards to male incomes declined over time, indicating that the average father's child support burden declined by considerably more than his income.

In related work, Philip K. Robins offers an alternative hypothesis:

the decline in new awards may have been a direct consequence of a rise in the ratio of female to male earnings and participation rates between 1961 and 1985,[86] which caused families and courts to shift the burden for support of children toward mothers who were perceived as increasingly able to provide for them. This is an interesting hypothesis and one to which the CPS data lend some support,[87] but there are several important reasons to suspect that this may not be the principal reason why real award amounts declined.[88] One reason for skepticism is that, judged by either guideline formulas or other marriage and divorce laws in force over this period, few states explicitly considered the mother's income in arriving at an award amount.[89] Another reason is that when we relate the real value of new awards to both the CPI and Robins's ratio of female to male earnings simultaneously, we find that the former is statistically significant but the latter is not.[90] In other words, although these two influences on awards are highly correlated and thus difficult to disentangle, we find that once we control for the impact of inflation per se, changes in new awards are unrelated to women's earnings relative to men's.

An alternative explanation for the secular decline in the real value of new awards is that the onset of no-fault divorce laws engendered a shift toward women in the burden of their children's financial support. Elizabeth Peters and Lenore Weitzman, among others, have argued that changes over time in the legal grounds for divorce have reduced the relative bargaining position of women and resulted in a lower level of interspousal transfers at marital dissolution, including alimony, child support, and property settlements.[91] As noted, this thesis is consistent with the pattern of lower child support awards observed in Western states, where no-fault divorce laws originated. It would also appear to be consistent with the declining value of new awards over time, as no-fault laws became more widespread during the 1970s.

To summarize, on average between 1958 and 1985, the current dollar value of new awards increased about half as fast as either consumer prices or male incomes, leading to a decline in the real value of new awards at an average annual rate of 3.4 percent. This finding is important for at least two reasons. First, it means that mothers newly eligible for child support increasingly find themselves bearing a greater share of the burden for the support of their children. Second, the decline in the real value of new awards is an important part of the explanation of why, among all women due support, the real value of support due declined between 1978 and 1985. It is to this topic that we now return.

Trends in the Value of Child Support Due: Policy Implications and Projections

We have argued that, largely as a result of a continuing decline in the real value of *new* awards, the average amount of child support *due* ever-married mothers declined by more than 22 percent between 1978 and 1985. In part a response to this decline, the very first provision of the Family Support Act of 1988 mandates that states make use of numerical guidelines in setting new award amounts and that they review the adequacy of existing awards on a periodic basis.[92]

To what extent could the decline in child support due between 1978 and 1985 have been prevented had one or both of these provisions already been in force? If all child support awards were not only reviewed but fully indexed to the price level, the real value of child support due in each of our four survey years would have been substantially greater. Specifically, suppose that all women due child support in 1978 had negotiated a fully indexed child support contract at the time of their marital disruption, automatically linking changes in their award amount each year to changes in the CPI. We calculate that rather than being due on average $3,360, they would have been due $4,445.[93] In other words, the real value of support due in 1978 was almost 25 percent less than it would have been had all awards established prior to 1978 included a full cost-of-living adjustment. Table 4.9 records similar calculations for each of the other three surveys. Because of the unusually high inflation rates that occurred between 1978 and 1981, the actual average value of child support due in 1981 was almost 32 percent less than it would have been with full indexation. With lower inflation rates after 1981, the value lost because of nonindexation is somewhat less—26.5 percent as of 1985. It is clear that indexation, or at a minimum periodic review, is an important reform that would raise the average amount of child support due.[94]

Nonetheless, it can also be seen from table 4.9 that simply requiring all awards to be fully indexed to the CPI would not have prevented most of the sharp decline in the real value of support due that occurred. Even with full indexation of all old awards, the average real value of child support due would have declined 20.2 percent between 1978 and

Table 4.9 Effect of Indexation on Value of Child Support Due
Ever-married Mothers by Year Support Due
(in 1985 dollars)

	Mothers Due Support in				% Change
	1978	1981	1983	1985	1978–1985
Actual value of child support due[a]	$3,360	2,755	2,750	2,606	−22.4%
Potential value of child support due with indexation[b]	$4,445	4,044	3,991	3,545	−20.2%
Percentage of potential value lost as a result of nonindexation[c]	24.4%	31.9%	31.1%	26.5%	—

[a] Mean values from unweighted regression sample, not directly comparable to weighted averages in table 2.5

[b] Current dollar value of child support due multiplied by ratio of CPI in 1985 to CPI in year of award (i.e., year of marital disruption)

[c] (2) − (1) as a percentage of (2)

1985. This is consistent with our earlier finding that most of the decline in support due cannot be attributed to an acceleration in inflation that eroded the real value of old awards, but rather to the failure of new awards to keep up with inflation. The real value of child support due would have remained constant across sample years (assuming indexation and barring changes in the composition of the population due support) only if the real value of new awards had not declined.

In both tables 4.7 and 4.9, we can see that more than 90 percent of the decline in the real value of child support due between 1978 and 1985 can be attributed to the failure of new awards to keep pace with rising prices. Moreover, as we have shown in table 4.8, the current value of new awards has also been rising substantially more slowly than male incomes. One obvious solution (which is included in the Family Support Act of 1988) is to require the courts to use formal guidelines (such as the Wisconsin formula) that establish new awards as a percentage of the obligor's income. This appears to be the single most important step toward stemming the decline in the real value of expected child support payments.

Recent aggregate data on the value of child support due in 1989 (released by the Census Bureau, Sept. 1991) hold some promise that improvements may already be under way. Among women due child support, the average real amount due rose 14 percent from 1985 to

1989.[95] This represents an extraordinary gain, especially in light of the declines that occurred up to 1985. Although it is not possible on the basis of aggregate data alone to identify the precise reasons for this change, we can offer some suggestions based upon our disaggregated analysis through 1985.

It is quite clear that the increase is not the result of compositional shifts in the population due support. Indeed, the most important shift that occurred was an increase in the proportion of mothers due support who were never married, up from 6.9 percent in 1985 to 11.8 percent in 1989. Assuming no other changes, this would have lowered the average value of support due by more than 2 percent.[96] Some of the increase in support may be the result of the relatively low inflation rates of the late 1980s: the CPI increased 15.2 percent from 1985 to 1989, less than its 18.4 percent rise from 1981 to 1985. As a result, although the real values of nonindexed existing awards declined as prices rose, they declined less than in earlier surveys, which helped to raise the real value of support due relative to 1985.

If, however, our analysis of trends in award amounts through 1985 is correct, then it is likely that neither compositional changes nor changes in the value of existing awards is the principal reason why the real value of support due increased. Rather, consistent with our earlier analysis, we conjecture that the 14 percent rise in average support due is largely the result of increases of similar magnitude in the value of newly made awards. To what extent these in turn are a result of the introduction of award guidelines (made advisory by federal law in 1984 and mandatory in 1988) awaits future research.

In this chapter we have used four years of cross-sectional data on women eligible for child support to study determinants, differentials, and trends in award rates and amounts. We provide a short summary of some of our most important findings here, but we postpone a more detailed summary to the end of chapter 5, where, after studying receipt rates and amounts, we will compare and contrast some of our findings for both awards and receipts.

We have shown that various socioeconomic characteristics of mothers—including education, age, location, and number and ages of children—and the incomes of fathers at the time of the marital disruption are significantly related to both the likelihood of having a child support award and the amount of support due (see tables 4.1 and 4.5). Taking account of racial and marital status differences in these factors can explain approximately two-thirds of the racial differential in award rates and amounts and somewhat less than half of the marital status differential (see tables 4.2 and 4.6).

We conclude that the aggregate award rate would have increased more during the 1980s had it not been for the disproportionate increase in the population of never-married mothers. Among ever-married mothers, about half of the increase in aggregate award rates can be attributed either to demographic shifts in the eligible population or to increases in the real incomes of fathers (see table 4.3). The other half is associated with a long-term secular increase in new award rates (see table 4.4). For child support due, we find that neither demographic shifts in the population due support nor changes in the inflation rate, which erodes the value of nonindexed old awards, explain very much of the decline; rather, support due declined because the current dollar value of new awards has been rising only about half as fast as prices and incomes (see tables 4.7 and 4.8).

We studied historical patterns in new award rates and amounts since 1958 for ever-married mothers. The likelihood of obtaining a child support award has been rising over time but rose faster for blacks than for nonblacks and slowed considerably after 1975. We attribute both the differential increase by race and the recent slowdown to changes over time in male real income (table 4.4). The value of new awards has failed to keep pace with either consumer prices or incomes: on average, dollars awarded have risen about half as fast as prices, and the ratio of new awards to male incomes has declined substantially (see table 4.8). From a public policy perspective, the introduction of mandatory guidelines in setting award amounts appears to be the most promising change to have been enacted in recent years. Yet the question of whether they may actually be expected to raise the value of awards awaits our consideration in chapter 6.

Child Support

Receipts:

Determinants,

Differentials,

and Trends

Child support awards are about promises made; child support receipts are about promises kept and promises broken. As we saw in chapter 2, only about half of all mothers due child support receive the full amount owed them in a given year, and at least one-fourth fail to receive anything. In this chapter we analyze the determinants of and differentials and trends in child support payments received by mothers with an award.

We study two different measures of receipts: first, the receipt rate—that is, the proportion of women due child support who receive any, and second, the amount received among women who receive some. For each receipt outcome, we look at estimates of the ceteris paribus effect of selected socioeconomic characteristics of mothers due child support. We also study the impact on receipts of variations in the amount of support due. We ask to what extent differences in average characteristics and in award amounts can account for observed receipt differentials by race and marital status, and to what extent changes over time in the composition of the population due support and in the real value of support due can account for observed changes in aggregate receipt outcomes between 1978 and 1985. We conclude with a summary of findings drawn from the analyses of both this and the previous chapter. We integrate our findings on each stage of the award and receipt process to consider how any mother eligible for child support can expect to fare overall.

We study receipts separately from awards for several reasons. First, racial and marital status differentials in awards and receipts tend not to be the same. For example, compared with the ever-married, never-married mothers are much less likely to have an award, but among those due support, they are no less likely to receive some. Second, awards and receipts can display different trends over time. For example, between the 1979 and 1984 surveys, the aggregate award rate fell while the aggregate receipt rate rose. Third, some of the factors that determine awards may be different from those that determine receipts. For example, awards are shaped by the economic circumstances of the father and mother at the time of the initial award, while receipts depend more upon their current economic well-being. Finally, we study awards and receipts separately because the relevant legal environment is different for each outcome. Awards are influenced by laws concerning marriage and divorce, paternity establishment, child custody, and child support guidelines, while receipts are affected by laws about child support enforcement and parental visitation.

There are several important differences between our analysis of receipts and awards that should be noted. First, unlike awards, for which we were able to study trends among the ever-married back to 1958, our analysis of trends in receipts is limited to the four years of survey data. Second, in analyzing racial and marital status differentials and trends in receipt rates and amounts, we make use of one piece of information that was not available in our analysis of awards—the amount of child support due. We will argue that this value can serve as an important proxy for the father's ability and desire to pay and for the mother's expected benefits and costs of obtaining support. We show that variations in receipts across mothers in a single year are closely tied to individual differences in the value of child support due, and we show that changes over time in the average real value of child support due are the most important causes of changes in the value of receipts.

Receipt Rates

Only about three out of four women due support receive any. Although ever-married and never-married mothers are equally likely to receive support, there is considerable variation in receipt rates by current marital status among the ever-married: for example, 81 percent of separated women receive support, but only 69 percent of remarried women do. Racial differences in receipt rates are modest and appear to be narrowing: on average between 1978 and 1985, 68 percent of black women compared with 74 percent of nonblack women receive some of the support they are due. This differential narrowed from 10 percentage points in 1978 to only 2 points in 1985. Overall, the aggregate receipt rate rose just 2.3 percentage points between 1978 and 1985.

We begin by examining the impact of a mother's characteristics on the likelihood that she receives support, making use of the statistical techniques explained in appendix B. Then, using these results, we decompose observed racial and marital status differentials in receipt rates into the portions that can and cannot be explained by differences in average characteristics. We show that more than half of the differential in receipt rates among subgroups of ever-married mothers can be attributed to observable demographic differences, but only 15 percent of the racial differential can. We also use the results of our initial statistical analysis to assess the impact of compositional changes and the decline in the real value of support due between 1978 and 1985 on the aggregate receipt rate. We find that for some marital status groups, none of their actual change in receipt rates would have been expected on the basis of these observed changes, suggesting that the enforcement environment per se improved over time.

Determinants of the Receipt Rate

In chapter 3 we argued that unlike awards, which might be expected to depend primarily upon the long-run economic position of the absent father and custodial mother, receipts depend more upon current economic circumstances. In a given year, a father is less likely to pay the support he owes if he experiences a temporary drop in income. A mother is less likely to take steps to ensure that her child's father pays if her own income, other than child support, exceeds her expectations or if she perceives the cost of collecting child support to be too high. Although we cannot observe the father's income or the mother's costs of collection directly, we approximate them by factors we can observe, including the mother's socioeconomic characteristics and the value of child support due. We hypothesize that, all else being equal, women due more child support are more likely to receive something.

Table 5.1   Effect of Selected Socioeconomic Characteristics of Mothers Due Child Support on Likelihood of Receiving Support, 1978–1985

	Not Controlling for Amount Due	Controlling for Amount Due
Education and age		
Years of education	2.0**	1.7**
College graduate[a]	−1.1	−1.8
Current age	0.6**	0.5**
Race and ethnicity		
Black[a]	−8.4**	−7.1**
Hispanic[a]	−5.9*	−5.3*
Current marital status		
Never-married[b]	0.1	3.0
Separated[b]	5.9**	6.2**
Remarried[b]	−2.9*	−2.7*
Number and ages of children		
Number	0.2	−1.5*
Age 6–17[a]	4.1**	3.3*
Location of residence		
Northeast[c]	10.6**	10.4**
North central[c]	4.0*	3.8*
South[c]	7.0**	7.1**
SMSA[a]	2.6*	1.7
Central city[a]	−3.0*	−2.7*
Years since marital disruption	−1.8**	−1.6**
Voluntary agreement[a]	21.8**	21.4**
Amount of support due ($1,000s)	—	2.8**
Mean receipt rate	73.3%	73.3%
Sample size	7,497	7,497

Note: Figures represent the percentage point change in the probability of receiving support for a unit change in a given variable, holding all others constant. Estimates are derived from probit regressions, which also control for the year of survey.

*(**) Indicates statistical significance at a 5% (1%) level.
[a] Relative to not having this characteristic
[b] Relative to being currently divorced
[c] Relative to living in the West

DEMOGRAPHIC DETERMINANTS. The estimates in the first column of table 5.1 do not control for the amount of support due, while those in the second column do. For most characteristics, the two estimates are nearly identical but when they are not, we discuss possible reasons for their differences. We turn now to a discussion of specific determinants of the receipt rate.[1]

Several of the mother's characteristics are likely to reflect differences in the father's ability to pay. We find her education and age to have significantly positive effects on the likelihood of receiving support. Each additional year of schooling raises the receipt rate by about 2 percentage points, and each year of age by about half of 1 percent. In part, race and Spanish ethnicity also reflect differences in ability to pay. We find that black mothers are 8.4 percentage points less likely than nonblacks to receive any support or, controlling for their lower amounts due, 7.1 points less likely. Similarly, Hispanic mothers have receipt rates that are 5.9 to 5.3 percentage points below otherwise similar non-Hispanics. For both minority groups, these ceteris paribus differences are roughly similar in magnitude to the overall differences reported in chapter 2, which suggests that racial or ethnic differentials in receipt rates cannot readily be attributed to differences in socioeconomic factors other than race or ethnicity. In the next section we try to account for the racial differential in receipt rates in greater detail.

Both a mother's need for support and a father's desire to pay are likely to vary with a mother's current marital status. Controlling for the influence of other socioeconomic factors, we find that, consistent with aggregate data in chapter 2, never-married and currently divorced mothers are still almost equally likely to receive support. But, among the ever-married, separated women are about 6 percentage points more likely and remarried women are 3 points less likely to receive support than otherwise similar divorced women. These ceteris paribus differentials are somewhat smaller than the aggregate differentials reported in table 2.9. Later we identify specific characteristics of subgroups of ever-married mothers that account for some of the differential in their receipt rates.

Regional and residential location differences in the likelihood of receiving child support may reflect variations in state laws and customs and in the mother's needs. Women in the West are less likely to receive support than otherwise similar women living elsewhere. The most favored group, women in the Northeast, are nearly 11 percentage points more likely to receive support. Women living within an SMSA are around 2.6 percentage points more likely to receive support than other women, although this advantage disappears once we also control for their higher than average awards. Women living in the central city of an SMSA are around 3 points less likely to receive support than otherwise similar women who reside in the suburbs of the SMSA, which, to the extent that central city residents have below-average incomes, may reflect differences in the father's ability to pay. To the extent central city residents are more willing to accept public assistance or find it more accessible, this may also reflect differences in the mother's needs.

When we do not control for differences in the amount of support due, we find that receipt rates are not affected by the number of children due support. But controlling for the amount due, the likelihood of receiving support falls significantly as the number of children rises. This change may reflect unobservable differences in the father's ability to pay: comparing two fathers who are obligated to pay the same total amount of support, the one with fewer children (who, therefore, owes more per child) is likely to have a higher income.

Three other socioeconomic characteristics are primarily expected to capture differences in the father's desire to pay. Fathers with children age six to seventeen are around 4 percentage points more likely to pay support. Fathers with voluntary rather than court-ordered agreements are nearly 22 percentage points more likely to pay. Finally, the likelihood a father pays falls off at the rate of around 2 percentage points per year for each year since the marital disruption.[2]

ECONOMIC DETERMINANTS. Whether or not support is received in a given year is likely to depend, in part, upon the long-term ability of the father to pay his support obligation and the anticipated needs of the mother for support. Both factors are likely to be related to the amount of child support due, since award levels usually depend upon the father's ability to pay and the mother's needs. In table 5.1, we show that the amount of child support due has a modest, but significantly positive, impact on the likelihood of receipt. Mothers are 2.8 percentage points more likely to receive support for each additional $1,000 of support they are due (measured in 1985 dollars). Fathers obligated to pay more child support tend to have higher permanent incomes and may feel a greater emotional attachment to their children as well. Mothers who are due more support may have greater long-term needs and a stronger incentive to ensure that at least some of it is received.

Although the long-term economic well-being of the father and mother affect payment behavior, current economic circumstances may have an even larger impact. Whether or not a father pays the support he owes in a given year is likely to depend upon his current level of income and household expenditures and perhaps upon his perception of the current financial position of his children's mother. Also, whether or not a mother seeks to ensure that the father fulfills his obligation may depend upon her current needs and her perception of his current ability to pay. We examine the relation between receipt rates and a variety of measures of current economic circumstances of the mother and father, holding constant the mother's demographic characteristics and value of support due.

Although we cannot observe the father's current economic circumstances directly, there is a close substitute in the 1979 CPS survey. In that survey, each mother was asked to estimate (within $5,000 intervals) the 1978 income of her children's father. For those mothers who responded, we related estimates of the father's income to whether or not support was received in 1978, while also controlling for the mother's socioeconomic characteristics and the amount of child support due. We find that each $5,000 increment to his income increases the likelihood of her receiving support by 2.7 percentage points.[3] To the extent that we hold constant a father's *long-term* ability to pay by controlling for the mother's characteristics (especially, education, age, ethnicity, and race) and the amount of support she is due, we can conclude that his *current* ability to pay has a separate positive and significant influence on the likelihood that he pays.[4]

The relation between receipts and the mother's income is a complicated one for several reasons. First, it is not clear whether we should expect the two factors to be positively or negatively related: one father may be more inclined to pay if he sees his children's mother also contributing to their support; another may try to take advantage of her contributions by reducing his support. Second, the direction of causation is unclear: does a mother's income affect her receipt rate or vice versa? In other words, while the father's payment behavior may be influenced by the overall level and particular sources of his children's mother's income, her own decision whether or not to work or to seek public assistance may also be influenced by whether or not he pays the support he owes. Finally, the relation between child support and AFDC income is even more complex. Because the state attempts to collect child support on behalf of mothers who are on AFDC, welfare mothers may not always know whether or not their children's father is paying support.

To examine the relation between a mother's income and her likelihood of receiving child support, we related whether or not she received support to several measures of her income, while also controlling for her socioeconomic characteristics and the value of support due, as in table 5.1.[5] We find that receipt rates are unrelated to either the mother's current total income (excluding child support) or her current labor market earnings. Thus, we conclude that variations in a mother's total current income and earnings have no systematic influence on the likelihood that the father pays the support he owes. In chapter 7 we study the relation between the mother's labor supply and child support income in greater detail.

In contrast to total income or earnings, we find that receipt rates are negatively related to the amount of AFDC income received: each $1,000 increase in AFDC benefits reduces the likelihood of the mother receiving child support by 3 percentage points. There are two ways to interpret this finding. One interpretation is that a father is less inclined to pay child support the more public assistance the mother receives (or, perhaps, that he does not pay so that she can get more). Another interpretation is that a mother who is less likely to receive child support is more likely to seek public assistance or is eligible for larger amounts. In chapter 7 we try to disentangle these two interpretations by studying in greater detail the relation between AFDC participation and child support receipts.

Accounting for Racial and Marital Status Differentials

RACIAL DIFFERENCES. As we saw in table 2.8, averaged over the period 1978–85, 68.3 percent of black women compared with 74.3 percent of nonblack women received at least some of the support due them. How much of this 6 point racial gap can be explained by observable differences between black and nonblack women? In table 5.2 we decompose the gap into the portions attributable to racial differences in socioeconomic characteristics and in the amount of child support due and the portion that cannot be attributed to either of these factors.[6]

Black women are more likely than nonblack women to live in the South, are more likely to be separated, are less likely to be remarried, and tend to have experienced more recent marital disruptions. As we saw in table 5.1, each of these characteristics is associated with a greater likelihood of receiving support. Offsetting these factors, blacks, on average, exhibit other characteristics that tend to lower their receipt rates relative to nonblacks. Blacks are less likely to be living in Northeast or north central states and are less likely to have a voluntary rather than a court-ordered settlement. When we control

Table 5.2 Accounting for Racial and Marital Status Differentials in Receipt Rates on the Basis of Differences in Mother's Characteristics and Amount of Child Support Due

Actual Differential[a]	Explained by Differences in[b]		Unexplained differential[c]
	Socioeconomic characteristics	Amount of support due	
Nonblack vs. black			
6.0 (100%)	−0.7 (−12%)	1.6 (27%)	5.1 (85%)
Separated vs. divorced			
6.2 (100%)	3.3 (53%)	0.2 (3%)	2.7 (44%)
Divorced vs. remarried			
5.9 (100%)	3.3 (56%)	1.0 (17%)	1.6 (27%)

[a] Receipt rate of first minus the second subgroup of mothers from table 2.8 or 2.9
[b] Racial or marital status difference in the means of the socioeconomic characteristics (table 5.1), or the amount of child support due evaluated by nonblack, separated, or remarried regression coefficients
[c] Actual minus explained differential

for the impact on receipt rates of all of these racial differences in socioeconomic characteristics together, we find that black women due support would actually be 0.7 percentage points *more* likely than nonblacks to receive at least some of the support due them.[7]

As we also saw in table 5.1, the smaller is the amount of child support due, the less likely is a woman to receive any. On average, black women were due $2,238 (measured in 1985 dollars) or $612 less than the $2,850 due nonblack women. This difference alone would account for a 1.6 percentage point lower receipt rate for black women.[8] Thus, together, racial differences in the amount of child support due and in the mother's characteristics account for just 0.9 percentage points or 15 percent of the overall 6 percentage point racial gap in receipt rates.

To the extent that we have not been able to control fully for racial differences in male incomes, race per se may reflect differences in the ability of black and nonblack fathers to pay support, especially given the higher unemployment rates of blacks. As noted previously, race might also reflect differences in their desire to pay, since black fathers are more likely to owe support to women who have had children by more than one man. Race may also reflect differences in the mother's current needs and in the costs of ensuring that child support that is owed is actually paid.

MARITAL STATUS DIFFERENTIALS. In table 2.9, we saw that 80.9 percent of currently separated women, 74.7 percent of divorced women, and 68.8 percent of remarried women due child support actually received payment between 1978 and 1985. Some of these differentials can be explained on the basis of other observable differences by current marital status. In table 5.2, we show that differences in the average amount of time since the marital disruption (which is shorter by 1.6 years for separated mothers), together with differences in other socioeconomic characteristics explain 53 percent of the total differential in receipt rates between separated and divorced women.[9] If we also take account of differences in child support due (separated mothers are due $93 more child support than divorced mothers), we can explain 3.3 percentage points, or 56 percent, of the 6.2 point differential. We also show that we can explain 4.3 percentage points, or 73 percent, of the 5.9 point differential in receipt rates between remarried and divorced women.[10] This explained differential is due primarily to the earlier marital disruptions (by 2.1 years) and smaller awards (by $396) of remarried relative to divorced mothers.

These unexplained residuals may be due, in part, to some unobservable differences in the mother's needs for and costs of collecting support. A remarried woman may have less incentive than a single mother to seek redress against a nonpaying father since her new husband is likely to be helping to support her children. A separated woman may anticipate lower costs of collecting support relative to a divorced or remarried woman since she is more likely to know the whereabouts of her children's father, especially if she is involved in ongoing divorce proceedings against him. These unexplained differentials may also be due, in part, to differences among fathers about which we have no data. A father who is separated rather than divorced may be more likely to have regular contact with his children and thus have a greater desire to pay. In addition, although we do not know the father's current marital status, it is quite likely that if the mother has remarried, he has too. If he also has a second family to support, he will be less able to pay the child support he owes.[11]

Table 5.3 Accounting for Changes in Aggregate Receipt Rate from 1978 to 1985 for All Mothers Due Support

| Actual Change[a] | Explained by Changes Over Time in[b] | | Unexplained change[c] |
	Socioeconomic characteristics	Amount of support due	
2.3 (100%)	1.7 (74%)	—	0.6 (26%)
2.3 (100%)	2.0 (89%)	−2.7 (−117%)	3.0 (128%)

[a] Weighted figures from table 2.8

[b] 1985 minus 1978 sample means of the socioeconomic characteristics (table 5.1) and amount of child support due evaluated at regression coefficients using 1978 data only, scaled to the weighted figures in the first column

[c] Actual minus expected change in receipt rates

Accounting for Trends in Receipt Rates across Survey Years

In chapter 2 we saw that the percentage of women due child support who received at least partial payment increased by 2.3 points between 1978 and 1985, from 71.7 to 74 percent. This aggregate receipt rate increased more for some subgroups than for others. It rose 9.5 percentage points for black women but only 1.4 percentage points for nonblack women. It increased 12.2 points for separated women, increased slightly for divorced women, fell slightly for remarried women, and fell 5.3 points for never-married women (see tables 2.8 and 2.9). Here we investigate the extent to which these changes could have been expected on the basis of demographic shifts in the population due support and the decline in the real amount of child support due between 1978 and 1985.

TRENDS OVERALL. In table 5.3 we decompose the 2.3 percentage point increase in the overall receipt rate from 1978 to 1985. The explained portion represents the change in receipt rates that could have been expected on the basis of changes over time in the characteristics of the population due support given the receipt environment prevailing in 1978, while the unexplained portion equals the actual minus the explained change. We offer two different estimates of the explained change. The first considers only the effect of changes in the socioeconomic characteristics of mothers due support, while the latter also includes the effect of changes in the real value of child support due.

According to table 5.3, had the enforcement environment prevailing in 1978 not changed, the overall receipt rate could have been expected to rise by 1.7 percentage points.[12] This rise is from a change in certain socioeconomic characteristics of women due support that were positively associated with the likelihood of receiving support in 1978. These include an increase in average years of education, the proportion of the eligible population living in the Northeast, the proportion of women with a voluntary agreement, and the proportion never-married. The only significant demographic shift that should have lowered receipt rates was an increase in the proportion of the eligible population that was black. Thus, on the basis of socioeconomic changes alone, roughly one-quarter of the 2.3 point rise in the receipt rate, or 0.6 percentage points, was unexpected.

Receipt rates are higher the higher the value of child support due (see table 5.1). This is because larger awards indicate both an absent father's greater ability to pay and a custodial mother's greater incentive to ensure that he pays. Unfortunately, the real value of child support due fell $785 (in 1985 dollars) between 1978 and 1985 (see table 2.4). To the extent that this decline across survey years in dollars due represents a decline in the average father's ability to pay or in the average mother's incentive to collect child support, we could expect the aggregate receipt rate to decline as well. Assuming that the relation between receipt rates and the value of child support due in 1978 also represents the relation that prevailed over time, we estimate that the sharp decline in average real dollars due between 1978 and 1985 could have been expected to lower the aggregate receipt rate by 2.7 percentage points. Combining this expected decline with an expected rise of 2 points owing to changes over time in the mother's socioeconomic characteristics,[13] the overall receipt rate could have been expected to decline 0.7 percentage points from 1978 to 1985. This means that the receipt rate was actually 3 percentage points higher in 1985 than would have been predicted on the basis of the enforcement environment prevailing in 1978.

To summarize, we calculate that there is an unexplained rise in the overall receipt rate of between 0.6 and 3 percentage points. The lower estimate ignores entirely the impact on receipts of changes in the value of child support due, while the higher one includes the impact of the almost 24 percent decline in dollars due between 1978 and 1985. Even if this decline was simply an unintended consequence of inflation, it must have reduced the mother's incentive to collect support, and thus the higher estimate may be more appropriate. In any case, at least

Table 5.4 Unexplained Changes in Receipt Rate from 1978 to 1985 of Women Due Support by Race and Marital Status

		Unexplained by Changes in	
	Actual Change[a]	Socioeconomic characteristics only[b]	Socioeconomic characteristics and decline in amount due[c]
Race			
Black	9.5	8.2	10.2
	(100%)	(86%)	(107%)
Nonblack	1.4	0.9	2.3
	(100%)	(64%)	(164%)
Marital status			
Ever-married	2.5	2.0	3.5
	(100%)	(80%)	(140%)
Separated	12.2	10.0	10.6
	(100%)	(82%)	(87%)
Never-married	−5.3	−5.8	−5.2
	(100%)	(109%)	(98%)

[a] 1985 minus 1978 receipt rates from tables 2.8 or 2.9

[b] Based on separate regressions for each racial group and marital status group using all four years of survey data, controlling for mother's socioeconomic characteristics (table 5.1). The unexpected change is derived from the probit coefficient on a dummy variable for the 1986 survey, scaled to the weighted data in the first column.

[c] Same as note (*b*), except also controlling for the value of support due

some (and perhaps all) of the increase in the receipt rate between 1978 and 1985 would not have been expected; rather, the explanation for its increase lies with social or legal changes that occurred during the 1980s.

TRENDS BY RACE AND MARITAL STATUS. As we have seen, changes in receipt rates from 1978 to 1985 show considerable variation by race and marital status, with black and separated women enjoying particularly large increases. In table 5.4, for various racial and marital status subgroups, we offer estimates of the change in receipt rates that would *not* have been expected—first, on the basis of changes in mother's socioeconomic characteristics alone, and second, on the basis of both changes in the mother's characteristics and the decline in the real value of child support due.[14] In general, consistent with the pattern found for all mothers in table 5.3, the unexpected change in receipt rates is larger when we include the impact of the decline in the value of support due.

Looking first at trends by race, we find that between 86 percent and 107 percent of the observed 9.5 percentage point increase in the receipt rate of black women and between 64 percent and 164 percent of the observed 1.4 percentage point increase in the receipt rate of nonblack women could not have been expected. For both races, small increases in receipt rates between 1978 and 1985 could have been expected on the basis of changes in the average characteristics of mothers due support, but these were more than offset by decreases expected on the basis of the decline in the real value of child support due.[15] The aggregate receipt rate in 1985 was 8.2 to 10.2 percentage points higher for black mothers and 0.9 to 2.3 percentage points higher for nonblack mothers than might have been expected (see table 5.4).

Turning to trends by marital status, we find that between 80 percent and 140 percent of the 2.5 percentage point rise in the receipt rate of ever-married mothers could not have been expected. Among the ever-married, currently separated mothers experienced the greatest rise in receipt rates, with an increase of 12.2 percentage points. We find that between 82 percent and 87 percent of this rise could not have been expected. The receipt rate of separated mothers could have been expected to rise 2.2 points given modest shifts in their demographic composition between 1978 and 1985, but part of this expected rise is offset by a 20.5 percent decline in the value of support due. Overall, by 1985 the receipt rate of separated mothers was 10.0 to 10.6 percentage points higher than expected.

In contrast to the general upward trend in receipt rates for most ever-married subgroups, never-married mothers experienced a decline in their receipt rate of 5.3 percentage points between 1978 and 1985. A small part of this decline could have been expected on the basis of an 8.5 percent decline in the value of child support due between 1978 and 1985.[16] This expected decline, however, is more than offset by changes in the average characteristics of never-married mothers due support, which could have been expected to increase their receipt rate. Overall, their receipt rate was 5.2 to 5.8 percentage points lower by 1985 than could have been expected.

ACCOUNTING FOR UNEXPECTED TRENDS. How can we account for these unexpected changes in receipt rates (in tables 5.3 and 5.4) that are not a result of observable changes in the characteristics of the population due support or changes in the value of child support due? They may have been caused by improvements in the economic, social, and legal environment surrounding the child support enforcement process. Separating these three factors from one another, however, turns out to be extremely difficult. Controlling for the mother's socioeconomic characteristics and the value of support due, we related whether or not a woman receives child support in a given year to a variety of contemporaneous aggregate economic conditions, including male unemployment rates (by state), inflation rates, and the increase in male (nominal and real) incomes. None of these factors, either together or separately, appeared to have a significant effect on the likelihood of receiving child support. Thus, we are led to conclude that current aggregate economic conditions have little impact on child support receipts, although, obviously, an individual's own economic circumstances may still have a strong impact. In the next chapter we examine to what extent changes in child support enforcement may have contributed to increases in receipt rates.

Receipt Amounts

Nonpayment of child support is not the only enforcement problem: many women who receive child support income report receiving less than they are due. On average between 1978 and 1985, among the three out of four women due support who received at least some payment, the average value of child support received was $2,520 (in 1985 constant dollars), which was about 83 percent of the average value of child support due of $3,004. Furthermore, the real value of receipts declined sharply over the period from an average payment of $2,960 in 1978 to $2,212 in 1985 (see table 2.11). Over this same period, the real value of support due (among mothers who received something) declined from $3,565 to $2,709, and the average ratio of amount received to amount due declined from .835 to .811 (see table 2.13).

Here we study the determinants of and differentials and trends in, the value of child support payments received among women who receive some child support. We show that the amount of child support received is largely determined by the amount of support due. Beyond their effect on award amounts, certain socioeconomic characteristics of mothers due support—particularly race and marital status—also influence receipts. On average, black and never-married women receive considerably less support than other women. We find that about half of the racial and all of the marital status differential in receipts can be accounted for by differences in the average characteristics of mothers and by the lower award amounts of black and never-married mothers. We also study trends in receipts from 1978 to 1985 for all women, as well as by race and marital status. We find that more than 80 percent of the average $748 decline in receipts overall could have been anticipated primarily on the basis of the sharp decline in real dollars due. Consistent with the decline over time in the ratio of dollars received to due, however, at least some of the decline in receipts remains unexplained by the decline in award amounts.

Determinants of the Value of Receipts

Between 1978 and 1985, among all women receiving support, child support income averaged $2,520 or $1,588 per child (table 2.11). Black, Hispanic, and never-married mothers received considerably less than average. Receipts—like awards—are likely to depend upon both the absent father's ability and desire to support the children and upon the custodial mother's needs for and costs of collecting support. Unlike awards, receipts may depend more upon the father's than the mother's current economic circumstances since it is he who decides whether or not to pay and how much to pay. Of course, the penalties he faces for nonpayment or for underpayment may vary with the behavior of the mother since she decides whether or not to initiate legal action against him.[17] Thus, in general, we would expect payments to vary across women with different socioeconomic characteristics to the extent these characteristics are correlated with the behavior of the father and the mother.[18]

For several reasons, child support payments are also likely to vary with the amount of child support due (in the year prior to the survey). First, since few fathers are likely to pay more than they are obligated to, the value of child support due represents an upper limit on receipts.[19] Second, the value of child support due may serve as a rather good proxy for the ability and desire of the father to pay support, characteristics that we are unable to observe or control for directly. Finally, all else being equal, mothers who are due more child support have a greater financial incentive to ensure that it is received.

Using multivariate statistical techniques, we related the value of child support received by mothers who received payment (in 1978, 1981, 1983, or 1985) to the value of child support due (in the same year) and to some observable socioeconomic characteristics of these mothers.[20] The results of these analyses appear in table 5.5.[21] The

Table 5.5 Effect of Selected Socioeconomic Characteristics of Mothers Receiving Child Support in 1978, 1981, 1983, or 1985 on Amount Received (in 1985 dollars)

	Among Mothers Receiving Child Support in		
	1978–1985	1978–1981	1983–1985
Education and age			
Years of education	35*	−9	73**
College graduate[a]	228**	376**	77
Current age	24**	18**	28**
Race and ethnicity			
Black[a]	−398**	−314*	−473**
Hispanic[a]	−258**	−276	−222*
Current marital status			
Never-married[b]	269**	314	310**
Separated[b]	176**	147	184**
Remarried[b]	−176**	−156*	−155**
Number and ages of children			
Number	35	122**	−74*
Age 6–17[a]	167**	28	261**
Region or location			
Northeast[c]	231*	−12	501**
North central[c]	67	18	118*
South[c]	72	−137	284**
SMSA[a]	111**	16	186**
Central city[a]	−14	134	−118*
Years since marital disruption	−30**	10	−65**
Voluntary agreement[a]	756**	359*	1,126**
Amount of support due ($100s)	81**	71**	94**
Mean amount received	$2,526	$2,718	$2,351
Sample size	5,481	2,620	2,861

Note: Figures represent the dollar change in the amount of child support received for a unit change in a given variable, holding all others constant. OLS estimates also control for the year of the survey and are corrected for sample selection bias (as explained in app. B).

  *(**) Indicates statistical significance at a 5% (1%) level.
  [a] Relative to not having this characteristic
  [b] Relative to being currently divorced
  [c] Relative to living in the West

estimates show the effect of child support due and the mother's characteristics on the value of support received (in 1985 dollars) based upon all four years of data. When the four years of data were analyzed separately, the estimated effects of some determinants showed considerable variation across survey years (especially 1981 and 1983), indicating that the underlying receipt behavior itself (influenced by the prevailing economic, social, and legal environments) may have changed over time. Thus, we present estimates of these ceteris paribus effects for mothers receiving support in 1978 or 1981 and separate estimates for 1983 or 1985. In the discussion that follows, we concentrate on the average effects in the first column of table 5.5 but note particular instances where effects appear to change over time.

DEMOGRAPHIC DETERMINANTS. Table 5.5 shows how the value of child support payments varies with selected socioeconomic characteristics of the mother when the value of child support due is held constant. More educated women receive more child support. On average, each additional year of schooling is associated with $35 more of child support received, and college-educated women receive an additional increment of $228. Older women also receive more support. Age increases support by $24 a year. Both mother's age and education are likely to be positively associated with the father's ability to pay and with the likelihood she can effectively use the legal system to ensure that he pays.

Even controlling for their lower award amounts, minorities receive less child support than other mothers. Averaged over the four years, blacks receive $398 less child support than nonblacks with similar socioeconomic characteristics, and Hispanics receive $258 less than other women. Between the 1978–81 and 1983–85 periods, the disadvantage faced by black mothers appears to widen (from $314 to $473). This is consistent with evidence presented earlier in table 2.13 that, on average, the ratio of child support received to the amount due is lower for minority women and that the ratio declined more for blacks than nonblacks over the four survey years. In the next two sections we investigate the sources of these racial differentials and trends in more detail.

Like race, a mother's current marital status also appears to have a direct influence on the value of her receipts. Never-married mothers receive considerably less support than other women (see table 2.11). Once we control for their lower award amounts in table 5.5, however, we find that they actually receive $255 more on average than divorced mothers with similar socioeconomic characteristics. Controlling for differences in award amounts, receipts also differ within the ever-married group: on average, a separated mother receives $176 more and a remarried mother $176 less than an otherwise similar divorced mother due the same amount. The separated mother may receive more because the emotional bond between the father and his children is still likely to be strong or because the father does not want to antagonize the judge he may face in divorce proceedings. A remarried mother may receive less because her new husband may be expected to provide at least some support for her children, especially in the form of shared goods, such as housing.

Receipts also vary by geographic region and residential location, but these differences appear to be significant only in the latter two survey years. Averaged over the four survey years, women in the Northeast receive $231 more child support than women in the West, all else being equal. Since women in the Northeast are less likely to have an award (table 4.1), those who do may be a select group who have greater needs or whose children's fathers have a greater ability to pay. In 1983 and 1985, women in other regions were receiving significantly more support than women in the West. On average, SMSA residents receive $111 more support than mothers living in rural areas, which may reflect differences in incomes between metropolitan and rural areas as well as differential access to legal assistance.

The emotional bond between the father and his children—or more generally, his desire to pay—directly affects child support payments. Controlling for the amount of support due, the number of children due support appears not to have a consistently positive influence on the amount received, but the presence of school-aged children does. On average, a father pays $167 more support if at least one of his children is between the ages of six and seventeen. He pays less support the more time has elapsed since his marital disruption: each additional year reduces receipts by $30.[22] If the original child support award was voluntarily agreed to, he pays $756 more than if the same level of support was court ordered.

ECONOMIC DETERMINANTS. As we have argued, differences in the value of support due are primarily likely to reflect long-term differences in the father's ability to pay and in the mother's need for support. Given the strong positive statistical association between amounts due and received (table 5.5), we conclude that long-term economic well-being is also directly related to child support receipts. But the current economic circumstances of each parent may be important too. A father may tend to pay less support if he is unemployed, suffers an unexpected decline in income for other reasons, or if he observes the mother's income to be higher than he had expected. In turn, a mother has less incentive to collect support if her current income is higher than anticipated.

Even so, once we control for the mother's socioeconomic characteristics and the amount of support due, we find little evidence that child support receipts vary with the current income of either the father or the mother. Using 1979 data—the only survey in which even indirect evidence about the father's income is reported—we find that receipt amounts are unrelated to the father's current income.[23] Using all four years of data, receipt amounts are also unrelated to either the mother's current total income (excluding child support) or her labor market earnings.[24] There is, however, a negative association between the value of child support received and the value of AFDC income received: each additional $1,000 in AFDC benefits is associated with a $116 reduction in child support receipts. This suggests either that fathers pay less support the more public assistance mothers receive or that mothers seek additional public assistance when fathers fail to pay the support they owe. The latter causation seems the more plausible given the failure of other income sources of mothers to affect receipts. We explore the causal relation between AFDC and child support in greater detail in chapter 7.

The Relation between Child Support Due and Received

As we might expect, variations in the amount of child support received are closely tied to variations in the amount of support due. In a statistical sense, among all of the factors listed in table 5.5, the amount of support due is by far the single most important determinant of the amount received. It alone explains over 77 percent of the total cross-sectional variation in receipt amounts.[25] This turns out to be of some interest because the relation between support due and support received appears to have changed over time and to have changed differently for nonblacks than for blacks.

Among all mothers receiving support between 1978 and 1985, every $100 increase in child support due was, on average, associated with an $81 increase in child support received (see table 5.5). This four-year average for all mothers, however, conceals both a significant change in the relation over time and by race. Among all mothers and among nonblack mothers (89% of all mothers) receiving child support in 1978 or 1981, every $100 increase in the value of child support due was associated with only a $71 increase in support received (see col. 2), while among those receiving support in 1983 or 1985, it was associated with a $94 increase in support received (see col. 3). By contrast, among black mothers, every $100 increase in support due was associated with an $83 increase in support received in 1978–81, but only a $65 increase in 1983–85 (results not shown).

The relation between the amount of child support due and received depends, in part, upon the prevailing child support enforcement environment. Changes over time in that relation indicate that there were some changes in the receipt process, although not what caused these changes.[26] As a result of changes in enforcement efforts (and possibly other changes) between 1978 and 1985, variations across all mothers and nonblack mothers in the value of their child support receipts became more closely associated with variations in their award amounts, while variations across black mothers in receipts became less closely tied to their award amounts. If we refer to mothers who are due the same amount of child support as equals and if we define justice as treating equals equally, then we might say that by 1985 child support enforcement had become more just—both overall and among nonblack mothers—but less just among black mothers.

The relation between dollars due and dollars received over the two subperiods among all women receiving support is pictured in figure 5.1. There is an important implication of the change over time in the relation shown in the figure. To understand this, however, we first need to distinguish between the *marginal* change in dollars received for a given change in dollars due (the slope of the received-to-due relation) and the *average* received-to-due ratio. Among mothers receiving child support between 1978 and 1985, the ratio of support received to support due averaged about .83 overall, declining slightly from .84 in 1978 to .81 in 1985 (table 2.13). It is important not to confuse this average ratio of received to due with the marginal relation, which may be very different, but it is also important that when the marginal is less (greater) than the average ratio of received to due, the average ratio declines (increases) as dollars due increase.[27]

The relation between the marginal and average ratio has implications for the distribution of receipt outcomes and child support enforcement generally. We have seen that the slope or marginal relation between dollars received and dollars due was .71 in 1978, while the average ratio of received to due was .84. This means that, among mothers receiving child support in 1978, the ratio of received to due

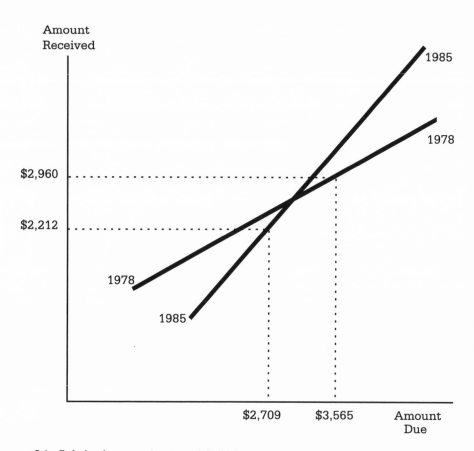

5.1   Relation between Amount of Child Support Due and Received, 1978 and
1985

was lower as the amount of child support due was increasing. By
contrast, in 1985 the marginal relation was .94 while the average ratio
was .81, which means that the ratio of received to due was rising with
dollars due. Thus, if we measure success by the ratio of child support
received to due, we might conclude that enforcement efforts showed
substantial improvement for mothers due more child support than
average but may have worsened for mothers with below average
awards. This interpretation is consistent with the idea that over time
fathers who are less willing and less able to pay support (and hence
have lower than average awards) were brought reluctantly into the
system.

Table 5.6 Accounting for Racial and Marital Status Differentials in Amount of Child Support Received on the Basis of Differences in Mother's Characteristics and Amount of Child Support Due

| Actual Differential[a] | Explained by Differences in[b] | | Unexplained differential[c] |
	Socioeconomic characteristics	Amount of support due	
Nonblack vs. Black			
$797 (100%)	$−193 (−24%)	$596[d] (75%)	$394 (49%)
Ever-married vs. Never-married			
$1,344 (100%)	$285 (28%)	$1,318[e] (91%)	$−259 (−19%)

[a] Value of child support received of nonblack minus black or ever-married minus never-married mothers from table 2.11.

[b] Difference of means of socioeconomic characteristics (from table 5.5), or amount of child support due evaluated by nonblack or ever-married regression coefficients, scaled to the weighted data in first column.

[c] Actual minus explained differential

[d] Racial difference in average support due is $735.

[e] Marital difference in average support due is $1,627.

Accounting for Racial and Marital Status Differentials

As we have seen, black women and never-married mothers receive substantially less child support than other women. On average between 1978 and 1985, black women received 30 percent less than nonblack women, and never-married mothers received 52 percent less than ever-married mothers (see table 2.11). Of course, black and never-married mothers are due substantially less support too. On average among women actually receiving support, blacks are due 24 percent less than nonblacks, and never-married mothers 53 percent less than ever-married mothers. In addition to their lower awards, black and never-married mothers are more likely to have some socioeconomic characteristics that tend to be associated with lower child support receipts, including youth and less education. Here we investigate to what extent smaller child support awards and socioeconomic disadvantages account for the lower average receipts of black and never-married mothers. Our results are summarized in table 5.6.

RACIAL DIFFERENTIALS. Among women who received some support between 1978 and 1985, black women received $797 less, on average, than nonblack women. The vast majority of this racial differential in receipts can be accounted for by the average $735 racial difference in the amount of support due. Holding constant socioeconomic characteristics, we have seen that each additional $100 of child support due is associated with an additional $81 of support received, both overall and among nonblacks. Evaluating racial differences in the amount of support due at this rate, we could expect a black woman to receive $596 less support, which represents 75 percent of the total racial gap in receipts.

Some racial differences in average socioeconomic characteristics contribute to higher expected receipts for nonblacks. On the one hand, compared with blacks, nonblack mothers have more education, are older, and are more likely to live in the Northeast, have school-aged children, and have voluntarily agreed to child support awards—all characteristics associated with higher receipts (table 5.5). On the other hand, black mothers are more likely to live within a metropolitan area (where compliance appears to be greater), to be separated or never married, and are less likely to be remarried. As we saw in table 5.5, controlling for dollars due, separated and never-married mothers receive more child support than divorced women, and remarried women receive less. When we evaluate the impact on receipts of all these racial differences in characteristics, holding constant differences in dollars due, we calculate that on average nonblacks would receive $193 less child support than blacks.[28] Combining the impact on receipts of racial differences in the mother's characteristics and of dollars due, we can account for $403 (or 51%) of the $797 racial differential in child support receipts, leaving $394 (or 49%) of the differential unexplained by these factors.

As noted, it may not be possible to control fully for racial differences in the absent father's ability to pay by simply controlling for observable differences in the mother's socioeconomic characteristics. Numerous studies have concluded that racial differences in male incomes exceed what could be expected on the basis of racial differences in characteristics alone.[29] Labor market discrimination and other cultural factors appear to depress black incomes below that of nonblacks with similar socioeconomic characteristics. Black men have significantly lower incomes, higher unemployment rates, and lower labor force participation rates than their nonblack counterparts. Thus, it might be expected that some portion of the racial gap in child support receipts is unexplained.

Some of the unexplained racial differential may also be attributable to differences in the mother's behavior. Black mothers, we have noted, may be less likely to seek legal assistance when absent fathers do not fulfill their child support obligation. In addition to the lack of information and mistrust of the legal system, it may be that with lower remarriage rates some blacks do not want to bring legal action because they hope to reestablish a relationship with their children's father. Furthermore, their expected benefits are lower, and many black women may not consider them worth the costs of collection.

MARITAL STATUS DIFFERENTIALS. On average, among women receiving support between 1978 and 1985, never-married mothers received $1,344 less than ever-married mothers. Most of this differential can be explained by never-married mothers being due $1,627 less child support. All else being equal, we have seen that each additional $100 of child support due raises receipts by approximately $81. If never-married and ever-married women differed only in the amount of support due, the average receipts of never-married women could be expected to be lower by $1,318,[30] or more than 90 percent of the total differential.

If we also take into account differences in average characteristics by marital status, we actually explain more than 100 percent of the total differential in receipts. Never-married women exhibit a number of characteristics that are associated with lower receipts. Compared with the ever-married, they are younger, have fewer years of education, are less likely to have older children, and are seven times as likely to be black. Taken together, these demographic differences lower expected receipts of never-married mothers by $285 relative to ever-married mothers due the same amount of support. Combining the effects of differences in the mother's characteristics and award amounts, we would expect never-married mothers to receive $1,603 less child support than ever-married mothers, which exceeds the actual difference by $259 (table 5.6).

The explanation for this may be that never-married women who receive child support are a highly select group. Indeed, they represent only 8 percent of all never-married mothers eligible for child support, compared with 43 percent of ever-married mothers. Those never-married mothers who have managed to overcome the enormous hurdles of obtaining an award and ensuring that at least some of it is paid are likely to be highly motivated mothers who know how to make use of the legal system. They are also likely to have support orders against men who are more able and more willing to comply. Finally, and perhaps most important, given the large increase in award rates for them between 1979 and 1986, it is likely that never-married mothers obtained their awards more recently, on average, than ever-married mothers—although we are unable to control directly for time since the award. As we have seen, payments are higher the more recent the award.

Accounting for Trends in Receipt Amounts across Survey Years

Between 1978 and 1985, the real value of child support received, like the real value due, declined sharply. Among all women receiving support, receipts fell 25.3 percent or by $748 (measured in 1985 dollars). The decline was smaller for black women than for nonblack women (17.5% vs. 25.1%), and smaller for ever-married than never-married women (23.8% vs. 28.7%).

Now we investigate why the real value of child support receipts declined so sharply and why these declines differed by race and marital status. As might be expected, the most important cause is the decline in award amounts. Another possible cause is shifts in the demographic composition of the population. If recipients of child support are increasingly women who are less likely to use the legal system to obtain help in collecting support or women whose children's fathers are less able to pay, then average receipts will decline over time. We show that although changes in demographic composition are not an important reason for the decline overall, they are somewhat important for some racial and marital status subgroups.

TRENDS OVERALL. Among all women receiving child support, measured in constant 1985 dollars, average receipts declined $748 or by 25.3 percent, while the average amount due declined $856 or by 24 percent (see table 5.7). We find that more than 80 percent of the decline in child support receipts between 1978 and 1985 could have been expected, and this almost entirely on the basis of the decline in the value of support due. It may be recalled that in 1978–81 each $100 change in child support due was associated with a $71 change in receipts (table 5.5). Assuming this relation had held to 1985, child support receipts would be expected to decline by $604. In addition, relatively minor changes in the demographic composition of the pop-

Table 5.7 Actual Decline in Amount of Child Support Received and Due and Unexplained Decline in Receipts from 1978 to 1985 among Women Receiving Child Support (in 1985 dollars)

	Actual Decline in Amount Received		Actual Decline in Amount Due		Decline in Amount Received Unexplained by Demographic Changes or Decline in Amount Due	
	$[a] (1)	%[b] (2)	$[c] (3)	%[d] (4)	$[e] (5)	%[f] (6)
All women	−748	25.3	−856	24.0	−131	17.5
Race						
Black	−373	17.5	−283	10.5	−25	6.7
Nonblack	−768	25.1	−908	24.7	−132	17.2
Marital status						
Never-married	−462	28.7	−242	14.1	−316	68.4
Ever-married	−716	23.8	−829	22.8	−108	15.1

[a] See table 2.11.

[b] Decline as a percent of amount received in 1978

[c] Based upon population-weighted data as in chap. 2

[d] Decline as a percent of amount due in 1978

[e] Based upon separate regressions by race and marital status, using all four years of data and allowing the effect of child support due to vary between the first two and last two survey years, as in table 5.5. The unexplained change is the coefficient on the dummy variable for the 1986 survey, weighted by an adjustment factor to be consistent with the population estimates from chap. 2.

[f] Unexplained as a percent of actual decline in amount received

ulation receiving support would be expected to reduce receipts another $13.[31] Altogether, this leaves a decline of $131 or 17.5 percent of the total decline not accounted for by the decline in support due and changes in the composition of the population (table 5.7).

In general, we can attribute this residual to changes over time in the receipt process or enforcement environment.[32] As we have already seen, one such change was that variations in receipts became much more closely tied to variations in awards, rising from .71 in 1978 to .94 in 1985 (see table 5.5). Using the relation between changes in dollars due and received that prevailed in 1985, we would have expected an overall decline in receipts of $805 or roughly 108 percent of the actual decline.[33] This suggests that other offsetting changes must also have taken place in the receipt environment between 1978 and 1985. We examine the contribution of changes in the legal environment in the next chapter.

TRENDS BY RACE AND MARITAL STATUS. Trends in receipts for nonblack women and ever-married mothers are nearly identical to trends overall, largely because 89 percent of all women receiving child support are nonblack and 95 percent have been married to their children's father. As shown in table 5.7, for nonblacks, the real value of child support received declined 25.1 percent or by $768 between 1978 and 1985, while the real value of support due declined 24.7 percent or by $908. For ever-married mothers, child support received declined 23.8 percent or by $716, while support due declined 22.8 percent or by $829. Largely on the basis of these declines in award amounts, we can explain over 82 percent of the actual decline in receipts for both groups. Changes over time in the mother's average characteristics were small and contribute little to the explained decline in receipts. Altogether, only 17.2 percent of the total decline in receipts for non-black mothers and 15.1 percent for ever-married mothers would not have been expected given the receipt environment prevailing in 1978.

Even a smaller portion of the decline for black women would not have been expected. As noted in chapter 2, the average value of receipts of black women declined considerably less than average—by just $373 or 17.5 percent. At the same time, among those who received child support, the value of support due also declined less than average—by $283 or 10.5 percent. Overall, the average ratio of support received to support due (which remained roughly constant for nonblacks) declined from .810 to .747 (see table 2.13). As a result, it might appear at first that the effectiveness of child support enforcement for black mothers actually deteriorated over time. This turns out not to be the case, however, once we also take account of the somewhat different relation between changes in support due and support received for blacks compared to nonblacks. It may be recalled that during the period 1978–81, holding all else constant, we found that each $100 change in child support due was associated with a $83 change in support received among black mothers compared to only a $71 change among nonblack mothers. Given this stronger association for blacks and considering both the decline in support due and compositional changes in the population receiving support, we can account for all but $25 or 6.7 percent of the total decline in the value of black receipts.

Among never-married mothers, the real value of child support received declined 28.7 percent, or by $462, between 1978 and 1985. This decline was even greater than the 14.1 percent or $242 decline in dollars due (see table 5.7). As a result, the average ratio of support received to support due declined substantially from .925 in 1978 to .745 in 1985 (see table 2.13). Given the relation between changes in support due and changes in support received for never-married mothers over the 1978–81 period, we find that more than half of the decline in receipts, or $316, would not be expected on the basis of the decline in dollars due and the changes in the composition of the population.[34] On the one hand, this suggests that effectiveness of the enforcement environment may have deteriorated. On the other hand, given the large increase in award and receipt rates of never-married mothers between 1978 and 1985, the average ability and desire to pay of fathers may have declined substantially, thereby exacerbating the problems of enforcement.

In both this chapter and chapter 4 we analyzed in detail four years of nationally representative cross-sectional data on mothers eligible for child support in order to look beyond the aggregate statistics presented in chapter 2. Specifically, we explored to what extent demographic (i.e., racial and marital status) differentials and trends across survey years in child support awards and receipts can be understood on the basis of the socioeconomic characteristics of mothers and other observable determinants of these outcomes. Drawing upon these analyses, we summarize some of our most important findings in tables 5.8 and 5.9.

DEMOGRAPHIC DIFFERENTIALS. As we saw in chapter 2, black and never-married mothers face disadvantages relative to nonblack and ever-married mothers at nearly every stage of the child support process. Blacks are less likely to have a child support award, have awards of much smaller value, are less likely to receive any of the support due them, and receive a smaller portion of what they are due. Never-married mothers have lower award rates and amounts; however, among those due support, they are as likely to receive some and to receive slightly more of what they are due. These aggregate demographic differentials, measured as average black or never-married child support outcomes minus average nonblack or ever-married outcomes, are summarized in table 5.8.

Table 5.8 also shows the extent to which these differences can be explained on the basis of differences in observable socioeconomic characteristics of mothers and for awards, the estimated income of fathers at the time of the award, and for receipts, the actual amount of support due. For example, we might expect blacks to have generally worse child support outcomes because they tend to have less education. This means that black fathers are less able to pay support and black mothers may be less able to use the legal system to secure and enforce an award. We might expect never-married mothers to have worse outcomes because they tend to have fewer children (fathered by the same man) and younger children. This means they may have less incentive to collect generally meager expected payments and their children's fathers (who perhaps never lived with them) may have less desire to pay.

Finally, the table shows how much of the differential has not been explained, presumably in part because we have not been able to control for all possible child support determinants and in part because of racial and marital status differences in the behavior of mothers and fathers. The latter are in turn shaped by the relevant social, cultural, and legal environments surrounding child support awards and receipts.

In general, demographic differentials in award rates are both much larger and better explained than differentials in receipt rates. Compared to nonblacks and ever-married mothers, far fewer blacks and never-married mothers have a child support award, but among those who do, blacks are only somewhat less likely to receive one and never-married mothers as likely. We are able to explain more than two-thirds of the racial differential in award rates but only one-third of the marital status differential. The racial differential in award rates is explained

Table 5.8 Summary of Racial and Marital Status Differentials in
Child Support Awards and Receipts

	Total Differential[a]	Explained Differential[b]	Unexplained Differential[c]
	Black vs. nonblack		
Rates			
Award	−35.7%	−26.1%	−9.6%
	(100%)	(73%)	(27%)
Receipt	−6.0%	−0.9%	−5.1%
	(100%)	(15%)	(85%)
Amounts			
Award due[d]	$−372	$−245	$−127
	(100%)	(66%)	(34%)
Received	$−797	$−403	$−394
	(100%)	(51%)	(49%)
	Never-married vs. ever-married		
Rates			
Award	−55.9%	−18.5%	−37.4%
	(100%)	(33%)	(67%)
Receipt	+0.4%	—	—
Amounts			
Award due	$−1,460	$−674	$−786
	(100%)	(46%)	(54%)
Received	$−1,344	$−1,603	$259
	(100%)	(119%)	(−19%)

Sources: See tables 4.2, 4.6, 5.2, and 5.6 for details.

[a] Average child support outcome of nonblack minus black or ever-married minus never-married mothers
[b] Explained by differences in the mother's socioeconomic characteristics and male incomes (awards) or dollars due (receipts)
[c] Total minus explained differential
[d] Among ever-married mothers only

largely by the higher proportion of blacks who are never-married or currently separated mothers, while the marital status differential is explained by the higher proportion of never-married mothers who are black, Hispanic, live in inner cities, have only young children, and have less education. By contrast, the relatively small racial differential in receipt rates is not well explained. While black women are less likely to receive support given their smaller average awards, they are more likely to receive it given their average socioeconomic characteristics (especially their more recent marital disruptions). These two effects are nearly offsetting, so that 85 percent of the overall racial gap in receipt rates remains unexplained.

At least half of the racial differential in both award and receipt amounts are explained on the basis of observable differences between blacks and nonblacks. Almost half of the differential in award amounts and more than 100 percent of the differential in receipt amounts by marital status are explained. We attribute the lower award amounts of black women to the greater likelihood of being never-married and (among the ever-married) to the lower incomes of their former husbands at the time of the award. In turn, the lower receipts of black women are largely explained by the lower award amounts, although this is offset somewhat by the effect of some socioeconomic characteristics (including a greater number of children). We attribute the lower award amounts of never-married mothers to the generally low socioeconomic status of both the mothers and fathers. Finally, the few never-married women who actually collect child support tend to receive more than would be expected on the basis of their socioeconomic disadvantages and the much lower value of their awards.

TRENDS OVER TIME. As we saw in chapter 2, award and receipt rates rose at least modestly, while the real value of child support awards and receipts declined sharply. In table 5.9 we summarize these trends for all women, as well as for black and never-married mothers separately. We show the change in each child support outcome across survey years, measured as 1985 minus 1978 levels (or, for award rates, 1986 minus 1979), and the change that can be explained on the basis of changes over time in some underlying determinants of child support, including socioeconomic characteristics of mothers, and, for award amounts, the cumulative inflation rate between the time of the award and the time of the survey or, for receipt rates and amounts, the value of support due.

We associate the unexplained changes in child support outcomes shown in table 5.9 with changes in the child support environment, although the relevant environment is different for awards than for receipts. For awards, because the aggregate award rate and amount of child support due in a given survey year represent the average experiences of mothers who became newly eligible for child support within the previous twenty-one years, the unexpected change reflects long-term changes in the underlying award process itself. For receipts, because the aggregate receipt rate and the amount received represent

Table 5.9 Summary of Trends in Child Support Awards and
Receipts between 1978 (79) and 1985 (86) by Race and Marital Status

	Total Change[a]	Expected Change[b]	Unexpected Change[c]
All mothers			
Rates			
Award	2.2%	−0.3%	2.5%
	(100%)	(−14%)	(114%)
Receipt	2.3%	−0.7%	3.0%
	(100%)	(−28%)	(128%)
Amounts			
Award due[d]	$−760	$−65	$−695
	(100%)	(9%)	(91%)
Received	$−748	$−611	$−131
	(100%)	(82%)	(18%)
Black mothers			
Rates			
Award[d]	10.3%	5.9%	4.4%
	(100%)	(57%)	(43%)
Receipt	9.5%	−0.7%	10.2%
	(100%)	(7%)	(107%)
Amounts			
Award due	$−596	—	—
Received	$−373	$−222	$−25
	(100%)	(60%)	(7%)
Never-married mothers			
Rates			
Award	7.8%	0.3%	7.5%
	(100%)	(4%)	(96%)
Receipt	−5.3%	−0.1%	−5.2%
	(100%)	(2%)	(98%)
Amounts			
Award due	$−131	—	—
Received	$−462	$−232	$−316
	(100%)	(50%)	(68%)

Sources: See tables 4.3, 4.7, 5.3, 5.4, and 5.7 for details.

[a] 1985 minus 1978, or for award rates, 1986 minus 1979
[b] Explained by changes in mothers' characteristics, male incomes or inflation (awards), and amounts due (receipts)
[c] Total minus explained change
[d] Among ever-married mothers only

the average experiences of mothers in the year before the survey, the unexpected change reflects differences in the enforcement environment prevailing in 1985 compared with 1978.

The aggregate award rate of all women rose just 2.2 percentage points between 1979 and 1986. This masked larger changes of 3.2 points for ever-married mothers and 7.8 points for never-married mothers because the latter subgroup—least likely to have an award—increased disproportionately. Given this increase, along with other smaller compositional shifts, we actually would have expected the aggregate award rate for all women to decline 0.3 points between 1979 and 1986, leaving an unexpected increase of 2.5 points, greater than the actual increase.

Some of the 10.3 percentage point gain in the award rate of ever-married black mothers would have been expected (due, in part, to a secular increase in black male income), but more than 40 percent would not have been expected. Almost none of the 7.8 percentage point rise in award rates of never-married mothers would have been expected. We attribute all of these unexpected increases to long-term improvements in the social and legal environments surrounding awards. Finally, we found that new award rates for ever-married mothers have been rising at least since 1958 (see table 4.4).

At the same time, the real value of child support due declined $760 among ever-married mothers between 1978 and 1985. Small compositional changes might have been expected to increase the average value of support due, while an acceleration of inflation (between 1978 and 1981) might have been expected to reduce it. Overall, we can explain only 9 percent of the actual decline on the basis of these two factors. We have argued that this unexplained decline is the result of the failure of new awards to keep up with rising consumer prices and male incomes at least since 1958 (see table 4.8).

Between 1978 and 1985, among all women due support, the aggregate receipt rate increased 2.3 percentage points; it rose 9.5 points for black mothers, but fell 5.3 points for the never-married. Some increase over time could have been expected solely on the basis of compositional shifts, but an even larger decrease could have been expected given the sharp decline in the real value of support due. Given these changes, receipt rates increased unexpectedly 3 percentage points for all women and 10.2 points for blacks and declined unexpectedly 5.2 points for the never-married. The unexpected increases in receipt rates suggest that, except for the never married, the enforcement environment improved between 1978 and 1985.

Among women receiving support, the real value of child support received declined for all demographic groups between 1978 and 1985—$748 (25%) for all women, $373 (18%) for blacks, and $462 (29%) for the never-married. We would have expected only small declines in receipts on the basis of compositional changes in the mother's characteristics but large declines on the basis of declines in the value of child support due. Overall, more than 80 percent of the decline in receipts would have been expected, but among blacks, more than 90 percent of the decline would have been expected. In other words, we find evidence of a smaller unexplained decline in receipts for blacks than for nonblacks, perhaps suggesting that enforcement efforts may be helping black women disproportionately. By contrast, among never-married mothers, more than half of the decline would not have been expected, reinforcing the earlier finding that never-married mothers are experiencing increasing problems collecting the support due them.

What lessons can be drawn from the disaggregated analysis of awards and receipts? First, we have seen it is not always possible to judge whether or not child support outcomes have improved over time simply on the basis of trends in aggregate outcomes for all women, since small changes in aggregate statistics can mask even larger changes for individual subgroups. Second, even when displayed by race and marital status, observed changes over time in child support outcomes can be misleading. Some changes in child support outcomes were simply the result of changes in their underlying determinants, including the socioeconomic characteristics of mothers, the real incomes of fathers, and the value of support due. Only changes that are unexplained by these factors can be attributed to changes over time in the social and legal environment governing awards and receipts.

Based on estimates of unexplained changes in award rates and amounts, as well as on trends in new awards among the ever-married, there appear to be some good news and some bad news about trends in the award process. The good news is that the likelihood of obtaining a child support award has been rising at least since 1958 and that most of this increase is not explained by changes in the socioeconomic characteristics of mothers or the real incomes of fathers but by changes in the social and legal environments. The bad news is that the real value of new awards, like the real value of child support due, has been declining over time. We offered several noncompeting hypotheses why the real value of new awards has been declining and analyzed the potential of child support guidelines for stemming this decline.

With regard to the receipt process, there is again some good news and some bad. First, unexplained increases in receipt rates for all demographic subgroups (except the never married) may indicate an improvement in child support enforcement between 1978 and 1985. Actual receipts declined, however, somewhat more than would have been expected given the accompanying decline in dollars due, especially among never-married mothers. Thus, on the one hand, among women receiving support it may be that the overall effectiveness of enforcement deteriorated slightly during the first half of the 1980s. On the other hand, given the rise in receipt rates, it may simply be that more reluctant payers were brought into the system who tend to pay a smaller proportion of what they owe.

In chapter 6 we explore to what extent the unexplained changes in award and receipt outcomes (summarized in table 5.9) can be attributed to changes in the legal environment. We relate child support awards and receipts not only to socioeconomic factors but also to specific child support laws and expenditures on child support programs within each state. For awards, we assess to what extent the recent introduction of mandatory guidelines may be likely to stem the decline in new award amounts and new laws regarding paternity establishment might help never-married mothers. For receipts, we identify specific laws among the set of provisions mandated by the 1984 Child Support Enforcement Amendments and the 1988 Family Support Act that appear to be most effective. It is to these legal analyses that we now turn.

The Legal
Environment

Child support awards are made and payments collected within an elaborate system of state and federal laws and regulations. These laws have been designed mainly to assist custodial parents in obtaining the support for their children that is their legal right. The entire bulwark of laws surrounding child support increasingly has been strengthened as awareness of the poverty of children living in single-parent families and its public consequences has grown.

Up to this point, in analyzing the determinants of child support outcomes, we have left the legal environment as part of the unobserved residual. Now we seek to characterize it in each state by existing laws and government spending on the child support enforcement program. The relevant legal environments differ between awards and receipts, with the former affected by laws concerning marriage and divorce, child custody, paternity establishment, and child support guidelines and the latter affected by laws about custody and visitation arrangements and child support enforcement. We focus here exclusively on laws pertaining to child support guidelines, paternity establishment, and child support enforcement.[1] We relate these laws and government spending in each state to the child support outcomes of individuals. With this analysis we seek to answer some important questions.

A most important question facing the public and individuals is whether recent federal legislation is likely to raise child support payments. New legislation passed in 1984 and 1988 required all states to introduce certain child support enforcement techniques and to adopt guidelines for award amounts. We provide evidence from 1978–85, before these laws were required, about which of them worked best and for whom, and which had perverse effects on child support outcomes. From this analysis we can infer the likelihood of success of recent federal legislation. We find that among the enforcement techniques mandated by the federal government, liens against property and wage withholding laws in effect for at least a couple of years have been the most effective. Although not required by federal law until 1992, criminal penalties for nonsupport have also been effective. Guidelines have been a double-edged sword, increasing the value of awards among the ever-married but slowing the growth of award rates among the never-married.

Another important question is whether the legal environment—laws and government spending—accounts for some of the changes in child support awards and receipts between 1979(78) and 1986(85), and specifically, whether the legal environment can explain the above-average gains of black mothers in awards and receipts or the progress of the never-married in establishing awards. We find that enforcement has been more effective for blacks than for nonblacks, and the legal environment generally appears to account for some of the increase in child support receipt rates among black mothers; however, changes over time in the legal environment surrounding awards does not appear to explain any of the increase in award rates among blacks and the never-married.

We begin with a brief history and overview of child support laws. We then analyze the effects on child support outcomes of child support enforcement, which is designed to increase collections; of guidelines, designed to arrive at more equitable and adequate child support award amounts; and of paternity establishment, designed to improve the low incidence of awards among never-married mothers. We study child support enforcement before guidelines and paternity laws because the government placed greater priority on the enforcement of existing awards than on the establishment of new ones during much of our period of analysis. Many states passed a variety of enforcement laws before adopting any guidelines. As a result, our analysis of the impact of guidelines is less elaborate than that of enforcement. Nonetheless, we discuss some of the many unresolved issues states must consider as they formulate and revise their child support guidelines.

History and Overview of Child Support Laws

Historical Growth in Importance of Laws

The federal government has increasingly come to view child support enforcement as an important weapon against poverty and welfare dependency. Before 1975, child support issues were viewed primarily as a matter of domestic law within the province of the states. But as attention increasingly focused upon the pervasive problems of non-payment, the widespread lack of awards, the low value of awards, the difficulty of interstate enforcement, and the special problems of never-married mothers, the federal government gradually began to take a more active role. These efforts culminated in the Family Support Act of 1988.

CHILD SUPPORT ENFORCEMENT. Federal initiatives to establish a national child support enforcement program began in 1975 with the passage of Title IV-D of the Social Security Act. Before this, like all family law issues, the enforcement of child support laws had been left chiefly to the states.[2] Even though they had a number of enforcement techniques at their disposal, states were believed to be doing an ineffective job.[3] Despite some adverse congressional sentiment, Title IV-D passed, in large part as a result of a recognition of the connection between the lack of child support and the growing burden of welfare. This connection was effectively summarized by Sen. Russell Long during debate on this legislation:

> Should our welfare system be made to support the children whose father cavalierly abandons them—or chooses not to marry the mother in the first place? Is it fair to ask the American taxpayer— who works hard to support his own family and to carry his own burden—to carry the burden of the deserting father as well? Perhaps we cannot stop the father from abandoning his children, but we can certainly improve the system by obtaining child support from him and thereby place the burden of caring for his children on his own shoulders where it belongs. We can—and we must— take the financial reward out of desertions.[4]

Title IV-D gave a major overseer role to the federal government but left the daily work of collecting child support to the states. It established both the federal Office of Child Support Enforcement to administer the nationwide program, and a Parent Locater Service. It also required each state to develop a program to assist in establishing paternity, to locate absent parents, to establish child support obligations, and to enforce such obligations. Further, it decreed that AFDC applicants or recipients must assign child support rights to the state and must cooperate in establishing paternity and securing support.

Each state was required to establish or designate a single separate child support agency, or so-called IV-D agency, and a state Parent Locater Service, which would use appropriate state and federal information to locate absent parents.

Sentiment in favor of an even more active federal role grew over the next decade, and in 1984 the Child Support Enforcement Amendments were passed unanimously by both houses and signed with great fanfare by President Reagan. Designed to strengthen the nation's child support enforcement system, this law required all states to use certain "strong, proven practices for collecting overdue child support."[5] In particular, it requires states to: (1) use automatic wage withholding to collect overdue child support; (2) employ expedited legal processes (e.g., administrative or quasi-judicial procedures) to establish and enforce support orders; (3) provide for collection of overdue support by intercepting state income tax refunds; (4) initiate a process for imposing liens against real and personal property; and (5) institute procedures for requiring a security, bond, or other guarantee. The law also reiterated that Title IV-D services were to be made available to non-AFDC families on an equal basis with AFDC families. The techniques incorporated in this legislation were deemed to be effective, although there was no actual evidence.

Strengthening the federal role remained a high priority, and four years later, child support enforcement was the first provision incorporated in the 1988 Family Support Act and was viewed as a welfare reform measure. The major advance on the enforcement front was to require that income withholding be immediate. This law also took an important first step in dealing with the difficult problem of interstate enforcement by establishing a commission to study the problem and to prepare a report.[6] It also included advances in guidelines and paternity establishment.

GUIDELINES AND PATERNITY ESTABLISHMENT. Before the recent era of guidelines or standards for determining their amount, child support awards were established on an individual basis with no uniform rationale. Awards often differed widely among noncustodial parents with equal ability to pay[7] and, as we showed in chapter 2, were low by any reasonable standards. The purpose of guidelines was to establish uniformity so that relevant factors such as the noncustodial parent's ability to pay support, rather than the whim of the judge or the persuasive power of an attorney, would determine awards. Another purpose was to raise awards to a level deemed adequate for meeting the expenses of the true costs of raising children, regardless of how such costs may be arrived at.

Guidelines for setting child support award amounts did not come until 1975 when they were established in the first states—Illinois and Maine. They contained the same basic elements still used today but were optional rather than presumptive. They became widespread only when states were required by the Child Support Enforcement Amendments of 1984 to adopt advisory guidelines. The Family Support Act of 1988 went further in mandating that guidelines be used as a "rebuttable presumption," that is, that they be adhered to unless there was a finding that their application "would be unjust or inappropriate in a particular case."[8]

To improve the adequacy of child support award amounts and remedy the problem of their declining value, the Family Support Act also mandated that a periodic review and adjustment for awards be enforced under Title IV-D beginning in 1990, by request and by 1993 automatically every three years. Further, it proposed that the secretary of Health and Human Services conduct a study of the feasibility of universal periodic review. The law also required that a state review its guidelines "every four years to ensure that their application results in the determination of appropriate child support award amounts."[9] The inclusion in the legislation of demonstration projects as well as a study of child-rearing costs[10] indicates that guidelines and their development are likely to continue to be an important policy issue well into the 1990s.

Since the enactment of Title IV-D in 1975, concern for children born outside of marriage has grown along with the proportion of AFDC cases needing paternity established before a child support award could be made.[11] State statute of limitations laws restricting paternity establishment to fairly young ages had already been declared unconstitutional before 1984[12] when the Child Support Enforcement Amendments required all states to permit the establishment of paternity up to the child's eighteenth birthday.[13] The Family Support Act of 1988 required states, beginning on 1 October 1991, to meet federal standards for establishing a minimum percentage of paternities, with the ultimate goal of reaching 50 percent.[14] It also required states to obtain the Social Security numbers of both parents when issuing a birth certificate and required all parties in a contested paternity case to submit to genetic testing at the request of any party.

Overview of Child Support Laws

CHILD SUPPORT ENFORCEMENT TECHNIQUES. The centerpiece of federal legislation to improve child support collections is a wage withholding law that allows a child support obligation to be withheld from a noncustodial parent's paycheck, much as taxes are withheld. The 1984 Child Support Enforcement Amendments mandated the use of wage withholding when there were arrearages (overdue payments).[15] It also allowed wage assignment when requested by a noncustodial parent. States were also allowed to extend withholding to other forms of income. The Family Support Act of 1988 went still further, mandating that, with two exceptions, wage withholding be immediate in all new or modified IV-D orders by October 1990. By 1 January 1994, new support orders issued in non-IV-D cases must also provide for immediate withholding. The exceptions are when good cause is found by a court or both parties agree to an alternate payment arrangement. High hopes were held out for the success of immediate wage withholding as witnessed by this statement of a sponsor of the bill, Sen. Daniel P. Moynihan: "Automatic wage withholding will help prevent many single-parent families from becoming public assistance recipients, as well as reduce welfare payments to others."[16]

Federal legislation also requires that states implement procedures to place liens against property—such as houses, vehicles, and land—of delinquent noncustodial parents who reside in and own property in that state. This may be especially useful in cases where a noncustodial parent has tangible assets but is not regularly employed and thus not easily subject to wage withholding. The lien comes into play mostly when the individual tries to transfer the property. "A child support lien converts the custodial parent from an unsecured to a secured creditor. As such, it gives the custodial parent priority over unsecured creditors and subsequent secured creditors."[17]

The 1984 law also required states to have two other enforcement provisions. First, a noncustodial parent must post security, bond, or other guarantee to secure payment of overdue support, another provision that is useful for individuals with assets but irregular or non-existent employment. Second, states must have procedures available to intercept state income tax refunds up to the amount of overdue child support.

Finally, 1984 federal legislation also required that states have available expedited judicial or administrative processes for establishing and enforcing support orders. States have generally met this requirement by setting up an administrative agency outside the courts or a quasi-judicial system in the courts. Michigan has implemented a respected model of the latter in its friend of the court. These procedures are intended to facilitate the movement of cases through the system.

A number of other child support enforcement techniques became available in some states but were not mandated by federal law. These include garnishment, attachments and executions, and criminal penalties. The first two involve a one-time seizure of wages or property to pay an arrearage. These have been superseded by automatic wage withholding and lien laws, which are ongoing rather than one-time weapons. The most notable enforcement technique passed over in federal legislation is having criminal penalties for nonsupport. In contrast to the other techniques, it is directly punitive, making it controversial. Further, the disadvantage of jailing as a penalty is that it can undermine the very objective it is meant to achieve by depriving a noncustodial parent of his or her livelihood.[18] Moreover, a woman on AFDC may be deterred from helping the agency locate an absent father if she knows he can be jailed for nonsupport, especially if he is contributing informally or in nonpecuniary ways to the support of the child. Despite these possible objections, criminal penalties have been successful at increasing child support receipts.

GUIDELINES AND PATERNITY ESTABLISHMENT LAWS. Guidelines for child support award amounts set a standard by which award amounts should be determined. They set awards in relation to the noncustodial parent's income. Other factors that may also be considered include the custodial parent's ability to support the child(ren), the needs of the child(ren), and whether the noncustodial parent has other children to support. During the period of our study, in most cases use of the guidelines was optional.[19]

Paternity establishment laws regulate the process of identifying the father of a child born out of wedlock.[20] Paternity "long-arm statutes" enable states to obtain jurisdiction over an individual residing in another state needed to establish paternity and set an award.[21] For cases in which this "long-arm" statute does not apply, some states have a provision for interstate establishment of paternity under the Revised Uniform Reciprocal Enforcement of Support Act (RURESA). Scientific tests to assist in paternity determination have become increasingly common and accurate, with a high probability that an incorrectly named father can be excluded from further scrutiny. Default judgments of paternity can be entered if the alleged father fails to show up when the paternity proceeding is a civil one. The move has been away from criminal proceedings to civil ones. During the period of study, states differed in their statutes of limitations on paternity establishment, restricting the initiation of a paternity action to periods "ranging from one year after birth to six years after majority."[22] As noted above, the 1984 law required states to permit the establishment of paternity anytime up to the child's eighteenth birthday. Specific state laws and statutes of limitations may, however, limit the amount of child support that can be recovered for the time prior to the establishment of paternity.[23]

AVAILABILITY OF LAWS. During our period of study, 1978–85, each state had established a particular set of child support laws. To describe them, we have assembled a unique data set based primarily on published and unpublished data from the National Conference of State Legislatures (NCSL). The NCSL data set contains information on the year child support enforcement techniques, guidelines, and paternity determination legislation were adopted in each state.[24] Table 6.1 shows the number of states with each child support law for each of the four years for which we have national data on child support payments—1978, 1981, 1983, and 1985.

All of the child support enforcement techniques required by federal legislation, as well as the others described here have been present in some states since at least 1978.[25] Some of the techniques had already gained popularity before being mandated by federal law, but others had not. The late 1970s and early 1980s witnessed the most rapid growth in wage withholding and state income tax refund offset laws. In these instances, passage of the federal law simply solidified an existing trend. After remaining relatively constant during the early eighties, liens on property, securities, bonds or other guarantees, and expedited processes grew widespread following the federal legislation that required them.

With respect to guidelines and paternity legislation, states appear to have been more followers than leaders. Whereas the number of states with guidelines for child support awards in 1978 was small and

Table 6.1   Number of States with Each Child Support Provision by Year, 1978–1985[a]

Provision	Year			
	1978	1981	1983	1985
Child Support Enforcement				
Automatic or mandatory income withholding[b] (AMW)	15	32	40	41
Automatic income withholding	7	13	13	32
Mandatory withholding	10	29	40	41
Voluntary wage assignment (VWA)	7	8	17	32
State income tax refund offset (TAX)	1	17	38	39
Liens on property (LIEN)	8	20	21	44
Security, bond, or other guarantee (SEC)	21	30	31	41
Criminal penalties for nonsupport (CRIM)	5	9	9	11
Expedited processes[b] (EP)	15	21	23	34
Administrative procedures	11	14	17	17
Friend of court and court trustees	4	9	9	18
Guidelines and Paternity Determination				
Guidelines[c]	6	11	12	34
Paternity long-arm statutes	11	18	19	21
Interstate determination of paternity	25	30	30	33
Default judgments	7	10	12	13
Limitations on recoveries	13	12	14	18
Scientific tests	18	29	36	41
Statutes of limitations	1	3	6	26

Source: NCSL, "State Legislation on Child Support and Paternity," chart, July 1985 (1985 data); NCSL, "State Legislation on Child Support and Paternity," chart, December 1983 (1981 and 1983 data); NCSL, *A Guide to State Child Support and Paternity Laws*, and unpublished data (1978).

[a] Covers the fifty states plus the District of Columbia

[b] These measures are created by combining the two (similar) measures directly beneath it. If the state has either measure, it is counted as having the technique.

[c] Three other states were listed as having guidelines according to the 1983 NCSL chart (one as of 1978 and two as of 1983) but were not recorded as having guidelines according to their 1985 chart. We chose to follow the information in the more recent chart.

by 1983, had only doubled, it nearly tripled in the year following the 1984 federal legislation requiring them. With the exception of scientific tests for establishing paternity, change in paternity legislation seems to have been relatively gradual between 1978 and 1983. Between 1983 and 1985, many states added statutes of limitations for paternity establishment, probably as a result of the 1984 federal legislation requiring them to do so.

Child Support Enforcement Laws

Child support enforcement laws provide techniques to force a delinquent obligor to pay and hence may increase a mother's receipts. Problems in collecting child support, documented in previous chapters, include nonpayment, irregular payment, and partial payment. In some cases, arrearages accumulate for many years and can range up to tens of thousands of dollars.[26] Making delinquent fathers pay can involve repeated attempts to bring them into court and many hours on the part of the custodial mother and various court personnel, including judges and lawyers. Beyond this, the mere existence of enforcement techniques may deter fathers from becoming delinquent in their payments. But even at the outset of the 1990s, when fathers tend to move out of state, enforcement continues to be a difficult problem.[27]

It is possible that child support enforcement techniques also have feedback effects on awards. Judges and other personnel involved in establishing and setting the level of awards probably know and take into account the court's ability to enforce such orders. The behavior of the parties involved in the agreement is also likely to be responsive to perceptions about the effectiveness of enforcement. By raising expected child support receipts, a stronger set of techniques might make the mother fight harder for an award or for a bigger one, and make the father resist an award more or seek a lower one. Thus, if for instance, wage withholding is known to facilitate collections, it may affect the likelihood that an award is established and its amount, although the direction of the effect is uncertain a priori.

Next, we address whether child support enforcement techniques and government spending are effective, whether child support enforcement techniques have any indirect effect upon awards, and whether a changing legal environment can account for those changes in receipts unexplained by socioeconomic factors, and particularly the above-average gains of black mothers. Before we try to answer these questions, we present a brief description of our methodology.

Evaluating the Effects of the Child Support Enforcement Program

As noted above, there has been considerable variation in enforcement techniques both across states at any given moment and over time. Using the basic framework of chapter 5, we can add measures of the legal environment in the state at the time when child support

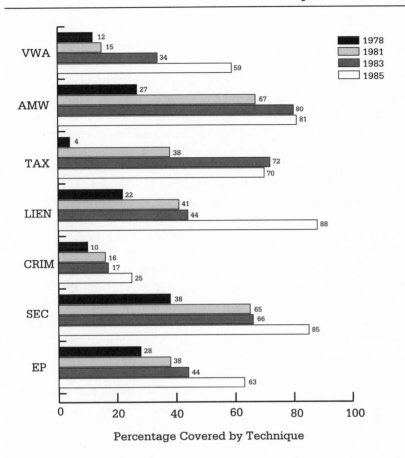

6.1 Percent of Women Due Support Covered by Child Support Enforcement Technique

payments were received to the socioeconomic factors already controlled for. Figure 6.1 presents the percentage of women due support covered by each child support enforcement technique in the year prior to each survey for the period 1978–85. The wide variation in laws during this period lends itself to multivariate statistical analysis of the impact of laws on child support receipts. In fact, this period is unique in this respect because most of these laws were soon to become available in all states to fulfill the federal mandate.

In evaluating the effect of laws on behavior, we need to be aware of a potential bias from reverse causality. Laws are not passed in a vacuum but may be initiated in response to a severe problem. For example, states with particularly poor payment records may initiate mandatory withholding in an effort to raise collections. If we consider only the contemporaneous relation between laws and receipts, we may find no effect of the law or even an apparently perverse one. To uncover the true relation, we might examine laws as of a given date and child support receipts at an earlier date. We would find that states with mandatory withholding laws had poor payment records and thus would not conclude that mandatory withholding was ineffective. Thus, to make certain that the measured contemporaneous effect of enforcement is real, we also examine the relation between laws as of a given date and receipts at an earlier date and net out this preexisting relation.[28]

We also explore certain variations on this basic model to examine other hypotheses. Assuming that the entire social climate surrounding child support has moved toward stricter enforcement, we test whether the contemporaneous effect of enforcement grew across the years of our surveys. Since laws may become effective only with a lag, allowing time for information about them to spread and regulations to be established, we also match child support payments in a given year with legal factors a few years earlier.

For a number of reasons, the effects we estimate must be considered a lower bound of the true effect. First, we have information only on the existence of laws, not on their implementation, usage, or enforcement. States have differed in how widely techniques are used and in whether they are made available to the entire child support population or only to the IV-D population—all AFDC mothers plus any non-AFDC mothers who avail themselves of the IV-D agency services. Also, some states have techniques available not by legislation but by practice, information we have only for one year. Hence, we treat states with these latter techniques as if they do not have them. We can test for their effectiveness only for that year. Finally, the legal measures pertain to the mother's state of residence, whereas around 30 percent of absent fathers are not subject to these same laws because they reside in a different state.[29] All of these limitations are likely to bias our estimates toward not finding an effect of the laws.

Effects of Child Support Enforcement Techniques on Receipts

Table 6.2 presents the estimated effect of child support enforcement techniques on the likelihood of receiving support and on the amount

Table 6.2 Effect of Child Support Enforcement Techniques on Child Support Receipts, 1978–1985

Enforcement Technique	Contemporaneous			Lagged	Preexisting	
	1978–1985	Subperiod 1 1978–1981	Subperiod 2 1983–1985	1981–1985	One period 1978–1983	Two periods 1978–1981
Receipt rate among women due support						
VWA	−.003	.034	−.021	−.016	.013	−.018
AMW	−.003	−.034*	.028	.031**	−.025	.004
TAX	.009	.009	.006	.014	.024*	.004
LIEN	.036***	.020	.048***	.038***	.021	.006
CRIM	.016	.003	.021	.013	−.015	.026
SEC	−.006	.003	−.021	−.003	.014	−.005
EP	−.021*	−.008	−.037**	−.005	−.001	−.017
Receipt amount (in 1985 dollars) among women receiving support						
VWA	24	−76	8	−52	26	8
AMW	11	81	−31	48	12	34
TAX	15	−12	23	−81	−25	41
LIEN	88*	170**	9	64	103*	65
CRIM	138**	302***	101*	141**	52	61
SEC	−40	−134*	1	−71	−75	−62
EP	63	57	101**	48	−3	62

Note: These estimates are derived by OLS regression on equations that also include the socioeconomic variables indicated in tables 5.1 or 5.5 and control for year of the survey.

*(**, ***) Significant at 10%, 5%, and 1% levels, respectively

of support received, controlling for the amount due between 1978 and 1985. That is, these estimates show the difference in receipts between women who live in a state with a certain child support enforcement technique and comparable women (i.e., with the same socioeconomic characteristics and due the same amount of support) who live in a state without it. We show the contemporaneous effect of enforcement across the four years of data and the effect in the first two and last two years of the period separately. To take account of lags, we look at the effect on child support receipts in 1981–85 of child support techniques that had been in effect for at least two years. To take into account any preexisting relations, we present the relation between the enforcement technique and child support receipts at least two years prior, in 1978–83, and at least four years prior, in 1978–81.[30] To avoid too many numbers, we do not present individual year-by-year analyses of the effect of enforcement techniques but discuss them in the text where they differ from the results obtained from the analyses based upon all four years of data combined.

Overall, at least three of the seven child support enforcement techniques were effective over our period of study. Liens and criminal penalties appear to have been effective both contemporaneously and with a lag, while mandatory withholding appears to have been effective only with a lag. In addition, securities, bonds, or other guarantee, which were negatively related to the amount received in 1981 and positively related in 1985, may have been becoming effective toward the end of our period of study.[31]

Liens on real and personal property were related both to a higher receipt rate and a larger amount received. Women in states with lien laws were about 3.6 percentage points more likely to receive support than other women and received about $88 more on average (col. 1). We find that liens were more effective in the latter half of the period, raising receipt rates 4.8 percentage points (col. 3). We also find a positive preexisting relation between lien laws and the amount of child support received two years earlier (col. 6), but not four years earlier (col. 7). Since, as shown in figure 6.1, the proportion of women in states with lien laws was basically the same in 1981 as in 1983, we place greater confidence in the latter results. Thus, we conclude that liens increased child support receipt rates and amounts.[32]

Over the entire period, women in states with criminal penalties received about $138 more child support on average. By individual year, criminal penalties were most effective in 1978, were relatively less effective in 1981, and were ineffective in 1983. One might be tempted to conclude that criminal penalties had become less effective and were perhaps superseded by the new techniques passed by the states were it not for the resumption of a small positive effect in 1985.[33]

Wage withholding is one technique that appears to become effective only with a lag.[34] Receipt rates were 3.1 percentage points higher in states with wage withholding laws in effect for at least two years (col. 4). This effect diminished over time, though, falling from 6.3 percentage points in 1981 to zero in 1985. A possible explanation is that by 1983, four out of five women were in states with such laws, leaving few to compare them with.

Using additional NCSL data collected in 1985, we also analyzed the effect on receipts of the number of wage withholding provisions in a state, which varied between 1 and 16, with 10 the average, and of four provisions separately: mandatory income withholding, automatic income withholding,[35] voluntary income withholding, and the requirement that withholding commence when an arrearage equals the amount of one month's support. Women in states with mandatory wage withholding provisions in 1985 were 7.4 percentage points more likely to receive support,[36] but the number of separate provisions did not affect receipts (results not shown). These results are only suggestive because we have just shown that over the entire period wage withholding provisions became effective only with a lag; thus, larger effects might be found for 1987 or later years. The effects of types of wage withholding provisions may be a fruitful area for further study.

A somewhat puzzling finding that reappears later is that expedited processes for establishing and enforcing support orders appear to have mixed effects—a negative effect on child support receipt rates and a positive effect on receipt amounts. Over the entire period 1978–85, women in states with expedited processes were 2.1 percentage points less likely to receive any support. In the latter half of the period, they were 3.7 percentage points less likely to receive support, but those who did received $101 more. Although this latter effect may appear desirable at first glance, it could simply be a result of the IV-D agency neglecting the more difficult cases. That expedited processes for establishing and enforcing child support orders are associated with lower receipt rates and higher receipt amounts raises some cause for concern and suggests that further research is needed to determine why.[37]

As mentioned earlier, one limitation of these analyses is that we have data only on techniques available by legislation, whereas some states employ child support enforcement techniques by practice. Data on techniques available by legislation and practice in 1984 were collected from state IV-D offices by the Office of Child Support Enforcement (OCSE) in a special one-time survey (known as the UPIP data). In that year, for example, fourteen states intercepted workman's compensation payments by practice, whereas only nine states did so by law. Analyzing these data we find that although techniques available by practice have similar effects to techniques available by legislation, they do not appear to be particularly effective, as none has statistically significant effects. Furthermore, controlling for practices for the most part leaves conclusions about the effectiveness of legislation unaltered, although it does change the magnitude of their effects somewhat.[38] Finally, none of our findings based upon the OCSE data conflicts with our findings based on NCSL data. For the most part, these findings confirm that our main estimates using NCSL data are not biased owing to our inability to control for enforcement techniques available by practice.

In conclusion, based upon the experience of states from 1978 to 1985, liens against property and wage withholding laws in effect for at least two years appear effective at increasing child support receipts. A security, bond or other guarantee may have become effective. These results suggest that these techniques, required by recent federal legislation, are likely to increase receipts in the future. State income tax intercept laws appear not to have been effective, and unexpectedly, expedited processes may have had unintended negative consequences for child support receipts. A more detailed examination of why these techniques, also required by recent federal legislation, did not help and may even have hurt receipts is clearly needed. Criminal penalties appear effective at increasing child support receipts, although their greatest impact was in 1978 when states had a limited number of other techniques at their disposal. Based upon these findings, we conclude that the neglect of criminal penalties in the 1984 federal law may have been a mistake.

Effects of Child Support Enforcement Techniques on Awards

Although designed primarily to improve child support receipts, child support enforcement techniques may also have intended or unintended feedback effects on awards. Laws that are believed to be effective are likely to set up an expectation that more of what is ordered can be collected. This may encourage the courts to set higher awards because they expect them to be collected, or lower awards, anticipating the collection of a higher proportion of that award. Thus, higher child support payments may result from the better enforcement of existing awards and higher initial awards. Alternatively, child support payments might be unchanged owing to the offsetting effects of child support enforcement on awards and receipts—if, anticipating that what is ordered will be collected, fathers resist larger awards more vigorously. We explore these potential feedback effects in two ways.

First, we examine the impact of laws on child support payments for all women receiving support. Estimates of the effect on amount received from a given award, derived by controlling for the amount of child support due, are presented in table 6.2 (lower panel). To explore the indirect effect of enforcement on payments through awards, we stop controlling for the effect of the amount due on the amount received (see table 6.3, col. 1). Any difference in estimates of the effects of the enforcement measures from those shown in table 6.2 can be deemed to be a result of the award amount itself. But since many of the awards of women currently receiving support were established before the laws, this estimate has to be considered a lower bound. We find that women in states with automatic or mandatory wage withholding laws received $234 more in child support payments on average than women in states without such laws.[39] Because (in table 6.2), withholding laws were unrelated to the amount of child support received controlling for the amount due, we can infer that wage withholding laws must raise awards by this amount.[40] Criminal penalties were also positively related to child support payments but had a significant positive preexisting relation with payments and, as shown in table 6.2, were positively related to the amount received from a given award. Thus, we would not conclude they had any effect on award amounts.

Second, we examine the direct effect of techniques in effect at divorce or separation on the award rate and amount for the subgroup of women who have divorced or separated since 1978, the initial year of our enforcement data. We find that among those eligible for support, voluntary wage assignment laws resulted in award rates that were 3.5 percentage points higher, and among those due support, resulted in award amounts that were $241 higher (table 6.3).[41] Securities, bonds, or other guarantees raised award amounts by $173. Comparing the contemporaneous to the preexisting effect suggests that criminal pen-

Table 6.3 Effect of Child Support Enforcement Techniques on Child Support Payments, 1978–1985

| | Payments among all women receiving support | | Awards among Women Divorced or Separated since 1978 | | | |
| | | | Award Rate among women eligible for support | | Amount due among women due support | |
Enforcement Technique	Contemporaneous	Pre-existing	Contemporaneous[a]	Pre-existing[b]	Contemporaneous[a]	Pre-existing[b]
VWA	144	53	.035**	.021	241*	−66
AMW	234**	146	−.010	−.026**	80	166
TAX	−17	−80	.016	−.015	150	−148
LIEN	83	−66	.011	.011	−25	36
CRIM	200*	282**	−.007	−.002	−8	257**
SEC	97	−113	.0001	−.013	173*	16
EP	−10	−6	−.002	.007	37	−30
Number of observations	5495	4057	6060	6797	3769	4375

Note: Equations also control for socioeconomic variables and year of the survey; for the recently divorced, they also control for income in the year of marital disruption in constant 1985 dollars.

*(**) Significant at 10% and 5% levels, respectively

[a] Sample consists of women divorced or separated between 1978 and 1986.

[b] Sample consists of women divorced or separated between 1975 and 1982; enforcement variables are measured 2–4 years in the future.

alties reduced award amounts. For this subgroup of women with recent marital disruptions, we find no significant contemporaneous effect of automatic wage withholding laws on award amounts.[42]

The results of both approaches suggest that the existence of certain enforcement techniques may have positive feedback effects on awards. Automatic or voluntary wage withholding, and securities, bonds, or other guarantees appear to create the expectation that awards will be paid, and as a result they can be set higher.

Effect of Government Spending on Receipts

Not only does the legal environment differ across states by the enforcement techniques available but also by the effort states devote to enforcing their IV-D programs. If a state spends more money enforcing existing child support orders or has a more efficient child support program, will that state have a higher receipt rate or collect more dollars owed? If a state devotes a higher proportion of its resources to its AFDC clientele, how will this be reflected in receipts for women residing in that state?

To represent the amount of government resources devoted to enforcement, we used two measures: total administrative expenditures of the IV-D program divided by the population in the state, and the proportion of total expenditures devoted to the AFDC population. To represent the efficiency of government enforcement efforts, we used the ratio of total collections to total administrative expenditures of the state IV-D program. Table 6.4 presents the averages of these measures by year of child support receipts for 1978–85. Average government spending on the child support enforcement program has increased rapidly since 1978, more than doubling in current dollars and increasing 30 percent in real terms between 1978 and 1985. Expenditures devoted to the AFDC clientele rose slightly less rapidly and actually declined as a proportion of total spending from .87 to .82 in 1983.[43] The ratio of collections to expenditures fell slightly during the early 1980s but rose significantly between 1983 and 1985.

Unfortunately, these data do not perfectly capture the states' effort. The ratio of collections to expenditures is an imperfect measure of the efficiency of the state enforcement agency.[44] First, if a state has a higher level of collections, it would almost necessarily need to have a higher receipt rate or receipt amount, and the causality may be re-

Table 6.4 Average Government Effort or Resources on Child Support Enforcement Program by Year, 1978–1985[a]

	1978	1981	1983	1985
Total administrative expenditures ($m)	14.3	20.5	27.9	30.6
(1985 $m)	23.6	24.3	30.1	30.6
AFDC expenditures ($m)	11.8	17.0	21.8	NA
(1985 $m)	19.5	20.1	23.5	NA
Total expenditures per 100,000 population (in current $)	0.136	0.232	0.316	0.363
(in 1985 $)	0.225	0.274	0.342	0.363
Proportion of expenditures on AFDC population	0.865	0.879	0.818	NA
Total collections relative to total expenditures	2.66	2.68	2.60	3.06

Source: HHS, *Child Support Enforcement, Annual Reports to Congress*, various issues: total expenditures and ratio (7th Annual Report, 53 and 88; and 11th Annual Report, 25 and 55); AFDC expenditures (3d Annual Report, 101; 6th Annual Report, 66; 8th Annual Report, 63); Census Bureau, Current Population Reports, series P-25, no. 998, *State Population and Household Estimates to 1985, with Age and Components of Change* (Washington, D.C.: U.S. GPO, 1986), table 3 (population estimates).

[a] Average state expenditures weighted by number of mothers eligible for child support in a given year, where the total equals 4,064 in 1985, 4,196 in 1983, 4,141 in 1981, and 3,539 in 1978.

NA = not available

versed. Second, and even more important, because states with higher ratios receive higher incentive payments from the federal government, they may seek to keep their ratios high by going after the easiest cases and spending the least amount possible for the greatest gain. A high ratio, thus, would not necessarily indicate a more efficient state program. Although we have no data to indicate whether states go after the easiest cases, we show later that they do not go after cases with higher awards. The two expenditure variables are also problematic. Expenditures in a state may be high relative to other states because noncompliance with child support orders is pervasive or because the state is more committed to enforcement. In the former case, expenditures may appear unrelated or even perversely related to child support outcomes. Unfortunately, high correlations in these measures over time preclude determination of whether there is such a preexisting relation.[45] A further limitation of these analyses is that government spending is clearly targeted for IV-D cases and would not pertain to cases handled by private attorneys.[46] There may, however, be spillover effects of state agency spending on the population at large. Because of their limitations, these measures are included only in the analyses of the effects of government spending per se and not in the analyses of the effects of enforcement techniques.[47]

Table 6.5 shows the estimates of the effects of differences across states in IV-D agency efficiency and resources on child support receipts; they control for differences in enforcement techniques, although this makes little difference in the estimates.[48] The figures in this table represent the percentage point change in the receipt rate for a one-unit change in the government spending measure, all else being equal.

In general, for all women, when the effects of IV-D agency resources and efficiency are examined together, the spending measures have little impact, but the collections ratio increases the child support receipt rate.[49] The average woman due support resides in a state that collects $2.81 per dollar of administrative expenditures. Doubling the average ratio would increase her likelihood of receipt by 2.8 percentage points, a surprisingly small amount. We also find, but do not show, that the ratio is unrelated to the receipt amount both controlling for and not controlling for the award amount. Thus, for a given expenditure, it appears that the more efficient state agencies collect in a higher proportion of cases but collect no more than do less efficient agencies. If these estimates are correct, however, the effect is so small as to limit the usefulness of increasing government efficiency as a means of increasing receipt rates.[50]

When the effects of IV-D agency resources on all women are examined without the efficiency measure, an increase in government expenditures per capita affects neither the receipt rate nor the amount, but an increase in the proportion of expenditures on the AFDC population reduces the receipt rate (results not shown). The absence of an effect of the former may be from the fact that the IV-D agency serves only some women and generally only lower-income women. Thus, possible effects on the IV-D population may be obscured when examining outcomes for all women. With respect to the latter, compared with no expenditure on the AFDC population, a state devoting all its resources to the AFDC population would have a 13 percentage point lower receipt rate.[51] This suggests that devoting a higher proportion

Table 6.5 Effect of IV-D Agency Expenditures on Child Support Receipt and Award Rates by Race and Marital Status, 1978–1986

Measure	Receipt Rate among Women Due Support[a]				Award Rate among Women Eligible for Support[b]			
	All	Nonblack	Black	Never-married	All	Nonblack	Black	Never-married
Collections relative to expenditures	.010***	.014***	−.020**	−.019	.009***	.007***	.016***	.012***
Expenditures per 100,000 population	−.055	−.090**	.195	.283	−.034	−.050*	−.033	.025
Proportion of expenditures on AFDC population	−.058	−.044	−.249	.037	.058*	.038	.076	.100
Number of observations	7,497	6,624	873	351	15,099	11,516	3,583	3,056

Note: Figures represent the percentage point change in the probability of receiving support of having an award for a one unit change in the government spending measure, holding all other variables constant. Estimates are derived from separate OLS regressions by demographic group, which also control for socioeconomic characteristics in table 5.1 or table 4.1 and year of the survey.

*(**, ***) Significant at the 10%, 5%, and 1% levels, respectively
[a] In the year prior to the survey
[b] In the year of the survey

of resources to the AFDC population understandably restricts a state's ability to raise collections. Controlling for this factor may bring the remaining variation in the state's collection ratio closer to the measure of efficiency of the IV-D agency that we seek.

In summary, variations in state government efforts in the child support enforcement program have no impact on the magnitude of child support payments among women overall. Variations in government spending have no impact on child support receipt rates, either, but more efficient IV-D agencies do appear to raise receipt rates by a small amount.

Legal Environment and Unexplained Changes in Receipts

In the previous chapter we showed that the socioeconomic characteristics of mothers and aggregate economic conditions accounted for only part of the change in child support receipts between 1978 and 1985. As we saw, receipt rates rose more than expected and amounts declined more. We now investigate whether any of these unexplained changes may be attributed to changes in state enforcement techniques and government spending over the period. The results of this analysis should be interpreted with caution because, although some enforcement measures attain significance individually, as a set they do not significantly improve our ability to explain variations in individual receipts at a point in time.[52] In table 6.6, we present the actual change in receipt rate and receipt amount between 1978 and 1985 for all women as shown in chapter 2. In subsequent rows, we present the percentage of the change unexplained by socioeconomic characteristics and the decline in the amount of support due only; by socioeconomic characteristics, amount due, and child support enforcement techniques; and finally, by all of these plus the three measures of government resources and efficiency.[53]

We find evidence that for all women the increasing availability of effective enforcement techniques significantly increased receipt rates between 1978 and 1985. Whereas socioeconomic factors could explain none of the 2.3 percentage point rise, child support enforcement techniques account for 83 percent, leaving only 17 percent of the rise unexpected. Unfortunately, government resources appear to work in the opposite direction, reducing the net benefit of the legal environment and enlarging the percent of the rise unexpected. Taking account of changes over time in the legal environment also increases the unex-

Table 6.6 The Legal Environment and Changes in Child Support Receipts between 1978 and 1985 by Race

	Receipt Rate among Women Due Support		Receipt Amount among Women Receiving Support[a]	
	All	Black[b]	All	Black[c]
Actual change[d]	2.3 (100%)	9.5 (100%)	−748 (100%)	−373 (100%)
Percentage unexplained by				
1. Socioeconomic character-istics and decline in amount due[e]	100%	95%	20%	16%
2. Socioeconomic charac-teristics, decline in amount due, and child support enforcement techniques	17	65	34	115
3. Socioeconomic charac-teristics, decline in amount due, child support enforcement techniques, and government spending (in current $)	87	11	37	123
4. Same as (3), except government spending (in constant $)	52	26	35	118

Note: These figures are coefficients on the intercept for the 1986 sample in OLS regressions on all four years of data, multiplied by an adjustment factor to bring them up to the weighted aggregate statistics in chap. 2, computed as a percentage of the actual change.

[a] These equations contain one edited observation on amount due. The regressions also allow the effect of the amount of child support due to vary between 1978–81 and 1983–85.

[b] Figures are from separate black regressions ($N = 873$).

[c] Figures are from regressions for all women with race interactions on the child support enforcement and IV-D variables.

[d] Equal to 1985 minus 1978 figures from tables 2.9 and 2.11

[e] These figures are comparable but not identical to those reported in table 5.10 because of the difference in estimation techniques.

plained decline in receipt amounts from 20 to 34 percent of the actual $748 decline. As we will see, the effect of the legal environment generally, shaped largely by the child support enforcement program, was particularly beneficial for black women.

The Legal Environment and Black Women

We noted in previous chapters that black women made substantial above-average gains in child support receipt rates between 1978 and 1985, although—after taking account of demographic shifts and the decline in amount due—their receipt amounts declined a comparable amount to those of other women. In this section, we explore to what extent their gains may be attributed to changes in the legal environment surrounding child support over the period.

We first examine whether child support enforcement techniques had a differential impact by race (see table 6.7).[54] Although ineffective among nonblacks, and as we saw earlier among all mothers, contemporaneous automatic wage withholding laws appear to have significantly increased the receipts from a given award for black mothers. Black mothers received around $330 more if they resided in a state with a wage withholding law than in a state without such a law (col. 5). Expressed differently, blacks in states with wage withholding laws received only around $280 less child support than nonblacks, whereas blacks in states without such laws received around $610 less. We also find, however, a large positive insignificant preexisting relation one period earlier and an even larger significant preexisting relation two periods earlier. Thus, we can not conclude that automatic wage withholding laws helped blacks more but rather that states that had withholding laws by 1983 or 1985 had already been collecting larger amounts of child support among the black population four to five years earlier.

We also find that the perverse effect of expedited processes on the child support receipt rate identified earlier seems to be stronger for the black population, especially in the latter part of the period. Over the entire period 1978–85, nonblack women living in states with expedited processes were only 1.2 percent less likely to receive support than in states without them, whereas black women were 8.2 percent less likely (col. 1). This substantially increases the 4.6 percentage point disadvantage blacks face relative to nonblacks in collecting support in

Table 6.7 Effect of Child Support Enforcement Techniques on Child Support Receipts by Race, 1978–1985

	Receipt Rate among Women Due Support				Receipt Amount among Women Receiving Support			
	Contemporaneous		Preexisting		Contemporaneous		Preexisting	
	1978–1985 (1)	1983–1985 (2)	One period 1978–1983 (3)	Two periods 1978–1981 (4)	1978–1985 (5)	1983–1985 (6)	One period 1978–1983 (7)	Two periods 1978–1981 (8)
Nonblack								
VWA	−.007	−.026	.009	−.021	31	25	12	6
AMW	−.008	.020	−.023	.008	−23	−44	−20	−27
TAX	.007	.003	.012	−.005	26	22	−25	35
LIEN	.037***	.054***	.025*	.004	87*	1	110*	62
CRIM	.017	.017	−.009	.031	150***	103*	39	38
SEC	.0001	−.021	.020	.006	−64	−1	−106	−94
EP	−.012	−.026*	.007	−.008	58	85*	15	82
Black								
BLACK	−.046	−.106	−.064	−.022	−607***	−390*	−802***	−1196***
VWA	.050	−.001	.079*	.054	−172	−169	17	−164
AMW	.021	.073	−.054	−.069	328**	140	285	550**
TAX	.020	.032	.119***	.072	−72	54	72	178
LIEN	.037	.026	−.002	.047	111	43	42	148
CRIM	.023	.066	−.073	−.021	36	33	202	288
SEC	−.050	−.005	−.012	−.060	191*	65	211*	243
EP	−.082*	−.117**	−.056	−.086	123	236	−207	−103

Note: See table 6.2.

*(**; ***) Significant at the 10%, 5%, and 1% levels, respectively. For the bottom panel, indicates the significance of the difference in the effect for blacks relative to nonblacks.

states without expedited processes. In the latter part of the period 1983–85, nonblacks in states with expedited processes were 2.6 percentage points less likely to receive support than in states without them, whereas the loss for blacks was a whopping 11.7 percentage points (col. 2). As for all women in table 6.2, the lower receipt rates in states with expedited processes during 1983–85 were accompanied by higher receipt amounts (col. 6); for blacks, this effect is revealed by comparing the large negative two-period preexisting effect (col. 8) to the positive contemporaneous effect.[55] A possible explanation for these findings is that obligations enforced outside of the courtroom are taken less seriously by absent fathers, especially among blacks.

In light of the strong focus of government spending on the AFDC population, which is disproportionately black, we explore next whether government spending on child support had any differential effect on blacks. Returning to the results in table 6.5, we find that the ratio of collections to expenditures—our proxy for efficiency—is positively related to the receipt rate of nonblack women only (col. 2) and is significantly negatively related to the receipt rate of black women (col. 3).[56] This perverse effect may highlight the problematic nature of this variable as a measure of efficiency. The causality may actually be reversed: where nonblack receipt rates are higher, collections to expenditures will be higher because nonblack fathers can pay more, but where black receipt rates are higher, collections to expenditures will be lower because black fathers are less able to pay. A IV-D agency that wants to increase federal incentive payments may pursue nonblack cases more. Raising the receipt rate among blacks may require greater and greater expenditures (e.g., owing to the need to establish paternity and the father may be harder to find) and result in smaller and smaller collections.

Controlling for the ratio of collections to expenditures, per capita expenditures by the IV-D agency have a significant negative effect on the receipt rate of nonblack women and a positive, albeit insignificant, effect on black women.[57] For nonblack women, an increase in expenditures of $.20 per 100,000 population (about 1 standard deviation from the mean) would decrease their receipt rate around 2 percentage points, while such an increase would raise it around 2.9 percentage points for black women. Although the negative effect of government spending on nonblacks may seem surprising, given the ratio of collections to expenditures, it may reflect a greater degree of noncompliance with child support orders or an inefficient state enforcement agency.

Finally, we return to table 6.6 (cols. 2 and 4) to examine how much of the unexpected changes in the receipts of black mothers between 1978 and 1985 can be explained by changes in the legal environment.[58] We find that whereas socioeconomic factors and the decline in the amount due could only explain 5 percent of the 9.5 percentage point rise in receipt rates between 1978 and 1985, child support enforcement techniques account for around 30 percent, and measures of OCSE performance for another 40 to 50 percent depending upon whether in current or constant dollars. This leaves only 11 to 26 percent of the rise unexpected. Child support enforcement techniques, especially the success of wage withholding, also enlarge considerably the unexplained decline in receipt amounts—from 16 percent when taking account of socioeconomic factors only to 115 percent of the actual change. Thus, despite the observed overall decline, the legal environment surrounding child support enforcement had a strongly favorable impact on the receipt amounts of black women between 1978 and 1985.

As we have shown, the impact of the legal environment surrounding child support enforcement on black mothers' receipts has, on balance, been favorable. The legal environment generally has increased their receipt rates and prevented an even greater decline in their receipt amounts. The one finding that raises some cause for concern is that expedited processes for establishing and enforcing support orders seems to reduce their chances of receiving support.

Guidelines and Paternity Laws

Recognition that the well-being of children can be substantially improved by adequate child support payments has encouraged the recent trend toward the development and implementation of state guidelines for child support award amounts. This trend, as well as the interest in paternity determination, postdate the emphasis on the effective enforcement of existing awards. As a result, our analyses of guidelines and paternity laws are more tentative than that of child support enforcement. Nevertheless, they constitute the first nationwide analytical work relating such laws to child support outcomes.[59] Next, we present more descriptive information concerning the development of guidelines, such as the choice of guideline models, issues related to the measurement of income, and the costs of raising children, including the treatment of second families.

Guidelines are multifaceted laws with a variety of provisions. Although the exact formula varies among the states, guidelines generally specify awards as a percentage of the income of at least one parent, usually the noncustodial father. In this study, however, we are limited to information only about whether or not and how long a state had guidelines. Future work should explore the relation between the various characteristics of guidelines and child support awards.

Although it is anticipated that guidelines will lead to greater equity in awards across families, they might also be expected to increase award amounts. Whether this is so or not depends upon whether the guideline percentage of income is set at or above that of the average award in the state and whether the guidelines are followed. Since, as shown in chapter 2, award amounts are too low by any reasonable standard and, at least at this writing, most states try to set guidelines on the basis of the amount actually needed to support children, we expect guidelines to increase award amounts. We find at least some evidence that they do.

What effect guidelines should have on award rates is less clear. Whether they result in more or fewer awards would probably depend upon how the guideline specifies the treatment of the lowest income noncustodial fathers. If it sets a nominal award for all noncustodial fathers even if below the minimum guideline percentage, that could result in a higher award rate. But if the guidelines applied a percentage of income to all fathers, judges might hesitate to take away the specified percentage of the poorest obligor's income and might instead make no award.[60] For noncustodial fathers at higher income levels, the expectation of a higher award under the guideline might cause them to resist an award more vehemently, but it might also cause custodial mothers to pursue an award more vigorously. Thus, a priori, the effect of guidelines on award rates is ambiguous.

The effect of paternity legislation on award rates of never-married mothers is also difficult to predict because prior to the 1984 Amendments, states showed relatively little interest in this aspect of enforcement. Paternity establishment is a necessary step before an award can be obtained for a never-married mother, but simply establishing paternity does not guarantee an award. Statutes of limitations at young ages are likely to restrict a state's ability to establish paternity, while scientific tests and statutes that facilitate interstate enforcement are likely to improve it. Thus, the former might be expected to decrease award rates and the latter two to increase them.

Evaluating the Effects of Guidelines and Paternity Legislation

We examine the effects of the legal environment surrounding child support awards in a similar manner to examining the legal environment surrounding receipts. In this case, however, it is more difficult to identify the relevant legal environment. For ever-married women, we can characterize the legal environment at the time of their marital disruption, and presumably their award, by relating the year guidelines were enacted to the year of the divorce or separation. For never-married mothers, the best we can do is to determine the legal environment in the year before the survey, since we do not know the year the award was made. The fact that we may not always measure the award environment correctly[61] may be expected to bias our results toward finding no effect, as will the advisory nature of the guidelines. For these reasons, our results must be viewed as a lower-bound estimate of the effects of guidelines and paternity laws.

Effects of Guidelines on Awards

About one in five women eligible for a child support award lived in a state with guidelines either at the time of marital disruption (14%) or, for the never-married, at the time of the survey (36%). Figure 6.2 shows the relevant data for divorced or separated women, and figure 6.3 for the never-married. As may be seen, until 1985, the majority of mothers were not covered by guidelines.[62]

Women in states with guidelines were slightly less likely to have an award, holding constant their socioeconomic characteristics (see table 6.8, col. 1).[63] In addition, the longer the guidelines were in effect, the lower the award rate: each additional year of guidelines lowered the award rate by 0.4 percentage points (col. 2). Thus, the earliest guideline, which was about ten years old at the time of the 1986 survey, would have lowered the new award rate by about 4 percentage points. Separate analyses by demographic group, however, show guidelines reduce award rates more for blacks than for nonblacks but significantly only for the never-married. They lowered the black award rate by 2.1 percentage points and the award rate of never-married mothers by 4.3 percentage points, more than for any other group; and each year in effect they lowered it by 0.7 additional percentage points for both groups.[64] These perverse effects raise some concern and may indicate a disincentive to apply guidelines to the lowest income obligors.

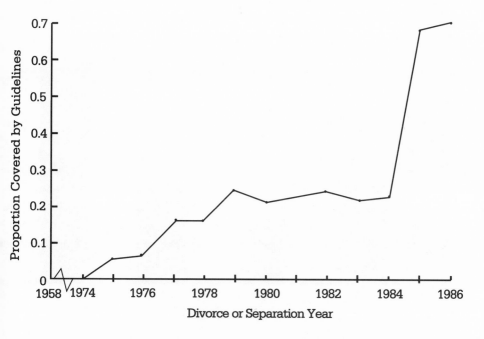

6.2 Proportion of Mothers Covered by Guidelines at Divorce or Separation

It is possible that these findings are a result of a preexisting relation between guidelines and award rates. Guidelines may be causing lower award rates, but states with lower award rates may face less opposition to the development of guidelines. To capture this effect, we relate guidelines that came into effect two years after the divorce or separation year of the ever-married, or the survey year for the never-married to the award rate,[65] controlling for existing guidelines.[66] We find no evidence of a preexisting negative relation between award rates and subsequently enacted guidelines. For blacks, we even find a positive, albeit insignificant relation, between subsequent guidelines and the award rate of 3.5 percentage points, suggesting that the true effect of guidelines is closer to a 6 than to a 2 percentage point reduction in their award rate.

Controlling for both the existence of guidelines and the number of years in effect at the same time, the effect of the former is estimated to be virtually zero, while that of the latter remains negative (results not shown). These results suggest that the older guidelines have had

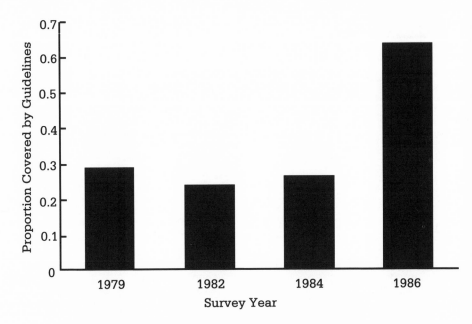

6.3   Proportion of Never-married Mothers Covered by Guidelines at Survey

the more perverse effect on the award rate of these more disadvantaged subgroups. This might be owing either to more never-married
mothers being exposed to the guidelines the longer ago they came into
effect or to the earlier guidelines failing to specifically treat cases in
which awards are less likely to be made, such as low-income obligors.
In the case of the latter, we would expect to find an increase in the
magnitude of the effect across survey years since a guideline established in, say, 1975 remains in effect longer. Although the differences
are not statistically significant, the negative effect of the guidelines'
years in effect becomes larger across surveys for blacks but not for
the never-married. Thus, our evidence seems to suggest that a combination of the cumulative exposure to guidelines for the never-married
and the fact that older guidelines had loopholes that resulted in fewer
awards among blacks caused the negative effect on the award rate.

   Controlling for differences in the socioeconomic characteristics of
women due support, awards were $228 higher in states with guidelines
than in states without them (see table 6.8, col. 3). Although the effect

Table 6.8 Effect of Guidelines on Child Support Awards by Race and Marital Status, 1978–1986

	Award Rate among Women Eligible for Support[a]		Award Amount among Women Due Support[b]	
	Contemporaneous 1979–1986	Preexisting 1979–1984	Contemporaneous 1978–1985	Preexisting 1978–1983
All Women				
Existence	−.012	.016	228*	30
Number of years	−.004*	—	29	—
Race				
Black				
Existence	−.021	.035	202	293
Number of years	−.007*	—	6	—
Nonblack				
Existence	−.007	.015	240*	−5
Number of years	−.002	—	36	—
Marital Status				
Never-married				
Existence	−.043**	.006	−31	124
Number of years	−.007**	—	21	—
Ever-married				
Existence	.005	.007	209*	17
Number of years	.0003	—	30	—

Note: Estimates are from separate OLS regressions by demographic group. Equations also include the socioeconomic variables indicated in chap. 4 and control for year of the survey; and for the ever-married, for real income in the year of marital disruption by race.

* (**) Significant at the 5% and 1% levels, respectively
a In 1979–1986
b In 1978–1985

is slightly smaller for blacks,[67] guidelines appear to raise the award amount due for all demographic subgroups except the never-married. Ever-married mothers' award amounts are $209 higher in states with guidelines.[68] Thus, guidelines appear to work as one would hope for the divorced and separated mother but to operate perversely for the never-married mother. Of course, based upon the contemporaneous relation alone, we cannot conclude that guidelines caused higher awards. It is potentially possible that states with higher awards found less resistance to enacting guidelines; however, we find no evidence of a positive preexisting relation for all women or for any demographic subgroup except blacks. Thus, we conclude that guidelines raised award amounts for ever-married nonblack mothers only.

In addition to reducing award rates of the disadvantaged groups somewhat less (unless the decline shows up with a lag), newer guidelines may increase award amounts of the ever-married somewhat more. Controlling for both the existence of guidelines and the number of years in effect at the same time raises the effect of new guidelines on awards of the ever-married to around $260, which diminishes $16 per year in effect (results not shown).[69]

For ever-married mothers, we can also determine whether the introduction of guidelines subsequent to the year of the divorce or separation results in any modification of the award. Controlling for both guidelines at the time of the divorce or separation and at the time of the survey, the effect of guidelines at divorce increases somewhat to around $270, but guidelines added since have no significant effect on awards (results not shown). These results reinforce the findings reported in chapter 2 and the appendix to chapter 4 (app. C), that a renegotiation of awards did not occur even when new guidelines came into effect that, based on our estimates, might raise awards by around $200.

Effects of Guidelines on Receipts

Guidelines may have unintended as well as intended feedback effects on child support receipts, just as child support enforcement laws may have such effects on awards. On the one hand, if guidelines raise awards so that some absent fathers are legally obligated to pay more than they desire, they may pay a lower proportion of their obligation or, in the extreme, not pay at all. On the other hand, guidelines could improve receipts if they lower award rates in such a way as to raise the average ability to pay of fathers with a support obligation, or if they make a father more willing to pay because he is convinced of the fairness of his obligation.

Controlling for the effects of state government enforcement effort, we find that women in states with guidelines at the time of their award have a somewhat higher receipt rate (3.4 percentage points) (see table 6.9, col. 3). Moreover, the longer the guidelines were in effect— perhaps gaining increased acceptability—the higher the receipt rate (the increase is 0.9 percentage points per year). We also find, however, that women in states with guidelines at the award received on average $122 less support from a given award, or $43 less per year the guidelines were in effect. These results suggest that guidelines may have both positive and negative consequences for child support receipts. Because they increase perceived fairness in setting awards, they may make fathers more likely to pay; however, the positive effect of guidelines on award amounts shown above appears to be partially offset by smaller receipts from a given award. We suggest that to guard against the potential for this unintended negative consequence of guidelines, states need to continue to improve enforcement.

In summary, we find that the typical ever-married nonblack mother benefits from guidelines. Her award amount is increased around $100 more than her amount received is lowered, and her receipt rate is increased by 3.4 percentage points. Black ever-married mothers appear not to gain and never-married mothers to lose. Their award rates are reduced up to 4.3 percentage points, and their payments are no higher than without guidelines.

Effect of Government Spending

To explore the question of whether state government enforcement efforts influence award outcomes, we return to table 6.5 where the effects of government spending measures on the award rate are shown. Since none affects the award amount, it is not shown. The problems of measurement discussed above continue to apply here. Similar to the impact on the receipt rate, more efficient state IV-D agencies increase the award rate. The ratio of collections to expenditures has a positive effect on the award rates of all groups, and the effect is largest for blacks.[70] A $1 increase in collections per dollar of expenditures (around half of 1 standard deviation from the mean of $2.76) raises the child support award rate by 0.9 percentage points for all

Table 6.9 Effect of Guidelines on Child Support Receipts, 1978–1985

Legal Measure	Receipt Rate among Women Due Support				Receipt Amount among Women Receiving Support			
	(1)	(2)	(3)	(4)	(5)	(6)	(7)	(8)
Guidelines								
Existence	.020	—	.034**	—	−107*	—	−122**	—
Number of years	—	.005	—	.009**	—	−39**	—	−43***
Government spending								
Collections relative to expenditures	—	—	.011***	.012***	—	—	−11	−15
Expenditures per 100,000 population	—	—	−.074*	−.071*	—	—	131	109
Proportion of expenditures on AFDC population	—	—	−.087*	−.084	—	—	114	92

Note: Equations also include the socioeconomic variables indicated in tables 5.1 and 5.5, the child support enforcement variables indicated in fig. 6.1, and year of survey.

*(**, ***) Significant at the 10%, 5%, and 1% levels, respectively

mothers (col. 5). The effect is one-third larger for the never-married (col. 8) and nearly twice as large for blacks (col. 7). These results suggest that the more efficient state governments are those that are more able to establish awards for the black and never-married populations.

Combining the effect of government spending on the award and receipt rate yields estimates of the total effect of IV-D agencies on child support payments. For all women and for nonblack women separately, IV-D agencies appear to have increased child support payments by increasing both award and receipt rates. But for blacks and the never-married, the effect of the government has been mixed. The negative effect of the collections ratio on the receipt rate roughly offsets the positive effect on the award rate. The effect, however, is still slightly beneficial because the number of women eligible for support is four times as large for blacks and ten times as large for the never-married as the number due support.

Paternity Determination Legislation and Award Rates of the Never-Married

Next we analyze what effect paternity laws have had on the award rates of never-married mothers. Paternity long-arm statutes, which enable states to reach across state lines to establish paternity, seem to have been the most effective. Never-married mothers have award rates that are 3.5 percentage points higher in states with these laws (see table 6.10, col. 1.).[71] In addition, we find a positive but insignificant preexisting relation one period earlier (col. 3) and no relation two periods earlier (col. 4). Since in some cases there is little change in the number of states with these laws over one period, we give stronger credence to the two-period results. Thus, we conclude that the paternity long-arm statute is the one important tool states have had for more successfully establishing the awards of never-married mothers.[72]

Statutes of limitation that restrict the age of the child until paternity can be established reduce the award rates of never-married mothers. Although the negative contemporaneous effect of statutes of limitation is itself insignificant, a significant positive preexisting relation is also found one period earlier (col. 3). The difference between the two suggests that these laws resulted in award rates that were 6.4 percentage points lower in states with such laws. Statutes of limitations in effect two to three years (col. 2) reduced award rates by 7.5 per-

Table 6.10 Effect of Paternity Determination Legislation on Award Rates of Never-married Mothers, 1979–1986

Statute	Contempo-raneous 1979–1986	Lagged 1982–1986	Preexisting	
			One-period 1979–1984	Two-periods 1979–1982
Paternity long-arm statute	.035**	.034	.024	.005
Interstate determination of paternity under RURESA	.019	.014	.021	−.009
Default judgments	.023	.030	.037*	.044*
Limitations on recoveries	.012	.008	.010	−.022
Scientific tests	−.007	−.002	−.005	.020
Statute of limitations	−.025	−.075**	.042**	.007

Note: Estimates derived by OLS regression on equations that also include the socioeconomic characteristics indicated in table 4.1 and control for year of the survey.

*(**) Significant at the 10% and 5% levels, respectively

centage points in 1982–86. This is a rather large effect relative to the average award rate among never-married mothers of only 16.8 percent over this period. Fortunately, only 5.5 percent of never-married mothers resided in such states. Although their purpose has been to protect a man from having to defend himself against a claim that he had fathered a child long ago, these laws clearly work against the interests of the child, the mother, and the public treasury. This has been recognized in recent federal legislation, which now requires states to allow paternity establishment up to a child's eighteenth birthday.

Unexplained Increase in Award Rates

In table 4.3 and again in the summary table 5.9, we saw that child support award rates rose more than expected on the basis of economic and demographic changes in the population due support between 1979 and 1986. Consistent with the finding that guidelines lower award rates, we find that their unexpected increase cannot be attributed to an increasingly favorable legal environment surrounding awards over this period; if anything, for all women, and also black women separately, the legal environment makes the unexpected increase even larger.[73] For the former, the unexpected increase of 2.4 percentage points, and for the latter 6.8 percentage points after controlling for socioeconomic characteristics increase to 3.5 and 9.5 percentage points, respectively, when guidelines and government spending measures are added to the equation. Among the never-married, the unexpected increase of 8.1 percentage points after controlling for socioeconomic characteristics, which is reduced to 7.2 points when government spending is added and to 6.9 points when the paternity legislation is added, returns to 8.1 points when guidelines are added. These findings suggest that the presence of guidelines outweighed the beneficial effect of IV-D agency spending and paternity determination legislation on the never-married mother's award rate between 1979 and 1986 and actually reduced the award rate among all women, as well as black women separately.

Although these results suggest that the early guidelines were not the panacea that might have been hoped for, nevertheless, since 1988, when states were required to have presumptive guidelines, much attention has been focused on their development. Guidelines have many different features, the most important of which is the percentage of income they require to be paid. We now proceed to a discussion of some of the issues involved in establishing and revising guidelines, which we hope will shed light on why they might perform as they do and provide ideas about how they might be made more effective. In chapter 8, we make some explicit recommendations.

Issues in Setting State Guidelines

In setting guidelines, states must choose the model on which the guideline is based and must decide issues concerning the measurement of income and the actual percentage of income that is awarded for each specified number of children. In this section, we briefly review: (1) the major models currently in use, (2) a variety of issues related to the measurement of income, and (3) the literature on costs of raising children, which forms the basis for determining the appropriate percentage of income in guidelines.

Guideline Models

As of 1990, states employed versions of one of three models[74]— the percentage of income model, the income shares model, and the Delaware-Melson model. These models will be discussed in turn.

PERCENTAGE OF INCOME. Sixteen states employ a variant of the percentage of income model, often associated with the state of Wisconsin. This model requires the noncustodial parent to pay a specified percentage of his or her income to the custodial parent as child support. This percentage increases with the number of children. The percentage may also vary with income level. Nine states use a flat percentage of income; six states, an increasing percentage; and one state, a decreasing percentage.

The primary advantage of this model is its simplicity. But, its simplicity also forms the basis for criticism because the obligor will pay the same dollar amount whether the custodial parent earns no income or an amount equal to that of the obligor. Advocates have countered that the model contains the implicit assumption that the custodial parent contributes his or her share of financial support directly.[75]

INCOME SHARES. Thirty-two states use the income shares model,[76] based upon the assumption that children have a right to share in their parents' incomes in equal proportion to what they would have had if the family had remained intact. The child support obligation is determined by the combined income of the parents and divided between them in proportion to their share of the total. Custodial parents are presumed to spend their share of the monetary total on the children as they provide physical care. The noncustodial parent's share is paid to the custodial parent as child support. The percentage of combined parental income is intended to reflect actual expenditures on children in an intact family (discussed further below). In thirty of the thirty-two states employing income shares, the percentage decreases as income rises, but two states use a flat percentage. This latter version reduces to a percentage of income model but explicitly acknowledges the expected financial contribution of the custodial parent to the children.

In addition to designating that both parents make a monetary contribution, the model is flexible in allowing for the apportionment between the parents of additional basic expenses such as work-related child care, extraordinary medical expenses, and a variety of custody arrangements.[77] A disadvantage to the most common version of this model with a decreasing percentage of income is that it may reduce the incentive for the custodial parent to increase her work effort because the increased income may lower child support payments. Moreover, it can bring about what may seem like perverse changes in the noncustodial parent's contribution. An increase in the noncustodial parent's income could result in a decrease in the amount of child support owed, and a decrease in income could result in an increase in the amount owed.[78] Any version of this model may be criticized for not acknowledging the nonmonetary contribution of the custodial parent in directly caring for the children.

DELAWARE-MELSON. Three states use the child support formula developed by Judge Elwood F. Melson in the state of Delaware. This model is like an income shares model in which a subsistence reserve is taken out for each parent to meet their basic needs and facilitate continued employment. Then they are required to use additional income to meet the basic needs of the child before keeping any additional income themselves. The primary child support amount to be paid is determined based upon the noncustodial parent's share of the total available net income of both parents after their subsistence amounts are subtracted. If the income of the noncustodial parent increases beyond that amount needed for his and his child(ren)'s subsistence, it is to be divided between the households so that children can share in the noncustodial parent's higher standard of living. This portion of the award is known as the Standard of Living Allowance (SOLA).

Of all the three models currently in use, the Melson model involves the most complex calculations. Moreover, it requires information on the amounts necessary for minimum subsistence as well as on the percentage of income allocated to children in intact families, as required by the other models.

Measurement of Income

Aside from the percentage of income, considered below, the most important factor in setting child support awards is the income base upon which awards are calculated. As of 1990, states were about equally divided between using an adjusted gross income base (23) and a net income base (24), with a handful of states using gross income.[79] Although the precise definition varies from state to state, the most commonly allowed deductions to arrive at adjusted gross income are prior support orders and health insurance. To arrive at net income, in addition to the deductions above, common deductions are taxes, mandatory retirement payments, and union dues.

Another issue regarding income is whether to consider the income of the custodial parent. In states employing the percentage of income model, they need not but may specify the income of the custodial parent as a reason for deviation from the guidelines. This may have at least symbolic value and could reduce the noncustodial parent's resistance to paying. Moreover, if the proportion of income spent on children declines as family income rises, then a lower award might be desirable in the case of high custodial parent earnings. But not including custodial parent income acknowledges the nonmonetary contribution of the custodial parent. If the proportion of income spent on children is constant over the income range, then regardless of whether custodial parent income is considered, the resulting award will be the same.[80] We will return to this issue later.

A final set of income-related issues of concern in setting guidelines is how to treat very high or very low incomes. The evidence suggests that judges hesitate to apply the guideline percentages uniformly in such cases.[81] Some states that have chosen to treat high incomes specifically have stipulated a cap on the amount of income to which the guidelines are to be applied, or a declining percentage of income as income rises. In some cases, "the support order may be fulfilled by transfers in a form other than present cash,"[82] possibly including such things as a trust fund for college education or the direct payment of tuition, camp, or fees for special lessons.

It may not be possible for a parent with a very low income to meet both his or her subsistence needs and a child support obligation based upon the same percentage of income as for higher income parents. As of 1990, thirty-five states set an income floor below which the guidelines are not uniformly applied. Usually the floor is a specified dollar amount below which the award is at the discretion of the court or is a lower percentage, often with a minimum award, such as $10 per month. Such nominal awards will at least establish an obligation and a regular pattern of payment. Furthermore, up to $50 per month is passed through to the family and thus will increase its well-being.

Costs of Raising Children

Although all of the issues discussed here are of concern, none is more critical than the percentages of income specified in the guidelines. It is generally believed that these percentages should reflect what parents actually spend on their children at various income levels, information that can be gleaned from the literature. Calling this "costs" is somewhat misleading, for we have data only on how much parents spend on children. Such expenditures increase as the parents' level of living increases because higher income families have different expectations about their children's needs or more money to meet these needs. (We will use the terms *expenditures* and *costs* interchangeably.)

Unfortunately, little or no consensus exists in the literature on what these expenditures are. Many household expenditures are either for shared consumption, such as housing or transportation, or others for which it is difficult if not impossible to measure separate expenditures such as food. What we do know is derived from elaborate and complex studies based upon Consumer Expenditure Survey data.[83] These studies differ in year of the CEX data used and in methodological approach, which results in a wide range of estimates of the percentage of income parents devote to their children. In the remainder of this section, we briefly review three of the methodological approaches, survey the findings of several major studies, and discuss their implications for guidelines. Later, in chapter 8, we offer policy recommendations for guidelines.

METHODOLOGICAL APPROACHES. Two of the three approaches estimate costs indirectly, and one estimates them directly. The indirect approaches, embodied in the Engel and Rothbarth methods, seek to ascertain child costs by finding a means of equating well-being across families of different sizes and in particular across families with and without children and with different numbers of children. The direct approach involves estimating costs for each category of consumption expenditures, without consideration of the level of family well-being.

The Engel method, also known as the "constant food-share" approach, is based upon the notion that families that devote an equal proportion of total consumption expenditures to food are equally well off.[84] To determine the cost of the first child, the proportion of total expenditures going to food is equalized between families with no children and families with one child. The addition to total expenditures needed to keep the larger family spending the same proportion of their budget on food is considered to be the cost of the child. A similar approach is applied to estimating the cost of the second child and so on. An assumption needed to implement this method is that the addition of children will not alter the way a family allocates its expenditures among food and other goods.[85] Some well-known economists such as Angus Deaton and John Muellbauer, however, argue that this approach tends to overestimate the costs of children because a child is a "largely food-consuming individual," and consequently, the family is overcompensated by the attempt to keep the food share down to the same level as in a childless family.[86]

The Rothbarth method is based upon the notion that families that devote an equal proportion of total consumption expenditures to adult goods are equally well-off. Adult goods are usually identified as adult clothing, alcohol, and tobacco—the only ones for which expenditures on adults can readily be separated from those on children. As in the previous method, the proportion of expenditures for the category of adult goods is equalized between childless and one-child families or between one-child and two-child families, and the addition to total expenditures needed to keep the larger family at the same level of well-being as the smaller one is deemed to be the cost of the children. Once again, the assumption that the addition of children will not alter adults' expenditures between the so-called adult goods and other categories is needed. Deaton and Muellbauer show that this method tends to underestimate the costs of children but believe that it is a useful starting point for measuring child costs.[87]

The Family Economics Research Group (FERG) of the U.S. Department of Agriculture (USDA) has been producing direct estimates of the costs of raising children for some time. They use a combination of the per capita approach, which divides an expenditure equally among family members, and the marginal approach, which attempts to determine the added expenditures attributable to children. Where expenditure categories exist that are recognizable as directly attributable to children—such as clothing or child care—or where studies are available that allow an estimation of costs for children specifically—such as health and food—they are used, otherwise the per capita approach is taken, as with housing, transportation, and other miscellaneous goods and services. Unfortunately, the per capita approach tends to overestimate the costs attributable to children, for it ignores economies of scale in consumption—the reduction in per person costs that comes with larger size (e.g., each family member does not need a bathroom or kitchen of its own).

In summary, of the three major approaches in use for estimating costs of children, the Engel and USDA methods are believed to provide an overestimate, and the Rothbarth method, to provide an underestimate. Thus, these approaches can be considered to provide an upper and a lower bound on parental expenditures on children.

ESTIMATES. We surveyed four studies completed during the 1980s, based upon the 1972–73 CEX data. The studies by Thomas Espenshade based on the Engel method and by Edward Lazear and Robert Michael based on a variant of the Rothbarth method have received the most attention.[88] The studies by Boone Turchi and Lawrence Olson are based on other methods.[89] We also surveyed two studies completed in 1990, based upon CEX data from the 1980s. David Betson conducted a study for the Department of Health and Human Services, pursuant to a provision of the Family Support Act of 1988, based upon CEX data from 1980 to the first quarter of 1987; we have used one of his estimates based upon the Engel method (Betson1) and one based on the Rothbarth method (Betson2).[90] Using data from the 1987 CEX, Mark Lino estimated costs of raising children by the USDA method.[91] Whether the percentage of income parents spend on children changes over time or not is unknown; thus, we need to examine studies that use the same methods at different times. The ways these studies present their results are not always comparable as some use socioeconomic status (SES) and some use income levels, but we can make them comparable by expressing expenditures on children as a proportion of total consumption expenditures.[92]

Estimates of child costs as a proportion of total consumption expenditures for middle-income families are presented in table 6.11. Expenditures on two children as a proportion of the total in a two-parent family based upon 1972–73 data equal 27 percent according to Lazear and Michael, 28 percent according to Turchi, 38 percent according to Olson, and 41 percent according to Espenshade. Based upon 1980s data, they equal 49 percent according to the Betson1 estimates, 35 percent according to the Betson2 estimates, and 43 percent according to USDA. As discussed above, estimates based upon the Rothbarth methodology (Lazear and Michael, and Betson2) may underestimate expenditures on children and should be considered the lower bound, whereas estimates based upon the Engel method (Espenshade and Betson1) and per capita methods (USDA) overestimate expenditures on children and should be considered an upper bound. The studies tend to find that expenditures on children vary proportionately with total current consumption expenditures, at least up to some fairly high income level.

According to all studies, expenditures increase as the number of children in the family increases, but not proportionately. Larger per child expenditure reductions are found as the number of children

Table 6.11 Expenditures on Children for Middle Income or SES Two-Parent Families

	Number of Children		
	1	2	3
As percent of total family expenditures			
1972–1973 CEX			
Turchi[a]	NA	28	NA
Espenshade[b]	26	41	51
Olson[c]	22	38	50
Lazear and Michael[d]	16	27	35
1980–1987 CEX			
Betson1[e]	33	49	59
Betson2[f]	25	35	39
1987 CEX			
USDA[g]	26	43	51
As percent of total family income			
Turchi[h]	NA	22	NA
Espenshade[h]	20	32	40
Olson[c]	18	30	40
Lazear and Michael[h]	13	21	28
Betson1[i]	23	34	41
Betson2[i]	18	25	27
USDA[g]	21	34	40

Note: Percentages are based on two-parent, average-expenditure families of average income or socioeconomic status (SES).

[a] Based on an average male child in a two-child family. These estimates do not differentiate by number of children.

[b] Percentages for two children are from Espenshade (1984, table 20), and for one and three children, from Williams (1987, table 7).

[c] Olson's estimates were presented as a percent of total income in a two-child family (1983, 44). To convert to a percent of total consumption, we divided by 0.789 (1989 *Economic Report of the President*, table B-26). To adjust this figure for number of children, we multiplied by (1/1.69) for one child and by (2.24/1.69) for three children (Olson, 3).

[d] Lazear and Michael (1988) report that in an average household (with 2.2 children and 1.93 adults), $38 is spent per child for every $100 spent per adult. Adjusting for a two-child, two-adult family, the child-adult consumption ratio is 0.375. Therefore the percent of expenditures attributable to two children is 0.27 or $(2 \times 37.5) / [(2 \times 37.5) + (2 \text{ adults} \times 100)]$. To adjust for number of children (Lazear and Michael, 86): 1 child = 0.16 or $(37.50 + 1.67) / [(37.50 + 1.67) + (2 \times 100)]$, 3 children = 0.35 or $[(37.50 - 1.67) \times 3] / [\{(37.50 - 1.67) \times 3\} + (2 \times 100)]$.

[e] Based on Betson's Engel (1) estimates that were the most directly comparable to Espenshade's estimates

[f] Based on Betson's Rothbarth (1) estimates that were the most directly comparable to Lazear and Michael's estimates

[g] Estimates were presented for the midpoint of the middle income range, $37,450. Annual child costs were determined by dividing expenditures from birth to age 18 by 18 years (Lino, table A). To convert to a percent of total consumption expenditures, see note (c) above.

[h] Converted to a percent of total income by multiplying figures above by 0.789. See note (c) above.

[i] The conversion was done by multiplying the figures above by 0.7, a smaller multiplier than the one we used for converting the other figures (Bassi and Barnow, 25).

increases from two to three than from one to two. The research evidence suggests that two children cost around 50 percent more than one child, while three children cost roughly 20 percent more than two.[93] Savings with a greater number of children come in part from economies of scale—that is, later children can use the same baby items, can wear hand-me-downs, and share rooms. They are also thought to result in part from parental preferences for maintaining a certain level of spending on themselves. (This notion has implications for the treatment of second families, which we consider below.) Most of the studies find that expenditures on children increase with children's age, but there is little concensus on the precise relation. Expenditures are generally found to be higher for older children, ages twelve to seventeen, than for younger children.

Expenditures also vary by family type. Studies that consider the mother's employment status find that families in which the mother works outside the home devote a higher proportion of expenditures to the children[94]—probably in part a result of work-related child care expenses. This finding is important for setting guidelines because a majority of mothers heading single-parent families with children under eighteen—67 percent as of March 1988—work outside the home[95] and are likely to have expenditure patterns more similar to those of two-parent families with an employed wife than to all two-parent families. The higher proportion of expenditures going to children in single-parent rather than in two-parent families is also thought to reflect in part the fact that single-parent families spend proportionately more on items like child care because they do not have a second parent to provide any of it.[96] Consistent with a narrowing difference in the need for work-related child care,[97] the difference in expenditures also appears to have narrowed over time.[98] But its continuance suggests that child care is not the only source of the higher proportion of spending on children in single-parent families.

IMPLICATIONS FOR ESTABLISHING CHILD SUPPORT GUIDE-LINES. Child costs as a proportion of current consumption expenditures must be converted to a proportion of income for establishing guidelines. Assumptions must be made about the relation between total current consumption and income or, alternatively, about the proportion of income going to taxes and savings. Since these latter two items tend to increase more than proportionately as family income rises, the percentage of income devoted to current consumption expenditures tends to fall. Hence expenditures on children probably tend to decline as a proportion of income, although expenditures on children tend to increase proportionately with total current expenditures. Yet especially in intact families a portion of the savings would also be intended for the children, and this should be taken into consideration in setting guidelines. Data are presented in table 6.11 converting expenditures from a proportion of total consumption to a proportion of total income, by number of children.

Estimates show that for a middle-income family, between 13 percent and 23 percent of income is spent on one child, between 21 percent and 34 percent on two children and between 27 percent and 41 percent on three children. The data are inconclusive as to whether these percentages should be expected to remain constant or decline with increases in income, especially if a share of savings is attributed to children. A recent study concludes that "further research is needed in order to develop definitive tests of how the costs of additional children as a proportion of family income change as family income increases."[99]

The data are strongly suggestive about the way that guideline percentages should increase with increasing numbers of children, although they are not as clear and are probably somewhat faulty in estimating how the percentages should vary with children's ages. Costs are probably higher for twelve- to seventeen-year olds, but the poor measurement of work-related child care costs makes us skeptical that we have an accurate estimate for preschoolers.[100]

Given the high rates of remarriage and out-of-wedlock births, many noncustodial parents will have second or later families. As we saw from studies on costs of raising children, expenditures on children in the same family increase with increases in the number of children but not proportionately. In addition, parents reduce expenditures on first children when second or later children are added to the family. Expenditures increase less than proportionately both because of economies of scale and parental preferences for maintaining a certain level of spending on themselves, such as cars, houses, and travel. Although the benefit of economies of scale does not extend across households, parental preferences for spending on themselves should apply across households. Of course, the noncustodial parent's second family is not the custodial parent's. Although balancing all these competing demands is difficult, one lesson we can learn from these findings is that the noncustodial parent's expenditures on children in prior families should be reduced somewhat by second families. They should not, however, be lowered as much as if the children were all in the same family.

As of 1990, most state guideline percentages fell within the range of the estimates of costs from the studies cited.[101] Yet many of the state percentages fell at or near the lower-bound cost estimates, which, as noted above, are believed to be an underestimate, and some were too low.[102] The implication is that at least some states need to raise their guidelines to enable children to approach a standard of living they had shared in the household with both parents.

Child support enforcement legislation became increasingly widespread during the late 1970s and early 1980s as a result of growing government efforts to get existing awards paid. The laws that were most successful at increasing receipts were liens against real and personal property, criminal penalties, and mandatory wage withholding that had been in effect for a couple of years. Withholding laws also appear to have raised awards. Federal legislation in 1984 and 1988 required all states to adopt liens and mandatory wage withholding laws, among other techniques, but neglected criminal penalties. Based on these findings, we expect the former techniques to raise child support receipts and possibly awards over the next decade, although laws added by mandate may be less effective than ones selected voluntarily. We believe, however, that strict criminal penalties of the type identified by NCSL would constitute a useful addition to the federal arsenal of child support legislation.

Given the emphasis on the largely black AFDC clientele, it is perhaps not surprising that enforcement has been somewhat more successful at increasing receipts among black than among nonblack mothers. Furthermore, increases in child support enforcement legislation and spending by IV-D agencies explain a considerable portion of the gains in the likelihood of receiving support among black mothers between 1978 and 1985. One notable exception is the perverse effect of expedited processes on their receipt rate. Because the child support system is continually evolving, this problem may have been handled already, but—in case not—we believe it would be advisable, at a minimum, to use this feature of state programs cautiously and to seek ways to improve it.

If the 1980s can be characterized as the decade of child support enforcement, then the 1990s might be characterized as the decade of guidelines. Guidelines were only advisory during the late 1970s and early 1980s and did not become widespread until after 1985 when federal law required them; federal law made them presumptive in 1988. At this writing, all states have implemented presumptive guidelines and, following the requirement to review them every four years, are considering their appropriateness. This process can be informed by our findings that at least until 1985, guidelines were a double-edged sword. They raised the amount of the award among nonblack divorced and separated mothers but lowered the award rate among black and, especially, never-married mothers. Furthermore, they raised the likelihood of receiving some support but lowered the amount received from a given award established. To guard against the negative effect on award rates, states need to treat low-income obligors explicitly in their guidelines. The higher receipt rate suggests that some fathers are more accepting of awards made under guidelines, but the lower proportion of the award paid suggests that more fathers may feel that the awards are set too high. These findings, as well as the discussion of guideline models, issues in the measurement of income, and costs of raising children, should be useful in the continuing process of revising and updating state guidelines for child support awards.

The time for widespread success in the area of paternity determination may not yet have arrived. Although there has been some progress and one technique that enabled states to reach across state lines to establish paternity seemed somewhat effective, award rates continue to be low. None of the other paternity determination laws was particularly effective during the late 1970s or early 1980s, and unfortunately, many state statutes of limitations significantly impeded the process of paternity determination and award establishment. The latter problem was eliminated by the 1984 federal legislation requiring states to allow paternity establishment up to the child's eighteenth birthday. The problem of establishing awards across state lines continues to be a difficult one, especially for this segment of the child-support-eligible population. Perhaps the attention being paid to interstate enforcement in the early 1990s will facilitate the states reaching federal goals set in the 1988 legislation for the increased proportion of paternities to be established.

The Economic

Consequences

of Child Support

Payments

> . . . for not an orphan in the wide world can be so deserted as the child who
> is an outcast from a living parent's love.
> —CHARLES DICKENS (*Dombey and Son*)

The economics of child support is not only the study of support; it is also about children. As such, the primary focus of this chapter differs sharply from previous ones. Up to this point we have attempted to explain how socioeconomic factors and the legal environment affect awards and receipts, why support outcomes differ so markedly by race and marital status, and what factors are responsible for observed changes over time in these outcomes. By contrast, in this chapter we take child support payments as a given and focus on the consequences of these payments (or lack thereof) for the economic well-being of the mother and her dependent children. The evidence provided here firmly documents the value of higher payments by showing how they improve the economic well-being of children.

Economic well-being is a multidimensional concept, related but not limited to total family income. Certainly, we want to examine to what extent child support payments augment the income of single mothers and their children and to assess by how much their incomes might rise if child support enforcement could be made more effective and awards increased. We will consider an increase in income to be beneficial not only for its own sake but also because higher income reduces the social and psychological risks associated with being poor and the social stigma that often accompanies the need to rely on public assistance. In addition, the receipt of child support may affect other dimensions of family behavior as well, including a mother's decisions regarding employment and whether or not to marry or remarry, and a child's decisions about his or her own schooling. In turn, these decisions affect not only current but also future well-being. Thus, child support payments have important implications for both the current and the future generation.

We investigate the extent to which child support payments raise the income of recipient families and reduce their likelihood of poverty and welfare dependency. We show that families with child support income are better off financially than those without and, perhaps surprisingly, are almost always better off by considerably more than the amount of child support they receive. Largely, this occurs because mothers who receive child support are more likely to work and to work longer hours than those without support. We also show that child support income has a rather complex impact upon remarriage but that at least for the 50 percent of mothers who have remarried five to six years after their divorce, child support seems not to deter remarriage. In the long-run, child support payments also appear to mitigate a portion of the adverse impact upon a child's education associated with living in a single-parent family.

We also investigate the consequences of several possible child support reforms. We assess how average total family income, poverty rates, and eligibility for and participation in welfare (AFDC) would be affected, first, if all existing child support orders were fully enforced but no new awards were established and, second, if awards were fully enforced and award rates and amounts were substantially increased. We conclude that even full enforcement of all existing support orders would reduce poverty rates and AFDC participation by only a small amount. Significant increases in award rates and amounts would be needed to produce meaningful increases in family income and concomitant reductions in poverty and welfare dependency.

In analyzing the impact of child support payments on family income, poverty rates, and economic behavior, we rely on the same four years of CPS data used in earlier chapters. Sometimes, however, particularly in assessing the behavioral consequences of various possible child support reforms, we use only one or two years of data. We do this when the analysis performed is considered exploratory rather than definitive, or when replicating the findings with each successive survey would be either difficult or simply repetitive.

The first section of this chapter discusses some conceptual issues regarding child support and economic behavior and then empirically examines the impact of child support on total family income and poverty rates. The next section estimates the impact of child support upon a single mother's decision to remarry, to participate in AFDC, and to work outside the home. Based on these analyses, we simulate the impact of selected changes in child support outcomes upon income, poverty rates, and AFDC participation. In the last section, we turn to what is perhaps the most important decision regarding children—their schooling. We look at the impact of child support on educational attainment and compare the schooling effects of child support with that of other income sources.

Child Support and Economic Well-Being

Child support has both direct and indirect effects on the economic well-being of a family. Directly, it is an important component of income. For many single mothers and their children, apart from the mother's earnings, child support is their largest source of income. For single mothers who do not work, child support payments (or alimony, for some) may be their primary form of support. For remarried mothers, although child support represents a smaller portion of total family income, it may still be the single largest component of nonwage income.

Child support, like other nonwage income (including interest, profits, dividends, and welfare benefits), is also expected to affect total family income indirectly through its effects on other economic decisions. For example, in most states, increases in nonwage income reduce potential AFDC benefits dollar for dollar and hence lower a mother's incentive to participate in welfare. Nonwage income also influences her decision to work: many previous studies have concluded that increases in nonwage income deter the mother's efforts to seek work.[1] The presence of nonwage income has been shown to affect a woman's likelihood of marriage or remarriage, and there is recent evidence that it may also influence the amount of schooling obtained by her children.

To the extent that child support is like other nonwage income, we can rely upon existing studies of welfare participation, labor supply, remarriage, and children's education to predict the impact of changes in child support upon economic behavior and family income. For example, because increases in nonwage income have been shown to reduce the effort to seek work and hence earnings, we might expect child support to do the same. However, as we will see, mothers who receive child support tend to work longer hours and have higher earnings than those who do not, and their children's educational attainment is increased more by child support than by other nonwage income. Evidence such as this suggests that while child support income shares certain similarities with other nonwage income, it also may have some distinctive characteristics.

Thus, it is also important to inquire how and why child support might affect economic behavior differently from other nonwage income. There are several factors to consider. First, child support is treated differently for tax purposes and welfare eligibility. Second, because many mothers fail to receive all the support due them, child support may be viewed as a relatively risky or less certain source of support. As we will argue, this uncertainty may have a direct influence on behavior. Third, child support may have a different effect upon behavior than other income because mothers who receive it may be trying to influence the likelihood that the child's father will continue to pay it. Finally, child support may simply appear to have a different effect because mothers who receive it and fathers who pay it might also be different in some other ways from those who do not.

How Child Support Differs from Other Nonwage Income

LEGAL DISTINCTIONS. Unlike other income, child support receipts are not subject to federal income taxes. (By contrast, the receipt of alimony is taxed; on the other hand, alimony payments, unlike child support, can be deducted from the taxable income of the party who pays.)[2] As a result, a dollar of child support income received is worth more than a dollar of other income, and thus we might expect child support income to have a greater influence on the recipient's behavior than an equivalent amount of other nonwage income. This is consistent with evidence about the relative effect of child support and other nonwage income on a child's education but not on the mother's labor supply.

Another legal issue is the treatment of nonwage income in computing welfare eligibility. For most of our period of study, any increase in nonwage income—including child support—would reduce potential AFDC benefits dollar for dollar. In other words, the so-called AFDC tax rate or benefit reduction rate was 100 percent on all sources of nonwage income. But beginning 1 October 1984, child support was treated differently than other income: the first $50 received per month was disregarded in calculating potential AFDC benefits. As a result, we might now expect child support to deter AFDC participation less than an equal amount of other nonwage income because it reduces benefits less.

CHILD SUPPORT AS AN UNCERTAIN INCOME SOURCE. Although few sources of income are completely certain, child support is probably subject to greater risk than other nonwage income. As we have seen, not all mothers due support actually receive it, and even among those who do, receipts average only about 80 percent of award amounts. Overall, about one in four mothers due support receives nothing, and another one in four receives less than the full amount due. In 1985, for example, 28 percent of mothers who received some child support income reported that payments were received only irregularly.

How does a relatively uncertain income source affect economic behavior? This question has been studied extensively in the context of labor supply.[3] It has been shown both theoretically and empirically that if nonwage income is subject to random fluctuations, then, all else being equal, an increase in its dispersion (variance) will increase the hours worked by risk-averse individuals. The intuition behind this result is that "individuals use the labor market as a hedge against uncertainty, [ensuring] themselves against a shortfall in nonwage income by increasing their labor income. The price paid for this insurance is the disutility [of labor]."[4] As a result, expected increases in an uncertain income source such as child support may appear to deter the mother's effort to seek work less than an equivalent increase in a certain income source such as AFDC payments because the former carries with it a greater risk that some or all of the increase will not be received.

CHILD SUPPORT AND STRATEGIC BEHAVIOR. As discussed in chapter 3, child support is often a source of conflict: the father worries that his children's mother may not be spending as much as he would like on them or not spending it the way he would like, and the mother worries that he may not pay the support he owes. Although he is unable to monitor her spending directly, he may adjust his payments on the basis of observable behavior. In turn, she may adapt her behavior in order to influence his payments. For example, to keep him paying the support he owes, she may be more inclined to work or work longer hours so as to demonstrate that she is doing all she can to help support their child.[5] She may also try to keep the children in school longer to please him. In other words, her actions may be part of some strategic behavior designed to increase the likelihood that he will pay the support he owes. As a result, child support may sometimes appear to have a different effect on her behavior than other sources of income over which she has no control.

CHILD SUPPORT AS AN INDICATOR OF OTHER CHARACTERISTICS. Mothers who receive child support and fathers who pay it may differ from those who do not in a number of ways. Some of these ways may be observable and thus readily controlled for, but some may not.[6] As a result, child support may simply appear to affect some types of behavior differently than other income because its presence signals or indicates something else about mothers who receive it and fathers who pay it. For example, mothers with child support are less likely to be on AFDC. This may be in part because of the lower AFDC benefits to which they are entitled, but it may also be because of differences in their attitudes: mothers who receive child support may have a greater sense of self-reliance and hence a greater aversion to accepting public assistance. As another example, we will see that children tend to get more education when their fathers pay child support. This may be in part a result of the direct effect of child support receipts on their mother's income, but it may also be that fathers who pay child support may have greater contact with their children and a stronger desire to see that they remain in school.

Child Support as an Income Source

The most immediate consequence of receiving child support is the increase in income for the mother-only family. We now look at total family income and its components, by mother's current marital status and whether or not she receives child support. We then compare the relative magnitudes of child support payments to other sources of income, and we look at how the real value of each source of income has changed over the period of study, 1978–85. Finally, we explore the relation between the award and receipt of child support and the likelihood of being poor.

Table 7.1 Average Incomes of All Mothers Eligible for Child Support as of April 1979, 1982, 1984, or 1986 by Current Marital Status and whether or not Receiving Child Support (in 1985 dollars)

| Income by Source[a] | All Mothers | Current Marital Status | | Among Single Mothers | |
		Re-married[b]	Single[c]	Receiving support[d]	Not receiving support
Total Family Income	$19,915	$35,770	$13,186	$17,375	$10,837
Total personal income of mothers	10,894	9,835	11,343	15,526	8,997
Earnings	7,946	7,755	8,027	10,536	6,620
AFDC payments	880	149	1,190	594	1,524
Child support	945	922	955	2,657	0
Alimony	132	20	180	401	55
Other	991	989	992	1,338	797
Sample size	15,026	4,477	10,549	3,791	6,758
	(100%)	(29.8%)	(70.2%)	(35.9%)	(64.1%)

[a] Income in the year prior to the survey (i.e., 1978, 1981, 1983, or 1985)

[b] Remarried mothers and mothers widowed after remarriage

[c] Currently separated, divorced, and never-married mothers

[d] Received some child support in 1978, 1981, 1983, or 1985

CHILD SUPPORT AND TOTAL FAMILY INCOME. Marital status obviously has an important impact upon total family income. As shown in table 7.1, among mothers eligible for child support between 1978 and 1985, total family income (measured in 1985 dollars) averaged $35,770 for those who had remarried, compared with just $13,186 for those who were single (i.e., separated, divorced, or never-married). The difference in family income is almost entirely a result of the presence or absence of a spouse. Indeed, excluding the earnings of all other family members, single mothers report higher personal incomes than remarried mothers.

Average child support payments received by remarried and single mothers are nearly the same, but given the much lower average incomes of the latter, they represent a far greater share of family income. As shown in table 7.1, average child support receipts were $955 for single mothers and $922 for remarried mothers. These represent about 7 percent of the total family income for all single mothers but less than 3 percent for all remarried mothers. The largest income source for remarried mothers is their husband's earnings (not shown), while the largest source for single mothers is their own earnings, accounting on average for 61 percent of their family's income. Among all single mothers, income sources in descending order of importance are personal earnings, earnings of other family members, AFDC payments, other nonwage income (interest, rent, profits, and dividends), child support, and finally, alimony.

For the approximately one in three single mothers who receive some payments, child support represents the largest source of financial support apart from their own earnings. In table 7.1, we compare total family income by source for single mothers receiving and not receiving child support. (Given the relative unimportance of child support for remarried mothers, we exclude them from this analysis.) On average, child support payments account for about 15 percent of total family income among all single mothers who receive any payment. Child support income is only about one-fourth as large as the mother's own earnings, but is one and a half times as large as the earnings of other family members, twice as large as other nonwage income, four and a half times as large as AFDC payments, and almost seven times as large as alimony income.

Single mothers who receive child support are better off than those who do not and by considerably more than the amount of child support received. Overall, total family income averaged $17,375 among those receiving support, which is $6,538 (or 60%) more than the average income of $10,837 among those without child support (see table 7.1). It is interesting that given average receipts of $2,657, child support accounts for only 41 percent of the total income differential between the two groups. Excluding child support, single mothers who receive child support still have $3,881 more income from other sources. This differential is largely a result of differences in the mother's earnings: those who receive child support earn an average of $3,916 more than those without any child support income.[7] Alimony and other nonwage income are also somewhat higher among those who receive child support, but these are offset by lower AFDC payments. Mothers with child support receive an average of $930 less AFDC income than mothers without child support.

One of the main empirical questions we pursue in this chapter is precisely how and why certain economic decisions such as work and welfare participation (and the income generated by these behaviors) are affected by child support receipts. Why do mothers with child support income also tend to have higher labor market earnings? Why do they report lower AFDC payments? And is the effect of child support on this behavior similar to or different from that of other sources of nonwage income? Before turning to this analysis, we look first at changes over time in the real value of child support relative to other income sources on which single mothers rely.

TRENDS OVER TIME IN INCOME. As we first saw in chapter 2, the real value of child support payments declined more than 25 percent between 1978 and 1985 (table 2.11). What impact did this decline have upon the economic well-being of mothers and their children? Did mothers who experienced a decline in their child support payments suffer a similar decline in their income overall, or did they offset some of this decline by increases in other sources of support? If so, the decline in child support payments we identified earlier might overstate changes in economic well-being. To investigate these questions, we examine income by source in each of the four survey years. These data—all expressed in 1985 dollars—are reported in table 7.2.

On average, among single mothers receiving child support, the real value of child support payments declined $822 between 1978 and 1985, while the real value of their total family income declined $1,411. Total family income fell by more than child support declined because at least two other sources of income fell as well—alimony and AFDC payments.[8] The mother's own earnings held relatively constant over time, while her other nonwage income increased somewhat.[9] (As shown in the table, mothers who received no child support experienced similar changes in these other income sources.) Thus, we may conclude that between 1978 and 1985, declining child support payments were not offset by increased income from other sources, but rather declines elsewhere reinforced the fall in child support, thereby decreasing the overall financial well-being of single mothers and their children even more.

CHILD SUPPORT AND POVERTY RATES. So far we have compared the incomes of remarried mothers with single mothers and of single mothers receiving child support payments with those not receiving any. We now turn to assess the adequacy of these incomes for meeting the needs of the mother and her children. One standard by which to evaluate adequacy is to compare total family income to poverty standards established by the federal government. In 1985, the official

Table 7.2   Average Incomes of Single Mothers Receiving and not Receiving Child Support in 1978, 1981, 1983, and 1985 by Year (in 1985 dollars)

Income by Type[a]	1978	1981	1983	1985	% Change 1978–1985
Single mothers receiving child support					
Total family income	$18,690	$17,300	$16,522	$17,279	−7.5
Mother's personal income	16,678	15,456	14,820	15,405	−7.6
Earnings	10,791	10,515	10,067	10,832	+0.4
AFDC payments	929	505	466	546	−41.2
Child support	3,197	2,598	2,572	2,375	−25.7
Alimony	541	435	420	241	−55.5
Other	1,221	1,402	1,296	1,411	+15.6
Single mothers not receiving child support					
Total family income	$12,235	$10,106	$10,451	$10,958	−10.4
Mother's personal income	9,939	8,283	8,759	9,281	−6.6
Earnings	7,062	5,990	6,507	7,056	−0.1
AFDC payments	2,062	1,504	1,353	1,329	−35.5
Child support	0	0	0	0	
Alimony	55	45	44	78	+41.8
Other	761	744	854	819	+7.6

[a] Income in the year prior to the survey (i.e., 1978, 1981, 1983, or 1985)

poverty threshold for a single mother was $7,410 if she had one related child under eighteen years, $8,662 if she had two children, and $10,941 if she had three.[10] The poverty rate is defined as the percent of a given population whose income is at or below the poverty threshold. Table 7.3 displays the poverty rates for the total eligible child support population for each of our four survey years. It presents data for all mothers and for remarried and single mothers separately and shows poverty rates by whether or not they have been awarded and are receiving child support.[11]

Overall, about 30 percent of *all* families with mothers eligible for child support are poor. (By comparison, in 1980 just 10% of all families were poor.[12]) Families headed by single mothers are about five times more likely than remarried mothers to have incomes below the poverty

Table 7.3 Percentage of Women with Family Incomes below the Poverty Line by Current Marital Status and Child Support Status, 1978, 1981, 1983, and 1985

Group (%)[a]	1978	1981	1983	1985
All Marital Groups (100)				
Total population (100)	27.8	30.6	33.3	31.8
Without an award (40.4)	42.1	45.3	45.4	48.9
With an award (59.6)	17.9	20.5	24.5	20.9
Receiving support (35.7)	14.3	17.1	18.7	18.3
Remarried mothers (26.7)				
Total population (100)	5.6	8.2	8.8	7.8
Without an award (21.6)	11.1	14.5	12.8	14.1
With an award (78.4)	4.0	6.4	7.4	6.4
Receiving support (40.4)	2.8	5.3	5.1	5.2
Single Mothers (73.3)				
Total population (100)	36.6	38.6	41.3	40.3
Without an award (46.4)	48.0	50.4	50.7	53.8
With an award (53.6)	26.0	27.9	32.7	28.9
Receiving support (34.3)	19.7	22.1	24.3	24.0

Sources: Census Bureau, CPR, series P-23, *Child Support and Alimony*, no. 112 (table 1), no. 140 (table 1), no. 148 (table 1), and no. 154 (table 1).

[a] Percentage of all mothers (or remarried or single mothers), averaged across the four survey years

threshold. Mothers with no child support award are more than twice as likely to be poor as mothers with an award and three times as likely to be poor as mothers who actually receive payments. Among all groups, poverty rates rose during the period from 1978 to 1983. They generally declined thereafter but still remained well above their 1978 levels.

Among *single* mothers eligible for child support, about 40 percent have incomes below the poverty threshold. Half or more of all single mothers without an award are poor, compared with slightly more than one-quarter of those with an award. Poverty rates are less than one in four if the mother actually receives payment. As has been noted, there are two principal reasons why poverty rates are lower for mothers with child support: they have higher incomes from child support directly, and they have higher incomes from others sources as well, most especially the mother's own labor market earnings.

We now look at some of the indirect effects of child support on some important choices mothers make that affect their family's well-being. We first consider the impact of child support on the likelihood of remarriage; next, we examine the effect of child support income on AFDC participation and labor supply; finally, we assess the potential impact of several broad changes in the nation's child support program upon AFDC participation, total family income, and poverty rates.

Child Support and Mother's Behavior

Remarriage

For most divorced mothers, remarriage is the surest way to raise their family's income and reduce their risk of being poor. Total family income for remarried mothers averages about three times that of single mothers (table 7.1), and their poverty rates are about one-fifth as high (table 7.3). Here, we study the impact of child support upon the decision to remarry. Specifically, we ask whether there is any evidence that mothers who have a child support award or who receive payments remarry less quickly than other mothers. If child support deters remarriage, then it is not clear that policies aimed at increasing child support payments will necessarily enhance the long-run economic welfare of the child support population.

A priori, child support might raise or lower a woman's chances of remarrying. Single mothers remarry for many reasons, but certainly financial considerations play some role, as economic analyses of marriage have shown.[13] On the one hand, whether or not a woman searches for a new spouse and the intensity of her search depend positively upon her expected gains from remarriage. These gains are likely to be larger for mothers who are not receiving child support than for those who are. On the other hand, remarriage is also affected by a woman's attractiveness as a mate. Mothers with children tend to have more difficulty remarrying because children are expected to impose a financial burden on the new spouse. Yet this burden is likely to be less for mothers with child support payments, which unlike alimony, do not legally stop with remarriage. Overall, then, it is not possible to predict how child support affects remarriage: all else being equal, child support income reduces a mother's likelihood and intensity of marital search, but it increases her attractiveness as a potential marriage partner. In the end, the effect of child support on remarriage is an empirical matter.

Table 7.4 summarizes the relevant results from an empirical analysis of remarriage among nonblack, ever-divorced mothers eligible for child support. (We excluded blacks because their marriage patterns

Table 7.4 Effect of Child Support on Likelihood of Remarriage among Nonblack, Ever-divorced Mothers by Number of Years since Divorce

Number of Years since Divorce Occurred (N)[a]	Percentage of Sample Currently Remarried[b]	Effect on Remarriage Rate of:		Effect on Remarriage Rate of:	
		Having an award[c]	Award amount (1,000s of 1985 \$)[d]	Receiving support[c]	Amount received (1,000s of 1985 \$)[e]
1 (889)	18.0%	−2.3%	+0.6%	−3.2%	−0.8%
2 (827)	25.3	−7.3	−1.4	−9.6**	−2.0*
3 (774)	34.5	−2.4	+0.2	−5.4	+0.2
4 (809)	43.1	+5.6	−0.7	−9.6*	+0.7
5 (680)	43.5	−1.8	−0.1	−4.6	+0.6
6 (702)	50.7	+0.2	−2.5*	−9.5*	−0.8
7 (582)	55.5	−7.9	−1.5	−12.6**	−0.6
8 (531)	59.1	−13.8*	−5.0**	−9.5*	−5.1**
9 (406)	64.5	+0.1	−3.5*	−14.7**	−1.8
10 (492)	55.5	+2.2	−3.6*	−0.2	−2.8
11 (332)	62.3	+5.7	−3.6*	−14.1*	−2.3
12 (326)	66.9	−19.4*	−7.1**	−16.3**	−1.9

*(**) Statistically significant at the 5% (1%) level

[a] Number of cases

[b] Remarried as of April 1979, 1982, 1984, or 1986

[c] Holding constant the mother's current age, race, ethnicity, education, geographic region, urban location, number and ages of children, and survey year

[d] Also controls for whether or not awarded child support

[e] Also controls for whether or not receiving child support

are quite different from those of nonblacks: on average, they are about half as likely to remarry.)[14] Controlling for the effect of relevant socioeconomic factors (discussed below), we isolated the impact of child support awards and receipts on the likelihood that a mother divorced *n* years ago (where *n* equals 1 to 12) is currently remarried. As shown in the first two columns, only 25 percent of mothers are remarried two years after their divorce. After six years, one in two are remarried, and after twelve years two in three are remarried.

Consistent with previous studies, we find that the likelihood of remarriage is influenced by a mother's ethnicity, age, education, geographic location, and the number and ages of her children.[15] But not all of these socioeconomic characteristics are significant for all divorce durations. One factor that is always significant is the mother's age: older women are much less likely to be remarried any given number of years after divorce. Women living in the Northeast, and with less frequency those in the north central states (regions with relatively more generous welfare benefits) are less likely than women in the West or South to have remarried. Central city residents, and to a lesser degree all urban residents, are also less likely to have remarried. Hispanics are less likely to be remarried within four years of their divorce. An increase in the number of children has a generally negative effect on remarriage, but the effect is insignificant. The presence of older children (ages 6 to 17), however, is associated with a greater likelihood of remarriage, but only within the first six years following a divorce.

In table 7.4, we summarize the ceteris paribus effect of child support awards and receipts on the likelihood of remarriage. Because it is almost certainly the *receipt* rather than the *award* of child support that affects remarriage, we would ideally like to know whether or not and how much child support a mother received before her remarriage. We know whether or not she is remarried as of the date of the survey, but if she is, we do not know precisely when she remarried. Also, we know how much child support she received in the year prior to the survey but not how much support she received before remarriage. If remarriage has no effect on receipts per se, we might simply assume that receipts before remarriage and receipts in the year prior to the survey were identical. But this is not likely to be true: as we saw in tables 5.1 and 5.5, remarried mothers are less likely to receive any child support and receive significantly less than other mothers. An alternative strategy is to substitute information about awards for receipts. Although awards are not a perfect proxy for receipts, at least they are not likely to be affected by current marital status, because an award is established at the time of divorce and thus generally before any remarriage decision.

There is little evidence that simply having a child support award has any systematic effect on remarriage, but there is some evidence that larger than average awards may delay remarriage. As shown in table 7.4, the estimated impact on remarriage of having an award is almost as likely to be positive as negative, shows little consistency in sign, and is seldom significantly different from zero. As shown in the fourth column of the table, during the first five years following divorce, award amounts appear to have no consistent or significant effect upon remarriage. After that, however, award amounts are negatively and significantly associated with remarriage rates. Although precise estimates vary by divorce duration, among those women awarded support, each additional $1,000 awarded reduces the likelihood of remarriage by 3 to 5 percentage points. Given the remarriage rates shown in column 2, this means that a mother who is due $1,000 more support than average is approximately 6 to 10 percent less likely to be remarried.

Turning from awards to receipts, we find that compared with mothers who receive no child support, those who receive some are less likely to be remarried at almost all divorce durations; but variations in the amount of support received (among those with positive receipts) have only a small effect. As shown in column 5, the impact on remarriage of receiving support is consistently negative, almost always significant, and gets stronger as the number of years since divorce lengthens. Correlation, however, need not imply causation. If the receipt of child support deters remarriage rather than the reverse, then we would expect higher amounts received to deter remarriage even more. In column 6, however, we find that although the impact on remarriage of larger receipt amounts is generally negative, it is not statistically significant. Thus, we conclude that the receipt of child support probably has a negligible impact upon remarriage.

To conclude, let us consider how the well-being of single mothers and their children would be served by public policy initiatives designed to raise child support payments. If average payments increase, then current income and hence short-term economic well-being will improve (insofar as increases in child support are not offset by decreases in other sources of income—a possibility we investigate in the next section). If, however, the increase in child support delays a mother's remarriage, then her family's long-term well-being may suffer. Fortunately, our evidence suggests that this is not likely to be the case. For the half of mothers who remarry within the first six years of divorce, child support appears to have almost no adverse impact on remarriage; for the half who do not, larger payments may delay their eventual remarriage, but only by a small amount. As a result, we would judge even the long-run effects of higher child support payments to be beneficial in almost all cases.

Welfare, Work Effort, and Well-being

Remarriage may have the largest impact upon total family income, but it is not the only way a single mother can improve her children's financial well-being. She makes two other interrelated economic decisions: whether or not to seek public assistance, and whether or not and how much to work. We investigate what impact child support payments have on each of these decisions and, more generally, on total family income. For example, if child support is found to raise the mother's work effort, then policies that increase average child support income will help raise her family's income by even more. Yet if child support reduces work effort or welfare participation, then her family's income will rise by less than the increase in child support payments alone.

In what follows we use data from the 1979 and 1982 CPS surveys to assess the effect of child support payments on welfare participation and annual hours worked by divorced and separated mothers.[16] Then, we use these cross-sectional findings to predict how certain changes in child support and welfare laws might be expected to affect AFDC participation, poverty rates, and the total family incomes of single mothers and their children. The changes we consider are: (1) welfare reform that fully disregards child support income in calculating potential AFDC benefits; (2) an increase in the effectiveness of child support enforcement generally that leads to full compliance with all existing awards; (3) full compliance and universal awards set at current average award levels; and (4) full compliance and universal awards set at 150 percent of their current levels.

THE EFFECT OF CHILD SUPPORT ON AFDC PARTICIPATION AND HOURS WORKED. In recent years economists have come to study welfare and work decisions of single women simultaneously.[17] Each decision imposes constraints upon the other. Welfare or public assistance can take many forms, including direct income transfers such as AFDC payments, and payments in-kind, such as food stamps, medicaid, and housing and energy assistance. We limit our welfare analysis to AFDC, by far the largest assistance program available to single mothers. The work decisions we study include both the decision whether or not to work and how many hours to work per year. Together earnings and AFDC benefits account for about 70 percent of total family income of a typical single mother (see table 7.1).

As shown more formally in the appendix to this chapter (app. D), a mother's decisions about whether or not to go on AFDC and how much to work (if at all) are related for at least two reasons: first, her AFDC income depends directly upon the value of her other income, including her earnings; and second, her work effort is affected indirectly by the value of her other income, including AFDC. Potential AFDC benefits vary by state of residence and according to the number of children, and they decline with increases in other income. In almost all states, nonwage income (including child support) reduces AFDC benefits dollar for dollar. A mother's earnings also lower her potential AFDC benefits, but the so-called AFDC tax or benefit reduction rate (which has varied over time and across states) has generally been less than 100 percent. Even so, most mothers who work full time (and even many who work only part time) are ineligible for AFDC because they earn too much. Work effort, in turn, can be shown to depend upon potential wage rates and nonwage income (including AFDC). All else being equal, a higher wage encourages work and higher nonwage income discourages it.

Economic theory predicts that child support—like all other nonwage income—should have a negative effect on both AFDC participation and work effort. Generally, increases in child support lower potential AFDC benefits by an equal amount, thereby reducing a mother's incentive to go on AFDC. All things being equal, higher child support payments can be expected to lower AFDC participation, but the exact magnitude of this association can only be estimated empirically. Like other nonwage income, child support will generally also deter work effort. As we show in appendix D, however, for a mother eligible for AFDC, an increase in child support or other nonwage income sufficient to get her off welfare may actually increase her work effort. She may be induced to work more because her effective wage rate has increased (now that her earnings are no longer "taxed" by a reduction in AFDC benefits). As a result of this ambiguity, not only the magnitude but also the direction of the effect of child support on hours worked remain empirical questions.

To measure the impact of child support on welfare and work behavior, we examined the decisions regarding AFDC participation and annual hours worked of currently divorced and separated mothers. To isolate the impact of child support on these decisions, we had to control for differences across mothers in nonwage income and potential AFDC benefits and for differences in potential hourly wages on and off AFDC.[18] We also needed to control for socioeconomic characteristics that might reflect differences in preferences for work and welfare.[19] Some of the results of this analysis are summarized in table 7.5. Mothers who are black, have more children, live in the Northeast, or reside in a central city are more likely to be on AFDC; mothers who live in the South, reside in an SMSA, or head a subfamily (in the home of their parents or other relative) are less likely to be on AFDC. We also found that annual hours worked are significantly lower for blacks, mothers who have more children—and most especially younger children—mothers who reside in an SMSA, and mothers who are currently separated or head a subfamily. Hours worked are higher for mothers who live in a north central or southern state.

How did child support and other nonwage income affect AFDC participation and annual hours worked? Twenty-eight percent of the sample reported receiving at least some AFDC during 1978 or 1981. All other factors being equal, we found that each additional $1,000 in either child support or other nonwage income (either of which lowers potential AFDC benefits by an equal amount) reduced the likelihood of being on AFDC by about 4.6 percentage points.[20] Sixty percent of the sample worked at least part of the year, and annual hours worked (including those who did not work) averaged 1,264 hours. Holding all else constant, we found that a $1,000 increase in AFDC benefits decreased the mother's work effort by 62 hours per year, a $1,000 increase in other nonwage income decreased the work effort by 69 hours per year, and a $1,000 increase in child support income decreased it by twenty-four hours per year.[21] In other words, all three sources of unearned income reduced hours worked, but the effect of child support was only about one-third the magnitude of the other two.[22] In the next two sections we use these estimates to simulate aggregate AFDC par-

Table 7.5 Effect of Selected Variables on Likelihood of AFDC Participation and on Annual Hours Worked by Divorced or Separated Mothers in 1978 or 1981

	Likelihood of AFDC Participation (%)	Annual Hours Worked (hrs/year)
Socioeconomic Factors		
Race or ethnicity		
Black[a]	10.7**	−97.9**
Hispanic[a]	− 0.4	18.9
Number of children		
Under age 3	2.4	−112.9**
Under age 6	5.9**	− 45.8
Under age 18	5.2**	− 33.7**
Location or region		
Northeast[b]	6.3**	− 31.7
North central[b]	3.3	110.9**
South[b]	− 9.0**	122.2**
SMSA[a]	− 6.0**	−102.3**
Central city[a]	9.3**	50.0
Living arrangements:		
Currently separated[a]	0.2	−223.2**
Subfamily head[a]	−16.5**	−201.1**
Wages and Nonwage Income		
Potential hourly wages[c]	0.1	401.9**
AFDC benefits ($1,000s)[d]	4.6**	− 61.6**
Child support ($1,000s)	− 4.6**	− 23.6**
Other income ($1,000s)	− 4.6**	− 69.0**
Sample Mean	28.3	1,264

Source: Adapted from Graham and Beller, "The Effect of Child Support Payments," tables 2, 3, and app. C.

*(**) Statistically significant at the 5% (1%) level

[a] Relative to not having this characteristic

[b] Relative to living in the West

[c] For AFDC participation, the difference between hourly wages on and off AFDC

[d] For AFDC participation, maximum potential benefits; for annual hours worked, actual benefits received

ticipation rates, poverty rates, and average total family incomes under alternative child support scenarios.

CAN INCREASED CHILD SUPPORT REDUCE THE WELFARE BUR- DEN? Traditionally, lawmakers and child support advocates have em- phasized the investment potential of increased government spending to improve the nation's child support system: if absent parents can be

Table 7.6 Predicted Effects of Changes in Child Support Outcomes on Eligibility for and Participation in AFDC by Single Mothers in 1978 and 1981[a]

Description of Child Support Environment	1978		1981	
	Percent eligible for AFDC	Percent receiving AFDC	Percent eligible for AFDC	Percent receiving AFDC
Currently prevailing award and receipt outcomes[b]				
With 100% AFDC tax on child support income	87	36	85	32
With a 0% AFDC tax on child support income	94	39	92	35
100% receipt rate but current award rate and amounts	83	35	80	30
100% receipt rate, 100% award rate and average awards, set at current levels[c]	65	29	61	24
150% of current levels	44	25	36	19

[a] Single means currently separated, divorced, or never-married.

[b] Currently prevailing refers to 1978 or 1981.

[c] Average award levels were $2,019 in 1978 and $2,386 in 1981.

made to support their own children, taxpayers will reap the dividends in the form of lower welfare expenditures. We examine now the validity of these claims by assessing the likely impact on AFDC participation in 1978 and 1981 of the several changes in welfare and child support laws that lead to improvements in award and receipt outcomes.

Eligibility and Participation Rates

As shown table 7.6, 36 percent of all single mothers with children from an absent father received some AFDC income during 1978; 32 percent received some in 1981. If they do not work, most single mothers are eligible for AFDC; they are ineligible only if their total nonwage income (including child support) exceeds the value of their state's AFDC guarantee. During 1978, 13 percent of all single mothers were ineligible on this basis, and 15 percent were ineligible in 1981. In table 7.6 we also show how eligibility for and participation in AFDC is likely to be affected by several possible child support reforms. First, we consider the consequences of a change in welfare laws that would exempt child support income in calculating eligibility for AFDC. Then we analyze the effects of higher average child support payments themselves, resulting either from the more effective enforcement of existing awards or from higher award rates and amounts.[23]

Until 1984, mothers on AFDC had little economic incentive to obtain a child support award or to ensure that their awards were enforced, since every dollar of child support they received reduced their AFDC payments by an equal amount. To create such an incentive, the Child Support Enforcement Amendments of 1984 ordered states to disregard the first $50 per month of child support paid in calculating potential AFDC benefits. This reform has two distinctly different possible effects on AFDC participation. On the one hand, by disregarding some child support income from the AFDC benefit calculation (or, equivalently, by lowering the AFDC tax rate on child support income), overall eligibility for AFDC increases and participation is likely to rise. On the other hand, by creating an incentive for mothers to cooperate with the state in locating their child's father, obtaining an award, and enforcing payment, the reform may ultimately raise child support payments enough to lower AFDC participation. Thus, on balance, it is not clear whether the disregard program would raise or lower the welfare rolls.

In table 7.6, we show the expected effect of a disregard program on AFDC eligibility and participation under two assumptions that might be expected to raise these rates the most: one, not only the first $50, but all of child support is ignored in calculating potential AFDC benefits; and two, even this complete disregard results in no net increase in child support receipts. What we find is that even under these extreme assumptions, expected AFDC participation does not increase much. Eligibility for AFDC rises from 87 to 94 percent in 1978 and from 85 to 92 percent in 1981, but participation rises only 3 percentage points in each year, from 36 to 39 percent in 1978 and from 32 to 35 percent in 1981.[24] Thus, we conclude that the much smaller $50 per month disregard program (which may also have raised child support payments) probably raised AFDC participation rates little.[25]

To what extent can increased child support collections help reduce AFDC participation? In table 7.6, we show AFDC eligibility and participation rates under the assumption that all current child support contracts are fully enforced (so that all mothers due support receive the full amount owed). As was true in 1978 and 1981, we also assume there is no disregard program, so that any increase in child support receipts reduces potential AFDC benefits by an (almost) equal amount.[26] The evidence presented there is strong that improved enforcement alone—without any increase in award rates or amounts—would have only a small effect: AFDC participation falls from only 36 to 35 percent in 1978 and from 32 to 30 percent in 1981; AFDC participation falls by so little because AFDC benefits decline by only a small amount. On average, maximum *potential* AFDC benefits (benefits paid at zero earnings) fall just 14 percent in 1978 or by $277, while child support receipts rise $280. In 1981, potential benefits fall $333 and child support receipts rise $338. The main reason average child support payments do not increase more is that only about 45 percent of single mothers were due support in either 1978 or 1981. Obviously, even full enforcement of existing awards cannot raise the receipts of mothers who are due nothing.

Substantial reductions in AFDC participation require not just better child support enforcement but also much higher award rates and amounts. The consequences of 100 percent enforcement and 100 percent award rates can be seen in table 7.6. In the next to last row, we assume that every mother has a child support award at least equal to $2,019 in 1978 or $2,386 in 1981, the average for all single mothers who were due support.[27] As a result, AFDC eligibility declines substantially, from 87 to 65 percent in 1978 and from 85 to 61 percent in 1981; AFDC participation declines from 36 to 29 percent in 1978 and from 32 to 24 percent in 1981.[28] What if the average child support award was increased to 150 percent of the current award levels?[29] As shown in the last row of the table, AFDC eligibility and participation rates would decline even more than before. In 1978, eligibility would fall by about one-half, from 87 to 44 percent, and participation would fall by almost one-third, from 36 to 25 percent. Expected changes would be even larger in 1981: eligibility falls from 85 to 36 percent and participation from 32 to 19 percent.

These hypothetical child support award outcomes are meant to provide benchmark projections, but it is important to recognize that such large increases in awards may not be feasible. First, it is unlikely that award rates would ever rise to 100 percent. Some mothers simply do not want an award, and some absent fathers may never be found or compelled to pay.[30] Second, the award amounts considered above are likely to be too high for many low-income fathers. Still, even if awards were 150 percent of current levels, this would represent only about 18 percent of average male income, a percentage consistent with guidelines adopted by many states after 1988 (see chap. 6). Overall, because actual child support payments are unlikely to rise by as much as assumed in table 7.6, the decline in AFDC participation must be expected to be less.

AFDC Expenditures

When child support payments rise and AFDC participation rates fall, government expenditures on AFDC are likely to decline. Expenditures decline both because the number of AFDC recipients falls and because average benefits paid to those who remain on AFDC are reduced. It is difficult to assess the precise magnitudes of these welfare savings because other factors that affect benefits—especially earnings—are also likely to change. In the long run, benefits may also be affected by changes in average family size, living arrangements, and even the propensity to divorce and remarry.[31] Moreover, to determine whether or not child support reforms are a good social investment requires knowledge not only about the potential savings from reduced welfare benefits, but also the additional costs of child support enforcement required to generate such outcomes. It is likely that achieving universal child support awards and full compliance with all support orders would be a difficult and expensive goal. Detailed calculations of these costs and benefits are, however, beyond the scope of the present analysis.

THE IMPACT OF CHILD SUPPORT REFORM ON INCOME AND POVERTY. Besides reducing welfare spending, higher child support payments will also raise the incomes of mothers and their children and reduce their risks of being poor. We now assess the impact of the child support reforms discussed above on poverty rates and on the average total incomes of families headed by a single mother. We look at the direct effects of higher child support payments on total family income, as well as at the indirect effects on hours worked and AFDC, which also affect income. We conclude that achieving significant reductions in poverty rates and increases in income will require not only better child support enforcement, but also significant increases in award rates and amounts.

Table 7.7 records the effect of several possible child support reforms on the income (in 1985 dollars) and poverty rates of single mothers with one to three own children under age eighteen from an

Table 7.7   Actual and Expected Incomes and Poverty Rates of Single Mothers with 1–3 Own Children under Age 18 in 1978 under Alternative Child Support Program Outcomes (in 1985 dollars)

	Average Total Family Income	Average Child Support Income	Percent at or below Poverty Line
Current child support program			
All mothers	$14,011	$1,241	37.5
Without an award	10,664	0	53.2
With an award	16,354	2,109	26.4
Receiving support	17,764	3,008	21.2
Alternative child support program outcomes assuming no changes in hours worked or AFDC participation			
1. Full compliance with current awards	14,514	1,744	35.0
2. Full compliance with 100% award rate and amounts set at			
a. current levels	16,384	3,614	21.7
b. 150% of current levels	17,847	5,077	13.5
Alternative child support program outcomes allowing for changes in hours worked and AFDC participation			
1. Full compliance with current awards	14,282	1,744	—
2. Full compliance with 100% award rate and amounts set at			
a. current levels	15,425	3,614	—
b. 150% of current levels	16,435	5,077	—

absent father in 1978.[32] For reference, it shows average total family income, child support payments, and poverty rates that actually prevailed in 1978 for mothers with an award, for mothers without an award, and for mothers receiving support. Among all mothers, child support payments averaged $1,241 or about 9 percent of their income of $14,011. More than one-third of all mothers had incomes below the poverty line, but those receiving child support had much higher incomes and a lower incidence of poverty than those without an award.

The middle panel of table 7.7 shows expected incomes and poverty rates for several alternative child support outcomes, under the assumption that changes in child support receipts have no feedback effects upon other sources of income. (We relax this assumption below.) If all current child support orders were fully enforced, average child support receipts would rise from $1,241 to $1,744, and the average total family income would rise from $14,011 to $14,514. As a result, the poverty rate would decline from 37.5 to 35 percent.[33]

As is true of welfare participation, significant reductions in poverty rates require not only the improved enforcement of existing awards but higher award rates and amounts as well. If all mothers had awards equal to the average award amount of mothers currently due support and if these awards were fully paid, average child support receipts would rise to $3,614, average total family incomes to $16,384, and the poverty rate would decline to 21.7 percent. Incomes would rise even more, and poverty rates would fall still further if awards were 150 percent of their current levels, or $5,077: average total family income would rise to $17,847—about equal to the average incomes of mothers who received support in 1978—and the poverty rate would decline to just 13.5 percent.

The bottom panel of table 7.7 shows the estimates of expected average total family income allowing for the changes in AFDC payments and earnings that are likely to occur as a result of increases in child support payments. As we discussed earlier, increases in child support reduce eligibility for and participation in AFDC, thus lowering average AFDC payments.[34] In addition, increases in child support are likely to affect annual hours worked, and hence earnings. Overall, the net effect of an increase in child support on earnings is expected to be small because, as shown in appendix D, an increase in child support reduces the hours worked by mothers who are not on AFDC, but it may raise hours worked by mothers who go off AFDC.

Under the assumption that all current child support orders are fully enforced (but no new ones established), the average total family income rises just $271 to $14,282 when child support payments increase by an average of $503 to $1,744. In contrast to the scenario in the middle panel, total income rises by less than the increase in child support receipts because together AFDC payments and earnings decline by $232 when child support receipts increase. We estimate that average AFDC payments decline by $228, from $1,432 to $1,204. This decline occurs because AFDC participation falls 1.4 percentage points from 35.9 to 34.5 percent of all mothers, and average benefits received by those on AFDC decline $498, from $3,989 to $3,491.[35] In addition, we estimate that the increase in child support and the fall in AFDC payments have nearly offsetting effects on hours worked. (Even though AFDC income declines less than child support receipts increase, the impact on hours of the former is stronger than that of the latter.)[36] Among all mothers, average hours worked fall by less than one hour per year, reducing average annual earnings by only about $4.

If all mothers were awarded support and received an amount equal to the average value of current awards, then just as in the middle panel, average child support payments would rise by $2,373 (to $3,614), but in this case total family income would rise by only $1,414 (to $15,425). The increase in child support income reduces average AFDC payments by $937 (to $495) because AFDC participation falls to 29.5 percent and average benefits received by AFDC recipients decline to $1,679. Once again, changes in child support and AFDC have nearly offsetting effects on hours and earnings: total work effort declines by three hours per year, and annual earnings fall just $22. If awards and receipts were raised to 150 percent of current levels, total family income would rise by $2,424 to $16,435. This occurs because, while as before child support receipts increase an average of $3,836, AFDC payments decline $1,382 and earnings fall $30.[37]

To summarize, we have simulated the impact of several alternative child support reforms on income and poverty rates among single mothers and their children. Any reform that raises average child support receipts is likely to raise the total income of the family, although by somewhat less than the increase in child support owing to feedback effects on AFDC participation and hours worked. Our analysis suggests that even minimal gains in family income and reductions in poverty rates will require substantial increases in average child support payments. Moreover, we have shown that such increases in child support cannot be achieved simply by improving the enforcement of existing orders but require much higher award rates and amounts as well.

Child Support and Children's Education

We now switch our attention from the custodial mother to the children themselves. Economists, psychologists, and sociologists agree—albeit from different perspectives—that living arrangements (i.e., family structures) have long-term consequences for the well-being of the children. There is accumulating evidence that children who have spent part of their childhood in a single-parent family are more likely to have a child out of wedlock, be a teenage parent, go on welfare, be poor, experience marital instability, and face difficulties in the labor market.[38] In particular, children from single-parent families are found to acquire less education than children who have spent their entire childhood in two-parent families.[39] This is important because education is known to be a good predictor of many future life-course events, including, especially, poverty and welfare dependency.[40]

We examine some of the educational decisions made by children in the eligible child support population. We compare their educational attainment with that of children who have always lived in a two-parent family. We measure education by the total number of years of school completed for children ages 16 to 20; for children 18 to 20, by whether or not they completed high school; and for high school graduates, by whether or not they entered college. We examine the impact on these educational outcomes of both their mother's current marital status and whether or not the child is now living or has ever lived in a single-parent family headed by a mother only. In addition, for the eligible child support population, we examine the impact of child support income (compared to other income) on educational outcomes. Specifically, we ask whether or not child support mitigates some of the negative impact on education of ever having lived in a mother-only family, and how its effect compares to that of other income.

Related Studies

Although children who have ever lived in mother-only families complete fewer years of schooling than those who have always lived in two-parent families, the precise magnitude of the schooling differential depends upon the population studied, the measures of schooling and living arrangements used, and the extent to which other factors are controlled for. Several studies find evidence of differential effects by gender and race: generally, the negative effect of living in a single-parent family appears to be larger for boys than girls and for blacks than whites.[41] Most studies agree that the length of exposure to single-parent living arrangements matter, but there is less consensus about the impact of the timing of the exposure.[42] In all studies, the estimated negative effect of living in a single-parent family is smaller when differences in family income are taken into account.

We might expect children who are living or who have lived in mother-only families to acquire less education as a result of their relative deprivation of both income and parental time. Children from low-income families tend to obtain less schooling and, as we have seen, single-parent families tend to have lower incomes than two-parent families. Children from mother-only families also tend to receive less attention from both parents than do those from two-parent families. The absence from the household of the father obviously reduces his contact with his children; less obvious, their mother may also spend less time with them. Traditionally, single mothers have been more likely to work than married women, although in recent years these differences in labor force participation have narrowed sharply. In any case, a single mother is less likely to have anyone to share in the household chores, which may strain and constrain the time she spends with her children.

This relative deprivation of income and parental time experienced by children who live in father-absent families is likely to be less if their mother receives child support income. As we have seen (table 7.1), single mothers who receive child support have higher incomes than those who do not, and the income difference between the two groups tends to be even greater than the amount of child support received. In addition, child support payments may also indicate greater parental involvement with the children. As some studies reviewed in chapter 3 suggest, a father who pays child support is more likely to have regular contact with his children. In addition, child support may help the mother afford to buy substitutes for her own time, such as quality child-care services while she works. Child support income may also provide her the means to purchase market goods that she can substitute for home production time, allowing her to spend more of her nonworking time with her children. Thus, we might expect the receipt of child support—through its impact on income and time—to mitigate some of the negative effects on children's education of living in a single-parent, mother-only family. Furthermore, we might expect child support to have a more positive impact than equivalent increases in other income sources because child support likely represents not only income per se but also greater parental involvement.

New Evidence

To test whether child support might reduce some of the negative influence on children's education associated with living in a mother-only family, we created a special mother-child data extract from the

1984 CPS.[43] This extract includes not only the sample of mothers eligible for child support that we have examined up until now, but also mothers from intact first marriages (and a small number of widows).[44] We matched each mother with her eldest child between the ages of 16 and 20. We excluded children under 16 because they are required by state law to be in school and over 20 because they are generally no longer eligible for child support. The resulting sample contains nearly five thousand mother-child pairs, described in greater detail in table 7.8. As shown there, 78 percent of the children in the sample are from intact two-parent families, 22 percent of them have ever lived in a single-parent mother-only family, and 15 percent currently live only with their mother.

As shown in table 7.8, the average number of years of schooling completed by children who have ever lived in a mother-only family is about one-half (0.6) year less than those who never did: 10.7 years compared with 11.3 years. There is no difference in the number of school years completed between children who have ever and those who currently live only with their mother. The proportion of children from all mother-only families who have completed high school is about 35 percent, compared with almost 50 percent from intact two-parent families; 20 percent of the former have entered college, compared with 33 percent of the latter. Of course, some of these differences are clearly related to differences in age distribution: children who have ever lived in mother-only families are slightly younger (by 0.3 years) and less likely to be of college age (33.7 percent of them are 19 or 20 years old, compared with 43.5 percent who have never lived in a mother-only family).

Some of the observed differences in education may also be related to differences in average characteristics by family type—most especially, race, mother's education, and total family income. Children who are black, whose mothers have less education, and who are poor might be expected to get less education. Overall, 11 percent of the sample is black, but 23 percent of children who have ever lived in mother-only families are black, compared with just 8 percent who have always lived in intact two-parent families. Single mothers tend to have somewhat less education. Among those who are currently single, the average educational attainment is 11.7 years compared with 12.1 years for those who have never been single mothers. In addition, single mothers have significantly less income. The average total family income is $16,425 for those mothers who are currently single, $22,717

Table 7.8   Selected Characteristics of Children Age 16–20 by Whether or not Ever Lived in a Mother-only Family, 1984

| | Lived in a Mother-only Family[a] | | |
| | Ever | | |
	All	Now	Never
Number of years of schooling completed	10.7	10.7	11.3
Percentage completed high school			
Total	35.1	35.7	49.6
18 years and older	62.1	60.8	76.2
Percentage entered college			
Total	20.1	21.4	33.0
High school graduates	57.2	60.0	66.6
Child's age (years)	17.8	17.9	18.1
Percentage black	22.6	30.6	8.1
Percentage male	49.3	50.0	52.5
Mother's education (years)	11.9	11.7	12.1
Mother worked in 1983 (%)	75.5	77.5	66.9
Total family income ($)[b]	22,717	16,425	37,278
Mother's earnings ($)[b]	8,458	9,069	6,511
AFDC income ($)[b]	501	699	38
Child support income ($)[b]			
Total	965	1,060	NA
Awarded support	1,445	1,698	NA
Receiving support	2,647	2,869	NA
Sample size	1,072	742	3,902
(%)	(21.6)	(14.9)	(78.4)

Source: Beller and Chung, "The Effect of Child Support Payments," table 1.

[a] *Ever* refers to children whose mother is ever-divorced, currently separated, or never-married; *never* refers to children whose mother is in an intact first marriage or widowed from first marriage; *now* refers to children whose mother is currently divorced or separated, widowed after remarriage, or never-married.

[b] Income received in 1983 (in 1983 dollars)

NA = not applicable

for those who have ever been single mothers, and $37,278 for those who have never been single.

To what extent do these various factors account for the observed differences in educational outcomes by family type? Table 7.9 shows the ceteris paribus effect of having lived in a mother-only family on total years of schooling among children 16 to 20, on the likelihood of having completed high school among children 18 to 20, and on the likelihood of having entered college among high school graduates. By

Table 7.9 Effect of Ever Having Lived in a Mother-Only Family or of Mother's Current Marital Status on Children's Educational Attainment

	Without Income		Controlling for Income	
	(1)	(2)	(3)	(4)
Total years of schooling completed (by children ages 16–20)				
Ever lived in a mother-only family[a]	−0.247***	—	−0.196***	—
Marital status[b]				
Divorced	—	−0.290***	—	−0.219***
Separated	—	−0.474***	—	−0.408***
Never-married	—	−0.373**	—	−0.311*
Remarried	—	−0.060	—	−0.063
Percentage high school graduates (among 18 years and older)				
Ever lived in a mother-only family[a]	−11.9***	—	−9.3***	—
Marital status[b]				
Divorced	—	−12.3***	—	−7.9**
Separated	—	−16.5***	—	−12.5**
Never-married	—	−19.7**	—	−15.7*
Remarried	—	−7.5*	—	−8.7**
Percentage entered college (among high school graduates)				
Ever lived in a mother-only family[a]	−8.7***	—	−6.0**	—
Marital status[b]				
Divorced	—	−6.5*	—	−1.8
Separated	—	−5.5	—	−1.0
Never-married	—	−1.3	—	−8.3
Remarried	—	−13.3***	—	−14.1***

Source: Beller and Chung, "The Effect of Child Support Payments," tables 3, 4, and A-1.

Note: Estimates also control for mother's age at child's birth, her education, employment status, and location; and child's age, gender, ethnicity, race, and number of siblings.

*(**, ***) Statistically significant at the 10%, 5%, and 1% levels

[a] Relative to those who never lived in a mother-only family

[b] Relative to mothers in an intact first marriage

ceteris paribus, we mean that we control for the child's age, sex, race, Spanish ethnicity, number of siblings, geographic region, and urban location. We also control for the mother's age at the birth of the child, her education, and whether or not she worked during the previous year. We present two sets of estimates, one that holds constant total family income (col. 3) and one that does not (col. 1).

The overall differentials in educational outcomes between children who have and have not lived in mother-only families (shown in table 7.8) shrink from 0.6 to about one-fourth of a year once we take account of differences in socioeconomic characteristics, and to one-fifth of a year when we also take account of the much lower incomes of mother-only families. Among eighteen- to twenty-year-olds, those who have spent some time in a mother-only family are 14.5 percentage points less likely to have completed high school overall, 12 points less likely controlling for socioeconomic characteristics, and 9 points controlling additionally for total family income. Among high school graduates, the overall differential in the likelihood of having entered college shrinks from 9.4 to 8.7 percentage points after controlling for socioeconomic characteristics and to 6 percentage points after controlling for family income as well.

Table 7.9 also shows ceteris paribus differences in children's education by the mother's current marital status (cols. 2 and 4). Currently divorced, separated, never-married, and remarried mothers constitute the population of mothers whose children have ever lived in a mother-only family. We compare the educational attainment of their children with that of married women in their first marriage—or equivalently, mothers of children who have never lived in a mother-only family. In general, these results tend to conform to earlier findings on the impact of having lived in a mother-only family. There is, however, one new result: unlike other children who have ever lived in a mother-only family, those whose mothers have remarried have completed almost as many years of school as those from intact two-parent families, and the difference is statistically insignificant. Yet we also find evidence that remarriage may complicate the college entrance decision. Children whose mothers have remarried are the least likely of all marital status groups to have entered college. We have seen that a mother's remarriage improves the economic well-being of her children by raising their total family income. Controlling for this income gain, we now find evidence that with the exception of college entrance, remarriage also helps to eliminate or at least to mitigate the negative effect on children's education associated with having lived in a mother-only family.[45]

To what extent might child support itself mitigate the negative effects of having ever lived in a mother-only family? In table 7.10, we look at the impact on a child's education of having a child support award and of the amount received. All else being equal, children who have lived in a mother-only family and who have no child support award have completed about 0.32 years less schooling than children from intact two-parent families (col. 1). Children who have lived in a mother-only family and who have a child support award have completed just 0.14 years less schooling than children from two-parent families (i.e., 0.178–0.315). Thus, it appears that the award of child support per se offsets more than half of the disadvantage incurred by living in a mother-only family. Controlling not only for the award of child support but also for the amount received (col. 2), we find that children whose mothers receive more support do even better: relative to children whose mothers have an award but receive no support, those whose mothers receive the average amount ($2,647) have completed 0.05 years more schooling.[46] Although this magnitude is small and lacks statistical significance, it represents one-third of the overall 0.14 year schooling disadvantage of children from mother-only families awarded child support relative to children from intact two-parent families.

The impact of child support on the chances of high school completion and of college entrance follows a similar pattern. Among eighteen-to twenty-year-olds who have ever lived in a mother-only family, child support awards offset half of the disadvantage (relative to children from intact two-parent families) in completing high school and 80 percent of the disadvantage in entering college. In addition, children who receive more child support tend to fare even better: each additional $1,000 of child support received raises the likelihood of high school completion by a significant 1.5 percentage points and of college entrance by an insignificant 0.75 percentage points.

In table 7.10, we also compare the impact on education of child support with that of other income. For all three outcome measures, child support income has a stronger positive effect on schooling than does all other total family income (col. 2). For example, each additional $1,000 of child support income is associated with 0.017 more years of schooling, while each additional $1,000 of other total family income is associated with just 0.004 more years. Considering each of the four

Table 7.10 Effect of Child Support and Other Income on Children's Educational Attainment, 1984 (in 1,000s of 1983 dollars)

	(1)	(2)	(3)
Total years of schooling completed (by children ages 16–20)			
Ever lived in a mother-only family	−0.315***	−0.316***	—
Awarded child support	0.178**	0.153**	—
Total family income excluding child support[a]	0.004***	0.004***	—
Child support income[a]	—	0.017	0.020*
Mother's earnings[a]	—	—	0.008***
AFDC benefits received[a]	—	—	−0.096***
Other nonwage income[a]	—	—	0.004
Percentage high school graduates (among 18 years and older)			
Ever lived in a mother-only family	−13.6***	−13.7***	—
Awarded child support	6.8*	4.6	—
Total family income excluding child support[a]	0.24***	0.25***	—
Child support income[a]	—	1.54**	1.62**
Mother's earnings[a]	—	—	0.23**
AFDC benefits received[a]	—	—	−2.86**
Other nonwage income[a]	—	—	0.23***
Percentage entered college (among high school graduates)			
Ever lived in a mother-only family	−13.2***	−13.2***	—
Awarded child support	10.6**	9.5**	—
Total family income excluding child support[a]	0.23***	0.23***	—
Child support income[a]	—	0.75	0.94
Mother's earnings[a]	—	—	0.28**
AFDC benefits received[a]	—	—	−4.41*
Other nonwage income[a]	—	—	0.21***

Source: Beller and Chung, "The Effect of Child Support Payments," tables 6–9.

Note: Estimates also control for mother's age at child's birth, her education, employment status, and location; and child's age, gender, ethnicity, race, and number of siblings. (Estimates in the third column do not control for mother's employment status, whether or not child support was awarded, or total income excluding child support.)

*(** ***) Statistically significant at the 10%, 5%, and 1% levels
[a] Income received in 1983 (in 1983 dollars)

components of total family income (child support, mother's earnings, AFDC, and other nonwage income) separately, child support has the strongest positive effect. For example, the impact of child support on total years of schooling completed is five times as large as that of other nonwage income and more than twice as large as that of mother's earnings. AFDC income actually appears to have a negative impact on education, although this may reflect, in part, unobservable differences between welfare recipients and others. The impact of child support relative to other income sources on the likelihood of high school graduation and college entrance follows a similar pattern.[47]

To summarize, children who have spent at least part of their childhood living in a father-absent family have completed less schooling than average. Although these children differ from those from intact two-parent families in a number of relevant respects—most especially age, race, and family income—at least half of their schooling disadvantage appears to be related directly to the effect of family structure itself. We find, however, that at least half of this disadvantage is eliminated for those children whose mother has a child support award, and among these children, educational outcomes rise with increases in the amount of child support received.

Regarding the policy implications of these findings, there is strong evidence that the award of child support and the payment of larger amounts mitigates the negative effect of living in a mother-only family on a child's educational attainment. Furthermore, this effect cannot be duplicated by income from other sources, especially not welfare. Thus, there is no substitute for an effective child support system when it comes to the future well-being of children as affected by their educational attainment.

We have looked at some of the direct and indirect effects of child support on the income and economic well-being of mothers and their dependent children. Single mothers who receive child support have higher incomes and are less likely to be poor than mothers who receive no support. Furthermore, the income differential between the two exceeds the amount of child support received. This occurs, in part, because mothers with child support tend to be more economically advantaged generally, are more likely to work, and earn considerably more when they do. It also occurs, in part, because child support reduces the likelihood of welfare participation, which in turn tends to increase work effort even more. In addition, child support income per se appears to deter work effort less than equivalent amounts of other nonwage income, although the reasons for this are not entirely clear.

For most single mothers, remarriage is the surest way to increase their family's income. About half of all divorced mothers remarry within the first five to six years after divorce. Within this time span, neither the award nor the receipt of child support appears to affect the chances of remarriage. Yet after the first six years, there is some evidence that the likelihood of remarriage is lower for mothers awarded and receiving higher than average child support payments.

Many single mothers, most especially those without any child support, are poor and turn to the welfare system for support. We have looked at the expected effect on poverty rates and AFDC participation of several potential changes in child support outcomes. Given the incidence and value of awards prevailing in 1978, we conclude that even if all obligations were paid in full, AFDC participation would only decline from 36 to 35 percent and the poverty rate from 37.5 to 35 percent. Significant reductions in AFDC and poverty rates require sizable increases in the proportion of mothers with an award and in the average value of these awards. With universal child support awards and amounts set at about 18 percent of the average male income, AFDC participation would decline by about one-third and poverty rates by almost two-thirds.

For children, one of the most important long-term consequences of living in a mother-only family is the adverse impact on their education. Several recent studies, confirmed by the results from our own analysis, suggest that children who have spent part of their childhood outside an intact two-parent family tend to acquire less schooling. We have shown, however, that children living in mother-only families who receive child support from their absent father tend to go further in school than those who do not. Child support offsets at least half of the disadvantage of living in a mother-only family, and it raises education much more than equivalent increases in income from other sources.

This chapter has only begun to explore some of the many important consequences of child support for mothers and children. Even still, our limited findings suggest at least two important conclusions. First, the beneficial effects of greater child support payments are likely to be more widespread than has generally been recognized. Not only does an increase in child support appear to help to reduce poverty and welfare dependency in the short run, it also tends to improve a child's educational outcomes in the long run. Moreover, these gains are not likely to be offset by any significant reduction in the likelihood of a mother's employment or eventual remarriage. The second important conclusion of this chapter is that many of the beneficial effects of child support are likely to remain rather modest unless average child support payments can be increased. We find that increasing child support will require not only a better enforcement of existing awards, but also an increase in the incidence and value of these awards.

A Policy Agenda

for Child Support

in the 1990s

Child support deserves the attention it may finally be starting to receive.[1] Pursuant to the Child Support Enforcement Amendments of 1984 and the Family Support Act of 1988, mechanisms are now in place to address the persistent widespread lack of awards, the low value of awards, and the extensive problem of nonpayment. As we have seen, progress throughout the 1980s in increasing the incidence of awards or the receipt of payments was limited, and the *real* value of awards and receipts fell because dollars awarded failed to keep up with rising prices. Whether more progress will be made during the 1990s depends in part upon how successful the new mechanisms turn out to be. At this writing, laws have been more successful in increasing receipts among women who have awards than at increasing awards, leading us to call for greater attention to establishing awards and making them adequate.

Particularly disadvantaged in the child support process are the mothers who can least afford it. Never-married and black mothers do worse than divorced or separated nonblack mothers at nearly every step. Fortunately, never-married and black mothers have also made somewhat more progress than other mothers in both awards and receipts, but only in their receipts can that progress be attributed to the legal environment. We believe that in the long run, a comprehensive approach to the child support problems of these groups is needed.

Unfortunately, the consequences for children of nonpayment of child support extend into adulthood. As we have seen, on average, single-parent families have lower incomes and are more likely to live in poverty and rely on welfare. The children in these families get less education, beyond that owing to their lower incomes. Child support helps to mitigate this negative effect and appears to do so more than income from other sources. For the benefit of the next generation, it is crucial that we find ways to get absent fathers to provide adequate support for their children.

A Policy Agenda

The following policy agenda for child support is intended to address these problems. It is not meant to be comprehensive but rather is limited primarily to recommendations that flow from our research. Also, while recognizing that a full analysis of policy requires consideration of the dollar costs of administering any resulting program as well as the expected benefits, we restrict our attention to the latter in keeping with the focus of this book.[2] We do, however, consider both advantages and disadvantages of policies we recommend.

The first three recommendations concern child support guidelines and awards to address the problems with the value of awards and award rates; the fourth recommendation deals with child support enforcement. The final three recommendations address racial and marital status differentials in awards and receipts and the consequences of payments for children. In each case we begin with a general recommendation, followed by an explanation of its rationale. Where applicable, we then make more specific recommendations and suggest the additional research that is most needed.

1. Continue to work on the development and full implementation of mandatory guidelines for child support awards.

We fully support the use of *presumptive* guidelines—those that must be followed unless there is a written finding against their application in a specific case—in order to treat the inadequacy and declining real value of *new* awards. We have seen that the failure of new awards to keep up with prices was the main reason why the amount of support due failed to keep up, which in turn was the primary cause of the decline in the real value of child support receipts over time. We have also seen that over the period 1978–85 awards were around $200 higher in 1985 dollars, or roughly 8 percent higher, in states with guidelines than in states without them, all things being equal. Substantial reductions in poverty and welfare dependency cannot be achieved without increases in award amounts to levels adequate for meeting the true costs of raising children.

But we also saw that these guidelines may have had unintended negative feedback effects on awards and receipts. They may have reduced the award rates of never-married and black mothers and the amount received from a given award made under guidelines for divorced or separated mothers. This latter effect may have occurred because as guidelines increase the amount of awards, the resistance of absent fathers is likely to increase. Based upon the functioning of existing guidelines and the costs of raising children, we make the following more specific recommendations.[3]

a. Incorporate in the guidelines the percentages of income that are based upon the latest reasonable estimates of the costs of raising children. At this writing, we would recommend a flat 18 percent of gross income for one child, 27 percent for two children, 32 percent for three children, and 36 percent for four children.

The most critical feature in setting adequate awards is the specification of these percentages.[4] The literature shows a wide range of estimates for the costs of children. For a middle-income family, they vary from 13 to 23 percent of gross income for one child, from 21 to 34 percent for two children, and from 27 to 41 percent for three children. Although we recommend a flat percentage of income, we allow an exception for the lowest-income obligors (see below). In 1990, the guidelines of most states fell within the range of these estimates, but some fell below and many were right at the lower bound, derived by the so-called Rothbarth method.[5] Our recommended percentages (discussed in chap. 6) are the same as the most recent Rothbarth estimates for one child but are slightly higher for two and three children.

b. Make explicit in the guidelines a provision for the treatment of low-income obligors by requiring at least a nominal award in all cases.

This recommendation is designed to address the possible negative feedback effect of guidelines on award rates of black and never-married mothers. Rather than applying a strict percentage of income to low-income obligors who may not be able to afford to pay, it appears that many judges elect to make no award instead. We believe it would be better to set a nominal award in such cases so that the absent father is brought into the system and can establish a pattern of regular payment. At such time as his income rises, his obligation can be adjusted upward.

c. Implement a uniform national system of guidelines in place of the present state-by-state system.

As with other aspects of child support enforcement, each state currently sets its own guidelines. Developing a uniform national system would mean that only one set of guidelines would need to be developed rather than fifty-one. The time and money saved could then be used to update child cost estimates every two to three years. Furthermore, no data are available for estimating the costs of raising children in individual states, only for the nation as a whole. Regional differences in prices tend to be reflected in incomes. Thus, a national system would reflect the reality of what we know about child costs just as well.

A national system of guidelines might even help to reduce the problems of interstate enforcement and facilitate the automatic updating of awards. First, every state would know precisely how much needs to be collected. Second, a widely accepted standard may make individuals more likely to pay and reduce their incentive to flee across state lines to get a better deal. Finally, a national guideline that defines gross income the same way across the country would reduce the administrative burden that is the main argument against specifying awards as a percentage of income for automatic updating as recommended below.

2. Fully implement the provision in the 1988 Family Support Act for the periodic review of existing awards established under the IV-D program and extend periodic review to all awards at the request of either party involved in the agreement.

The implementation of the periodic review of *existing* child support orders directly addresses the problem of the declining value of *old* awards. We have seen that in the past the renegotiation of awards did not occur even after a state had adopted new guidelines that could potentially have raised the average award by $200 per year in 1985 dollars. Although this amount may appear small in the face of the costs of renegotiating an award, it may not be when its present value over the course of the child's life is considered. The expense of renegotiation, however, may have kept mothers from pursuing this avenue. The Family Support Act of 1988 mandated the periodic review and updating of Title IV-D (publicly enforced) child support orders every three years and required the secretary of Health and Human Services to carry out a study on the feasibility of updating all old orders under new guidelines. We recommend that the updating of old non-IV-D orders be done only at the request of either party involved in order to limit the administrative burden. Below we recommend that *future* orders incorporate a provision for automatic updating, which would supplant the need for the periodic review and renegotiation of individual awards.

a. Move toward a policy of automatic updating of awards.

Automatic updating of awards would substantially reduce the added workload and eliminate the lag in adjustment created by periodic review once every three years. Automatic updating could be accomplished either by tying awards to the Consumer Price Index, to an index of real income, or by denominating initial awards as a percentage of the income of the obligor. The third alternative would be preferable in our opinion. First, although the costs of raising children will rise with the CPI, the noncustodial parent's income may not rise at the same rate. Thus, child support could become an increasing or decreasing burden. An index of real incomes would better reflect the average father's ability to pay but clearly not that of each particular father. Specifying awards as a percentage of income would reflect the circumstances of the individual father. If he were still living with his children, they would suffer the same loss of income as he does or benefit from the same increase. Therefore it seems appropriate that they still share in his good or bad fortune.[6]

Arguments against this approach center on the administrative burden that would be created. In IV-D cases, it would be difficult for the agency to know whether the correct amount was being paid. In interstate cases, since there would be no specified dollar amount and because every state defines income differently, it would be difficult to collect. But immediate income withholding, which will be part of all new orders beginning in 1994, should facilitate the updating of awards specified on a percentage basis, just like income tax withholding helps to deter tax avoidance. A national child support guideline, as recommended above, would address the problem of enforcing across state lines orders written as a percentage of income.

3. Place higher priority on increasing awards to never-married mothers.

Never-married mothers constitute the fastest growing segment of the child-support-eligible population. The frequent lack of awards and their low value places this group at a major disadvantage relative to ever-divorced or separated mothers. Unwed mothers face the particular problem of establishing paternity. As we have shown, their lower award rates cannot be explained solely on the basis of their socioeconomic disadvantages, and the legal system has had no discernible beneficial effect. In fact, guidelines (as recalled above) and statutes of limitations on paternity establishment (as discussed below) have had some negative effects. At a minimum, these perverse effects should be eliminated. It may not be easy, however, to find ways to improve the situation, for many of these mothers have indicated they do not even want an award.

a. Require all states to adopt paternity long-arm statutes.

b. Require states to disseminate information that paternity can now legally be established for any child up to age eighteen.

c. Require states to obtain the Social Security numbers of both parents at the child's birth.

Based upon evidence from 1978 to 1985, paternity long-arm statutes, appear to have been the single most effective technique that states had at their disposal for establishing paternity. But statutes of limitations operated perversely, reducing the incidence of awards among the never-married, probably because many restricted paternity establishment to fairly young ages. By 1984, when the Child Support Enforcement Amendments required all states to permit paternity establishment up to the child's eighteenth birthday, many more restrictive statutes had already been declared unconstitutional. To assure maximum impact, it is important to make certain that the relevant population and the legal community become aware of this change in the law. Obtaining both parents' Social Security numbers at the child's birth is required by the Family Support Act of 1988 and should help later in locating parents. Seeking to establish paternity early on, when the father often is proud and the parents generally still have a relationship, is a strategy some states have tried.[7]

d. Raise the amount of child support disregarded in determining welfare benefits to one-half the poverty level for the first child, which equaled $81 per month in 1990.[8]

Never-married mothers eligible for welfare face a particular disincentive to establish paternity and secure a child support award because at present only the first $50 per month is passed through to the family (i.e., disregarded), while the rest goes to reimburse the state for AFDC payments. Thus, the economic well-being of the mothers and children is enhanced by only a small amount. Moreover, the value of this pass-through (like welfare benefits generally) has declined in real terms since it was introduced in 1984. We have shown that increasing the disregard would not raise welfare participation rates very much, largely because most mothers who work would still be ineligible. The disregard should be specified, not in nominal terms, but in terms of a value that changes over time to reflect changes in the costs of raising a child at a poverty level of living. Tying the disregard to the first child avoids building in an incentive for having more children but acknowledges that the existing child should be supported at a minimum adequate level. Besides increasing the value of the disregard, the federal government should permit it to be applied in other welfare programs such as Food Stamps and Medicaid as well.

Further Research

Many unanswered questions remain about guidelines. We were only able to look at the effect of *advisory* guidelines through 1985. One fruitful avenue for research is an evaluation of the effects of the new *presumptive* guidelines: do they, like advisory guidelines, increase award amounts but lower award rates and receipt amounts? Another is the evaluation of the effectiveness of various guideline models, the percentages absent parents are required to pay, and the treatment of key factors by the states in raising awards. As suggested above, examining the possible source of the unintended negative feedback effects of guidelines on award rates of the low-income groups would also be desirable. Another need is to study how to design and implement a uniform national system of guidelines. Furthermore, guidelines embody many normative judgments, such as whether or not a mother of young children should be expected to work outside the home.

Research should determine the values inherent in the various guideline models and evaluate their effect on the well-being of children.

Since the percentage of income to be paid is the most important feature of guidelines in calculating support and there are many unanswered questions about costs of raising children, further research in this area is needed to address the following questions: (1) Are the methodologies most widely used to estimate these costs reliable, or should other approaches be pursued? (2) Do we need continually to update the estimates of costs of raising children, or do the percentages of income devoted to children remain relatively constant over time? (3) How well do these estimates, which are largely based upon the expenditure patterns of two-parent families, fit the needs of single-parent families? (4) To what extent are these estimates realistic in taking account of the direct expenses noncustodial parents incur for visitation and nontraditional custody arrangements? (5) How well do these estimates accommodate the needs of second families, that is, subsequent children of the obligor?

4. Continue the vigorous enforcement of effective child support techniques—liens against property; automatic wage withholding; a security, bond, or other guarantee; and criminal penalties.

Certain child support enforcement techniques have been successful at increasing receipt rates, preventing receipt amounts from declining more than they have, and possibly even increasing award amounts. Those techniques have had beneficial effects at least through 1985 and should continue to be vigorously enforced. Further, specific recommendations are made for income withholding, criminal penalties, and expedited processes.

a. Have the federal government monitor state implementation of income withholding and, if possible, provide incentives for and guidance on its implementation. State governments should recognize that the mere existence of withholding laws may be insufficient and actively promote their use and acceptance.

b. Fully implement immediate income withholding in all child support orders initially issued in a state by 1994 and consider extending it to all orders issued or modified in a state.

For the most part, automatic wage withholding laws have become effective only with a lag. The first specific recommendation is designed to speed their operation. Since 1988, automatic wage withholding after an arrearage has been superseded by immediate wage withholding in all IV-D cases. By 1994, the latter will be required for all orders initially issued in a state; in addition, a study of the feasibility of making it mandatory in all cases should have been conducted.

c. Add criminal penalties (of the type identified as exemplary by the National Conference of State Legislatures) for nonsupport to the federally mandated arsenal of enforcement weapons.

During the period 1978–85, criminal penalties appeared to be the single most effective technique states had to increase the amount of child support received. Despite their apparent success, such provisions were not among the techniques required of the states by the federal government in 1984. Although all states had statutes making nonsupport of one's dependents a crime, only a limited number had criminal nonsupport statutes with all of the features considered important by NCSL.[9] Criminal penalties can act as more of a deterrent to noncompliance than the techniques that were required. This deficiency in federal law has recently been remedied with respect to interstate cases. As of October 1992, bill S1002, which makes nonpayment of child support across state lines a federal crime, had been signed into law. In recommending criminal penalties, we would restrict jailing to weekends so that it does not interfere with the noncustodial parent's ability to hold a job and pay child support.

d. Exercise caution in the use of expedited processes until further research can establish under what circumstances this technique lowers receipt rates.

Expedited processes for establishing and enforcing awards, such as administrative or quasi-judicial procedures, are designed to speed the child support collection process by eliminating the need to go to court before a judge. Such processes seem to have reduced receipt rates, especially in the black population, although they have increased receipt amounts among those who receive some. Taken in combination, these two effects suggest that expedited processes may be permitting those who are less able to pay to get away without paying at all. It is possible that men do not take awards made outside court as seriously as court-ordered awards.

e. Encourage innovative approaches to child support enforcement, especially for the self-employed and chronically unemployed.

Various states have found new strategies to assure payment. In 1991, the state of Illinois passed a law requiring all individuals who apply for a professional license in the state to sign a statement that they are not in arrears on child support payments.[10] The state of Washington has instituted a statewide program to be used against child support debtors who cannot be reached through wage withholding. Through a combination of warning letters, liens, and ultimately the seizure and sale of property (such as automobiles, boats, and other vehicles), the state IV-D office has collected a substantial amount of back support.[11] Several states now require fathers to join job-search programs.[12] More such innovative methods need to be developed and implemented widely in order for enforcement to become more effective.

Further Research

Continuing research into the effectiveness of existing child support enforcement mechanisms and a search for innovative ways to handle unsolved problems are desirable. We have analyzed the effectiveness of enforcement through 1985, but as more recent data become available, it will be useful to examine the impact of legal changes made since then. As suggested above, research into the reason for the perverse effects of expedited processes would be useful. Research should also be conducted on three problems in the matter of child support enforcement that continue to plague government officials: how to tap the resources of fathers with child support obligations who are beyond the reach of traditional mechanisms because they are either self-employed, frequent job changers, or working in the underground economy; how to handle fathers who have few resources because they are unemployed or low-skilled; and how to establish and effectively enforce orders across state lines. Although progress has been made in the latter area, since interstate enforcement is at least required, it is still more difficult than enforcement within a single state. A recent government report documents a lower receipt rate among women in interstate cases.[13]

5. Address the child support problems facing never-married and black mothers in a broader framework.

As we have shown, even if mothers received all the child support they were due, poverty rates would not decline substantially because award rates and amounts are much too low. For many poor and never-married and poor and black mothers, awards are low or nonexistent because their children's fathers are also poor. In the long-run, the economic problems faced by these families need to be addressed in a broader framework that includes the high incidences of both out-of-wedlock births and minority poverty.

a. Seek to reduce out-of-wedlock births, especially among teenagers.

This would reduce the number of children born who need but are unlikely to receive child support. In addition to disseminating better information about birth control, one strategy is to conduct an educational campaign, both in the schools and through other means, about the financial and parenting responsibilities incurred by having children. If teenagers recognized that having children results in an eighteen-year financial obligation for their rearing, it might serve as a deterrent to the teens becoming parents too soon.

b. Improve policies designed to narrow income differences by race and gender.

Reducing the racial differential in earnings among men will help reduce differentials in child support outcomes because, as we have shown, part of the reason for the lower awards of black and never-married mothers is the low income of black and young unmarried men. Furthermore, reducing the gender gap in earnings will help to raise the economic well-being of children in mother-only families because the largest single source of income for these families is the mother's own earnings. One strategy would be to enforce more vigorously equal employment opportunity and affirmative action laws. Another would be to provide training for the mother at public expense and yet another to improve opportunities for investing in the human capital of children from poor families.

c. Continue to provide public support for the lowest income families.

There are some men who cannot afford to pay child support adequate to meet children's needs, even at a poverty-level income. As we showed in tables 7.6 and 7.7, welfare will continue to be an important source of income for the lowest income families.[14]

An alternative program under consideration at this writing is known as an assured benefit, also sometimes called child support assurance or insurance. An assured benefit experiment was designed for the state of Wisconsin but has not been implemented at this writing.[15] Under this program, each child with an absent parent is assured a minimum level of support. To the extent possible, this payment comes from the absent parent, but any deficit is made up by the state. This program assures that children will be supported at least at a minimum adequate level. Such a program has certain advantages over welfare, such as the absence of a disincentive for the mother to work because, in contrast to the welfare benefit, the child support payment would not be reduced by increases in the mother's earnings. The final report of the National Commission on Children released in 1991 stopped short of recommending immediate implementation of such a program but instead recommended that the federal government undertake a large demonstration of "an insured child support plan" and, if proved effective, adopt an "insured child support benefit in every state."[16]

Further Research

Further examination of the sources of differentials in child support outcomes between demographic groups is needed. Large portions of the differentials remained unexplained after taking account of racial or marital status differentials in socioeconomic characteristics, income, and legal factors. This suggests that even the narrowing of income differentials by race may not fully eliminate these differentials in child support outcomes. One possible explanation for the marital status differential in award amounts is that many judges routinely have ordered lower awards for children born outside a marriage. Since the Family Support Act required mandatory guidelines, the Office of Child Support Enforcement has made it clear that this practice violates federal law. Research should be conducted on whether the law reduces the marital status differential. In addition, interdisciplinary research would be most useful in exploring the differences in culture and attitudes that may explain differences in child support outcomes. For instance, the question of why many never-married mothers do not seek a child support award needs to be examined. Knowing whether the reluctance is due, for instance, to an ethic of self-reliance or a desire to have no further contact with the child's father would be useful information in setting child support policy.

6. Develop and implement policies that facilitate greater investments in the education of children in single-parent families.

Nonpayment of child support has negative consequences for children, who suffer from lower incomes and a greater incidence of poverty and dependence on welfare. Children from low-income families are more likely to be poor as adults. For these reasons, many of the above recommendations should help both in the short-run and the long-run, but additional policies are still needed.

Children from single-parent families generally achieve less education. Evidence suggests that they are more likely to fall behind grade for their age, drop out of high school, be less likely to graduate high school, and be less likely to enter college. This problem may be able to be addressed publicly by government programs but can also be addressed privately. As we have shown, the payment of child support mitigates this negative effect; thus, we offer the following specific suggestions to strengthen this relationship.

a. Develop policies that encourage increased contact with the noncustodial parent.

More frequent contact with the noncustodial parent is associated with better outcomes generally for children. Fathers who see their children frequently are more likely to pay support. This in turn is associated with the higher educational attainment of children. The final report of the National Commission on Children concludes, "because parents' personal involvement, in addition to their material support, is important for children's development, enhanced child support enforcement may prove to be an effective strategy for holding absent parents accountable in more than just the financial sense."[17] Of course, the law cannot mandate the attitudes of the father: forcing a relationship may make him more antagonistic. Moreover, in some cases there is good cause, such as domestic violence, not to pursue an award. Research is needed to determine what policies encourage contact between noncustodial parents and their children and why child support income increases children's educational attainment considerably more than other sources of income.

b. Extend child support beyond age eighteen for students enrolled full time in high school.

Children in low-income, single-parent families are more likely to fall behind grade for their age. Child support should not be terminated at age eighteen if children are still in high school, because education is the most common route out of poverty.

c. Extend child support to age twenty-two for students enrolled full time in any postsecondary education and require the noncustodial parent to pay a proportionate share of expenses up to the tuition and fees at the major state university in the state; or

d. Establish a trust fund as part of child support agreements to provide savings for children who are expected to enroll full time in postsecondary education.

College entrance and attendance decisions usually come at the time the child attains the age of legal majority. Evidence from studies by Judith Wallerstein in California indicates that even some fathers who maintained contact with and paid child support to their children all along and who could afford to continue providing support refused to pay for college.[18] Yet a college education is increasingly important to compete successfully in the labor market.

Some states already follow the first of these two strategies (e.g., Missouri). The second strategy also makes a good deal of sense. Analyses of the costs of raising children indicate that although the proportion of income for current consumption may indeed decline as income rises, saving increases with income, and a portion of that should be allocated for future child expenses, such as college tuition.[19] Recognizing that the level of saving will be reduced by divorce, the share that would have accrued to the child should be a specified part of the child support award. In the case of a child that is expected to attend college, a trust fund should be established for a college education. In states where guidelines specify a cap or a declining percentage of income as the income of the noncustodial parent rises, the noncustodial parent should set up the trust fund. In states where guidelines require a flat percentage of income, it may be specified that at high incomes, the custodial parent set up a trust fund for the purpose.[20]

7. Address children's well-being in a broader framework.

Several related policies would benefit children in all single-parent families, regardless of race or marital status.[21] Improving the labor market opportunities for women is the surest way to improve the economic well-being of single-parent families. Parental leave policies that would allow parents to take time off for a short period after childbirth without losing their jobs may keep some poor women from having to go on welfare. Of course, if the leave is unpaid, this is useful only for those who can afford it. Improving the availability of affordable quality child care would enable working mothers heading single-parent families to find high-quality alternative care. This would facilitate investment in the human capital of both mother and child.[22]

Is Success within Our Reach?

Much progress remains to be made in the child support arena—from getting awards for the never-married, to increasing the value of awards to reflect the actual costs of raising children, to getting existing awards fully paid. Much of the legislation needed to accomplish these goals already exists, although changes still need to be made. But the missing key to future progress and the one that has allowed the inadequate provision of support to go unchecked for too many years is the lack of a national commitment to the economic well-being of children, our primary national resource. Until and unless a national consensus is reached that puts our children's well-being first, we may find that new laws and regulations cannot bring about improvements in the award and payment of child support of the magnitude that is so desperately needed.

CPS March/April
Match Files

Because of errors in survey design, some women with children aged twenty-one or older were unintentionally included in the sample. We adjusted the sample to exclude these by requiring women to be sixty-five and under at the time of the survey and, for those who had been married, to have undergone a marital disruption less than twenty-two years ago. This adjustment is intentionally conservative, excluding only women who are clearly ineligible for child support.

We considered, but rejected, an alternative adjustment based upon children's ages. This is a less conservative strategy that excludes more women who might not be eligible for child support, but also excludes some women who are eligible. At issue is whether women with children over age eighteen only now should be considered eligible for child support. Many states terminate the requirement for child support when the child reaches majority at the age of eighteen. But, some states do not. For example, Missouri makes provision for child support to continue to age twenty-two if the child is a full-time student. Moreover, nearly one-third of eligible women with no child under eighteen present as of the census surveys are due child support and 58 percent of those with an award are still due support. Consequently, we chose not to eliminate women who did not have children present under age eighteen.

In addition to imposing the above sample restrictions, we modified the sample or data in other ways to remedy inconsistencies between the March and April portions of the records. We excluded eight women in 1979 and ten in 1982 who had children present in the household from an absent father according to the April record but were reported to live only with unrelated individuals according to the March record. These differences may have arisen because the demographic infor-

Table 2.A1 National Estimates of the Child Support Population for 1978, 1981, 1983, and 1985 (Census Bureau and revised)

Award and Recipiency Status	1978 Census Bureau[a] N (mil.)	% Dist.	1978 Revised Estimate N (mil.)	% Dist.	1981 Census Bureau[a] N (mil.)	% Dist.	1981 Revised Estimate N (mil.)	% Dist.	1983 Census Bureau[a] N (mil.)	% Dist.	1983 Revised Estimate N (mil.)	% Dist.	1985 Census Bureau[a] N (mil.)	% Dist.	1985 Revised Estimate N (mil.)	% Dist.
Total	7.080	100.0	6.950	100.0	8.361	100.0	8.234	100.0	.690	100.0	8.528	100.0	8.808	100.0	8.646	100.0
Awarded	4.188	59.2	4.123	59.3	4.961	59.3	4.914	59.7	5.015	57.7	4.928	57.8	5.396	61.3	5.316	61.5
Supposed to receive payment	3.419	48.3	3.394	48.8	4.039	48.3	4.018	48.8	3.995	46.0	3.957	46.4	4.381	49.7	4.344	50.2
Not supposed to receive payment	0.769	10.9	0.729	10.5	0.922	11.0	0.896	10.9	1.020	11.7	0.971	11.4	1.015	11.6	0.972	11.3
Not awarded	2.892	40.8	2.827	40.7	3.400	40.7	3.320	40.3	3.675	42.3	3.600	42.2	3.412	38.7	3.330	38.5
Supposed to receive payment	3.419	100.0	3.394	100.0	4.038	100.0	4.018	100.0	3.995	100.0	3.958	100.0	4.381	100.0	4.344	100.0
Actually received	2.454	71.8	2.432	71.6	2.900	71.8	2.885	71.8	3.037	76.0	3.014	76.2	3.243	74.0	3.215	74.0
Full amount	1.674	49.0	1.659	48.9	1.885	46.7	1.874	46.6	2.018	50.5	2.000	50.5	2.112	48.2	2.094	48.2
Partial amount	0.780	22.8	0.773	22.7	1.015	25.1	1.011	25.2	1.019	25.5	1.014	25.7	1.131	25.8	1.121	25.8
Did not receive	0.965	28.2	0.962	28.4	1.138	28.2	1.133	28.2	0.958	24.0	0.944	23.8	1.138	26.0	1.129	26.0

Source: 1979, 1982, 1984, and 1986 crs March/April Match Files.

[a] Our estimates are slightly under Census Bureau estimates owing to the omission of 8 cases in 1979 and 10 cases in 1982 with inconsistencies in the record.

mation was retained from the March file although the supplement data were obtained from the April file. (Census Bureau and revised estimates appear in table 2.A1.)

Another inconsistency was that some women classified as a member of a primary family in March actually appear to be a head or wife of head of a subfamily according to the April data. Obviously, information on the number of children in various age categories pertaining to the primary family will not generally be the same as such information pertaining to the subfamily. An example is a family that includes a mother, her daughter, and the daughter's two children. The mother has one adult child living at home while the daughter has two presumably young children living at home. For such women, we treated the family data as missing.

Certain inconsistencies appeared in the data themselves. In general, we used the data as we found them. We discovered, however, that a few outlier observations were causing inconsistent results in the analyses of aggregate data in chapter 2. On the basis of other information in the record, we altered one observation on the amount of child support due a remarried black mother in 1978 from $18,000 to $1,800 (the same as the amount she received). In addition, we excluded twelve women for whom the ratio of child support received to child support due exceeded four from the analyses of the ratio.

*A Brief Guide
to Regression and
Decomposition
Analysis*

In this appendix we review two analytical tools that are used extensively in subsequent chapters. We use regression analysis to study the determinants of child support outcomes and we use decomposition analysis to account for differentials and trends over time in these outcomes. We describe each of these tools briefly and illustrate how they can be used to study determinants, differentials, and trends in child support awards and receipts.

Regression Analysis

Suppose we hypothesize that a variable Y is determined by another set of variables x_1 to x_m. We call Y the dependent variable and the set of Xs the independent variables. Further, suppose we hypothesize the following linear causal relation:

$$Y = b_0 + b_1x_1 + b_2x_2 + \ldots + b_mx_m + e \tag{1}$$

In equation 1, b_0 to b_m are referred to as the coefficients and e represents an error term (with zero mean and constant variance). The coefficient b_i can be interpreted as the effect on Y of raising or lowering x_i by one unit, holding all other independent variables constant. That is, b_i represents the ceteris paribus effect of x_i on Y. The error term summarizes all other influences on Y besides x_1 to x_m.

In regression analysis, we use observations on the dependent and independent variables to estimate the set of coefficients b_0 to b_m. Suppose we have information on the values of Y and the Xs for many different individuals. In the classical regression model (known as ordinary least squares or OLS), the coefficients are chosen (or estimated) to minimize the sum of the squared *residuals,* where the residual is the difference between the actual value of Y and its predicted value derived from evaluating equation 2, using the actual Xs and the estimated coefficients. We can also compute standard errors associated with the coefficient estimates that allow us to construct confidence intervals: for example, 95 percent of the time the true coefficient will lie within an interval bounded by the estimated coefficient plus or minus twice its standard error.

Both Y and the Xs can be either continuous variables, or discrete ones. Discrete variables can take on only a limited number of values, and are sometimes called "dummy variables." For example, X may be assigned the value 1 if a woman is black and 0 if she is not; Y may equal 1 if a woman has a child support award and 0 if she does not. Discrete independent variables present no new estimation problems, but dummy dependent variables do. It can be shown that estimation of equation 1 by OLS is no longer appropriate if Y is limited in range. If Y is a dichotomous (two-valued) dummy variable, an appropriate alternative is known as probit. In probit, we construct the following continuous index function:

$$I = a_0 + a_1 x_1 + a_2 x_2 + \ldots + a_m x_m + e \qquad (2)$$

where $Y = 1$ if $I > 0$ and $Y = 0$ if $I \leq 0$. The probit coefficients a_0 to a_m are estimated by maximum likelihood methods available on many computer statistical programs. The probability of observing $Y = 1$ is given by $F(\hat{I})$, where the F is the cumulative distribution function of the standard normal distribution and $\hat{I}$ is the fitted value of equation 2, using the Xs and the estimated probit coefficients.

Another important difference between OLS and probit is the interpretation of the estimated coefficients. We can interpret the OLS coefficient b_i as the ceteris paribus or partial effect on Y of raising x_i by one unit, holding all other Xs constant. Unfortunately, the probit coefficient itself does not have this natural interpretation. Rather, the equivalent ceteris paribus effect of x_i on Y is given by $f(\hat{I})a_i$, where $f(\hat{I})$ is the standard normal density function evaluated at $\hat{I}$.[1]

In subsequent chapters we use probit to estimate whether or not a woman has a child support award and whether or not she receives payment, and we use OLS to estimate the value of support due and received. Estimation, however, of the last child support outcome—the value of support received—introduces one additional complication. Because we can observe the value of child support received (CS_r) only for mothers actually receiving support, we estimate the determinants of CS_r conditional on $CS_r > 0$, which violates one of the standard assumptions of OLS. One method of estimation when the independent variable is subject to this type of sample selection is known as Tobit analysis. We follow an alternative method proposed by James Heckman.[2] Heckman suggèsts a simple two-step procedure: first, estimate the probability of sample inclusion by multivariate probit; and second, include an additional regressor called *lambda* in OLS estimates of the original independent variable, where lambda is the inverse Mill's ratio formed from the probit equation. In our case, we first define the likelihood of receiving child support as

$$R^* = a_0 + a_1x_1 + a_2x_2 + \ldots + a_mx_m + e \tag{3}$$

where $R = 1$ if $R^* > 0$ and $R = 0$ if $R^* \le 0$, and estimate equation 3 by probit. Then, we define lambda as $f(aX)/F(aX)$, and we include it in OLS estimates of CS_r:

$$CS_r = b_0 + b_1z_1 + \ldots + b_mz_m + b_{m+1} \; lambda + e \tag{4}$$

Decomposition Analysis

In the next two chapters we also make frequent use of another tool known as decomposition or *means-coefficients* analysis to study expected differentials in child support outcomes across subgroups of women and to study trends over time.[3] That is, we use this analysis to understand why awards and receipts differ by race and marital status and why aggregate award and receipt outcomes change over time.

It is easiest to explain this technique in terms of a specific example. Suppose we want to understand why, on average, black women have smaller child support awards than nonblack women. We might hypothesize that for both blacks and nonblacks the value of an award, **Y,** depends upon observable factors x_1 to x_m, but that the effect of any specific x_i might differ by race. That is, for nonblacks (denoted w), we hypothesize that

$$\mathbf{Y}^w = c_0^w + c_1^w x_1^w + \ldots + c_m^w x_m^w + e^w \tag{5}$$

and for blacks (denoted b) we hypothesize that

$$\mathbf{Y}^b = c_0^b + c_1^b x_1^b + \ldots + c_m^b x_m^b + e^b \tag{6}$$

(In some cases, rather than estimating separate equations by race, we might estimate a single equation for both races together. In this case, we would include a dummy variable for race, which is equivalent to allowing the intercepts $[c_0]$ but not the slopes $[c_1$ to $c_m]$ to differ between the two equations above.)

If we may estimate equations 5 and 6 separately by OLS, we then obtain two sets of estimated coefficients (denoted $\mathbf{C}^w$ and $\mathbf{C}^b$). One property of these estimated coefficients is that when equations 5 and 6 are evaluated at the mean of $\mathbf{Y}$ (denoted $\overline{\mathbf{Y}}$) and the mean of the Xs (denoted $\overline{\mathbf{X}}$), the residual term is zero. In other words,

$$\overline{\mathbf{Y}}^w = \mathbf{C}^w \overline{\mathbf{X}}^w, \text{ and} \tag{5'}$$

$$\overline{\mathbf{Y}}^b = \mathbf{C}^b \overline{\mathbf{X}}^b \tag{6'}$$

where the right-hand side in each equation uses vector notation to express the summation in a more compact form. (That is, $\mathbf{C}$ is a row vector of estimated coefficients and $\mathbf{X}$ is a column vector of sample means.)

Call $(\overline{\mathbf{Y}}^w - \overline{\mathbf{Y}}^b)$ the observed racial differential in average child support awards. Subtracting equation 6' from 5', it can be shown that

$$(\overline{\mathbf{Y}}^w - \overline{\mathbf{Y}}^b) = \mathbf{C}^w(\overline{\mathbf{X}}^w - \overline{\mathbf{X}}^b) + \overline{\mathbf{X}}^b(\mathbf{C}^w - \mathbf{C}^b) \tag{7}$$

Equation 7 is the fundamental equation of decomposition analysis. It says that the total racial differential in awards can be decomposed into two parts, the first owing to racial differences in the means of the explanatory variables and the second a result of racial differences in coefficients (or equivalently, their effects).[4] Alternatively, the first term represents the differential in awards that can be *explained* by racial differences in average explanatory variables, while the second term represents the difference that remains *unexplained* by these factors. (When a single equation is estimated rather than separate equations by race, the coefficient on the racial dummy variable itself represents the unexplained difference.)

Finally, when the decomposition represents changes over time rather than racial differentials in the value of child support awards, the above decomposition has a slightly different interpretation. Suppose we rewrite equation 7 as:

$$(\overline{\mathbf{Y}}^2 - \overline{\mathbf{Y}}^1) = \mathbf{C}^1(\overline{\mathbf{X}}^2 - \overline{\mathbf{X}}^1) + \overline{\mathbf{X}}^2(\mathbf{C}^2 - \mathbf{C}^1) \tag{8}$$

where 1 and 2 refer to two different years. According to equation 8, the change over time in the average value of child support awards can be decomposed into two parts. The first term represents the change in awards that could be expected or explained on the basis of changes over time in the determinants of awards, when these changes are evaluated at the environment (i.e., coefficients) prevailing in the earlier year. The second term represents the unexpected or unexplained change in awards, which in turn can be associated with changes over time in the award environment itself (i.e., changes over time in the coefficients).

Are Child Support

Awards

Renegotiated?

In table 2.6 we offered some preliminary evidence that, on average, the values of child support currently due and initially awarded are the same. Here we test this hypothesis more fully. We show that, on average, women (with identical socioeconomic characteristics) who were divorced or separated in the same year but due support in different years are due the same amount. This suggests that initial award amounts tend not to be readjusted over time. Of course, this does not mean that no one received an adjustment but only that any increases were offset by comparable decreases so that in the aggregate the nominal value of awards remained unchanged.

More formally, combining all four years of survey data, we use regression analysis to relate the *nominal* (current dollar) value of child support due to (1) the socioeconomic characteristics of the mother, (2) the year of her marital disruption, and (3) the year she was surveyed.[1] If dollars due in the year before the survey are identical to dollars originally awarded, then the coefficient on the survey year will be insignificantly different from zero. In other words, if knowing the date of the survey does not improve our ability to explain cross-sectional variations in nominal dollars due (controlling for a mother's characteristics and the year of her marital disruption), then we can conclude that initial award amounts remain unchanged over time. The results of this analysis appear in appendix table 4.A1.

Controlling for differences in socioeconomic characteristics, but not for the year of the marital disruption (see row 2), we find that we can explain little of the overall increase across surveys in nominal dollars due. For example, compared with a woman due child support in 1978, a woman with exactly the same socioeconomic characteristics

Table 4.A1   Explaining Differences across Sample Years in Amount of Child Support Due Ever-married Mothers (in current dollars)

	Relative to 1978, additional support due in:		
	1981	1983	1985
Total unadjusted difference[a]	295*	527*	546*
Difference after controlling for socioeconomic factors[b]	258*	506*	561*
Difference after controlling for socioeconomic factors and year of the marital disruption by[c]			
1. Linear time trend,[d] or	21	136	42
2. Average price level,[e] or	−10	76	−51
3. Average male incomes[f]	−1	87	−48

* Different from zero at a 5% significance level

[a] Unweighted regression sample figures and thus not directly comparable to figures reported in chap. 2.

[b] Includes mother's socioeconomic characteristics listed in table 4.5.

[c] We restrict all marital disruptions to have occurred within 22 years of the date of the initial 1979 survey.

[d] Linear time trend tied to the year of mother's marital disruption beginning with 1958 = 1

[e] CPI in year of mother's marital disruption, with 1967 = 100

[f] Mean income of year-round, full-time male workers, by race, in year of mother's marital disruption

is due $258 more in 1981 or 87 percent of the unadjusted difference, and she is due $561 more in 1985 or 103 percent of the unadjusted difference. Thus, it appears that changes in the socioeconomic characteristics of the population due support do not account for changes over time in nominal dollars of child support due.

By contrast to socioeconomic characteristics alone, the addition of an indicator of the year of the mother's marital disruption explains all of the change, no matter whether this indicator is a simple linear time trend, the level of prices, or male income in that year. We find that once we also control for the year of the mother's marital disruption (or consumer prices or male incomes in that year), differences in dollars due across surveys are no longer significant. In other words, controlling for socioeconomic characteristics and some indicator of the year of the marital disruption, we do not improve our ability to explain variations across women in support levels by including the survey year that support is due. Thus, we conclude that, on average, initial awards are neither renegotiated nor automatically adjusted over time.[2]

A Theory of
Welfare, Work,
and Child Support

A single mother's welfare and work choices are shown pictorially in figure 7.A1. Suppose her family's well-being (or utility, as defined in chap. 3) depends positively upon total family income (Y) and her leisure time (L), where leisure represents all time not spent working (for pay) outside the home. An indifference curve (such as $U_0 U_0$ or $U_1 U_1$) represents all combinations of Y and L that generate the same level of utility. The horizontal axis in figure 7.A1 divides her total time (L') between leisure (measured left to right) and work (H, measured right to left). The vertical axis shows her total family income, which consists of her personal earnings (wH, where w is her wage rate), plus nonwage income (N). In the absence of AFDC, the budget constraint is the straight line NY'. Subject to this constraint, the mother chooses L and Y to maximize utility or, equivalently, to get to her highest indifference curve. If this choice is at point N (so that $L = L'$ and $Y = N$), she does not work and has only nonwage sources of income. If this choice is at point E_1, she works H_1 (and enjoys $L' - H_1$ leisure time) and has $wH_1 + N$ total income.

AFDC offers a minimum income guarantee G (shown in fig. 7.A1), which varies by state of residence and family size. If a mother chooses not to work, she is eligible to receive AFDC benefits (G') equal to $G - rN$, where r is the AFDC tax rate on nonwage income.[1] ($r = 1$ in most cases.) If she works, her benefits are further reduced by twH where t is the AFDC tax rate on earnings. (t varies by state and has varied over time as well.) In figure 7.A1, point B is the so-called break-even point where actual AFDC benefits received would be reduced to zero. (AFDC payments received are shown by the vertical distance between GY'' and NY'.) With an AFDC program, the mother's overall budget

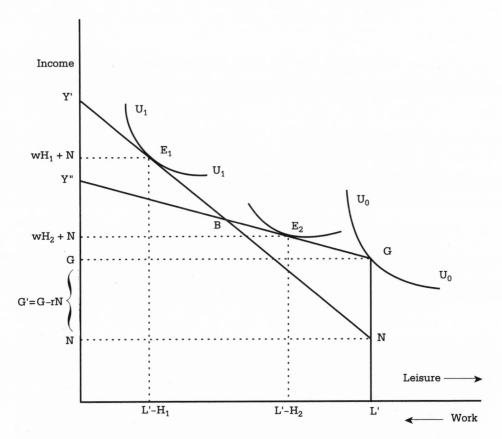

7.A1   AFDC Participation and Hours Worked

constraint is the nonlinear GBY'. If utility is maximized along line segment BY'—say at point E_1—then she chooses not to go on AFDC and works H_1 hours. If utility is maximized along line segment GB—say at point E_2—then she goes on AFDC and works H_2 hours. Finally, if utility is maximized at G, then she goes on welfare and does not work.

How does an increase in child support income affect the work and welfare decisions shown in figure 7.A1? Recall that child support is a component of nonwage income. Without an AFDC program, an increase in child support raises N and causes a parallel upward shift in the budget constraint (from NY' to N'Y''', as shown in figure 7.A2. For a mother who works, the new utility maximizing point is E'_1, assuming

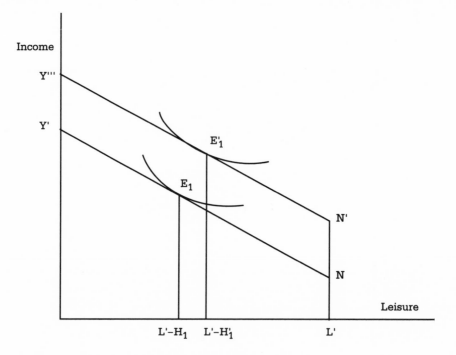

7.A2 Increase in Nonwage Income without AFDC

that both more leisure and income are preferred. Hours of work decrease from H_1 to H_1', while total family income rises from Y_1 ($= wH_1$
$+ N$) to Y_2 ($= wH_1' + N'$). Total family income rises, but by less than
the increase in child support payments because hours of work and
hence earnings decline.

The impact of child support is more complicated if an AFDC program exists, as shown in figure 7.A3. For a mother not on AFDC, the
increase in child support still reduces the total hours worked. But for
a working mother on AFDC, an increase in N (owing to an increase in
child support) reduces her potential welfare benefits ($G - rN$) and
causes the breakeven point (defined above) to shift to the left from B
to B'. This, in turn, reduces the likelihood of AFDC participation. If

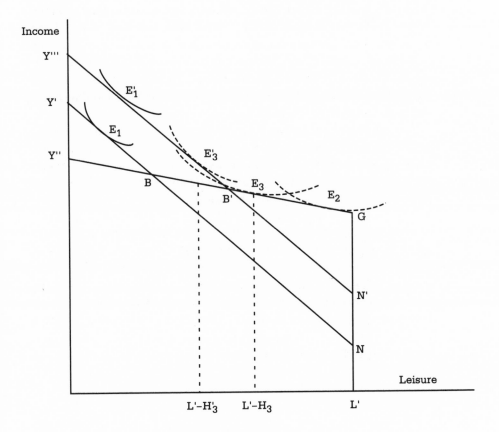

7.A3 Increase in Nonwage Income with AFDC

she remains on AFDC at E_2, then the increase in N has no effect on hours worked. Yet if the increase in N is sufficient to induce her to stop participating in AFDC (i.e., to shift from E_3 on line segment GB to E_3' on B'Y'''), it may actually result in an increase in hours worked (from H_3 to H_3'). Thus, to summarize, economic theory predicts that an increase in child support income unambiguously reduces the likelihood of AFDC participation but may either raise or lower the number of hours worked. In other words, the effect of child support on hours worked is an empirical rather than a theoretical question.

Do all forms of nonwage income have the same effect on welfare participation? Historically, nearly all state-run AFDC programs taxed all forms of nonwage income, including child support, at 100 percent (i.e., $r = 1$), so that any rise in nonwage income would reduce potential AFDC benefits by an equal amount. Since 1984, however, as mandated by federal law, the benefit reduction calculation now disregards the first $50 per month of child support income. As a result, among mothers with little or no child support income, increases in child support payments can be expected to reduce AFDC participation less than equal increases in other nonwage income.

Do all forms of nonwage income have the same effect on the number of hours worked? For mothers not on AFDC, increases in either child support or other nonwage income raise N by the same amount and thus should affect work effort identically. For mothers on AFDC, work effort is affected by both nonwage income and potential AFDC benefits [i.e., $N + G' = G - (r - 1)N$]. On the one hand, if all forms of nonwage income are taxed at 100 percent, then increases in N are offset by equal decreases in G', leaving the work effort of mothers who remain on AFDC unaffected (although as shown above in fig. 7.A3, mothers who quit AFDC may increase their hours worked). On the other hand, if child support income is not taxed or is subject to an initial disregard, then increases in child support—unlike other nonwage income—raise $N + G'$ for mothers on AFDC and may reduce their work effort if they remain on AFDC.

AFDC	Aid to Families with Dependent Children
AMW	automatic or mandatory income withholding
ASPE	Office of the Assistant Secretary for Planning and Evaluation
ASSA	Allied Social Science Association
BLS	U.S. Bureau of Labor Statistics
CEX	Consumer Expenditure Survey [data set]
CFR	Code of Federal Regulations
CPI	Consumer Price Index
CPS	Current Population Survey [data set]
CPR	Current Population Reports
CRIM	criminal penalties for nonsupport
DEFRA	Deficit Reduction Act
DSTREND	indicator of marital disruption year
EP	expedited processes
FERG	Family Economics Research Group
FTMRATIO	female-to-male earnings ratio
GPO	Government Printing Office
HHS [DHHS]	U.S. Department of Health and Human Services
KID6TO17	one or more children aged six to seventeen
LAW	indicator of marital disruption year, if after 1975
LIEN	liens on property
NBER	National Bureau of Economic Research
NCSL	National Conference of State Legislatures
NICHD	National Institute of Child Health and Human Development
NLS72	National Longitudinal Study of the High School Class of 1972 [data set]
OCSE	Office of Child Support Enforcement
OLS	ordinary least squares
PHS	Public Health Service
PSID	Panel Study of Income Dynamics [data set]
RURESA	Revised Uniform Reciprocal Enforcement of Support Act
SEC	security, bond, or other guarantees
SES	socioeconomic status
SIPP	Survey of Income and Program Participation [data set]
SMSA	Standard Metropolitan Statistical Area
SOAP	Survey of Absent Parents [data set]

SOLA	Standard of Living Allowance
SSA	Social Security Administration
TAX	state income tax refund offset
UPIP	Uniform Program Improvement Project
USDA	U.S. Department of Agriculture
USDL	U.S. Department of Labor
VWA	voluntary wage assignment
YEAR86	observation from 1986 CPS

Notes

Chapter 1: Introduction

1. According to the U.S. Bureau of the Census, *Statistical Abstract of the United States,* single-parent female-headed families (including widows) increased from 4.5 million in 1960 (1973 ed., table 58) to 8.7 million in 1980 (1985 ed., table 68). In 1980, 14.6 out of 29.3 million poor persons were members of families headed by a woman with no husband present (1982–83 ed., table 728).

2. In 1960, 52% of all single-parent female family heads were widows but by 1980 only 29% were. Census Bureau, *Statistical Abstract of the United States,* 1973 (table 58) and 1985 (table 68).

3. Census Bureau, Current Population Reports, Special Studies, series P-23, no. 106, *Child Support and Alimony: 1978* (Advance Report). Washington, D.C.: GPO, 1980.

4. Census Bureau, CPR, Special Studies, series P-23, no. 112, *Child Support and Alimony: 1978.* Washington, D.C.: GPO, 1981, 5.

5. Authors' calculations from own data.

6. Census Bureau, *Statistical Abstract of the United States,* 1982–83, table 555.

7. Henrietta J. Duvall, Karen W. Goudreau, and Robert E. Marsh, "Aid to Families with Dependent Children: Characteristics of Recipients in 1979," *Social Security Bulletin,* April 1982, chart 1.

8. In a 1979 survey of the AFDC population, only 7.5% of recipient children had fathers who were deceased or incapacitated, down from 14.2% in 1973. See Duvall, Goudreau, and Marsh, "Aid to Families with Dependent Children," table 3.

9. See, e.g., Sheila Fitzgerald Krein and Andrea H. Beller, "Educational Attainment of Children from Single-Parent Families: Differences by Exposure, Gender and Race," *Demography* 25:221–34; Sara S. McLanahan, "Family Structure and Dependency: Early Transitions to Female Household Headship," *Demography* 25:1–16; Sara S. McLanahan and Larry L. Bumpass, "Intergenerational Consequences of Family Disruption," *American Journal of Sociology* 94:130–52; and Gary D. Sandefur, Sara S. McLanahan, and Roger A. Wojtkiewicz, "Race and Ethnicity, Family Structure, and High School Graduation," Institute for Research on Poverty Discussion Paper 893–89, Aug. 1989.

10. In fact, the trend was so strong in this direction that it raised the

concern of at least one seasoned observer (Harry D. Krause, "Child Support Reassessed: Limits of Private Responsibility and the Public Interest," in *Divorce Reform at the Crossroads,* ed. Stephen D. Sugarman and Herma Hill Kay, [New Haven: Yale University Press, 1990], 166–90). He argued that many of the absent fathers simply could not afford to support their children, and in such cases the government should provide the support. In making his argument, he offered a rationale as to how the public loses when these children are not supported.

11. U.S. National Center for Health Statistics, *Vital Statistics of the United States, 1984,* vol. 3, Marriage and Divorce. Washington, D.C.: GPO, 1988, table 2–1.

12. UN, *1986 Demographic Yearbook,* 38th ed., New York, 1988, table 19.

13. U.S. National Center for Health Statistics, *Vital Statistics of the United States, 1986,* vol. 1, Natality. DHHS pub. no. 88–1123, Public Health Service, Washington, D.C.: GPO, 1988, tables 1–1 and 1–31.

14. Census Bureau, CPR, series P-20, no. 437, *Household and Family Characteristics: March 1988.* Washington, D.C.: GPO, 1989, table 1; ibid., no. 218, *Household and Family Characteristics: March 1970.* Washington, D.C.: GPO, 1971, table 1.

15. In 1988, an additional 3% of each group lived with their fathers only. Census Bureau, CPR, series P-20, no. 433, *Marital Status and Living Arrangements: March 1988.* Washington, D.C.: GPO, 1989; ibid., no. 212, *Marital Status and Family Status: March 1970.* Washington, D.C.: GPO, 1971.

16. Arthur J. Norton and Paul C. Glick, "One-Parent Families: A Social and Economic Profile," *Family Relations* 35:9–17; Irwin Garfinkel and Sara S. McLanahan, *Single Mothers and Their Children* (Washington, D.C.: Urban Institute, 1986), 8.

17. This fact is a main theme of two recent books. See I. Garfinkel and S. S. McLanahan, *Single Mothers and Their Children,* and Harrell R. Rodgers, Jr., *Poor Women, Poor Families* (New York: M. E. Sharpe, 1986).

18. Census Bureau, CPR, series P-23, no. 154, *Child Support and Alimony: 1985.* Washington, D.C.: GPO, 1989, table 1.

19. Diane Pearce, "The Feminization of Poverty: Women, Work and Welfare," *Urban and Social Change Review* 11:28–36.

20. Census Bureau, CPR, series P-23, no. 112, *Child Support and Alimony: 1978,* 7.

21. According to popularly cited figures, income in relation to needs decreases 73% after divorce for women and children but increases 42% for men (Lenore J. Weitzman, *The Divorce Revolution,* New York: Free Press, 1985). Other research shows a 30% drop for the former (Saul D. Hoffman and Greg J. Duncan, "What *Are* the Economic Consequences of Divorce?" *Demography* 25:641–45.)

22. The second Census Bureau survey on child support was conducted in April 1982; subsequently, they have been conducted every two years. All the statistics in this paragraph were obtained from the Bureau, CPR series P-23, no. 112, *Child Support and Alimony: 1978;* ibid., series P-60, no. 173, *Child*

Support and Alimony: 1989. Washington, D.C.: GPO, 1991. The latter report was released in Sept. 1991.

23. The actual statistic is 58.3 for women 18 and over, calculated from the data in table 1, and 57.7 for women 15 and over.

24. This rise may need to be viewed with caution owing to some possible change in the way the Census Bureau measured the amount of child support received, which may break comparability with earlier data (Daniel R. Meyer, "Data Adjustments in the Child Support Supplement of the Current Population Survey," University of Wisconsin, Feb. 1992.)

25. This section is based upon information contained in U.S. House of Representatives, Committee on Ways and Means, *Background Material and Data on Programs within the Jurisdiction of the Committee on Ways and Means*. Washington, D.C.: GPO, 1989, sect. 8.

26. Authors' calculations based upon data collected by the National Conference of State Legislatures. See table 6.1 for more details on mandatory wage withholding and other enforcement techniques.

27. U.S. Department of Health, Education and Welfare, Office of Child Support Enforcement, *First Annual Report to the Congress on the Child Support Enforcement Program,* 111; U.S. Department of Health and Human Services, Office of Child Support Enforcement, *Child Support Enforcement, Twelfth Annual Report to the Congress for the Period Ending 30 Sept. 1987,* vol. 2, table 20.

28. HHS, Office of Child Support Enforcement, *Child Support Enforcement, Fourth Annual Report to the Congress for the Period ending 30 Sept. 1979,* 99; ibid., *Child Support Enforcement: Twelfth Annual Report,* vol. 2, table 19.

29. Still, by 1986, spending on child support programs represented less than one-tenth of 1% of all government spending. See *Economic Report of the President,* Jan. 1987, table B-77.

30. Seven of the thirteen articles on child support indexed in the 1986 edition of the *Reader's Guide to Periodical Literature* appeared in the black-oriented magazine *Jet*.

31. For example, *The Oprah Winfrey Show,* "Unpaid Child Support," Chicago: Harpo Productions, 13 Jan. 1989. Transcript 610.

32. Recent attempts to explain why marital patterns differ increasingly among the races may be found in "The Growing Racial Differences in Marriage and Family Patterns," by Reynolds Farley and Suzanne M. Bianchi, Research Report no. 87–107, Population Studies Center, University of Michigan, April 1987; and Neil Bennett, David Bloom, and Patricia Craig, "The Divergence of Black and White Marriage Patterns," *American Journal of Sociology* 95:692–722.

33. On the one hand, gains among AFDC recipients would for the most part be deemed a public benefit because as a condition for going on AFDC a woman must assign her child support rights to the state. Except for the first $50 per month, child support collected on behalf of a woman reduces her AFDC benefits dollar for dollar. On the other hand, gains among the non-AFDC population would be largely a private benefit, directly increasing the income

of women and children. Of course, to the extent that state IV-D offices help non-AFDC women stay off welfare, some of these benefits may be deemed public as well.

34. In 1985 less than 3% of ever-divorced or currently separated women received alimony income (Census Bureau, CPR, series P-23, no. 154, *Child Support and Alimony: 1985*. Washington, D.C.: GPO, 1989, table C).

35. Andrea H. Beller and John W. Graham, "The Determinants of Child Support Income," *Social Science Quarterly* 67:353–64. The questions on property settlements in the 1979 survey were dropped subsequently.

36. Gary S. Becker, *A Treatise on the Family* (Cambridge, Mass.: Harvard University Press, 1981). See also, G. S. Becker, "A Theory of the Allocation of Time," *Economic Journal* 75:493–517.

37. At the extreme, as is the case in Hungary, a divorced father can be made so badly off that he cannot afford to remarry and even sometimes must return home to live with his parents. Ferenc Kamaras, deputy chief, Population Statistics Section, Hungarian Central Statistical Office, interview with AHB, Budapest, 24 July 1987.

38. Barbara R. Bergmann presents data from a survey conducted with Sherry Wetchler of 520 Maryland residents that reveals a general consensus that fathers should pay more child support than they now do and that remarriage should not reduce their obligation. "How Big Should Child Support Payments Be?" Paper presented at the First Annual Women's Policy Research Conference, Institute for Women's Policy Research, Washington, D.C., May 1989.

39. For some international comparisons, see Peter Dopffel, "Child Support in Europe: A Comparative Overview," in *Child Support: From Debt Collection to Social Policy,* ed. Alfred J. Kahn and Sheila B. Kamerman, Newbury Park, Calif.: Sage, 176–226. Also, e.g., the interests of the child are given a high priority in Hungary, where fathers are compelled to transfer large proportions of their incomes to children living with their former wives, according to Kamaras (interview with AHB, Budapest, 24 July 1987).

40. Census Bureau, CPR, series P-60, no. 173, *Child Support and Alimony: 1989,* fig. 3, p. 15.

41. Absence from the household may be due to divorce, separation, or never being married, but not to death or married but living elsewhere. By contrast to this latter reason, separation includes "those with legal separations, those living apart with intentions of obtaining a divorce, and other persons permanently or temporarily estranged from their spouses because of marital discord." (Census Bureau, CPS March/April Match File: Alimony and Child Support, Technical Documentation, Washington, D.C., 1988, 115.) It is interesting to note, however, that spouses living apart are more likely to divorce subsequently than those living together (Ronald R. Rindfuss and Elizabeth H. Stephen, "Marital Non-Cohabitation: Separation Does not Make the Heart Grow Fonder," Carolina Population Center Paper no. 88–30, Dec. 1988.)

42. It was also repeated in 1988 and 1990, but neither of these data sets was available at the time we performed these analyses.

43. Although both the Survey of Income and Program Participation (SIPP) and the Panel Study of Income Dynamics (PSID) are also nationally representative, the former is too new to allow study of child support before 1984 and the latter is too small (5,000 families) to allow study of various population subgroups, and for much of its history, it has failed to separate child support from alimony. Other relevant data sets include the pilot study from the Survey of Absent Parents (SOAP) and the National Longitudinal Study of the High School Class of 1972 (NLS72), but neither of these surveyed all women eligible for child support.

44. In some states child support legally terminates at age eighteen, but see our discussion in app. A.

45. See also Graham and Beller, "A Note on the Number and Living Arrangements of Women with Children under Twenty-One from an Absent Father: Revised Estimates from the April 1979 and 1982 Current Population Surveys," *Journal of Economic and Social Measurement* 13:209–14.

46. U.S. National Center for Health Statistics, *Vital Statistics of the United States: 1986,* vol. 1, Natality. DHHS pub. no. (PHS) 88–1123, Public Health Service, Washington, D.C.: GPO, 1988, table 1–34.

47. This group was included in the 1988 and 1990 surveys.

48. Census Bureau, CPR, series P-70, no. 13, *Who's Helping Out? Support Networks Among American Families.* Washington, D.C.: GPO, 1988, table F.

49. Yoram Weiss and Robert J. Willis, "An Economic Analysis of Divorce Settlements," National Opinion Research Center, University of Chicago, April 1989.

50. Although a question on whether health insurance was included in the child support agreement was added to the CPS survey in 1984, we do not make use of it since it was not consistently available across all survey years. In the 1986 survey, 44.5% of women with an award said that health insurance was included as part of the award. (Census Bureau, CPR, series P-23, no. 154, *Child Support and Alimony: 1985.* Washington, D.C.: GPO, 1989.)

51. In this sample, around one-quarter of the fathers carry medical insurance for the children on a regular basis. (Kathleen M. Paasch and Jay D. Teachman, "Gender of Children and Differential Forms of Child Support," paper presented at the Population Association of America Annual Meetings, Toronto, May 1990.)

52. Jay D. Teachman, "Intergenerational Resource Transfers across Disrupted Households: Absent Fathers' Contributions to the Well-Being of Their Children," Johns Hopkins University, n.d.

53. In the 1979 survey, mothers were asked two questions about their children's fathers: (1) whether or not the father had any other children to support; and (2) what was the value of the father's income in 1978. In subsequent surveys these questions were dropped because the responses to them were deemed unreliable. Beller and Graham ("The Determinants of Child Support"), however, found them to be significant and reliable determinants of both awards and receipts.

54. Andrew Cherlin, Jeanne Griffith, and James McCarthy, "A Note on

Maritally-Disrupted Men's Reports of Child Support in the June 1980 Current Population Survey," *Demography* 20:385–89; Weiss and Willis, "An Economic Analysis."

55. This information was collected beginning with the 1988 survey.

56. In chaps. 2 and 4 we offer some evidence that few awards are readjusted over time, which permits us to approximate initial award amounts by the amount currently due. In studying trends in receipts, we must restrict our attention to the period since 1978.

57. Cassetty, *Child Support and Public Policy* (Lexington, Mass.: Lexington Books, 1978); and Chambers, *Making Fathers Pay: The Enforcement of Child Support* (Chicago: University of Chicago Press, 1979).

58. Nancy M. Gordon, Carol A. Jones, and Isabel V. Sawhill, "The Determinants of Child Support Payments," Working Paper no. 992–05, Washington D.C., Urban Institute, 1978; Annemette Sorensen and Maurice MacDonald, "An Analysis of Child Support Transfers," in *The Parental Child Support Obligation,* ed. Judith Cassetty (Lexington, Mass.: Lexington Books, 1983), 35–58; June O'Neill, "Determinants of Child Support" final report under grant 1RO1 HD 16840–01, NICHD, 1985; Beller and Graham, "The Determinants of Child Support Income," *Social Science Quarterly* 67:353–64; and Freya L. Sonenstein and Charles A. Calhoun, "Determinants of Child Support: A Pilot Study of Absent Parents," *Contemporary Policy Issues* 8:75–94.

59. Weiss and Willis, "Children as Collective Goods and Divorce Settlements," *Journal of Labor Economics* 3:268–92; and Weiss and Willis, "An Economic Analysis."

60. Beller and Graham, "Child Support Awards: Differentials and Trends by Race and Marital Status," *Demography* 23:231–45; Beller and Graham, "Child Support Payments: Evidence from Repeated Cross-Sections," *American Economic Review* 78:81–85; James L. Peterson and Christine Winquist Nord, "The Regular Receipt of Child Support: A Multistep Process," *Journal of Marriage and the Family* 52:539–51; and Philip K. Robins, "Why Are Child Support Award Amounts Declining?" *Journal of Human Resources* 27 (Spring 1992): 362–79.

61. Philip K. Robins, "Child Support, Welfare Dependency, and Poverty," *American Economic Review* 76:768–88; Kurt Beron, "Applying the Economic Model of Crime to Child Support Enforcement: A Theoretical and Empirical Analysis," *Review of Economics and Statistics* 70:382–90; and Beller and Graham, "The Effect of Child Support Enforcement on Child Support Payments," *Population Research and Policy Review* 10:91–116.

62. Philip K. Robins and Katherine P. Dickinson, "Child Support and Welfare Dependence: A Multinomial Logit Analysis," *Demography* 22:367–80; Graham and Beller, "The Effect of Child Support Payments on the Labor Supply of Female Family Heads: An Econometric Analysis," *Journal of Human Resources* 24:644–88; Andrea H. Beller and Seung Sin Chung, "The Effect of Child Support Payments on the Educational Attainment of Children," paper presented at the Population Association of America Annual Meetings, New Orleans, April 1988; and John W. Graham, Andrea H. Beller, and Pedro Hernandez, "The Relationship between Child Support Payments and Offspring

Educational Attainment," paper presented at the Conference on Child Support and Child Well Being, Airlie House, Va., 5–7 Dec. 1991.

63. The data do not permit us to examine the effect on (first) marriage behavior.

Chapter 2: Aggregate Differentials and Trends in Child Support Payments

1. See, e.g., Joseph I. Lieberman, *Child Support in America* (New Haven: Yale University Press, 1986), p. ix.

2. Ibid.

3. In this chapter only, we use the March supplement weights, designed by the Census Bureau to give each observation its appropriate weight in the whole U.S. population. Changes in the weighting scheme in accord with 1980 census figures were first implemented in the 1986 sample. This must be borne in mind with regard to comparability to earlier years Census Bureau, CPR, series P-23, no. 152, *Child Support and Alimony: 1985 (Advance Data from March-April 1986 Current Population Surveys)*. Washington, D.C.: GPO, 1987.

4. Our adjustments to the census data are discussed in app. A.

5. Hispanic women may be of any race.

6. Reasons for not having an award were first explored in the 1984 survey, but the 1986 data used here provide greater detail.

7. Other types of settlements include property settlements in lieu of child support (2%) and joint custody (3%).

8. Although paternity establishment can be an issue for the never-married, inability to establish paternity is an infrequently cited reason for having no award (5%). Of course, those who cannot locate the father might also have difficulty establishing paternity. Other reasons for having no award significantly more common among the never-married than among other marital status groups are that they did not go to court or try for child support (3%) and the father is living in the household (3%).

9. The 1984 award rate seems somewhat low by comparison with those in adjacent survey years. Besides the unexpectedly low award rate, the award amount and receipt rate are also unexpectedly high in 1984. Census Bureau officials could give no explanation why the 1984 survey data might differ from the 1982 or 1986 data.

10. In 1986, among separated mothers, 30% of those with no award said the reason was that the final agreement was pending, whereas only 3% of ever-divorced mothers cited this reason.

11. In our data, the average separation among black mothers had lasted 5.8 years, whereas among nonblacks, it had lasted 3.4 years. Separation is sometimes referred to as the poor women's divorce.

12. Although remarried black mothers constitutes a relatively small group and is thus subject to considerable sampling variability, this difference in means is significant at the 5% level. We say that a difference in means is statistically significant if the difference is sufficiently large so that it would

have occurred by chance in less than a set percent of cases, such as 5%. Usually, when a difference of this type is discussed in the text, it is statistically significant. Other differences that may appear large in the tables but are not mentioned in the text are not statistically significant.

13. Ideally, historical trends should be studied using a sample of women with children *ever* eligible for child support rather than *currently* eligible as collected in the CPS. This latter restriction limits the coverage of women divorced or separated a number of years before the survey to those who had young children at the time.

14. 1958 is the earliest year of divorce or separation permitted by our sample restriction that the disruption year be no more than twenty-one years prior to the survey date for women in the 1979 survey. Owing to small sample sizes for the earliest years, however, we must combine the data for those years with later years. 1985 is the latest disruption year for women in the 1986 survey since we exclude from these analyses women whose disruption occurred in the survey year itself.

15. Alfred J. Kahn and Sheila B. Kamerman, *Child Support: From Debt Collection to Social Policy* (Newbury Park, Calif.: Sage, 1988), 12.

16. HHS, Office of Child Support Enforcement, *Child Support Enforcement Statistics: Fiscal 1979*, 1980, table 1; *Child Support Enforcement, Eleventh Annual Report to Congress, for the Period Ending September 30, 1986*, vol. 2, tables 24 and 26.

17. Trends among the never-married can be observed only for the survey years since their records contain inadequate information to identify the year in which the award could be presumed to have been made.

18. HHS, Office of Child Support Enforcement, *Child Support Enforcement, 7th Annual Report to Congress for the Period Ending September 30, 1982*, 70 and 82.

19. That is, these data do not allow us to determine the rate at which women were able to escape from AFDC owing to their obtaining an award (i.e., the transition probability).

20. Overall, the proportion of women eligible for child support who were on AFDC declined from 27% in 1979 to 24% in 1986. By marital status, the proportion declined for the ever-married from 22% to 15% (the largest decline for any demographic group) but fluctuated for the never-married beginning at 49% and ending at 52%. The proportion of nonblack women on AFDC declined from 20% to 17%.

21. HHS, *Child Support Enforcement, Seventh Annual Report*, 76.

22. In each of the four surveys, only women who responded that they were supposed to receive child support in the year prior to the survey were asked: "In total, how much in child support payments were you supposed to receive in [last year]?" In other words, the CPS collected data on dollars of child support due in a particular year only among women due support in that year and not the value of child support originally awarded. What are the implications for our estimates? In each year, about 20% of the women awarded support are not due it because the award was not made until the year of the

survey, their children are over the age limit, the father is deceased (and made no provision for payments to continue), or some other reason. As many of these women are likely to have older children, on average, their awards will have been made longer ago and thus be smaller. Excluding these women's awards from our calculations would tend to bias our figures upward slightly. On another point, the restrictions we place on our samples have limited impact for this sample because women with older children will tend to be the ones no longer due child support and will drop out of the sample. Our restrictions eliminate less than 1% of the sample of women due support.

23. Harry D. Krause, *Child Support in America* (Charlottesville, Va.: Michie, 1981), 23–24.

24. As reported, the survey includes only women who had a child out of wedlock and are *currently* never-married, excluding those who subsequently married. Thus, never-married mothers is a relatively young and adversely selected group, in the sense that for a given age, they are the ones with the poorest marriage prospects. (For a discussion of marriageability issues see, e.g., Becker, *A Treatise on the Family,* chap. 4.)

25. We use nonblack mothers as the reference group for Hispanics since the values for non-Hispanics (not reported) are similar to those for nonblacks.

26. Census Bureau, CPR, series P-60, no. 159, *Money Income of Households, Families and Persons in the United States: 1986.* Washington, D.C.: GPO, 1988, table 29.

27. Care must be taken when considering the figures for some small racial-marital status groups such as never-married mothers of a given race in a given year. Although the change in amount due between 1978 and 1985 is not significant for either race, the amount due is significantly lower for black than for nonblack mothers in 1978 but not in 1985. This indicates that changes over the period narrowed the racial differential.

28. A potential exists for reverse causality here because women with lower child support awards may be more likely to remarry quickly, presumably to restore a better level of living for themselves and their children (Beller and Graham, "Variations in the Economic Well-Being of Divorced Women and Their Children: The Role of Child Support Income," in *Horizontal Equity, Uncertainty, and Measures of Well-Being,* ed. Martin David and Timothy Smeeding, NBER Studies in Income and Wealth Series, vol. 50, Chicago: University of Chicago Press, 1985, 471–509).

29. The CPI is an index of the general price level measured by pricing the items on a list of goods and services purchased by a representative urban household. This index can be used to deflate nominal monetary figures so that they can be compared in real terms over time.

30. These "per child" numbers should not be interpreted to indicate the amount that would be awarded for one child. It is generally recognized that an additional child costs less than a first child. See, e.g., Edward P. Lazear and Robert T. Michael, *Allocation of Income within the Household* (Chicago: University of Chicago Press, 1988). In table 4.7, we show the average amount of child support awarded by the number of children due support.

31. This increase for Hispanics primarily reflects changes in the Census Bureau weighting scheme that gave them greater population weights as of 1984.

32. This cutoff was selected so that we would have at least forty observations in each survey year–disruption year cell.

33. Owing to the Census Bureau sampling procedures, women whose marital disruption took place in 1976 who were still due child support in 1985 were likely to have older children and consequently perhaps fewer children, accounting for some of the decline we observe. While this is true to some extent, the basic point remains. On a per-child basis for marital disruptions that took place in 1976, the average award declined from $2,239 in 1978 to $1,795 in 1981 and to $1,452 in 1985, although the 1983 value of $1,934 exceeded the 1981 value.

34. We do not report the numbers for the survey year and the previous year because many such awards covered only part of the year and thus tend to be abnormally low.

35. But Lieberman (*Child Support in America*) presents evidence that *voluntary* unemployment or lowered earnings have not been considered justifiable grounds for lower awards.

36. Lenore J. Weitzman, "Child Support Myths and Reality," in *Child Support,* ed. Kahn and Kamerman, 256.

37. Carol S. Bruch, "Developing Normative Standards for Child-Support Payments: A Critique of Current Practice," in *The Parental Child-Support Obligation,* ed. Judith Cassetty (Lexington, Mass.: D. C. Heath, 1983), 119–32; National Conference of State Legislatures, *In the Best Interests of the Child: A Guide to State Child Support and Paternity Laws,* by Carolyn Royce Kastner and Lawrence R. Young, Oct. 1982; Lieberman, *Child Support in America.*

38. Census Bureau, Current Population Reports, series P-60, no. 159, *Money Income of Households,* table 29. This assumes that the average income of all men is a good approximation for the average income of noncustodial fathers. But the latter may be younger, more subject to unemployment, and have lower labor force participation rates. Thus, this income measure is likely to be an overestimate.

39. Irwin Garfinkel and Sara S. McLanahan, *Single Mothers and Their Children,* Washington, D.C.: Urban Institute Press, 1986. To get an idea of just how low even these figures are, we compare them to figures for another country, Hungary, where the proportion of income legislated for one child is 20%, with 40% for two children, and 50% for three or more children (Ferenc Kamaras, Hungarian Central Statistical Office, interview with AHB, Budapest, 24 July 1987).

40. See Thomas J. Espenshade, *Investing in Children* (Washington, D.C.: Urban Institute Press, 1984), table 5; and Lazear and Michael, *Allocation of Income within the Household* (Chicago: University of Chicago Press, 1988), table 6.5.

41. There are, however, some differences in the sample selected. Espen-

shade selects two-parent families only, while Lazear and Michael also include one-parent families in their sample.

42. The Espenshade estimates are based upon Engel's food share method, and the Lazear and Michael estimates upon Rothbarth's adult goods method. Angus S. Deaton and John Muellbauer argue that the former overestimates costs, while the latter underestimates them. See "On Measuring Child Costs: With Applications to Poor Countries," *Journal of Political Economy* 94:720–44.

43. We use the overall cpi to convert the published estimates of each author into 1985 dollars. Because Espenshade has already converted his estimates into 1981 dollars using price indexes for specific categories of consumption—whereas Lazear and Michael present their results in 1972–73 dollars—the conversions are slightly different for the two studies.

44. Census Bureau, cpr, series P-60, no. 156, *Money Income of Households, Families and Persons in the United States: 1985.* Washington, D.C.: GPO, 1987, table 23.

45. During the third quarter of 1990, median weekly earnings of wives who worked full-time were $366 compared with $336 for women who maintain families. bls, News, usdl 90–557, Washington, D.C., 29 Oct. 1990, table 1.

46. Some married couples use fathers as a source of child care and some use shift-work, which permits a certain amount of child care by the father. Census Bureau, cpr, series P-70, no. 20, *Who's Minding the Kids? Child Care Arrangements: 1986–87.* Washington, D.C.: GPO, 1990; Harriet B. Presser, "Can We Make Time for Children? The Economy, Work Schedules, and Child Care," *Demography* 26:523–43.

47. The official poverty line is that level of income below which a family of a given size and number of related children under 18 is considered not to have enough money to attain a decent standard of living. The poverty threshold for a single-parent family with two children was $8,662 in 1985 (Census Bureau, cpr, series P-60, no. 158, *Poverty in the United States, 1985.* Washington, D.C.: GPO, 1987, table A-2, p. 163.) This is likely to be an underestimate because in 1990 the official poverty line, which is based upon spending patterns that existed around 1960, was being challenged in Congress as too low. (Patricia Ruggles, *Drawing the Line: Alternative Poverty Measures and their Implications for Public Policy,* Washington, D.C.: Urban Institute Press/University Press of America, 1990.)

48. Philip K. Robins, "Child Support, Welfare Dependency, and Poverty," *American Economic Review* 76:768–88.

49. Irwin Garfinkel and Marygold S. Melli, "The Use of Normative Standards in Family Law Decisions: Developing Mathematical Standards for Child Support," *Family Law Quarterly* 24:157–78.

50. Although these never-married mothers are likely to be a select group, it is not on the basis of observable characteristics; that is, they are younger, less educated and more likely to be black than ever-married mothers due support. The selectivity, then, must be on the basis of unobservable characteristics, such as greater initiative and determination of the mother or perhaps the greater ability or desire of the children's father to pay.

51. David Chambers shows that fathers who have more frequent contact with their children are more likely to pay support (*Making Fathers Pay,* Chicago: University of Chicago Press, 1979). See also Judith A. Seltzer, Nora Cate Schaeffer, and Hong-wen Charng, "Family Ties after Divorce: The Relationship between Visiting and Paying Child Support," *Journal of Marriage and the Family* 51:1013–32.

52. Although we have only 23 remarried black mothers in our sample in 1978 and 34 in 1985, this increase in the receipt rate is significant at the 5% level.

53. In our sample, among women due support, the average number of years since separation for black mothers is 5 compared with 3 for nonblack mothers.

54. Women who can afford a private attorney would probably use one as each public attorney has many IV-D cases to handle and thus cannot devote too much time to any one case. (Comments to AHB by Thomas M. Vaught, assistant attorney general, state of Illinois, 10 Aug. 1990.)

55. Although AFDC recipients are required to cooperate with the IV-D agency, prior to the initiation of the $50 disregard in 1984, in which that amount of child support was passed through to the mother, she may not always have known whether her child's father was paying support; thus, prior to 1985 receipt rates among AFDC recipients may be biased downward.

56. Of course, during the 1980s, changes in the AFDC program itself tended to reduce the number and proportion of women on AFDC, so that not all of this change is necessarily attributable to the child support enforcement program.

57. This latter increase is not statistically significant.

58. There is reason to believe that this per child comparison may be somewhat misleading for never-married mothers. According to the "sibling deeming" provision of AFDC, enacted as part of the Deficit Reduction Act of 1984 (DEFRA), if any child in a family receives child support, that money is deemed available to support all of the children and must be counted in determining AFDC benefits. Thus, it does not matter how many children are covered by the child support award. Moreover, since the vast majority of the increase in the number of children for never-married mothers occurs after 1984, it may be a spurious increase reflecting the fact that after that date all of their children had to be counted in determining the welfare grant.

59. Never-married nonblack mothers receiving support is a small but growing group. Our sample contains 16 in 1978 and 45 in 1985. Despite the small size of the group, the decline is statistically significant at the 10% level.

60. Remarried black mothers receiving support is a very small group, 13 in 1978 and 26 in 1985, and the increase in amount received is not significantly different from zero.

61. By contrast to the ratio of the average amounts, the average ratio shows how the proportion received varies, independently of level of child support due. Since the average amounts are affected by the level of child support, their ratio may give a different picture.

62. There is some ambiguity here as to just how women might report the

amount due. They could give the amount specified in their written agreement or they might give the amount they informally renegotiated with their children's absent father. For a very small proportion of women in our sample (1.5%), the amount received is greater than the amount due, suggesting that at least some women are giving the former amount (or that the father is paying arrears).

63. By contrast to the receipt rate, the ratio of child support received to child support due does not appear to decline as years go by since the marital disruption. Thus, although some fathers cease to pay as the years pass, those who continue to pay do not tend to reduce the proportion paid.

64. Census Bureau, CPR, series P-60, no. 173, *Child Support and Alimony: 1989*. Washington, D.C.: GPO, 1991. As pointed out in the notes to chap. 1, however, there may be some problems of comparability in the data.

Chapter 3: An Economic Model of Child Support

1. Census Bureau, *Statistical Abstract of the United States, 1982–83*, Washington, D.C.: GPO, 1982, table 73; and ibid., 1987, table 68.

2. Roger A. Wojtkiewicz, Sara S. McLanahan, and Irwin Garfinkel, "The Growth of Families Headed by Women: 1950–1980," *Demography* 27:19–30.

3. Given our focus upon child support, we ignore individuals without children in making income comparisons by household type.

4. Census Bureau, CPR, series P-60, no. 157, *Money Income and Poverty Status of Families and Persons in the United States: 1986*. Washington, D.C.: GPO, 1987, table 1.

5. See, e.g., Gary S. Becker, Elisabeth M. Landes, and Robert T. Michael, "An Economic Analysis of Marital Instability," *Journal of Political Economy* 85:1141–88.

6. Eleanor E. Maccoby, Charlene E. Depner, and Robert H. Mnookin, "Custody of Children Following Divorce," in *Impact of Divorce, Single Parenting and Stepparenting on Children,* ed. E. Mavis Hetherington and Josephine D. Aresteh (Hillsdale, N.J.: Lawrence Erlbaum, 1988), 91–114.

7. Census Bureau, CPR, series P-70, no. 13, *Who's Helping Out: Support Networks among American Families*. Washington, D.C.: GPO, 1988, table D.

8. See Lenore J. Weitzman, *The Divorce Revolution* (New York: Free Press, 1985); and Saul D. Hoffman and Greg J. Duncan, "What *Are* the Economic Consequences of Divorce?" *Demography* 25:641–45.

9. Census Bureau, CPR, series P-60, no. 157, *Money Income and Poverty Status of Families and Persons in the United States: 1986,* table 7.

10. This section draws heavily upon ideas developed by Saul Hoffman in "An Economic Model of Child Support Payments," University of Delaware, June 1990, and from similar themes developed in "Children as Collective Goods and Divorce Settlements," by Weiss and Willis, *Journal of Labor Economics* (July 1985): 268–92.

11. Hoffman shows that if the mother's own utility function is Cobb-Douglas, this spending pattern will prevail.

12. That is, there is both a substitution effect and an income effect at work.

13. Although total costs are sure to increase as she asks for more and more support, it is not clear that her marginal or incremental costs would also increase: over some range, marginal costs could be constant or even declining, since securing additional dollars of support may get easier rather than harder. Fortunately, stability in fig. 3.6 requires only that the slope of the marginal cost curve exceed the slope of the marginal benefit curve.

14. If there is an unanticipated decline in his long-run ability to pay, he is likely to seek a permanent change in the support order.

15. H. Elizabeth Peters and Laura M. Argys, "Changes in Child Support Payments after Divorce: Compliance and Modifications," paper presented at the Allied Social Science Association annual meetings, Washington, D.C., December 1990.

16. Frank F. Furstenberg, Jr., "Supporting Fathers: Implications of the Family Support Act for Men," paper presented at the Population Association of America annual meetings, Toronto, Canada, May 1990.

17. Kurt J. Beron, "Applying the Economic Model of Crime to Child Support Enforcement: A Theoretical and Empirical Analysis," *Review of Economics and Statistics* 70:382–90.

18. The effect on receipts of contacting the IV-D office is examined in Philip Robins, "Child Support, Welfare Dependency, and Poverty," *American Economic Review* 76:768–88.

19. Becker, *A Treatise on the Family* (Cambridge, Mass.: Harvard University Press, 1981). See chap. 4, "Assortative Mating in the Marriage Market," esp. pp. 75–76.

20. See, e.g., William Julius Wilson, *The Truly Disadvantaged: The Inner City, the Underclass and Public Policy* (Chicago: University of Chicago Press, 1987).

21. Prior experience with the 1979 CPS data supports the claim that the mother's characteristics serve as useful proxies for father's income. In that survey mothers were actually asked to estimate father's income. When we introduced this income measure into our analyses, we found that the effects of the mother's characteristics on child support outcomes were significantly reduced, suggesting that the latter are good proxies for the father's income. These findings are reported in Beller and Graham, "Variations in the Economic Well-being of Divorced Women and Their Children: The Role of Child Support Income," in *Horizontal Equity, Uncertainty and Measures of Economic Well-Being,* ed. Martin David and Timothy Smeeding, NBER Studies in Income and Wealth, vol. 50 (Chicago: University of Chicago Press, 1985), 471–509.

22. In addition, many of the fathers in our sample are likely to be members of the baby-boom generation who have experienced smaller-than-average income growth.

23. Frank F. Furstenberg, Jr., and Kathleen Mullan Harris, "The Disappearing American Father? Divorce and the Waning Significance of Biological Parenthood," University of Pennsylvania, March 1990.

24. As discussed in chap. 1, this means that we have to rely solely on the

mother's report of how much child support he pays, which may differ from his own report.

25. See Freya L. Sonenstein and Charles A. Calhoun, "Determinants of Child Support: A Pilot Survey of Absent Parents," *Contemporary Policy Issues* 8:75–94; and Martha S. Hill, "The Role of Economic Resources and Dual-Family Status in Child Support Payments," paper presented at the Population Association of America annual meetings, New Orleans, April 1988.

26. Ron Haskins, "Child Support: A Father's View," in *Child Support,* ed. Kahn and Kamerman, 306–27.

27. Hill, "The Role of Economic Resources."

28. Catherine R. Albiston, Eleanor E. Maccoby, and Robert R. Mnookin, "Does Joint Legal Custody Matter?" *Stanford Law & Policy Review* (Spring 1990): 167–79. See esp. table 10.

29. See Sonenstein and Calhoun, "Determinants of Child Support"; Frank F. Furstenberg, Jr., James Peterson, Christine Nord, and Nicholas Zill, "The Life Course of Children of Divorce: Marital Disruption and Parental Contact," *American Sociological Review* 48:656–68; and Judith Seltzer, Nora Schaeffer, and Hong-wen Charng, "Family Ties after Divorce: The Relationship between Visiting and Paying Child Support," *Journal of Marriage and the Family* 51:1013–32.

30. See Haskins, "Child Support," 318–9 for a summary of several studies. See also Furstenberg and Harris, "The Disappearing American Father."

31. Perhaps surprisingly, child support payments reported by a father are no higher among men who characterize their relationship with a mother as "very friendly," than among fathers who say their relationship is less than "very friendly."

Chapter 4: Child Support Awards: Determinants, Differentials, and Trends

1. Throughout the text, we reserve the term *significant* to denote statistical significance, as defined in app. B.

2. As discussed in app. B, when the dependent variable is dichotomous (i.e., takes a value of 1.0 for women with an award and 0 for women without an award), the relation can be estimated with a probit function. The probit coefficients—adjusted appropriately—can then be interpreted as the *ceteris paribus* effect.

3. From the full sample of 15,658 mothers used to generate aggregate statistics in chap. 2, we excluded 283 ever-married mothers missing data on marital disruption year and another 276 mothers missing data on their children's ages, leaving 15,099 eligible mothers. In addition, unlike the nationally representative aggregate estimates given in chap. 2, our regression estimates are based upon unweighted sample data. Although the decomposition analyses reported in tables 4.2 and 4.3 also use unweighted data, we have rescaled the figures reported in those tables to conform to the aggregate differentials from chap. 2. This rescaling is done by multiplying the unweighted figures by the ratio of weighted to unweighted sample means.

4. In general, our socioeconomic variables do not do a very good job explaining differences in award status among the never married.

5. That is, four times the coefficient on years of education (2.8%) minus the coefficient on college graduate (6.9%).

6. We use a linear time trend, DSTREND, to control for the year of the marital disruption. DSTREND equals the last two digits of the marital disruption year minus 57, and thus, given our sample restrictions on the divorce or separation year, ranges from 0 to 29.

7. Casual observation would suggest that this is true of many different types of legislation.

8. Our analysis uses the decomposition technique discussed in app. B.

9. We estimated separate award rate equations by race using multivariate probit analysis. The racial differences in average characteristics can then be evaluated with (i.e., multiplied by) coefficients from either the black or non-black regression. The figures in the table and the text use the nonblack coefficients. When the black coefficients are used, we can explain 51% of the overall racial difference. We used the nonblack coefficients because, individually and as a group, they were estimated with more statistical precision.

10. Among the ever-married only, racial differences in mother's characteristics account for less of the explained differential than they do among all mothers because a large part of that differential is owing to the disproportionate presence of never-married mothers among the black subgroup.

11. Mean male income, in current dollars, of year-round full-time workers age 15 and over (14 and over prior to 1980), by race, from 1958 to 1986 comes from the Census Bureau, CPR, series P-60, no. 159, *Money Income of Households, Families and Persons in the United States: 1986*. Washington, D.C.: GPO, 1988, table 29. For blacks, we used the "nonwhite" income series, and for nonblacks, the "white" series. This approximation assumes that the distribution of income around the mean did not change over the period and that the income of full-time workers can be used to represent the income of ever-married fathers.

12. This estimate is obtained by multiplying the $8,000 racial difference in income by the 1.0 percentage point estimate of the effect of a $1,000 increase in income, derived from the probit coefficient on male income in an equation for nonblacks only.

13. Weiss and Willis, "An Economic Analysis of Divorce Settlements," University of Chicago, April 1989, 16.

14. See Elmer P. Martin and Joanne Mitchell Martin, *The Black Extended Family* (Chicago: University of Chicago Press, 1978).

15. Neil G. Bennett, David E. Bloom, and Patricia H. Craig, "The Divergence of Black and White Marriage Patterns," *American Journal of Sociology* 95:692–722.

16. This estimate uses the regression coefficients from the ever-married probit to evaluate the difference in means. When we use the coefficients from the never-married probit, we explain only 1% of the overall differential.

17. This estimate is based upon probit coefficients for ever-divorced

women only. When probit coefficients for currently separated women are used instead, only 4.3 points of the 35.6 percentage point differential is explained.

18. Census Bureau, CPR, series P-60, no. 156, *Money Income of House-holds, Families, and Persons in the United States: 1985*. Washington, D.C.: GPO, 1987, table 33. Of course, not all fathers of children of never-married mothers are never-married themselves, but this is their most likely marital status.

19. We evaluate the impact on award rates of income differences by marital status on the same basis we evaluated income differences by race—i.e., at a rate of 1 percentage point in award rates for each $1,000 in income.

20. The results in table 4.3 are based upon separate probit regressions for each racial and marital status group. For all women and for never-married mothers, these are the same probits used to generate table 4.1. For ever-married mothers as a group, and by race, we replace the year of the marital disruption in table 4.1 with male real income in the year of the disruption, by converting to constant dollars the income series described in note 11 above.

21. This equals the difference between the 1986 and 1979 predicted prob-abilities of having an award, where the predicted probabilities are obtained by evaluating the probit function using the 1986 and 1979 weighted means of the socioeconomic variables listed in table 4.1 (holding never-married constant at the 1979 level).

22. This calculation is similar to that explained in the preceding note, except that all socioeconomic variables except for the percent never married are held constant at their 1979 levels.

23. These demographic changes are evaluated using the probit coefficients from a separate never-married regression using all four years of CPS data.

24. The average marital disruption in the 1979 survey occurred in 1973, while in the 1986 survey, it occurred in 1980. It may be recalled from table 2.7 that the real incomes of men stagnated after 1973. Thus, average male income associated with disruption year changed little between the 1979 and 1986 surveys.

25. That is, we take the difference between the probit function at the 1979 and 1986 values of male income, holding the socioeconomic variables constant at their 1979 levels.

26. Most exits occur because the children are no longer eligible for support; most entries occur through new marital disruptions.

27. In addition, some women already in the pool who did not negotiate an award at the time of their marital disruption may have obtained one since. This source of change is not likely to be very important, however, because, as evidence presented in note 28 below shows, few mothers appear to obtain an award subsequent to their marital disruption.

28. Some of the statistical analysis underlying table 4.1 provides further, albeit indirect, evidence that most mothers sought their awards at the time of their marital disruption. Initially we found that ever-married mothers in the 1986 survey were more likely to have an award than mothers in the 1979 survey, even after controlling for differences in their socioeconomic charac-

teristics. Once we also controlled for the date of their marital disruption, however, differences in award rates by survey year disappeared. This means, for example, that a woman divorced in 1975 and surveyed in 1986 is no more likely to have an award than another woman (with similar characteristics) also divorced in 1975 but surveyed in 1979. Thus, if the award rate of a given divorce cohort (i.e., 1975) has not changed between 1979 and 1986, we might conclude that few mothers without an award at the time of their marital disruption (or at least by 1979) obtained one after that.

29. Since there is nothing comparable to disruption year for never-married mothers (who represent about 20% of the eligible population), we exclude them from the present analysis. A possible proxy for the date of their child support award might be survey year minus the age of the child. There are, however, several important problems with this proxy. First, for women with more than one child, it is not clear which child's age should be used, since the survey does not identify which child the award applies to. Second, even if she has only one child, it is not clear that she obtained, or tried to obtain, an award at the date of the child's birth since most states allow a women to establish paternity and seek an award at any time up to the child's eighteenth birthday.

30. Census Bureau, CPR, series P-60, no. 159, table 29.

31. Census Bureau, *Statistical Abstract of the United States: 1982–83.* Washington, D.C.: GPO, 1982, tables 60 and 124.

32. Although many of these new laws were designed to enforce existing obligations rather than to establish new ones, one might argue that attention to child support enforcement generally is likely to have a positive impact on award rates. Another possibility is that the introduction of effective child support enforcement per se slowed the upward trend in new award rates. When child support orders are not strongly enforced, the cost of agreeing to one is negligible; but if a father knows that he will actually have to pay, he may be less likely to agree to an award in the first place.

33. In the following analysis, we exclude women whose disruptions occurred during the year of the survey (since many are separated mothers still in the process of negotiating an award), which reduces our total sample from 12,043 to 11,496 cases.

34. If the presence of younger children reduces (raises) the probability of an award, then our estimate of the annual percentage point change in new award rates will be biased upward (downward), unless we control directly for the effect of age. We do this using a variable called KID6TO17, which equals 1.0 if at least one child is between the ages of 6 and 17, and 0 if all children are under 6 or older than 17. It should be noted that KID6TO17 may be measured with some error, since some of the children in the household may not be the ones eligible for child support.

35. The estimates are derived from separate probit regressions for blacks and nonblacks, which relate whether or not a woman has a child support award to a linear time trend tied to the year of her marital disruption (DSTREND, as defined earlier), while at the same time controlling for her socioeconomic characteristics, as in table 4.1. The estimates given in table 4.4 equal the probit

coefficient on DSTREND multiplied by the standard normal density function evaluated at the sample mean of the award rate.

36. In the unweighted regression samples, black women are only 15% of ever-married women but 33% of separated women.

37. This was accomplished by including not only DSTREND but also LAW in the separate racial probit regressions, where LAW equals the last two digits of the year of the marital disruption minus 75.

38. We also experimented with splitting the period at other dates, but the split after 1975 provided the best fit to DSTREND and LAW.

39. Less successfully, we also tried male unemployment rates and the ratio of female to male incomes in the year of the disruption.

40. That is, we reestimate the probit equations underlying table 4.4 by relating whether or not a woman has a child support award not only to a simple linear time trend but also to male real incomes in the year of her marital disruption. The estimated effect of the latter captures the relation between changes in new award rates and changes in male incomes, while the former captures the trend in new awards that cannot be explained by changes in male incomes.

41. For all ever-married women, the probit coefficient had a t-value of 3.59. Among nonblacks only, the effect of $1,000 of income was 1.0% (with a t-value of 3.33), and among blacks the effect was 0.52% (with a t-value of 0.54).

42. More precisely, 0.29 and 0.35 represent the annual percentage point increases in new award rates that remain *unexplained* by socioeconomic characteristics or male real incomes.

43. Census Bureau, CPR, series P-60, no. 159, table 29.

44. To see this, observe that the aggregate award rate of ever-married mothers is simply a weighted average of the new award rates of all women currently eligible for support, where the weights depend upon the relative sizes of each new award (or marital disruption) cohort. If these weights (which sum to 1) remain constant over time, the aggregate award rate will necessarily rise at the same rate as new award rates. But if the weights assigned to more recent disruptions decline over time owing to a secular decline in the rate of marital dissolution, then the aggregate award rate will rise more slowly than new award rates.

45. As noted in chap. 1, divorce rates peaked in 1981. One way to see the effects of this in our surveys is to notice from table 3.4 that, for all ever-married mothers eligible for child support, the average years since marital disruption increased from 6.0 years in 1979 to 6.4 years in 1986.

46. For reasons noted in chap. 2, not all women awarded child support are due it. In this section we examine support levels for the latter group only.

47. As discussed in app. B, we use ordinary least squares, where the dependent variable is the value of child support due (measured in 1985 dollars) and the independent variables are the socioeconomic characteristics of women due support listed in table 4.5. Sample sizes, which are noted in the table, are smaller than in chap. 2 because we excluded 64 women for whom we do not know the ages of their children and 145 women for whom we do not know

the year of their marital disruption. In addition, unlike the means in chap. 2, our regressions use unweighted data. The decomposition results in tables 4.6 and 4.7 are also based upon these unweighted regression samples, but figures in those tables have been adjusted by the ratio of weighted to unweighted means to correspond to the aggregate differentials in chap. 2.

48. The value of child support awarded is likely to depend upon the father's income at the time of the initial award. Thus, even if we could observe his current income, it is not clear that it would be a better proxy than her characteristics for his ability to pay at the time of the award.

49. For all women due support, the overall racial difference in awards is $589, which is less than the ceteris paribus difference of $653. This suggests that, on average, black women exhibit other characteristics that tend to raise their award amounts relative to nonblacks. We investigate these factors later in this chapter.

50. Edward P. Lazear and Robert T. Michael, *Allocation of Income within the Household* (Chicago: University of Chicago Press, 1988), table 5.11, panel B.

51. Of course, as noted in chap. 2, the causation could be reversed: women due less support may be more likely to have remarried in order to have a new source of support for their children. We examine this issue in more detail in chap. 7.

52. Although the relative advantage of the first two regions also appears in the overall means, the southern advantage does not. The reason for this is that, on average, women in the South exhibit other characteristics (such as a greater likelihood of being black) that would tend to lower awards relative to women in the West.

53. H. Elizabeth Peters, "Marriage and Divorce: Informational Constraints and Private Contracting," *American Economic Review* 76:437–54.

54. The ceteris paribus central city disadvantage exceeds the overall disadvantage of women in central cities, suggesting that on average the other characteristics of women in central cities would tend to raise their award amounts.

55. We ran separate award regressions by race. The figure in the text is obtained by multiplying the coefficient on "never-married" from the black regression of $-935 by the racial difference in the fraction of the population never married of -.21, and then dividing by the total differential of $612.

56. The difference in average characteristics is evaluated at the black coefficients.

57. We converted nominal male income to real 1985 dollars the same way we converted nominal dollars due into real 1985 dollars. That is, for women due child support in 1978, we multiplied both male income and child support due by 1.649, which represents the CPI in 1985 relative to 1978. For women due support in 1981, we multiplied both by 1.183, and for women due support in 1983, we multiplied both by 1.080.

58. That is, we multiply the black income coefficient of .0618 by the racial difference in average incomes of $5,903, and then adjust this product by the ratio of the weighted to unweighted total differential ($372/$333).

59. See Francine D. Blau and John W. Graham, "Black-White Differences in Wealth and Asset Composition," *Quarterly Journal of Economics* 105:321–39.

60. See Graham and Beller, "The Effect of Child Support Payments on the Labor Supply of Female Family Heads: An Econometric Analysis," *Journal of Human Resources* 24, app. C. See also Philip Robins, "Child Support, Welfare Dependency, and Poverty," *American Economic Review* 76 (1986), table 1.

61. See Robert Moffitt, "An Economic Model of Welfare Stigma," *American Economic Review* 73:1023–35, table 2.

62. As discussed in chap. 2, given the way the Census Bureau posed the child support and paternity questions to never-married mothers, it is not possible to determine if all of the children present have the same father, nor if the child support award applies to all or only one of the children. Thus, while a never-married mother with two or more children present may report having a child support award, it is possible that the award applies to only one of her children.

63. Because so few never-married mothers were due support, we used the coefficients from the regression for all marital status groups combined (table 4.5, col. 1), rather than from separate regressions by marital status, to evaluate differences in means of the socioeconomic characteristics between never-married and ever-married mothers.

64. The unexplained differential is the $797 coefficient on "never-married" reported in table 4.5, col. 1, adjusted by the factor ($1,460/$1,480.7), which is the ratio of the weighted to unweighted sample differential in award amounts.

65. Some mothers may have obtained their award subsequent to the date of their disruption, but we have no way of detecting this since the CPS data do not provide the date of the original award. In our analysis of award rates we offered some indirect evidence that suggests most awards were obtained at the time of the marital disruption. We assume this to be the case in the analysis that follows.

66. It can be shown mathematically that, under fairly general conditions, the real value of new awards and child support due will decline at the same rate. See the mathematical appendix to Graham and Beller, "Trends in the Value of Child Support Awards," paper presented at the Population Association of America Annual Meetings, Toronto, Canada, 3 May 1990.

67. This measure was first used by Philip K. Robins in "Why are Child Support Award Amounts Declining?" Institute for Research on Poverty, Discussion Paper no. 885–89, June 1989.

68. The results reported in table 4.7 are derived from a standard decomposition analysis based upon separate regressions by survey year. As discussed in app. B, this allows us to decompose the change in the dependent variable (dollars due) across survey years into an explained portion owing to changes in the means of the independent variables and an unexplained portion resulting from changes in the coefficients. An alternative procedure would be to estimate a single equation with all four years of data, allowing for intercept differences

by including dummy variables for the survey year. Here, the coefficients on the survey year dummies would represent the unexplained change. Robins follows this latter procedure in "Why are Child Support Award Amounts Declining?" but he neglects to include survey year dummies, which incorrectly constrains his independent variables to explain the full change across surveys in dollars due, leaving him with no unexplained change.

69. In other words, we evaluate the demographic changes that occurred between 1978 and 1985 and between 1978 and 1981 based on the coefficients from a child support due regression using 1978 data only. We evaluate demographic changes between 1981 and 1985 based on regression coefficients using 1981 data only.

70. In a regression of all women due child support using 1978 data only, never-married mothers were due $962 less support than other women with identical characteristics. The $33 figure in the text equals $962 times .034, the increase in the percentage never-married.

71. Following this procedure, we estimate that among mothers due child support in 1978 each percentage point of inflation from the date of their award to 1978 lowered the real value of child support due in 1978 by $15.97 (measured in 1985 constant dollars). A separate statistical analysis conducted for women due support in 1981 finds that each percentage point of inflation from the date of their award to 1981 lowered the real value of support due in 1981 by $7.14 (again, measured in 1985 dollars).

72. This is because, on average, women in 1981(85) had experienced 17.4 (8.11) percentage points more inflation since their award than women in 1978, and each percentage point of inflation lowers the real value of child support due per year by $15.97.

73. That is, we multiply a 9.29 percentage point decline in the cumulative inflation rate times the $7.14 inflation effect estimated for mothers due support in 1981 (see note 71 above).

74. Formally, according to the theory of decomposition analysis presented in app. B, the unexplained change between, say 1978 and 1985, is due to changes in the child support due regression coefficients between 1978 and 1985.

75. To express awards in 1985 constant dollars, we multiply current dollars due by the ratio of the CPI in 1985 to the CPI in the year of the award. The value of new awards expressed in 1985 constant dollars would also equal the nominal value of child support due in 1985 if all awards were fully indexed to the CPI.

76. Controlling for the socioeconomic characteristics in table 4.5, we related the natural log of the nominal value of child support due to the simple linear time trend, DSTREND, defined as the last two digits of the marital disruption year minus 57. The regression coefficient on DSTREND represents the annual rate of increase in the value of new awards.

77. This estimate is derived from a regression of the log of the real value of new awards on DSTREND and the socioeconomic control variables listed in table 4.5, where 3.5% is the coefficient on DSTREND.

78. We related the natural log of the value of new awards made to ever-

married mothers between 1958 and 1985 (expressed first in current and then in 1985 constant dollars) to the natural log of the CPI in the year of the award, holding socioeconomic characteristics constant. The regression coefficient on the log of the CPI represents the percentage increase in the value of new awards associated with a 1% increase in the CPI.

79. That is, we defined a spline function that allowed the estimated coefficient on the natural log of the CPI to differ before and after 1980.

80. Another way to study this question is to estimate the award relation for each of the four surveys separately. Because more than half of all mothers in any survey were divorced or separated within six years of the date of the survey, the estimated relation obtained from each survey separately primarily reflects the experiences of the most recent six cohorts. In general, we find that the association between prices and awards by survey year is roughly the same as for the full sample, suggesting a stable relation over time.

81. Lieberman, *Child Support in America*.

82. Robert D. Thompson and Susan F. Paikin, "Formulas and Guidelines for Support," *Juvenile and Family Court Journal* 36:33–40.

83. These estimates are obtained from relating the natural log of the value of new awards (in both current and constant dollars) to the natural log of the current value of male incomes, holding constant socioeconomic characteristics. In work not shown, we also related the value of new awards to the simple ratio of female to male incomes of full-time workers in that year because some states also considered the mother's income in arriving at an award amount. This ratio variable was statistically significant, but its t-value was not as large as that of male incomes alone. When we related the log of child support to the log of male income and the ratio of female to male incomes together, only the log of male income was statistically significant.

84. Following our earlier analysis of awards and prices, we also experimented to see whether the association between increases in nominal award amounts and increases in male incomes had changed over the period. We could find very little evidence of any structural shift in that relation.

85. That is, we regressed the log of new awards in 1985 constant dollars on a linear time trend (DSTREND) and the log of male real income in the year of the award (INCOME85), along with the mother's socioeconomic characteristics from table 4.5. The estimated coefficient on DSTREND is $-.0365$ with a t-value of 14.55, and the coefficient on INCOME85 is .5997 with a t-value of 3.31.

86. Robins, "Why Are Child Support Award Amounts Declining?"

87. When we regress the real value of new awards against Robins's ratio of female-to-male earnings (FTMRATIO) and the socioeconomic variables in table 4.5, the coefficient on FTMRATIO is -10173.8 with a t-value of 11.75.

88. In addition to those explanations given in the text, there is reason to believe that Robins's female-to-male earnings ratio series (which increases from .136 in 1961 to .419 in 1985) overstates the increase in the relative earnings capacity of single mothers. He adjusts the median earnings of women by the labor force participation rate of married women. It is not clear that "potential" earnings should be adjusted by participation rates at all, and if they are

adjusted, it is not clear that the participation rate of married women is preferred to that of single mothers, which was higher and did not rise as rapidly.
Unadjusted by any labor force participation rates, the ratio of female-to-male
median earnings rose from .380 in 1961 to .525 in 1985.

89. According to Lieberman, *Child Support in America,* 4–5, before 1974
the only legal responsibility for the financial support of the child was that of
the father, and by 1986, only eight states had encoded the mother's financial
responsibility into law in the Uniform Marriage and Divorce Act.

90. The t-ratio on the log of the CPI is 1.86, while that on FTMRATIO is
only 0.90.

91. Peters, "Marriage and Divorce"; and Lenore J. Weitzman, *The Divorce
Revolution: The Unexpected Social and Economic Consequences for Women
and Children* (New York: Free Press, 1985).

92. For a summary of the Family Support Act, see HR, Committee on
Ways and Means, *Background Material and Data on Programs within the
Jurisdiction of the Committee on Ways and Means.* Washington, D.C.: GPO,
1989, 590–600.

93. This estimate equals the mean of new awards expressed in 1985 dollars
among all women due support in 1978. In other words, for each woman due
support in 1978, we multiply the nominal value of support due by the CPI in
1985 divided by the CPI in the year of her marital disruption.

94. The periodic review requirements in the Family Support Act stop far
short of full indexation since review is mandated only for cases processed
through the IV-D system, and then only every three years.

95. Census Bureau, CPR, series P-60, no. 173, *Child Support and Alimony:
1989.* Washington, D.C.: GPO, 1991, table F.

96. Assuming that the average amount of support by marital status remained unchanged between 1985 and 1989, (that is, $2,494 overall, $2,575
ever-married, and $1,419 never-married), given the increase in never-married
mothers to 11.8% of all those due support in 1989, the average amount of
support due overall could have been expected to fall to $2,439.

*Chapter 5: Child Support Receipts: Determinants, Differentials, and
Trends*

1. The regression sample of mothers due support contains 7,497 cases,
214 less than in chap. 2 owing to missing data on child's age and the value of
child support due. In addition, unlike chap. 2, these regressions are based
upon unweighted data. In tables 5.2–5.4, we have rescaled our estimates to
conform to those reported in chap. 2 by multiplying by the ratio of the weighted
means in chap. 2 to the unweighted means of chap. 5.

2. We define "years since marital disruption" to be zero for never-married
mothers. Thus, when we compare never-married to ever-married women, we
are comparing, more precisely, the never-married to ever-married women
whose disruption occurred less than one year ago.

3. The details of these estimates are reported in table 15.2 in Beller and
Graham, "Variations in the Economic Well-Being of Divorced Women and

Their Children: The Role of Child Support Income," in *Horizontal Equity, Uncertainty and Economic Well-Being,* ed. Martin David and Timothy Smeeding (Chicago: University of Chicago Press, 1985), 471–506.

4. Using all four years of data, we also related receipt rates to several aggregate proxies for the father's income and employment status—including (for each sample year) the male unemployment rate in the mother's state of residence, the annual rate of increase of male incomes, and the annual inflation rate. None of these aggregate variables was significantly related to receipt rates. It may simply be that no aggregate statistic is able to capture individual differences in the father's current ability to pay. In one study in California in which the father's characteristics are known, his unemployment experience was found to be the most important predictor of whether or not he paid. (For details, see Peters and Argys, "Changes in Child Support Payments," 9.)

5. That is, we added several income variables to the basic regression underlying the second column of table 5.1. These variables were the mother's total personal income excluding child support and income by source—i.e., earnings, public assistance, and other nonwage income. The analysis in this section does not imply a direction of causation between income and receipts but rather simply tests whether or not receipts and income are related at all.

6. This decomposition is based upon separate regressions by race, using the black regression coefficients to evaluate the differences in the means of the independent variables. For a more complete discussion of decomposition analysis, see app. B.

7. The racial difference in means of socioeconomic characteristics is evaluated at the nonblack regression coefficients. A very similar magnitude is explained using black coefficients.

8. This result is obtained by evaluating the racial difference in child support due using nonblack regression coefficients. Among nonblacks, each additional $1,000 of support due raises the receipt rate by almost 2.7 percentage points. We could explain even more of the differential using black coefficients: among blacks, each $1,000 of support due raises receipt rates by 3.3 points.

9. We ran separate regressions for divorced and separated women. The results reported in table 5.2 use the coefficients from the separated regression to evaluate the differences in means of the independent variables. The explained difference is considerably smaller when the divorced regression coefficients are used to evaluate differences in means.

10. We ran separate regressions for remarried and divorced women. The results reported in table 5.2 use the coefficients from the remarried regression to evaluate the differences in means.

11. Recent evidence also suggests that some remarried fathers tend to from strong emotional bonds with the children from their new marriage to the neglect of the children of their former marriage. See Furstenberg, "Supporting Fathers."

12. That is, we are evaluating the changes in the means of the socioeconomic variables using the coefficients from a regression sample of women due support in 1978.

13. When we control for the amount of child support due, the change in the receipt rate expected on the basis of changes in socioeconomic characteristics is slightly larger (2.0 points) than when we do not (1.7 points) owing to differences in some of the underlying regression coefficients.

14. Unlike our usual analysis of trends, which is based upon separate regressions by sample year, we use all four years of data together to estimate trends for the marital status subgroups because sample sizes become quite small for some subgroups using only 1979 data. In the combined four-year data set, we use dummy variables to control for sample year. In this formulation, the coefficient on YEAR86 (indicating 1985 data) can be interpreted as the change in the receipt rate that is unexplained by other factors.

15. The real value of child support due fell 21.6% for blacks and 23.6% for nonblacks.

16. Changes in the value of child support due never-married mothers also help explain some of the changes in their receipt rate across individual surveys: between 1978 and 1981 the receipt rate declined 17.4 points, while the value of support due declined 17.9 percent; between 1981 and 1985 the receipt rate rose 13.1 points, while the value of support due rose 11.5% (see tables 2.4 and 2.8).

17. If the mother is on AFDC, it is the state that decides whether or not to initiate legal action.

18. Table 3.1 summarizes our expectations about the sign of the effect of particular socioeconomic characteristics on child support receipts.

19. In around 1% of the sample, women report receiving more child support in a given year than they report being due. This may be because current receipts include payments that were due in an earlier period or because receipts reflect prior informal agreements to provide more support.

20. Since the sample consists only of women receiving child support, there is the potential of selection bias to the extent that women who receive support differ in unobservable ways from women who do not. We correct for this using a technique proposed by James J. Heckman in "Sample Selection Bias as a Specification Error," *Econometrica* 47:153–61, as discussed more fully in app. B. We found evidence of selection bias in table 5.5, cols. 1 and 3 but not in col. 2.

21. For all of the regression analyses reported in this section, we excluded 135 mothers missing data on their child's age from the full sample of 5,629 represented in table 2.11. We excluded another 13 mothers for reasons explained in the note to table 2.13. Sample sizes are noted in table 5.5. Unlike the estimates in chap. 2, the regressions are based upon unweighted data. For consistency with the figures in chap. 2, aggregate differentials and trends reported in tables 5.6 and 5.7 are then adjusted by the ratio of weighted to unweighted means.

22. As in our analysis of receipt rates, we define "years since marital disruption" to be zero for never-married mothers.

23. These results are reported in Beller and Graham, "Variations in the Economic Well-Being of Divorced Mothers," 481–86.

24. To the basic receipt regression underlying col. 1, table 5.5, we added

either mother's current income excluding child support or income by source—earnings, AFDC benefits, and other nonwage income.

25. When child support due is the only independent variable (other than a constant term) in the receipt amount regression, the R^2 is .772. The addition of the socioeconomic variables in table 5.5 raises the R^2 to .782.

26. The goodness of fit, or R^2, also increases from .727 in the first sub-period to .860 in the second.

27. In fig. 5.1, the ratio of received to due can be represented as the slope of a ray from the origin to a point on the 1978 or 1985 line. At the sample means of due and received, these rays (approximately) have the slope of .84 in 1978 and .81 in 1985. Because the slope of the 1978 line (i.e., the marginal relation) is .71 (which is less than .84), these rays become progressively flatter as the value of child support due increases. Because the slope of the 1985 line is .94 (which is greater than .81), these rays become progressively steeper as the value of child support due increases.

28. These differences are evaluated at the nonblack regression coefficients.

29. See, e.g., Mary Corcoran and Greg J. Duncan, "Work History, Labor Force Attachment, and Earnings Differences between the Races and Sexes," *Journal of Human Resources* 14:3–20.

30. The decomposition analysis is based upon separate regressions for ever-married and never-married women. We evaluate differences in the means of the explanatory variables at the ever-married coefficients.

31. This estimate is obtained by subtracting from the total decline ($748), the amount explained by the decline in dollars due ($604), and the amount unexplained ($131), represented by the regression coefficient on the dummy variable for the 1986 survey year.

32. In other words, to changes over time in the coefficients in the receipt regression.

33. That is, the regression coefficient on dollars due of .94 (from last col., table 5.5) times the $856 decline in dollars due.

34. Among never-married mothers only, we find that the marginal relation between changes in the amount of support due and changes in the amount received rose from .86 in 1978–81 to .90 in 1983–85.

Chapter 6: The Legal Environment

1. For a recent study of the effect on child support payments of individual variation in legal custody arrangements see, Judith A. Seltzer, "Legal Custody Arrangements and Children's Economic Welfare," *American Journal of Sociology* 96:895–929.

2. U.S. House of Representatives, Committee on Ways and Means, Subcommittee on Human Resources, *The Child Support Enforcement Program: Policy and Practice,* Washington, D.C.: GPO, 1989, 55.

3. Sanford N. Katz, "A Historical Perspective on Child-Support Laws in the United States," in *The Parental Child-Support Obligation,* ed. Judith Cassetty (Lexington, Mass.: Lexington Books, 1983), 17–28.

4. Russell B. Long, Remarks in the Senate, *Congressional Record,* v.

118, 14 March 1972, 8291, as quoted in HR, *The Child Support Enforcement Program,* 56.

5. HHS, Office of Child Support Enforcement, Secretary's Symposium on Child Support Enforcement, 16–17 Aug. 1984, mimeo.

6. After holding hearings, the U.S. Commission on Interstate Child Support made recommendations in a preliminary report in Sept. 1991 and is scheduled to send to Congress a list of final proposals by Feb. 1992 ("Child Support Panel Offers Way to Collect," *New York Times,* 8 Sept. 1991, national ed., 12).

7. See, e.g., Lucy Marsh Yee, "What Really Happens in Child Support Cases: An Empirical Study of Establishment and Enforcement of Child Support Orders in the Denver District Court," *Denver Law Journal* 57(1): 21–68.

8. HR, *Family Support Act of 1988,* rep. 100–998, 28 Sept. 1988, 5.

9. Ibid.

10. Some results from the study that was conducted are presented later in this chapter.

11. HR, *The Child Support Enforcement Program,* 86.

12. NCSL, *A Guide to State Child Support and Paternity Laws,* 106–7.

13. The Family Support Act of 1988 further required that the permission be made retroactive to cases brought since 1984 if they were denied the first time.

14. HR, *The Child Support Enforcement Program,* 18.

15. The material in this section draws heavily on HR, *The Child Support Enforcement Program,* 33–50.

16. Ibid., 37.

17. Ibid., 38.

18. This technique, or jailing for civil contempt of court, has nonetheless been used effectively by some judges. For example, Judge Robert Steigmann, formerly circuit court judge in Champaign County, Illinois, jailed delinquent fathers for the weekend and let them out only to go to work during the week. It was amazing how quickly fathers found the money to pay large amounts of overdue support in the face of such prospects. Jim Dey, "Program Prompts Fathers to Pay," *Champaign-Urbana News-Gazette,* 15 Aug. 1982, A2.

19. National Conference of State Legislatures, *A Guide to State Child Support,* 26.

20. We consider only those laws for which we have data for several years. National Conference of State Legislatures, *A Guide to State Child Support,* 82–107.

21. For the long-arm statute to apply, the alleged father must have had "significant minimal contacts" with the custodial parent's state, as, e.g., if the conception took place there. HR, *The Child Support Enforcement Program,* 15.

22. National Conference of State Legislatures, *A Guide to State Child Support,* 105.

23. According to the National Conference of State Legislatures (*A Guide to State Child Support,* 104), the preferable situation is to leave it up to the

judge based upon each party's claims rather than to impose arbitrary limitations.

24. OCSE also publishes data on the availability of child support enforcement techniques, but we chose to abide by the definitions adopted by the NCSL, which uses criteria designed to select legislation that is "exemplary." For example, a piece of legislation may need to have three separate provisions for NCSL to regard it as satisfactory.

25. We omitted from our analyses two techniques present in nearly every state—garnishment, and attachments and executions.

26. For example, in one case heard in Champaign County Court, Illinois, 5 Sept. 1990, there was an arrearage of $10,000 since 1980, with no regular payment since 1982. The award had been set at $60 biweekly. In another case, the arrearage was $16,432. (Observation of AHB).

27. See "Child Support Panel Offers Way to Collect," *New York Times*.

28. For a more technical presentation of this model, see Beller and Graham, "The Effect of Child Support Enforcement on Child Support Payments," *Population Research and Policy Review* 10(2): 97–100. Our treatment here follows that presentation except that here we employ OLS regressions, do not correct the receipt amount equations for possible sample selection bias, and use four rather than only two years of data on child support.

29. Martha S. Hill, *PSID Analysis of Matched Pairs of Ex-Spouses: The Relation of Economic Resources and New Family Obligations to Child Support Payments,* Report to the Department of Health and Human Services, ASPE, 1984.

30. The first of these probably does not capture a preexisting relation for all child support enforcement techniques because, as seen in fig. 6.1, some of them changed little in availability between 1981 and 1983, while others changed little between 1983 and 1985.

31. Women in states with such laws in 1985 received around $200 more support than women in states without them.

32. When we perform these analyses on a year-by-year basis instead of pooling together all the years of data, we find no significant effect of liens on the receipt rate (the effect is positive in three out of the four years, which explains how it becomes significant when the four years are combined). Once we take account of preexisting relations, however, we find receipt rates higher in states with lien laws in 1985.

33. In separate year-by-year analyses, we find receipts higher in states with criminal penalties by $400 in 1978, by $163 in 1981, and by $150 in 1985; the coefficients for 1978 and 1985 are significant at the 5% level and for 1981, at the 10% level.

34. The one exception is that in separate year-by-year analyses, after taking account of the preexisting relation, we find that women in states with contemporaneous wage withholding laws in 1981 received more child support.

35. We combined the first two together in our other analyses.

36. This effect is significant at the 10% level.

37. There are no significant preexisting relations between expedited pro-

cesses and child support receipts. Thus, we can rule out the possibility that the states that initiated expedited processes did so in response to extreme backlogs in their court system that were reducing receipt rates.

38. We do find a significant positive relation between workman's compensation intercept legislation and receipt rates in 1985 that disappears when laws available by practice are included in the equation.

39. We also find a significant positive relation between wage withholding laws lagged two to three years and payments received in 1981–85 of $183. In earlier work, we found a similar but larger effect ($704) between wage withholding laws in effect by 1978 and payments received three years later in 1981 (Beller and Graham, "The Effect of Child Support Enforcement," 111).

40. Although the estimates in col. 2 show a smaller positive preexisting relation between awards and wage withholding laws, it is not statistically significant, leaving our conclusion unaltered.

41. In cols. 4 and 6, we find no significant preexisting relations for these estimates; however, voluntary wage assignment is positively related to award rates two to three years earlier, and this effect approaches significance.

42. These results are probably owing to the differences in the sample rather than to an inconsistency with the earlier results because withholding laws are also unrelated to amount received, not controlling for amount due for this more limited sample. This sample contains only women with recent marital disruptions who were due support, whereas the previous sample covers women from all disruption years who received support. We do, however, find a significant negative preexisting relation between wage withholding laws and child support award rates. Award rates appear to be 2.6 percentage points lower two to four years prior to the measurement of withholding laws. This suggests that states that initiated wage withholding laws in the late 1970s and early 1980s had lower award rates initially. This preexisting effect, however, is not significantly different from the negative contemporaneous effect.

43. Since data on AFDC expenditures are not available for fiscal year 1985, in our statistical analyses we relate data for fiscal year 1983 to receipts in 1985. This overestimates the proportion of expenditures devoted to the AFDC population in 1985 because according to the U.S. average, this proportion fell from .79 in fiscal year 1983 to .69 in fiscal year 1986. (HHS, *Eighth Annual Report to Congress,* 58 and 60, and *Eleventh Annual Report to Congress,* vol. 2, 30.)

44. According to Kurt Beron, this variable might be interpreted "as representing the state's perceived enforcement environment and providing an indicator of general deterrence" ("Policy Issues and Child Support Payment Behavior: Empirical Findings," *Contemporary Policy Issues* 8:128).

45. Alternatively, this problem of mutual causation between expenditures and outcomes can also be handled in a simultaneous equations framework, but that is beyond the scope of this study.

46. It is not possible to identify IV-D cases in all survey years.

47. Although the inclusion of these measures of government spending does not alter the substantive findings, it does alter somewhat the relative magni-

tudes and significance of the effects of various enforcement techniques on the receipt rate. In particular, the inclusion of the collections-to-expenditure ratio increases the negative effect of expedited processes and reduces the positive effect of liens by around 30%.

48. These estimates use government expenditures in current rather than constant dollars, but this also makes little difference in the estimates.

49. Beron ("Policy Issues," 131) finds a similar effect of the collections ratio for 1983 alone.

50. This may be an indication that the way state agencies raise their collections ratio is not always through more efficient operations.

51. This effect is significant at the 1% level. Owing to the possibility that the proportion of expenditures on the AFDC population might be serving as a proxy for the proportion of the population in the state on AFDC, we added a control for AFDC recipiency. The proportion of expenditures on AFDC recipients remained negative and significant.

52. The F-test for the addition of the child support enforcement variables to the receipt rate equation equaled 2.15 with a critical value of 3.23 at the 5% level; the F-test for the addition of the state spending measures equaled 6.72 with the critical value at the 5% level of 8.53.

53. These data are computed from the coefficient on the intercept for the 1986 sample in a pooled OLS regression of all four years of data. Because the estimation method differs from that used in the previous chapter, the percent of changes unexplained by socioeconomic characteristics may not be identical.

54. We examine the effects of child support enforcement techniques on black women by interacting race with the child support enforcement variables in regressions for all women.

55. Taking account of the ratio of collections to expenditures for the black population, discussed below, expedited processes have a significant negative effect (-2.6 percentage points) on the nonblack population that is an insignificant amount more negative for the black population. This suggests that expedited processes affect the ratio of collections to expenditures, perhaps contributing to its negative effect on blacks.

56. Although the ratio of collections to expenditures is insignificant in a separate regression on the amount received for black women, it is significantly different at the 10% level in a positive direction from the negative effect of the ratio on nonblacks when black is interacted with the OCSE variables only. When black is also interacted with the enforcement variables, this difference becomes insignificant.

57. Although the positive effect of per capita expenditures by the enforcement agency on the receipt rate of black women is insignificant, according to regressions with black interactions on the OCSE variables, it is significantly different at the 5% level from the negative effect on nonblack women. But when we add black interactions on the child support enforcement techniques to the equation, this difference is no longer significant. This suggests that part of the impact of spending by the IV-D agency on the receipt rate of black women comes through their use of child support enforcement techniques.

58. We use separate regressions for black women to examine the effect of laws on the unexpected changes in receipt rates but use interaction terms with race in regressions for all women to examine the effect on receipt amounts.

59. Based upon data from court records for four Ohio counties, researchers found no change in award rates but an increase in award amounts between 1985 and 1987–88 after the implementation of federally mandated guidelines in 1987. (Kathryn Stafford, Golden Jackson, and Sharon Seiling, "The Effects of Child Support Guidelines: An Analysis of the Evidence in Court Records," *Lifestyles: Family and Economic Issues* 11:361–81.) Although suggestive, this type of analysis is clearly inconclusive because there is no cross-sectional variation in the presence of guidelines and no time-series analysis to determine whether there was any trend toward an increase over time in award amounts in these counties prior to the guidelines.

60. Point made by Aviva Futorian, chair, Guidelines Subcommittee of the Illinois Child Support Advisory Committee, conversation with AHB, Chicago, April 1990.

61. We also may not have the correct award environment for ever-married women if their award was not obtained at the divorce or separation.

62. Actually, all states were required to have formulas for determining the amount of the child support obligation in AFDC cases since 1975. These formulas had to take into account eight factors that are roughly like those in most guidelines (e.g., income, earning potential, needs of a child, and existence of other dependents [45 CFR, sect. 302.53 (1991)]). These formulas were in effect over the entire period of our study, and according to one knowledgeable observer, many states were confused about whether to use the formula or the guideline they had developed (Paula Roberts, memo to AHB, 13 Dec. 1991).

63. Since many states added guidelines in 1985, we examined these relations for the first three surveys alone, excluding the 1985 data. The results were basically the same.

64. These effects are not significantly different from those for nonblack mothers or ever-married mothers, respectively, when both groups are included in the same regression equation.

65. Actually, for the never-married it is guidelines in effect at the next survey. So for the 1979 survey, that is actually three rather than two years later in 1982.

66. This is a slightly different approach to capturing the preexisting effect than the one used for the child support enforcement laws. We were unable to use this method—which doubles the number of variables—for enforcement because of the large number of different laws relative to the number of states (or degrees of freedom).

67. The difference is not statistically significant, however.

68. These estimates are based upon separate equations for the ever-married. Based upon an interaction term in the equation for all women, the estimated effect of guidelines on award amount of ever-married mothers is $249, which is significant at the 1% level. The separate equation allows us to control for income in the year of the divorce or separation, which we do in constant 1985 dollars. If we instead measure income in current dollars or

replace it with a time trend, we find no significant effect of guidelines on award amounts. We prefer the former version because a time trend is a kind of unexplained change itself and guidelines may be the source of at least part of this unexplained change. We found a similar relation when we omitted divorces and separations that occurred in 1985, the year many states added guidelines, or 1986.

69. The coefficient on existence of guidelines is significant at the 10% level and on the number of years guidelines are in effect is insignificant.

70. When we allow the effect of the measures of government spending to vary by year, the proportion of expenditures on the AFDC population also has a significant positive effect on the award rate of the never-married in 1982.

71. There is some evidence of an increase in the effect of this provision in 1982 and 1984.

72. When we allow the effect of these paternity measures to vary over time, default judgments are found to have a positive effect on the award rate in 1984.

73. Our estimates are based on the coefficient on a dummy variable for the 1986 survey year in a regression over all four years of data. We examine how this coefficient changes as we add guidelines, paternity determination, and government spending variables to the analysis.

74. As used here, *state* refers to the fifty states plus the District of Columbia.

75. Barbara R. Bergmann, "Can Child Support Payments Make a Dent in the Poverty of Women and Children?" in *First Annual Women's Policy Research Conference, Proceedings,* Washington, D.C.: Institute for Women's Policy Research, 1990, 57–70; and Irwin Garfinkel and Marygold S. Melli, "The Use of Normative Standards in Family Law Decisions: Developing Mathematical Standards for Child Support," *Family Law Quarterly* 24:157–78.

76. This model was developed by Robert G. Williams, *Development of Guidelines for Child Support Orders: Final Report,* Washington, D.C.: HHS, Office of Child Support Enforcement, 1987, and is sometimes known as the Williams Model.

77. Williams, *Development of Guidelines,* 1987.

78. Laurie J. Bassi and Burt S. Barnow, "Expenditures on Children and Child Support Guidelines," paper presented at the Western Economic Association International 66th Annual Conference, Seattle, July 1991, 22. Bassi and Barnow point out that this is also possible with the percentage of income guideline when the percentage declines with income.

79. Although it would seem the simplest, even the gross income base is not entirely straightforward. In addition to wages and other cash compensation from an outside employer, difficulties may arise over how to compute or whether to include the value of fringe benefits, the measurement of income from self-employment, the potential income from low- or nonincome producing assets, and means-tested income.

80. Although this is true, considering the custodial parent's income might still provide the necessary information to apportion extra add-on expenses

that may be shared between parents, such as child care and extraordinary medical expenses.

81. Harry D. Krause, "Child Support Reassessed: Limits of Private Responsibility and the Public Interest," in *Divorce Reform at the Crossroads,* ed. Stephen D. Sugarman and Herma Hill Kay (New Haven: Yale University Press, 1990), 166–90.

82. Massachusetts does the latter in cases where the obligor's annual income exceeds $75,000 (Marilyn Ray Smith and Jon Laramore, "Massachusetts' Child Support Guidelines: A Model for Development," in *Essentials of Child Support Guidelines Development: Economic Issues and Policy Considerations* [Washington, D.C.: Women's Legal Defense Fund, 1987], 304.)

83. The CEX, conducted by the Bureau of Labor Statistics (BLS), collects data from a national sample of households of the civilian noninstitutional population on consumer expenditures by category, income, and household characteristics. For nearly a century the BLS had been conducting these surveys every ten years, but in 1980 they began collecting data annually.

84. Ernst Engel, "Die Productions und Consumtionsverhaltnisse des Konigsreichs Sachsen," *Zeitscrift des Statistischen Bureaus des Koniglich Sachishen Ministeriums des Innern* 3(1857).

85. Technically, this assumption is know as separability in consumption.

86. Angus S. Deaton and John Muellbauer, "On Measuring Child Costs: With Applications to Poor Countries," *Journal of Political Economy* 94:720–44.

87. Through an empirical investigation, Julie Nelson ("Separability, Scales and Intra-Family Distribution: Some Empirical Evidence," Working Paper Series 346, Department of Economics, University of California, Davis, October 1989) shows that the assumptions of this model lead to estimates of expenditures for some goods that are not believable and argues that adults are likely to shift their consumption expenditures away from adult goods and toward categories of goods from which all family members can benefit when children are present. Results similar to those of Deaton and Muellbauer for both the Engel and Rothbarth methods are found by Panos Tsakloglou, "Estimation and Comparison of Two Simple Models of Equivalence Scales for the Cost of Children," *Economic Journal* 101:343–57.

88. Espenshade, *Investing in Children;* Lazear and Michael, *Allocation of Income.*

89. Turchi's study is based on a variant of the Prais-Houthakker model (Boone A. Turchi, *Estimating the Cost of Children in the United States,* Final Report to the National Institute of Child Health and Human Development, June 1983). Olson specifies a particular utility function (Lawrence Olson, *Costs of Children* [Lexington, Mass.: Lexington/D.C. Heath, 1983]).

90. David M. Betson, *Alternative Estimates of the Cost of Children from the 1980–1986 Consumer Expenditure Survey,* HHS, Office of the Assistant Secretary for Planning and Evaluation, September 1990.

91. Mark Lino, "Expenditures on a Child by Husband-Wife Families," *Family Economics Review* 3:2–18.

92. Estimates from the Espenshade, Olson, and Turchi studies are pre-

sented by socioeconomic status level, while those from the USDA study are presented by income range and from the Lazear and Michael study by income level.

93. The Betson2 estimates, which we take as the starting point for our recommendations in chap. 8, do not appear to have a large enough increment between two and three children. For three children, they actually fall in the bottom of the range of estimated expenditures.

94. Expenditures on children increase around 20% with the employment of the second adult (Lazear and Michael, 89; Espenshade, 31).

95. USDL, BLS, *Handbook of Labor Statistics* (bull. 2340), Washington, D.C.: GPO, 1989, table 58.

96. Based upon 1972–73 data, Lazear and Michael (pp. 90 and 98) found the proportion of expenditures going to children in a two-child family rose from 27% in a two-parent to 53% in a single-parent family.

97. In 1972–73, the labor force participation rate was 53% for single mothers compared to 41% for married spouse-present mothers with children under 18; by 1988, the rates had increased to 67 and 65 percent, respectively. (U.S. Department of Labor, *Handbook of Labor Statistics,* 1989, tables 57 and 58.)

98. Based upon data from the 1980s, when single-parent families were more prevalent and had work patterns more similar to those of mothers in two-parent families but using a similar estimation technique, Betson found the proportion of expenditures going to children in a two-child family rose from 35% to 53% as the number of parents in the household decreased from two to one (L. J. Bassi and B. S. Barnow, "Expenditures on Children," 15).

99. Anne R. Gordon and Irwin Garfinkel, "Child Costs as a Percentage of Family Income: Constant or Decreasing as Income Rises?" Institute for Research on Poverty, Discussion Paper no. 889–89, 1989, 31.

100. See Beller, Phipps, and Krein, *An Analysis of Child Support,* 92–93, for details.

101. This type of information has not been collected for the earlier years upon which our analytic work is based.

102. Bassi and Barnow, "Expenditures on Children," 1991, 27–32.

Chapter 7: The Economic Consequences of Child Support Payments

1. For a summary of these studies, see Mark R. Killingsworth, *Labor Supply* (Cambridge: Cambridge University Press, 1983), chaps. 3 and 4.

2. There is another important distinction between child support and alimony. When a divorced mother remarries, her alimony payments legally cease, but her child support payments do not. This means that although large alimony payments may be a deterrent to remarriage, child support should not be.

3. See, e.g., Michael K. Block and John M. Heineke, "The Allocation of Effort Under Uncertainty: The Case of Risk-Averse Behavior," *Journal of Political Economy* 81:376–85; and Peter C. Coyte, "The Supply of Individual Hours and Labor Force Participation under Uncertainty," *Economic Inquiry* 24:155–71.

4. Coyte, "The Supply of Individual Hours," 166.

5. We are indebted to Gary Becker for this suggestion, letter to authors, 15 Dec. 1989.

6. Some other differences may not be observable, but we may still be able to control for their effects indirectly using advanced statistical techniques to control for the effects of sample selection bias (see app. B for a full description).

7. Mothers with child support are more likely to work and earn more if they work; e.g., in 1985, 83% of mothers receiving child support worked, compared with just 65% of mothers not receiving support. Among mothers who worked, average earnings were $13,037 if they received child support and $10,891 if they did not.

8. Average AFDC payments declined sharply between 1978 and 1985, falling 41% among mothers with child support income and 36% among those without. Average AFDC payments declined both because participation rates fell and because average benefits received by those on AFDC declined. Among all single mothers, the AFDC participation rate fell from 37% to 31%; and real benefits received by AFDC participants declined from $4,410 to $3,362.

9. Real earnings remained relatively constant between 1978 and 1985, both for those receiving and those not receiving child support. This constancy conceals some small changes over time in labor force participation rates and real earnings of those mothers who worked. The percentage of all single mothers who worked fell from 72% in 1978 to 71% in 1985, while over the same period real earnings of those who worked rose from $11,700 to $11,799.

10. See, e.g., Census Bureau, CPR, series P-23, no. 154, *Child Support and Alimony: 1985 Supplemental Report*. Washington, D.C.: GPO, 1989, table A-2.

11. These data are Census Bureau estimates adapted from CPR, series P-23, nos. 112, 140, 148, 154 (table 1 of each report).

12. Census Bureau, *Statistical Abstract of the United States, 1982–83*. Washington D.C.: GPO, 1982, table 734.

13. See Becker, Landes, and Michael, "An Economic Analysis of Marital Instability," pp. 1141–87; and Robert Hutchens, "Welfare, Remarriage, and Marital Search," *American Economic Review* 69:369–79.

14. For an analysis of why marriage behavior differs by race, see Neil Bennett, David Bloom, and Patricia Craig, "The Divergence of Black and White Marriage Patterns," *American Journal of Sociology* 95:692–722.

15. Hutchens, "Welfare, Remarriage, and Marital Search," looks at the probability of remarriage within two years and controls for many of the same socioeconomic characteristics we do. Becker, Landes, and Michael, "An Economic Analysis of Marital Instability," control for fewer factors but look at remarriage rates after 2, 5, 10, and 15 years following the divorce.

16. This analysis was performed before the availability of the 1984 and 1986 CPS data. Some of the results in this section were first reported in Graham and Beller, "The Effects of Child Support on the Labor Supply of Female Family Heads: An Econometric Analysis," *Journal of Human Resources* 24:664–88.

17. See, e.g., Robert Moffitt, "An Economic Model of Welfare Stigma," *American Economic Review* 73:1023–35.

18. For mothers who did not work, we estimated potential wages based upon their characteristics and the wages of mothers who did work. For more details, see Graham and Beller, "The Effects of Child Support on the Labor Supply," app. A.

19. Following previous studies, these characteristics include mother's age, education, race, ethnicity, marital status, residential location, previous work experience, and the number and ages of her children.

20. AFDC participation depends upon potential AFDC benefits that equal the smaller of either the state's payment standard minus total nonwage income or the state's maximum AFDC payment level. Since total nonwage income equals child support plus other nonwage income, this means that child support and other nonwage income will have the same effect (but opposite sign) on AFDC participation as potential AFDC benefits do.

21. Our estimation allowed AFDC benefits, other nonwage income, and child support to have different effects on hours worked but constrained them to have the same effect on AFDC participation.

22. It is important, however, to emphasize that these are *partial* effects. To calculate the *total* effect on hours worked of a change in either child support or other nonwage income *for a mother on AFDC,* recall that given the 100% AFDC tax rate, a $1,000 increase in either reduces potential AFDC benefits by an equal amount. Thus, for AFDC recipients, we predict that if nonwage income rises (and AFDC falls) by $1,000, annual work effort would decline by just 7 hours (i.e., 62–69), while if child support rises (and AFDC falls) by $1,000, annual work effort would actually increase by 38 hours (i.e., 62–24).

23. The simulations in this section are for all single mothers, including the never married. Thus, we assume that the work and welfare effects estimated above for divorced and separated mothers are applicable to never-married mothers as well.

24. That is, potential AFDC benefits rise by the average amount of child support received, which was $742 in 1981 and $627 in 1978. Changes in participation rates are found by multiplying by −0.046, the cross-sectional estimate of the effect of AFDC benefits on participation from table 7.5.

25. Of course, total welfare expenditures may have increased somewhat since the average potential AFDC benefits were increased by the amount of the disregard. We consider this possibility at the end of this section.

26. The changes in AFDC benefits and child support are not identical, because the actual benefit reduction calculation is nonlinear. Some states impose a maximum benefit that is less than the potential benefits to which women with very little nonwage income would be entitled. For more details, see Graham and Beller, "The Effects of Child Support on the Labor Supply," app. B.

27. That is, awards are 12.6% (11.5%) of the median income of year-round, full-time male workers in 1978 (1981).

28. These changes occur because as child support receipts increase, av-

erage maximum potential AFDC benefits fall by $1,550 for 1978 and by $1,823 for 1981.

29. That is, awards are 18.9% (17.3%) of the median income of year-round, full-time male workers in 1978 (1981).

30. For example, 38% of mothers without an award as of April 1986 said they did not even want one.

31. We can establish some boundaries for these potential welfare savings. In 1979, 3.428 million families received a total of $11.1 billion in AFDC and approximately 83% of these families were headed by single mothers eligible for child support. (Census Bureau, *Statistical Abstract of the United States, 1982–83*, tables 557 and 559.) If we might assume that 83% of AFDC payments, or $9.2 billion, went to the 36% of all single mothers who received support in 1978, and if each recipient received the same amount of support, then each 1 percentage point reduction in AFDC participation would save $255 million, assuming that remaining beneficiaries continue to receive the same level of support. Thus, because the changes in table 7.6 that we considered reduced AFDC participation between 1 and 11 percentage points, the expected decline in expenditures would be between $0.255 and $2.805 billion.

32. We chose 1978 because we need to use the estimated effects of child support on AFDC and labor force behavior from table 7.5. We excluded re-married mothers, mothers who only have children age eighteen and over, and mothers with four or more children: remarried mothers have much higher incomes and a much lower risk of being poor; only children under eighteen are eligible for AFDC; and we were unable to construct an exact poverty threshold for mothers with four or more children for whom the precise number of children is not known.

33. We estimated the poverty rate by first calculating total family income for each single-mother family and then looking at the percentage of families who fall below the official poverty threshold (given earlier in the text).

34. Averaged across all mothers, AFDC payments decline both because the percentage on AFDC falls and because benefits received by those who remain on AFDC fall by approximately the increase in child support received.

35. When average child support payments increase $503, potential AFDC benefits decline $498 in 1985 dollars (or $302 in 1978 dollars). As a result, AFDC participation should decline by 1.4 percentage points based upon the impact of AFDC benefits (expressed in 1978 dollars) on AFDC participation shown in table 7.5.

36. From table 7.5, each $1,000 decrease in potential AFDC benefits (mea-sured in 1978 dollars) increases annual hours worked by 61.6, while each $1,000 increase in child support reduces hours worked by 23.6. Averaged among all mothers, the decline in potential AFDC is just $108 (i.e., the $302 benefit change discussed in note 36 above times the 35.9% who receive it), while the average change in child support income is $305 (in 1978 dollars). Thus, the change in hours worked is estimated as (61.6 hours) × (−.108) + (23.6 hours) × (.302) = −0.5 hours.

37. The estimates of average total family income in the bottom panel are

not calculated to permit us to estimate poverty rates. But since these income estimates are not too different from those in the middle panel, it is likely that poverty rates would be roughly the same.

38. For an economic perspective, see Heather L. Ross and Isabel V. Sawhill, *Time of Transition: The Growth of Families Headed by Women* (Washington, D.C.: Urban Institute, 1975); for a psychological one, see E. M. Hetherington, K. A. Camara, and D. L. Featherman, "Achievement and Intellectual Functioning of Children in One-Parent Households," in *Achievement and Achievement Motives: Psychological and Sociological Approaches,* ed. J. Spence (San Francisco: W. H. Freeman, 1983); for a sociological one, see Irwin Garfinkel and Sara McLanahan, *Single Mothers and Their Children: A New American Dilemma* (Washington, D.C.: Urban Institute, 1986).

39. See, e.g., Lois B. Shaw, "High School Completion for Young Women: Effects of Low Income and Living with a Single Parent," *Journal of Family Issues* 3:147–63; Sara S. McLanahan, "Family Structure and the Reproduction of Poverty," *American Journal of Sociology* 90:873–901; and Sheila F. Krein and Andrea H. Beller, "Educational Attainment of Children from Single-Parent Families: Differences by Exposure, Gender and Race," *Demography* 25:221–34.

40. Mary J. Bane and David T. Ellwood, *The Dynamics of Dependence: The Routes of Self-Sufficiency,* report prepared for assistant secretary for planning and evaluation, HHS, 1983.

41. See Krein and Beller, "Educational Attainment of Children"; McLanahan, "Family Structure and"; and Martha S. Hill and Greg J. Duncan, "Parental Family Income and the Socioeconomic Attainment of Children," *Social Science Research* 16:39–73.

42. See Shaw, "High School Completion"; McLanahan, "Family Structure"; and Krein and Beller, "Educational Attainment of Children."

43. The analysis reported here is based upon Andrea H. Beller and Seung Sin Chung, "The Effect of Child Support Payments on the Educational Attainment of Children," paper presented at the Population Association of America annual meetings, New Orleans, April 1988 (rev. June 1988).

44. There are 198 mothers widowed after their first marriage; these cases are included with intact two-parent families (to whom their socioeconomic characteristics are most similar).

45. More details on the impact of remarriage on children's education can be found in Andrea H. Beller and Seung Sin Chung, "Family Structure and Educational Attainment of Children: Effects of Remarriage," *Journal of Population Economics* 5:39–59.

46. That is, the child support coefficient 0.017 times $2,647.

47. For more details, see Beller and Chung, "The Effect of Child Support Payments." New evidence based upon 1988 CPS data essentially supports these findings. See John W. Graham, Andrea H. Beller, and Pedro Hernandez, "The Relationship between Child Support Payments and Offspring Educational Attainment," paper presented at the conference on Child Support and Child Well Being, Airlie House, Virginia, 5–7 Dec., 1991.

Chapter 8: A Policy Agenda for Child Support in the 1990s

1. Child support even made the cover of *Newsweek* in May 1992 (Steven Waldman, "Deadbeat Dads: Fathers on the Lam—From Their Own Kids," *Newsweek,* 4 May 1992, 46–52).

2. A framework to evaluate costs along with benefits and effects of the child support enforcement program has been developed by the U.S. General Accounting Office, *Child Support Enforcement: A Framework for Evaluating Costs, Benefits, and Effects,* GAO/PEMD-91-6, Report to the Assistant Secretary for Family Support Administration, DHHS, March 1991.

3. An important related recommendation, which does not emanate from our research, is that—as long as there is no national health insurance plan—awards should make explicit provision for health insurance coverage for the child.

4. As used here, income refers to the absent parent's income in states employing the percentage of income model and to the combined income of both parents in states employing the income shares or Melson models. Based upon available evidence, we prefer a flat percentage of income, which would yield the same child support award regardless of model.

5. Bassi and Barnow, "Expenditures on Children."

6. A recent study finds that payments are higher under child support orders expressed in percentage rather than fixed terms (Judi Bartfeld and Irwin Garfinkel, *Utilization and Effects on Payments of Percentage-Expressed Child Support Orders,* Institute for Research on Poverty, Special Report no. 55, July 1992).

7. The state of Washington has used this approach successfully. New York City plans an experimental program using nurses and social workers to persuade unwed fathers to sign papers acknowledging paternity (Celia Dugger, "Establishing Paternity Earlier to Gain Child Support Later," *New York Times,* Friday, 3 Jan. 1992, sec. 1, local ed.).

8. Census Bureau, CPR, series P-60, no. 175, *Poverty in the United States: 1990.* Washington, D.C.: GPO, 1991, table 23.

9. NCSL, *A Guide to State Child Support and Paternity Laws,* 138–44.

10. HB2486, 87th General Assembly. 1991 Illinois Laws 3109.

11. The IV-D agency personnel who do this have got so good at it that they can seize a car in under two minutes (HHS, Office of Child Support Enforcement, "'Seize-and-Sell' in Washington, A Tough Enforcement Technique for Tough Cases," *Child Support Report* 13 [Aug. 1991], 1 and 5.)

12. Waldman, "Fathers on the Lam," 49.

13. U.S. General Accounting Office, *Interstate Child Support: Mothers Report Receiving Less Support from Out-of-State Fathers,* GAO/HRD-92-39FS, Fact Sheet for Congressional Requesters, Jan. 1992.

14. An alternative is to enhance the earning ability of absent parents by targeting job training programs toward them. The Family Support Act authorizes demonstration projects on targeting training programs to certain low-income individuals (Paula Roberts, letter to AHB, 3 Jan. 1992).

15. Wisconsin was a leader in experimenting with immediate income with-

holding and percentage of income guidelines. For a review of the Wisconsin program, see Irwin Garfinkel, Sara McLanahan, and Philip K. Robins, *Child Support Assurance: Design Issues, Expected Impacts, and Political Barriers as Seen from Wisconsin,* Urban Institute Press, 1992.

16. National Commission on Children, *Beyond Rhetoric: A New American Agenda for Children and Families,* Final Report. Washington, D.C.: GPO, 1991, 98. This also appears as one component of a recent proposal for major reform of the child support enforcement system introduced by members of the House of Representatives (*The Downey/Hyde Child Support Enforcement and Assurance Proposal,* 12 May 1992) and is the subject of a recent book (Irwin Garfinkel, *Assuring Child Support: An Extension of Social Security,* New York: Russell Sage Foundation, 1992).

17. National Commission on Children, *Beyond Rhetoric,* 99.

18. Judith S. Wallerstein and Shauna Corbin, "Father-Child Relationships after Divorce: Child Support and Educational Opportunity," *Family Law Quarterly* 20:109–28.

19. Other such expenses might include braces, weddings, and the like (Barbara R. Bergmann, "Can Child Support Payments Make a Dent in the Poverty of Women and Children?" in *First Annual Women's Policy Research Conference, Proceedings,* Washington, D.C.: Institute for Women's Policy Research, 1990).

20. This recommendation is adapted from Beller, Phipps, and Krein, *An Analysis of Child Support.*

21. For a recent comprehensive treatment of children's well-being and proposed policy responses, see Sylvia Ann Hewlett, *When the Bough Breaks: The Cost of Neglecting Our Children,* Basic Books, 1991.

22. Edward Zigler identifies the child care system as "the third institution" after the family and the school "that determines what a child is to become." He argues that quality child care can promote the child's optimal development ("Shaping Child Care Policies and Programs in America," *American Journal of Community Psychology* 18(2): 187).

Appendix B: A Brief Guide to Regression and Decomposition Analysis

1. G. S. Maddala, *Limited-Dependent and Qualitative Variables in Econometrics* (Cambridge: Cambridge University Press, 1983), 23.

2. James J. Heckman, "Sample Selection Bias as a Specification Error," *Econometrica* 47:153–61.

3. This technique has been widely used in labor economics to study the impact of discrimination on racial and gender differences in earnings. A classic reference is Alan S. Blinder, "Wage Discrimination: Reduced Form and Structural Estimates," *Journal of Human Resources* 8:436–55.

4. Notice that the difference in means of the explanatory variables is evaluated at the nonblack coefficients, while the difference in coefficients is evaluated at the black means. It is also possible to rewrite the equation: $(\bar{Y} - \bar{Y}) = \mathbf{C}^b(\bar{X}^w - \bar{X}^b) + \bar{X}^w(\mathbf{C} - \mathbf{C}^b)$, which simply reverses the weights.

In general, these two versions give different results, but there is no reason to favor one set of weights over the other.

Appendix C: Are Child Support Awards Renegotiated?

1. That is, we use the same set of socioeconomic factors as in table 4.5 for ever-married women.

2. Some women due child support (1.2% of the cases) report receiving more child support than they are due. One reason for this may be that initial awards were informally renegotiated upward. To test for the presence of informal renegotiation, we replaced dollars due with dollars received when the latter was greater and reestimated the regression equation discussed in the text. (We omitted twelve cases where the ratio of received to due exceeded 4.0 since the likelihood of a coding or response error is high.) The results of this analysis were virtually identical to those reported in table 4.8. Thus, we conclude that even informal renegotiation is rare.

Appendix D: A Theory of Welfare, Work, and Child Support

1. Fig. 7.A1 assumes that $G' > 0$, or equivalently, $G > rN$. If $G' < 0$, a mother is not eligible for AFDC, even if she does not work.

References

Adrian, Arthur A. *Dickens and the Parent-Child Relationship*. Athens, Ohio: Ohio University Press, 1984.

Albiston, Catherine R., Eleanor E. Maccoby, and Robert R. Mnookin. "Does Joint Legal Custody Matter?" *Stanford Law & Policy Review* (Spring 1990): 167–79.

Bane, Mary J., and David T. Ellwood. *The Dynamics of Dependence: The Routes of Self-Sufficiency*. A report prepared at the request of the Assistant Secretary for Planning and Evaluation, Department of Health and Human Services, 1983.

Bartfeld, Judi, and Irwin Garfinkel, *Utilization and Effects on Payments of Percentage-Expressed Child Support Orders*, Institute for Research on Poverty, Special Report no. 55, July 1992.

Bassi, Laurie J., and Burt S. Barnow. "Expenditures on Children and Child Support Guidelines." Paper presented at the Western Economic Association International 66th Annual Conference, Seattle, July 1991.

Becker, Gary S. "A Theory of the Allocation of Time." *Economic Journal* 75 (Sept. 1965): 493–517.

———. *A Treatise on the Family*. Cambridge: Harvard University Press, 1981.

Becker, Gary S., Elisabeth M. Landes, and Robert T. Michael. "An Economic Analysis of Marital Instability." *Journal of Political Economy* 85 (Dec. 1977): 1141–87.

Beller, Andrea H., and Seung Sin Chung. "The Effect of Child Support Payments on the Educational Attainment of Children." Paper presented at the Population Association of America Annual Meetings, New Orleans, April 1988.

———. "Family Structure and Educational Attainment of Children: Effects of Remarriage." *Journal of Population Economics* 5 (Feb. 1992): 39–59.

Beller, Andrea H., and John W. Graham. "Variations in the Economic Well-Being of Divorced Women and Their Children: The Role of Child Support Income." In *Horizontal Equity, Uncertainty, and Measures of Well-Being*, NBER Studies in Income and Wealth Series, ed. Martin David and Timothy Smeeding, vol. 50, 471–509. Chicago: University of Chicago Press, 1985.

———. "Child Support Awards: Differentials and Trends by Race and Marital Status." *Demography* 23 (May 1986): 231–45.

———. "The Determinants of Child Support Income." *Social Science Quarterly* 67 (June 1986): 353–64.

———. "Child Support Payments: Evidence from Repeated Cross-Sections." *American Economic Review* 78 (May 1988): 81–85.

———. "The Effect of Child Support Enforcement on Child Support Payments." *Population Research and Policy Review* 10(2) (1991): 91–116.

Beller, Andrea H., Barbara J. Phipps, and Sheila Fitzgerald Krein. *An Analysis of Child Support Guidelines and Costs of Raising Children.* Illinois Department of Public Aid, 1991.

Bennett, Neil G., David E. Bloom, and Patricia H. Craig. "The Divergence of Black and White Marriage Patterns." *American Journal of Sociology* 95 (Nov. 1989): 692–722.

Bergmann, Barbara R. "How Big Should Child Support Payments Be?" Paper presented at the First Annual Women's Policy Research Conference, Institute for Women's Policy Research, Washington, D.C., May 1989.

———. "Can Child Support Payments Make a Dent in the Poverty of Women and Children?" In *First Annual Women's Policy Research Conference, Proceedings,* 157–70. Washington, D.C.: Institute for Women's Policy Research, 1990.

Beron, Kurt J. "Applying the Economic Model of Crime to Child Support Enforcement: A Theoretical and Empirical Analysis." *Review of Economics and Statistics* 70 (Aug. 1988): 382–90.

———. "Policy Issues and Child Support Payment Behavior: Empirical Findings." *Contemporary Policy Issues* 8 (Jan. 1990): 124–34.

Betson, David M. *Alternative Estimates of the Cost of Children from the 1980–1986 Consumer Expenditure Survey.* A report prepared at the request of the U.S. Department of Health and Human Services, Office of the Assistant Secretary for Planning and Evaluation, Sept. 1990.

Blau, Francine D., and John W. Graham. "Black-White Differences in Wealth and Asset Composition." *Quarterly Journal of Economics* 105 (May 1990): 321–39.

Blinder, Alan S. "Wage Discrimination: Reduced Form and Structural Estimates." *Journal of Human Resources* 8 (Fall 1973): 436–55.

Block, Michael K., and John M. Heineke. "The Allocation of Effort under Uncertainty: The Case of Risk-Averse Behavior." *Journal of Political Economy* 81 (March/April 1973): 376–85.

Bruch, Carol S. "Developing Normative Standards for Child-Support Payments: A Critique of Current Practice." In *The Parental Child-Support Obligation,* ed. Judith Cassety, 119–32. Lexington, Mass.: D.C. Heath, 1983.

Cassetty, Judith. *Child Support and Public Policy.* Lexington, Mass.: Lexington Books, 1978.

Chambers, David L. *Making Fathers Pay: The Enforcement of Child Support.* Chicago: University of Chicago Press, 1979.

Cherlin, Andrew, Jeanne Griffith, and James McCarthy. "A Note on Maritally-Disrupted Men's Reports of Child Support in the June 1980 Current Population Survey." *Demography* 20 (Aug. 1983): 385–89.

Corcoran, Mary, and Greg J. Duncan. "Work History, Labor Force Attachment, and Earnings Differences between the Races and Sexes." *Journal of Human Resources* 14 (Winter 1979): 3–20.

Coyte, Peter C. "The Supply of Individual Hours and Labor Force Participation under Uncertainty." *Economic Inquiry* 24 (Jan. 1986): 155–71.

Deaton, Angus S., and John Muellbauer. "On Measuring Child Costs: With Applications to Poor Countries." *Journal of Political Economy* 94 (Aug. 1986): 720–44.

Dodson, Diane. "A Guide to the Guidelines." *Family Advocate* 10 (Spring 1988): 4–10.

Dopffel, Peter. "Child Support in Europe: A Comparative Overview." In *Child Support: From Debt Collection to Social Policy,* ed. Alfred J. Kahn and Sheila B. Kamerman, 176–226. Newbury Park, Calif.: Sage Publications, 1988.

The Downey/Hyde Child Support Enforcement and Assurance Proposal: Promoting Parental Responsibility and Securing a Better Future for Children in America, issued by Rep. Thomas J. Downey of New York and Rep. Henry J. Hyde of Illinois, 12 May 1992.

Duvall, Henrietta J., Karen W. Goudreau, and Robert E. Marsh. "Aid to Families with Dependent Children: Characteristics of Recipients in 1979." *Social Security Bulletin,* April 1982.

Economic Report of the President, Jan. 1987. Washington, D.C.: GPO.

Engel, Ernst. "Die Productions und Consumtionsverhaltnisse des Konigsreichs Sachsen." *Zeitscrift des Statisticshen Bureaus des Koniglich Sachishen Ministeriums des Innern* 3 (1857).

Espenshade, Thomas. *Investing in Children: New Estimates of Parental Expenditure.* Washington, D.C.: Urban Institute, 1984.

Farley, Reynolds, and Suzanne M. Bianchi. "The Growing Racial Differences in Marriage and Family Patterns." Research Report 87–107, Population Studies Center, University of Michigan, April 1987.

Furstenberg, Frank F., Jr. "Supporting Fathers: Implications of the Family Support Act for Men." Paper presented at the annual meeting of the Population Association of America, Toronto, May 1990.

Furstenberg Frank F., Jr., and Kathleen Mullan Harris. "The Disappearing American Father? Divorce and the Waning Significance of Biological Parenthood." University of Pennsylvania, March 1990.

Furstenberg, Frank F., Jr., Christine Winquist Nord, James L. Peterson, and Nicholas Zill. "The Life Course of Children of Divorce: Marital Disruption and Parental Contact." *American Sociological Review* 48 (Oct. 1983): 656–68.

Garfinkel, Irwin. *Assuring Child Support: An Extension of Social Security.* New York: Russell Sage Foundation, 1992.

Garfinkel, Irwin, and Sara McLanahan. *Single Mothers and Their Children: A New American Dilemma.* Washington, D.C.: Urban Institute, 1986.

Garfinkel, Irwin, Sara McLanahan, and Philip K. Robins. *Child Support Assurance: Design Issues, Expected Impacts, and Political Barriers as Seen from Wisconsin.* Washington, D.C.: Urban Institute Press, 1992.

Garfinkel, Irwin, and Marygold S. Melli. "The Use of Normative Standards in Family Law Decisions: Developing Mathematical Standards for Child Support." *Family Law Quarterly* 24 (Summer 1990): 157–78.

Gordon, Anne R., and Irwin Garfinkel. "Child Costs as a Percentage of Family Income: Constant or Decreasing as Income Rises?" Discussion paper 889–89, Institute for Research on Poverty, 1989.

Gordon, Nancy M., Carol A. Jones, and Isabel V. Sawhill. "The Determinants of Child Support Payments." Working paper 992–05, Washington D.C., Urban Institute, 1978.

Graham, John W., and Andrea H. Beller. "A Note on the Number and Living Arrangements of Women with Children under Twenty-one from an Absent Father: Revised Estimates from the April 1979 and 1982 Current Population Surveys." *Journal of Economic and Social Measurement* 13 (July 1985): 209–14.

———. "The Effect of Child Support Payments on the Labor Supply of Female Family Heads: An Econometric Analysis." *Journal of Human Resources* 24 (Fall 1989): 664–88.

———. "Trends in the Value of Child Support Awards." Paper presented at the annual meeting of the Population Association of America, Toronto, May 1990.

Graham, John W., Andrea H. Beller, and Pedro Hernandez. "The Relationship between Child Support Payments and Offspring Educational Attainment." Paper presented at the Conference on Child Support and Child Well Being, Airlie House, Va., Dec. 1991.

Haskins, Ron. "Child Support: A Father's View." In *Child Support: From Debt Collection to Social Policy,* ed. Alfred J. Kahn and Sheila B. Kamerman, 306–27. Newbury Park, Calif.: Sage Publications, 1988.

Heckman, James J. "Sample Selection Bias as a Specification Error." *Econometrica* 47 (Jan. 1979): 153–61.

Hetherington, E. M., K. A. Camara, and D. L. Featherman. "Achievement and Intellectual Functioning of Children in One-parent Households." In *Achievement and Achievement Motives: Psychological and Sociological Approaches,* ed. J. Spence. San Francisco: W. H. Freeman, 1983.

Hewlett, Sylvia Ann. *When the Bough Breaks: The Cost of Neglecting Our Children.* New York: Basic Books, 1991.

Hill, Martha S. *PSID Analysis of Matched Pairs of Ex-Spouses: The Relation of Economic Resources and New Family Obligations to Child Support Payments.* A report to the Department of Health and Human Services, Assistant Secretary for Planning and Evaluation, 1984.

———. "The Role of Economic Resources and Dual-Family Status in Child Support Payments." Paper presented at the annual meeting of the Population Association of America, New Orleans, April 1988.

Hill, Martha S., and Greg J. Duncan. "Parental Family Income and the Socioeconomic Attainment of Children." *Social Science Research* 16 (March 1987): 39–73.

Hoffman, Saul D. "An Economic Model of Child Support Payments." University of Delaware, June 1990.

Hoffman, Saul D., and Greg J. Duncan. "What *Are* the Economic Consequences of Divorce?" *Demography* 25 (Nov. 1988): 641–45.

Hutchens, Robert. "Welfare, Remarriage, and Marital Search." *American
Economic Review* 69 (June 1979): 369–79.

Kahn, Alfred J., and Sheila B. Kamerman. *Child Support: From Debt Collection to Social Policy.* Newbury Park, Calif.: Sage Publications, 1988.

Kastner, Carolyn Royce, and Lawrence R. Young. *In the Best Interests of
the Child: A Guide to State Child Support and Paternity Laws.* National
Conference of State Legislatures, Oct. 1982.

Katz, Sanford N. "A Historical Perspective on Child-Support Laws in the
United States." In *The Parental Child-Support Obligation,* ed. Judith Cassetty, 17–28. Lexington, Mass.: Lexington Books, 1983.

Killingsworth, Mark R. *Labor Supply.* Cambridge: Cambridge University
Press, 1983.

Krause, Harry D. *Child Support in America.* Charlottesville, Va.: Michie,
1981.

———. "Child Support Reassessed: Limits of Private Responsibility and the
Public Interest." In *Divorce Reform at the Crossroads,* ed. Stephen D.
Sugarman and Herma Hill Kay, 166–90. New Haven: Yale University Press,
1990.

Krein, Sheila F., and Andrea H. Beller. "Educational Attainment of Children
from Single-Parent Families: Differences by Exposure, Gender, and Race."
Demography 25 (May 1988): 221–34.

Lazear, Edward P., and Robert T. Michael. *Allocation of Income within the
Household.* Chicago: University of Chicago Press, 1988.

Lieberman, Joseph I. *Child Support in America.* New Haven: Yale University
Press, 1986.

Lino, Mark. "Expenditures on a Child by Husband-Wife Families." *Family
Economics Review* 3 (Sept. 1990): 2–18.

Maccoby, Eleanor E., Charlene E. Depner, and Robert H. Mnookin. "Custody
of Children Following Divorce." In *Impact of Divorce, Single Parenting,
and Stepparenting on Children,* ed. E. Mavis Hetherington and Josephine
D. Aresteh, 91–114. Hillsdale, N.J.: Lawrence Erlbaum, 1988.

Maddala, G. S. *Limited-Dependent and Qualitative Variables in Econometrics.* Cambridge: Cambridge University Press, 1983.

Martin, Elmer P., and Joanne Mitchell Martin. *The Black Extended Family.*
Chicago: University of Chicago Press, 1978.

McLanahan, Sara S. "Family Structure and the Reproduction of Poverty."
American Journal of Sociology 90 (Jan. 1985): 873–901.

———. "Family Structure and Dependency: Early Transitions to Female
Household Headship." *Demography* 25 (Feb. 1988): 1–16.

McLanahan, Sara S., and Larry L. Bumpass. "Intergenerational Consequences of Family Disruption." *American Journal of Sociology* 94 (July
1988): 130–52.

Meyer, Daniel R. "Data Adjustments in the Child Support Supplement of the
Current Population Survey." University of Wisconsin, Feb. 1992.

Moffitt, Robert. "An Economic Model of Welfare Stigma." *American Economic Review* 73 (Dec. 1983): 1023–35.

National Commission on Children. *Beyond Rhetoric, A New American Agenda for Children and Families,* Final Report. Washington, D.C.: GPO, 1991.

Nelson, Julie. "Separability, Scales and Intra-family Distribution: Some Empirical Evidence." Working Paper Series 346, Department of Economics, University of California, Davis, Oct. 1989.

Norton, Arthur J., and Paul C. Glick. "One-Parent Families: A Social and Economic Profile." *Family Relations* 35 (Jan. 1986): 9–17.

O'Neill, June. "Determinants of Child Support." Final report under grant 1RO1 HD 16840–01, National Institute of Child Health and Human Development, 1985.

Olson, Lawrence. *Costs of Children.* Lexington, Mass.: Lexington/D.C. Heath, 1983.

Paasch, Kathleen M., and Jay D. Teachman. "Gender of Children and Differential Forms of Child Support." Paper presented at the annual meeting of the Population Association of America, Toronto, May 1990.

Pearce, Diane. "The Feminization of Poverty: Women, Work and Welfare." *Urban and Social Change Review* 11 (Feb. 1978): 28–36.

Peters, H. Elizabeth. "Marriage and Divorce: Informational Constraints and Private Contracting." *American Economic Review* 76 (June 1986): 437–54.

Peters, H. Elizabeth, and Laura M. Argys. "Changes in Child Support Payments After Divorce: Compliance and Modifications." Paper presented at the annual meeting of the Allied Social Science Association, Washington, D.C., Dec. 1990.

Peterson, James L., and Christine Winquist Nord. "The Regular Receipt of Child Support: A Multistep Process." *Journal of Marriage and the Family* 52 (May 1990): 539–51.

Prais, S.J., and Hendrick S. Houthakker. *The Analysis of Family Budgets.* Cambridge: Cambridge University Press, 1955.

Presser, Harriet B. "Can We Make Time for Children? The Economy, Work Schedules, and Child Care." *Demography* 26 (Nov. 1989): 523–43.

Rindfuss, Ronald R., and Elizabeth H. Stephen. "Marital Non-Cohabitation: Separation Does Not Make the Heart Grow Fonder." Carolina Population Center Paper 88–30, Dec. 1988.

Robins, Philip K. "Child Support, Welfare Dependency, and Poverty." *American Economic Review* 76 (Sept. 1986): 768–88.

———. "Why Are Child Support Award Amounts Declining?" Discussion Paper 885–89, Institute for Research on Poverty, June 1989.

———. "Why Are Child Support Award Amounts Declining?" *Journal of Human Resources* 27 (Spring 1992): 362–79.

Robins, Philip K., and Katherine P. Dickinson. "Child Support and Welfare Dependence: A Multinomial Logit Analysis." *Demography* 22 (Aug. 1985): 367–80.

Rodgers, Harrell R., Jr. *Poor Women, Poor Families.* New York: M. E. Sharpe, 1986.

Ross, Heather L., and Isabel V. Sawhill. *Time of Transition: The Growth of Families Headed by Women.* Washington, D.C.: Urban Institute, 1975.

Ruggles, Patricia. *Drawing the Line: Alternative Poverty Measures and Their Implications for Public Policy.* Washington, D.C.: Urban Institute Press/ University Press of America, 1990.

Sandefur, Gary D., Sara S. McLanahan, and Roger A. Wojtkiewicz. "Race and Ethnicity, Family Structure, and High School Graduation." Institute for Research on Poverty Discussion Paper 893–89, Aug. 1989.

Seltzer, Judith A. "Legal Custody Arrangements and Children's Economic Welfare." *American Journal of Sociology* 96 (May 1991): 895–929.

Seltzer, Judith A., Nora Cate Schaeffer, and Hong-wen Charng. "Family Ties After Divorce: The Relationship between Visiting and Paying Child Support." *Journal of Marriage and the Family* 51 (Nov. 1989): 1013–32.

Shaw, Lois B. "High School Completion for Young Women: Effects of Low Income and Living with a Single Parent." *Journal of Family Issues* 3 (June 1982): 147–63.

Smith, Marilyn Ray, and Jon Laramore. "Massachusetts' Child Support Guidelines: A Model for Development." In *Essentials of Child Support Guidelines Development: Economic Issues and Policy Considerations,* 267–328. Washington, D.C.: Women's Legal Defense Fund, 1987.

Sonenstein, Freya L., and Charles A. Calhoun. "Determinants of Child Support: A Pilot Study of Absent Parents." *Contemporary Policy Issues* 8 (Jan. 1990): 75–94.

Sorensen, Annemette, and Maurice MacDonald. "An Analysis of Child Support Transfers. In *The Parental Child Support Obligation,* ed. Judith Cassetty, 35–58. Lexington, Mass.: Lexington Books, 1983.

Stafford, Kathryn, Golden Jackson, and Sharon Seiling. "The Effects of Child Support Guidelines: An Analysis of the Evidence in Court Records." *Lifestyles: Family and Economic Issues* 11 (Winter 1990): 361–81.

Teachman, Jay D. "Intergenerational Resource Transfers across Disrupted Households: Absent Fathers' Contributions to the Well-Being of Their Children." John's Hopkins University, n.d.

The Oprah Winfrey Show. "Unpaid Child Support." Chicago: Harpo Productions, 13 Jan. 1989. Transcript 610.

Thompson, Robert D., and Susan F. Paikin. "Formulas and Guidelines for Support." *Juvenile and Family Court Journal* 36 (Fall 1985): 33–40.

Tsakloglou, Panos. "Estimation and Comparison of Two Simple Models of Equivalence Scales for the Cost of Children." *Economic Journal* 101 (March 1991): 343–57.

Turchi, Boone A. *Estimating the Cost of Children in the United States.* Final Report to the National Institute of Child Health and Human Development. June 1983.

U.S. Bureau of the Census, Current Population Reports

Series p-20, no. 212. *Marital Status and Family Status: March 1970.* Washington, D.C.: GPO, 1971.

Series P-20, no. 218. *Household and Family Characteristics: March 1970.* Washington, D.C.: GPO, 1971.

Series P-20, no. 433. *Marital Status and Living Arrangements: March 1988.* Washington, D.C.: GPO, 1989.

Series P-20, no. 437. *Household and Family Characteristics: March 1988.* Washington, D.C.: GPO, 1989.

Series P-23 (Special Studies), no. 106. *Child Support and Alimony: 1978* (Advance Report). Washington, D.C.: GPO, 1980.

Series P-23 (Special Studies), no. 112. *Child Support and Alimony: 1978.* Washington, D.C.: GPO, 1981.

Series P-23 (Special Studies), no. 140. *Child Support and Alimony: 1981.* Washington, D.C.: GPO, 1985.

Series P-23 (Special Studies), no. 148. *Child Support and Alimony: 1983* (supplemental report). Washington, D.C.: GPO, 1986.

Series P-23 (Special Studies), no. 152. *Child Support and Alimony: 1985* (Advance Data from March–April 1986 Current Population Survey). Washington, D.C.: GPO, 1987.

Series P-23 (Special Studies), no. 154. *Child Support and Alimony: 1985* (supplemental report). Washington, D.C.: GPO, 1989.

·Series P-60, no. 156. *Money Income of Households, Families, and Persons in the United States: 1985.* Washington, D.C.: GPO, 1987.

Series P-60, no. 157. *Money Income and Poverty Status of Families and Persons in the United States: 1986* (Advance Data from March 1987 Current Population Survey). Washington, D.C.: GPO, 1987.

Series P-60, no. 158. *Poverty in the United States: 1985.* Washington, D.C.: GPO, 1987.

Series P-60, no. 159. *Money Income of Households, Families and Persons in the United States: 1986.* Washington, D.C.: GPO, 1988.

Series P-60, no. 173. *Child Support and Alimony: 1989.* Washington, D.C.: GPO, 1990.

Series P-60, no. 175. *Poverty in the United States: 1990.* Washington, D.C.: GPO, 1991.

Series P-70, no. 13. *Who's Helping Out: Support Networks Among American Families.* Washington, D.C.: GPO, 1988.

Series P-70, no. 20. *Who's Minding the Kids? Child Care Arrangements: 1986–87.* Washington, D.C.: GPO, 1990.

Census Bureau. *Statistical Abstract of the United States, 1973, 1982–83, 1985, 1987.* Washington, D.C.: GPO.

———. Technical Documentation. Current Population Survey. *March/April Match File: Alimony and Child Support.* Washington, D.C.: GPO, 1988.

U.S. Congress. House. Committee on Ways and Means, Subcommittee on Human Resources. *The Child Support Enforcement Program: Policy and Practice.* Washington, D.C.: GPO, 1989.

———. House. Committee on Ways and Means, *Background Material and Data on Programs within the Jurisdiction of the Committee on Ways and Means.* Washington D.C.: GPO, 1989, Section 8.

———. House. *Family Support Act of 1988, Report 100–998.* Washington, D.C.: GPO, 28 Sept. 1988.

U.S. Department of Health and Human Services, Office of Child Support Enforcement. *First Annual Report to the Congress on the Child Support Enforcement Program,* 30 June 1976.

———. *Fourth Annual Report to the Congress for the Period Ending 30 Sept. 1979.*

———. *Seventh Annual Report to Congress for the Period Ending 30 Sept. 1982.*

———. *Eighth Annual Report to Congress for the Period Ending 30 Sept. 1983.*

———. *Eleventh Annual Report to Congress for the Period Ending 30 Sept. 1986,* vol. 2.

———. *Twelfth Annual Report to the Congress for the Period Ending 30 Sept. 1987,* vol. 2.

———. *Child Support Enforcement Statistics: Fiscal 1979,* 1980.

———. "'Seize-and-Sell' in Washington, A Tough Enforcement Technique for Tough Cases." *Child Support Report* 13 (Aug. 1991).

———. Secretary's Symposium on Child Support Enforcement. 16–17 Aug. 1984. Washington, D.C. Mimeo.

U.S. Department of Labor. Bureau of Labor Statistics. *Handbook of Labor Statistics* (Bull. 2340). Washington, D.C.: GPO, 1989.

———. *News,* USDL 90–557. Washington, D.C.: GPO, 29 Oct. 1990.

U.S. General Accounting Office, *Child Support Enforcement: A Framework for Evaluating Costs, Benefits, and Effects,* GAO/PEMD-91-6, Report to the Assistant Secretary for Family Support Administration, DHHS, March 1991.

———. *Interstate Child Support: Mothers Report Receiving Less Support from Out-of-State Fathers,* GAO/HRD-92-39FS, Fact Sheet for Congressional Requesters, Jan. 1992.

U.S. National Center for Health Statistics. Public Health Service. *Vital Statistics of the United States,* 1984, vol. 3, Marriage and Divorce. Washington, D.C.: GPO, 1988.

———. *Vital Statistics of the United States,* 1986, vol. 1, Natality. Washington, D.C.: GPO, 1988.

United Nations. *1986 Demographic Yearbook,* 38th ed. New York, 1988.

Vaught, Thomas M. Comments to author (AHB). Chicago, 10 Aug. 1990.

Waldman, Steven. "Deadbeat Dads: Fathers on the Lam—From Their Own Kids." *Newsweek,* 4 May 1992.

Wallerstein, Judith S., and Shauna Corbin. "Father-Child Relationships after Divorce: Child Support and Educational Opportunity." *Family Law Quarterly* 20 (Summer 1986): 109–28.

Weiss, Yoram, and Robert J. Willis. "Children as Collective Goods and Divorce Settlements." *Journal of Labor Economics* 3 (July 1985): 268–92.

———. "An Economic Analysis of Divorce Settlements." National Opinion Research Center, University of Chicago, April 1989.

Weitzman, Lenore J. *The Divorce Revolution: The Unexpected Social and Economic Consequences for Women and Children.* New York: Free Press, 1985.

———. "Child Support Myths and Reality." In *Child Support: From Debt*

Collection to Social Policy, ed. Alfred J. Kahn and Sheila B. Kamerman, 251–76. Newbury Park, Calif.: Sage Publications, 1988.

Williams, Robert G. *Development of Guidelines for Child Support Orders: Final Report.* A report prepared for the U.S. Department of Health and Human Services, Office of Child Support Enforcement. Washington, D.C.: GPO, 1987.

Wilson, William Julius. *The Truly Disadvantaged: The Inner City, the Underclass and Public Policy.* Chicago: University of Chicago Press, 1987.

Wojtkiewicz, Roger A., Sara S. McLanahan, and Irwin Garfinkel. "The Growth of Families Headed by Women: 1950–1980." *Demography* 27 (Feb. 1990): 19–30.

Yee, Lucy Marsh. "What Really Happens in Child Support Cases: An Empirical Study of Establishment and Enforcement of Child Support Orders in the Denver District Court." *Denver Law Journal* 57 (Fall 1979): 21–68.

Zigler, Edward. "Shaping Child Care Policies and Programs in America." *American Journal of Community Psychology* 18 (April 1990): 183–93.

Index

Page numbers in italics refer to figures and tables.

HKJ

NW JKV